SEX, SIN AND SUFFERING

Sex, Sin and Suffering brings together for the first time a series of fascinating studies on the social history of venereal disease in modern Europe and its former colonies. The book explores the responses of legal, medical and political authorities to the 'Great Scourge' and, in particular, discusses how such responses reflected and shaped social attitudes towards sexuality and the social relationships of class, gender, generation and race.

Topics covered include:

- the discourses surrounding VD and prostitution in late-nineteenth-century and early-twentieth-century Europe using case studies of France, Sweden and the Netherlands
- the impact of VD on wartime and interwar social hygiene initiatives
- the balance between moral and medical imperatives in public health initiatives, in Germany, Italy, Russia and the UK
- the social history of VD within the colonial context – including Hong Kong, Shanghai, Singapore and Uganda
- the interaction of metropolitan and colonial ideologies, and the interface between race, gender and disease
- the relationship between VD and social change since the Second World War
- the social construction of disease and promiscuity in post-war Europe and the debate surrounding VD within the 'permissive society', and after.

This wide-ranging and illuminating book will be an invaluable resource for researchers in a number of disciplines including: history, history of medicine, social policy, welfare, gender and sexuality, politics and cultural studies.

Roger Davidson is Reader in Economic and Social History at the University of Edinburgh. His previous publications include *Whitehall and the Labour Problem in Late-Victorian and Edwardian Britain* and *Dangerous Liaisons: The Social History of VD in Twentieth Century Scotland*. **Lesley A. Hall** is Senior Assistant Archivist (Outreach), Archives and Manuscripts, Wellcome Library, and Honorary Lecturer in the History of Medicine at University College London. She is the author of *Sex, Gender and Social Change in Britain since 1880*; *Hidden Anxieties: Male Sexuality 1900–1950*; and co-author, with Roy Porter, of *The Facts of Life: The Creation of Sexual Knowledge in Britain, 1650–1950*.

ROUTLEDGE STUDIES IN THE SOCIAL HISTORY OF MEDICINE

Edited by Bernard Harris
Department of Sociology and Social Policy, University of Southampton, UK

The Society for the Social History of Medicine was founded in 1969, and exists to promote research into all aspects of the field, without regard to limitations of either time or place. In addition to this book series, the Society also organizes a regular programme of conferences, and publishes an internationally recognised journal, *Social History of Medicine*. The Society offers a range of benefits, including reduced-price admission to conferences and discounts on SSHM books, to its members. Individuals wishing to learn more about the Society are invited to contact the series editor through the publisher.

The Society took the decision to launch 'Studies in the Social History of Medicine', in association with Routledge, in 1989, in order to provide an outlet for some of the latest research in the field. Since that time, the series has expanded significantly under a number of editors, and now includes both edited collections and monographs. Individuals wishing to submit proposals are invited to contact the series editor in the first instance.

1 NUTRITION IN BRITAIN
Science, scientists and politics in the twentieth century
Edited by David F. Smith

2 MIGRANTS, MINORITIES AND HEALTH
Historical and contemporary studies
Edited by Lara Marks and Michael Worboys

3 FROM IDIOCY TO MENTAL DEFICIENCY
Historical perspectives on people with learning disabilities
Edited by David Wright and Anne Digby

4 MIDWIVES, SOCIETY AND CHILDBIRTH
Debates and controversies in the modern period
Edited by Hilary Marland and Anne Marie Rafferty

5 ILLNESS AND HEALING ALTERNATIVES IN WESTERN EUROPE
Edited by Marijke Gijswit-Hofstra, Hilary Marland and Hans de Waardt

SEX, SIN AND SUFFERING

Venereal disease and European society
since 1870

*Edited by Roger Davidson and
Lesley A. Hall*

London and New York

First published 2001
by Routledge
11 New Fetter Lane, London EC4P 4EE

Simultaneously published in the USA and Canada
by Routledge
29 West 35th Street, New York, NY 10001

Transferred to Digital Printing 2003

Routledge is an imprint of the Taylor & Francis Group

© 2001 Roger Davidson and Lesley A. Hall for selection and editorial matter;
individual contributors for their contribution

Typeset in Baskerville by Taylor & Francis Books Ltd
Printed and bound in Great Britain by TJI Digital, Padstow

All rights reserved. No part of this book may be reprinted or
reproduced or utilized in any form or by any electronic, mechanical,
or other means, now known or hereafter invented, including
photocopying and recording, or in any information storage
or retrieval system, without permission in writing
from the publishers.

British Library Cataloguing in Publication Data
A catalogue record for this book is available from the British Library

Library of Congress Cataloging in Publication Data
Sex, sin and suffering : venereal disease and European society since 1870 / edited by
Roger Davidson and Lesley A. Hall.
p. cm – (Routledge studies in the social history of medicine; 11)
Includes bibliographical references and index.
1. Venereal diseases–Europe–History–20th century. 2. Sexually transmitted
diseases–Europe–History–20th century. 3. Prostitution–Europe–History–20th century.
I. Davidson, Roger, 1942– II. Hall, Lesley A. III. Series.
RA644.V4 S3675 2001
616.95'1'0094–dc21   00-062803

ISBN 0–415–23444–1

CONTENTS

CONTENTS

FIGURES

CONTRIBUTORS

Andrew Aisenberg is Assistant Professor of History, Scripps College, Claremont, California.

Frances Bernstein is Assistant Professor of History, Drew University, New Jersey.

Ramón Castejón-Bolea is Honorary Collaborator in the Department of Public Health, University of Miguel Hernandez, Alicante.

Roger Davidson is Reader in Economic and Social History at the University of Edinburgh.

Petra de Vries is Lecturer in Women's Studies in the Political Science Department, University of Amsterdam.

David Evans is Visiting Fellow, Faculty of Health and Social Care, University of the West of England.

Michaela Freund has recently obtained her doctorate from the Department of History, University of Hamburg, and now works as a journalist for a national newspaper in Hamburg.

Lesley A. Hall is Senior Assistant Archivist (Outreach), Archives and Manuscripts, Wellcome Library, and Honorary Lecturer in the History of Medicine at University College London.

Philippa Levine is Professor of History, University of Southern California.

Anna Lundberg is a postdoctoral research associate in the Department of Historical Studies, University of Umeå, Sweden.

Kerrie L. MacPherson is Associate Professor of History, University of Hong Kong.

Lutz D. H. Sauerteig is Lecturer and Research Fellow, Institute for the History of Medicine, University of Freiburg, Germany.

Michael W. Tuck is Assistant Professor of History, Northeastern Illinois University.

Bruno P. F. Wanrooij is Professor of Humanities and Social Sciences, Syracuse University Florence Program.

ACKNOWLEDGEMENTS

The editors would like to thank the Wellcome Trust, the Wellcome Institute for the History of Medicine Academic Unit, and the Faculty of Social Sciences Research Initiative Committee of the University of Edinburgh for providing financial and logistical support for our International Colloquium on VD and European Society held at the Wellcome Institute in March 1999, at which early versions of the chapters in this volume were discussed. We are also indebted to Gayle Davis for providing a summary of the proceedings for editorial purposes and for other literary assistance, and to Virginia Berridge, Elspeth Heaman, and Sarah Hodges who also attended and provided valuable comments on the papers. Additionally, we are grateful to the Editor of *Russian Review* for permission to use material which previously appeared in article form in that journal in Frances Bernstein's chapter in this book.

INTRODUCTION

Roger Davidson and Lesley A. Hall

Venereal disease (VD) has played a substantial role in the social and cultural history of modern civilization. As Allan Brandt has rightly observed, in its social constructions, it has both reflected and reinforced society's 'most basic assumptions and beliefs' and its 'fears about class, race, ethnicity, and in particular, sexuality and the family'.[1] Thus, VD has been, and continues to be, of interest to more than the medical historian. Not only has it been significant in shaping and articulating perceptions of sexuality generally, it has also provided a rich field for the study of the state's response to perceived threats to public health occasioned by what were deemed to be inappropriate and dangerous forms of sexual and gender behaviour.

Over the last thirty years, VD has produced a considerable historiography. Rosebury provided an early overview of the history of VD designed 'for ordinary people rather than for specialists or scholars'. Although informative, it adopted a somewhat 'whiggish' approach to the development of venereology and lacked theoretical engagement.[2] Oriel, approaching the topic as a clinician rather than as a professional historian, provided a wide-ranging synthesis and bibliographical survey of more recent research. However, while he furnished a revealing account of progress in the medical understanding of sexually transmitted diseases, his comparative treatment of the development of venereology and VD controls in Britain, continental Europe and the USA was limited.[3]

The social history of VD in Britain has been the subject of a number of important studies. Until recently, these have primarily focused on the arguably atypical decades during which a system of regulated prostitution was in place in certain garrison and port towns under the Contagious Diseases Acts (1866–86) as a means of protecting the health of Her Majesty's armed forces.[4] Walkowitz, McHugh, Spongberg, and sections of Mort, have all used this episode and the debates it produced to illuminate a number of contemporary issues relating to medicine, morality, the position of women, and the political process.[5] In addition, Bland has consolidated her previous analyses of the feminist and social purity discourses surrounding VD in the aftermath of the repeal of the Acts.[6]

The contentious question of VD controls in Britain during the First World War, both in the military and the civilian population, has also been the focus of considerable research. This was not merely an *ad hoc* crisis when silence was breached in the interests of a nation at war. As argued by Hall in this volume, it also signified concerns which were powerfully inflected by pre-existing social anxieties; anxieties which both informed and reflected the celebrated proceedings of the Royal Commission on Venereal Diseases. Additional research has addressed the issue of prophylaxis in wartime and the immediate post-war years as a means of documenting the shifting moral and medical assumptions surrounding sexual politics.[7]

Arguably, somewhat less attention has been paid to the broader context of military concerns over VD. However, Harrison does address the military discourses surrounding VD and reveals the contingent nature of policies pursued in different theatres of action.[8] In addition, Hall explores the 'association of war, vice and venery as associated disruptions of natural order', the significance of VD in defining the interface between military and civilian health and sexuality, and the impact of war on the surveillance and regulation of sexual behaviour. More broadly, Levine deals with the important role of empire and racial questions in British military attitudes towards these diseases.[9]

The history of venereology and VD provisions in mid- and later-twentieth-century Britain is still incomplete. Clinicians with a historical turn of mind and venereologists in reminiscent mood have provided valuable information on the creation and development of the VD services.[10] More recently, David Evans has analysed the development of the VD clinic system established in 1916 in response to the report of the Royal Commission on Venereal Diseases.[11] Meanwhile, Davidson has focused on the distinctive Scottish experience in relation to VD with its 'culture of compulsion' shaped by differing political, social and religious traditions.[12]

During the 1980s, the advent of AIDS/HIV provided additional stimulus to the historical investigation of VD in Britain. Berridge and Strong lay stress on the influence of previous experience in the administration of VD in determining a voluntarist approach to AIDS amongst policy-makers.[13] Davenport-Hines placed the twentieth-century debates surrounding VD within the longer-term perspective of British attitudes to dangerous sexualities from the Renaissance to the present. However, strongly coloured by the AIDS hysteria of the late 1980s, he depicted a monolithic, almost ahistorical, culture of stigmatization.[14]

Apart from a limited analysis of the impact of the continental system of licensed prostitution upon the origins of the Contagious Diseases Acts and of the moral outrage surrounding 'white slavery' upon their repeal, few of these specifically British studies locate the social history of VD within an international context. However, Davidson attempts to place the Scottish experience within a comparative (primarily British Dominion) perspective, focusing on dimensions of stigmatization and control including gender, generation, class and race.[15] Taithe furnishes a comparative study of the discourses surrounding prostitution and disease in nineteenth-century Britain and France and their role in structuring deviancy and crime.[16] Davidson and Sauerteig also attempt to explore the

2

varying relationship between law, medicine and morality in England, Germany and Scotland in their responses to VD and their relative weighting of public health priorities and civil liberties.[17] In addition, in the course of his wide-ranging study of sexually transmitted diseases in Australia, Lewis to some extent locates British ideologies and practices within an international perspective, although revealing little on the patterns and processes of the diffusion of medical and social hygiene ideas.[18]

The social history of VD in many other European countries has also attracted increasing attention in recent years. Thus, Sauerteig has published extensively on the development of venereology and VD policy in late-nineteenth-century and twentieth-century Germany.[19] Bernstein has explored the (highly gendered) response of the newly established Soviet regime in Russia to the threat of VD to civil society.[20] Forrai has also provided some initial, albeit restricted, insights into the origins of modern VD policy in Hungary.[21]

Adopting a more sociological approach, Mooij provides a wide-ranging analysis of 'the characters and narrators' shaping VD discourses in the Netherlands. This is a particularly interesting case study. As the result of French influence during the Napoleonic era, the Netherlands followed a regulationist strategy of controlling prostitution for much of the nineteenth century, but was subsequently strongly influenced by the British abolitionist movement as well as changes in the attitudes and ideas of public health physicians. Mooij focuses on the social response to VD and its victims in what she defines as a 'socio-genetic' perspective, emphasizing the historical circumstances and social structures within which specific responses arose. She registers the rise and fall of public interest and the social function of periodic shifts in concern over VD, stressing the interconnections as much as the polarities between moral and biomedical responses to VD. Her analysis is strongly indebted to the sociological theories of Norbert Elias and Abram de Swaan, a refreshing change from the usual reliance on a Foucauldian theoretical framework. Thus, her stress is on the impact of the growing interdependency of modern society upon successive epidemiological models which informed the debate over sexually transmitted diseases, with the 'wheel' of infection radiating from the bodies of a vicious cluster of prostitutes being supplanted by the 'chain' of infection of a more generally promiscuous society, to be superseded in turn by the 'network' of transmission in the era of AIDS.[22]

Quétel has provided a valuable synthesis of French cultural responses to syphilis. Although his work fails fully to engage with earlier historiographical debate, and his comparative analysis is limited, he does advance the important thesis that, despite its influence upon VD debate across Europe, and in particular its position as a role model for many commentators within the UK and the USA, the French system of regulating prostitution was by no means a reliable prophylactic measure.[23]

A more wide-ranging study of VD in European society has been provided by Baldwin in his magisterial overview of contagion and the state in Europe during the period 1830–1930, in which he deploys syphilis as one exemplar of the differential responses to epidemic and contagious diseases mediated through specific national political and cultural traditions (he focuses particularly on Britain, France, Germany and Sweden). He argues that 'prophylactic divergence' between nations and the various competing theories of disease and its control did not necessarily map neatly, as is frequently alleged, onto authoritarian and liberal political cultures. He makes the point that apparently similar preventive strategies (across and within different nations) could be based on very diverse ideological assumptions, and were often the product of strategic alliances between groups at very different points on the political spectrum (as Mooij's work on the Netherlands also attests). Inevitably, national and regional historians will disagree with some aspects of Baldwin's typology. For example, the positioning of Britain in his analysis pays scant regard to divergent aspects of the Scottish experience. Swedish scholars will take issue with his argument that Sweden 'went back to the future' in modelling legislation such as Lex Veneris of 1918 on an earlier tradition of sanitary statism. Furthermore, it is questionable how far the patterns of government growth identified correspond to the everyday experience of the diseased within European society. Nevertheless, this is a thought-provoking and theoretically sophisticated overview which is bound to influence all subsequent debates.[24]

It is therefore apparent that, although there is a rich historiographical tradition relating to VD, with the notable exception of Baldwin's work, comparative studies of the social response to VD in Europe in different cultural settings remain limited.[25] This volume seeks to go some way to make good this omission. The editors decided at an early stage to deal with a limited historical period. Responses to VD have always been powerfully inflected by local and historical contingencies which can often become muted in too broad an overview. The twentieth century has seen a range of medico-scientific developments in venereology of major importance including the development of the Wassermann diagnostic test for syphilis, the discovery of Salvarsan, and the subsequent rise of antibiotic therapies; advances which have often required substantial administrative and legislative initiatives. It has also witnessed two world wars in which VD controls became a major issue of military and racial efficiency for the contending forces and raised fundamental and contentious issues (often gender-specific) relating to the relationship between public health and civil liberties.

Yet a purely twentieth-century focus for a volume seeking to address the relationship of VD to modern European society would be inappropriate. Significant strands of continuity with nineteenth-century beliefs and practices continued to inform medico-moral discourses surrounding VD well after the First World War, and need to be acknowledged. Hence the starting date of 1870.

Regulationism, or the attempted control of the spread of VD through the medical policing of prostitutes, which originated in France, was widespread through much of late-nineteenth-century Europe. In addition, it was employed in various forms within the colonial context. Aisenberg's chapter shows how this strategy was deeply embedded in French concepts of citizenship, civic

4

responsibility, and the protection of the health of the state. He explores the theories of Parent-Duchâtelet that inspired the French system of regulated prostitution (which continued until after the Second World War). However, the decline or modification of the classical regulationist system in other European countries from the late nineteenth century onwards suggests that the system in France itself was deeply embedded in specifically French cultural, political, and social discourses which made it less susceptible to overthrow or alteration.

In Britain, 1870 marked a significant turning point in the history of the Contagious Diseases Acts which sanctioned a system of local experiments in regulation. Although there were powerful advocates for its extension and even universalization, major challenges had emerged. Moreover, as many of the case studies in this volume demonstrate, this 'Abolitionist' discourse, albeit with varying inflections, acquired considerable influence in other European and European colonial countries, with the rise of an international movement opposed to the regulation of prostitution. Typically (see, for example, the chapters by Aisenberg, Castejón-Bolea, de Vries, Levine and Wanrooij) the debate is seen to be 'as much a social as medical dispute' involving wide-ranging issues relating to social order and the policing of social space and sexual behaviour.

The later nineteenth century also witnessed dramatic developments in medical knowledge relating to VD. The gonococcus was identified in the 1870s, thus enabling the definitive differentiation of gonorrhoea from syphilis. Meanwhile, improving standards of clinical observation and the rise of morbid pathology were revealing the hitherto barely suspected extent to which syphilis was responsible for late neurological and cardiological symptoms, as well as the prevalence of congenital infection, well before the Wassermann Test enabled this to be demonstrated in the laboratory.

The state of knowledge concerning syphilis in the final decades of the century, though constantly expanding, was conducive to pessimism, if not medical nihilism. In the mid-nineteenth century, the leading European authority, Philippe Ricord, an eminent French syphilologist, had promoted a basically optimistic model of syphilis as limited, treatable and controllable. However, his successor, Alfred Fournier, presented an altogether more pervasive and pessimistic view of syphilis and its curability. Attempts to introduce 'syphilization' techniques analogous to vaccination for smallpox had largely dissipated following the death of Auzias-Turenne in 1870 and that of his Norwegian adherent, Boeck, in 1875.[26] Syphilis therefore came to operate as a potent cultural metaphor for complex feelings of *fin de siècle* unease on an international scale. It was a significant theme in novels in several European languages, and Ibsen's *Ghosts* and Brieux's *Les Avariés (Damaged Goods)* were widely translated and produced on stage.

There was also a transition in ideas concerning public health during this period. The nineteenth century had seen many successes in the war against disease. Improved sanitation and water supplies had largely eradicated the epidemics which had seemed so devastating in the earlier decades of the century.

Isolation hospitals further prevented the spread of infectious diseases, while vaccination (albeit a contested practice) had made significant headway in eradicating smallpox. However, the failures of the sanitarian movement were the more glaring in the light of these obvious successes. Increased surveillance of health revealed the extent to which chronic conditions were endemic among populations. In particular, as Sauerteig's contribution indicates in the case of Germany, VD posed a potent threat to the efficiency and welfare agendas of European nation states.

Both Sauerteig and de Vries emphasize growing medical opposition to a moral regulatory system administered by the police, reflecting both advances in the medical knowledge underpinning public health administration and in the professional authority of medical expertise. In particular, it is evident that the conditions under which the examination of prostitutes took place were seldom adequate for reliable diagnosis, and were sometimes as likely to cause cross-infection as to identify disease. There was a subculture of concealment among the prostitute community. In addition, the position of examining surgeon was of notoriously low status (indeed, one that the proponents of regulation would have been loath to occupy) and frequently attracted incompetent doctors.

While bacteriologists were identifying the causative organisms of many illnesses, the origin of syphilis remained unknown. As many of the case studies document, throughout Europe the persistence of syphilis (like that of tuberculosis and cancer) fed into anxieties fuelled by Darwinian doctrines. If the concept of the survival of the fittest initially seemed to confer an evolutionary basis for the superiority of the industrialized West, it also posed the threat that other organisms might endanger that hegemony. Thus, eugenic and degenerationist discourses at the turn of the century were powerfully influenced by the increasingly apparent congenital ravages of syphilis. Moreover, the impact of VD on contemporary social theories was powerfully reinforced by a multilateral flow of ideas and information on the issue. Medical conferences, and in particular those devoted to venereal issues, such as those held in Brussels in 1899 and 1902, were vital in articulating international concerns.

The failure of traditional regulationism as a 'prophylactic strategy' was becoming apparent as medical surveillance by the state and insurance companies increased, as the system came under attack on feminist, libertarian and moral grounds, and as new paradigms of public health, medical practice and social welfare emerged. However, in the late nineteenth and early twentieth centuries, alternative strategies that could offer immediate advances in the control of VD were not readily to hand. The task of improving national morals promised to be a protracted one. In most European countries, any form of preventative sex education was liable to be contested and, apart from exceptional measures to protect military and naval forces, the use of condoms or chemical prophylaxis was primarily regarded as an inducement to immorality and corrosive of public and racial health.

This was the context in which, in 1905, the causative organism of syphilis and

6

its sequelae, such as general paralysis of the insane, were finally identified by Schaudinn and Hoffmann. In the following year, the Wassermann Test for serum diagnosis of syphilis was evolved and revealed not only the prevalence of latent asymptomatic syphilis but the extent to which traditional mercurial treatment had left the spirochaete active. In 1909, Paul Ehrlich and his co-workers finally discovered the so-called 'magic bullet', Salvarsan '606', with its allegedly miraculous remedial effects. However, the new therapy was problematic and it took many years to establish optimum levels of dosage and duration of treatment. There were also cultural and logistical problems in securing patient access to and compliance with a therapy that required specialized and often protracted and painful treatment. Furthermore, the outbreak of the First World War in 1914 had serious implications for the supply of Salvarsan to countries at war with Germany and its allies.

While in some countries the advent of Salvarsan led to the demise of regulationism, in others it survived, in some instances even into the age of antibiotics. As Baldwin has argued, at least three different approaches can be distinguished: 'regulationism, tempered by its eventual reform' as in France and Germany, 'abolition and a strictly voluntary approach in Britain', and 'sanitary statism' in Scandinavia, where, as eventually in Germany, broadly regulationist techniques were applied to the entire sexually active population.[27] These chapters and previous comparative studies of contagious diseases – pre-eminently those of Ackerknecht and Baldwin[28] – suggest a range of variables that might explain such divergence: the balance between libertarianism and authoritarianism within political culture; the conjuncture of concerns over VD and prostitution with issues of national identity/unification and efficiency; the nature of the military system; and the social politics and leverage of abolitionist forces. Most recently, Baldwin has also emphasized the influence on 'prophylactic strategies' of 'geo-epidemiological location' both in relation to 'the epidemic currents of contagious disease' and to the topography required to make certain preventive controls work.[29]

The pattern of government growth associated with VD policy and the relationship between public concern and legislative action varied between European countries and between their colonial territories. In the United Kingdom, a lengthy campaign by concerned groups, reinforced by the arrival of Salvarsan, finally secured a Royal Commission in 1913, followed by government action to introduce an entirely new system of voluntary disease controls from 1916. However, in Germany, although medical pressure groups were advocating more coercive control strategies to protect the Fatherland at an earlier date, new regulations were not fully implemented until 1927. Such delay between the first voicing of concern and the introduction of official measures contrasts strongly, as Tuck reveals, with the immediacy of legislation by chiefs in Uganda, and doubtless reflects the need of governments in complex mass democracies to be sensitive to a wide range of diverse and conflicting interests and opinions. VD legislation also varied in its efficacy between different cultures. Swedish cooperation with public health controls, as illustrated by Lundberg, contrasts with the slippage Wanrooij points to between legislative measures and actual practice in Italy, reflecting in part the greater centralization of the political process in Sweden in comparison to the continuing strength of regional identities in Italy.

Despite the ostensible shift of twentieth-century policy-makers towards a more gender-neutral approach to the issue of VD controls, they continued to bear more heavily upon women, and especially upon women who transgressed conventional boundaries of acceptable behaviour. Many contributions in this volume illustrate the degree to which new interventionist measures focused on protecting men and their families, with 'loose women', broadly defined to include all sexually active single women, continuing to be located as the primary source of infection and thus undeserving of health care in their own right. Thus, Bernstein, in her account of the iconography of anti-venereal propaganda in the early years of the Soviet regime in Russia, indicates that these roles were not among the legacies of the past overturned or even much moderated by the Marxist-Leninist remaking of society. Similarly, Sauerteig's and Freund's chapters on Germany powerfully reveal the extent to which women who contravened the sexual norms of respectable womanhood were perceived and policed as a polluting force, even where they were the unwitting victims of wartime upheavals. Freund reveals how, even in the age of antibiotics, sexually active German women continued to be seen as active agents of infection and subjected to authoritarian and punitive measures, whereas occupying troops were regarded as innocent victims. Evidence thus suggests that, in many European countries, the early-twentieth-century feminist critique of male sexual power and irresponsibility as the root cause of VD in society had been rapidly eroded and recast within public health ideologies. Certainly, a leitmotiv of many of the chapters in this volume, including those relating to Sweden, Germany and the United Kingdom, is a continuing discordance between the apparently gender-neutral language of much twentieth-century VD legislation, and the gender-specificity of its eventual implementation.

It is also evident that not only sexually active women, but all 'marginal' groups whose social/sexual behaviour was unorthodox, remained liable to scapegoating within the medical and moral discourses surrounding VD. Consistent with the classic thesis of Mary Douglas, the greatest potential to pollute continued to be located in the minds of social commentators and policy-makers with 'persons in a marginal state ... people who [were] somehow left out in the patterning of society, who [were] placeless'.[30] Thus, whether it was vagrants in early-twentieth-century Sweden or, as in Evans's contribution, single male Caribbean immigrants in 1950s' Britain, 'bodies' who deviated from and disrupted established social patterns were particularly identified with venereal contagion.

In some respects, VD and the social concerns surrounding it have provided an important peg upon which to hang broader debate over sexuality and society.

However, this role has in many countries been persistently constrained by a powerful counter-discourse in which the public discussion of VD, however relevant to national health and efficiency, has been perceived as in itself obscene and corrupting. The task of enlightening and warning the public continued to fall foul of fears, frequently, as in Italy, Germany and Spain, orchestrated by the Churches, that the information would get into the 'wrong' hands and contaminate the innocent rather than cautioning the guilty. Sauerteig describes the sensational and voyeuristic qualities of some German anti-VD propaganda, with visitors to health exhibitions fainting at the sight of hyper-realistic wax models of diseased genitals. Propagandists deployed modern methods of disseminating propaganda such as film, but as Hall and Sauerteig emphasize, anxieties over the morality of cinema and mass communications generally led to constraints on exhibition. Wanrooij identifies similar processes at work in late-twentieth-century Italy.

This volume does not set out merely to provide a set of narrative histories of VD policy in the various countries, although it does fulfil a valuable role in mapping the pattern of governmental responses to VD in much of modern Europe. It aims to integrate the range of local and national studies of the social history of VD in Europe and its former colonies, and to develop comparative perspectives. Patterns of continuity and change, and of similarity and contrast within the European and colonial experience, interweave throughout the various chapters and furnish new insights into how VD both reflected and shaped social attitudes to sexuality and social relationships.[31]

Feminist and Foucauldian analyses have been extensively deployed to interpret the use of pollution fears of VD as a threat to public health to regulate and police deviant bodies. In addition, there has been increasing awareness that many dimensions of stigmatization and control, apart from gender, intersected in the social politics surrounding VD, including class, age and race. Policy and provisions have come to be seen as much more than just uncomplicated misogynist products of a patriarchal system, and as contingent upon a range of socio-economic factors connected with the ecology and social pathology of the modern city.

Class issues and prejudices played a crucial role in shaping VD policy. As Aisenberg, de Vries and Wanrooij indicate, within late-nineteenth-century discourses surrounding contagion, concepts of disease and immorality were conflated with the corrupting effects (both moral and political) of the working-class urban environment. In some of the chapters there is evidence that, as the twentieth century advanced, there was some democratization of the content and processes of debate surrounding VD. However, in most instances, the pluralistic aspects of policy-making, including the shaping of propaganda, were fairly circumscribed. While VD increasingly shifted from being an issue of public order to one of public health, in many ways the medicalization of the issue served to elevate the power of the medical profession and its emerging specialties over working-class sexual behaviour.

Moreover, given the bourgeois ideology which underlay the social hygiene movement in many European countries, it was specifically *working-class* female sexuality within the urban environment which was the object of surveillance and stereotyping by public health and police authorities. Social historians have increasingly located responses to VD within a spectrum of concerns about the 'working girl' as both morally endangered herself and as a source of moral and medical danger to others, leading to a complex framework of regulatory, reformative and medical provisions and procedures (both statutory and philanthropic) aimed at containing this transgressive and unruly figure. Thus, in many countries, institutions with an overtly philanthropic agenda of 'rescuing' and redeeming prostitutes, or preventing girls in moral danger from actual 'fall', subjected them to a quasi-punitive regime of hard physical labour, moralization and the inculcation of bourgeois standards of appropriate conduct.[32]

Concerns over youth culture and sexual behaviour also figured prominently in VD debates across Europe. Within Britain, in particular, the 'problem' or 'vicious' girl forms a recurrent motif in moral panics, from the heated debates of the late nineteenth century over the age of consent, through the fears over adolescents maddened with 'khaki fever' pursuing soldiers during the First World War, to the widely sensationalized 'yellow golliwog' badges of the early 1960s flaunting schoolgirls' loss of virginity.[33] Both in Europe and in colonies such as Uganda, adolescents of both sexes were the object of regulatory mechanisms as societal changes seemed to indicate the breakdown of traditional family and community controls over a group newly emancipated by economic change. Moreover, as Davidson indicates in his analysis of the epidemiology and control of VD in late-twentieth-century Scotland, this preoccupation with the 'sexual licence' of youth also shaped medical and educational developments. It became central to the rising concern over the emergence of resistant strains of gonorrhoea and of a new generation of sexually transmitted diseases. It was also often central to the ongoing debate over the wisdom, timing, content and delivery of sexual health education.

A more nuanced interpretation of VD debates within Europe after 1870 also serves to locate the role of male sexuality, and of assumptions about the sexual behaviour of men, within contemporary concerns. Thus, Hall and de Vries indicate that, in both Britain and the Netherlands, the abolitionist discourse which became so influential throughout much of northern Europe at the turn of the nineteenth century not only positioned the promiscuous male as the conduit by which VD penetrated the bourgeois family but also featured the 'debauched aristocrat' as a deviant form of masculinity associated with decadence and disease. As Castejón-Bolea indicates, this perception of the male as the source of congenital infections subsequently influenced Spanish social hygienists in their campaign against VD. While Hall and Wanrooij record that, in the early twentieth century, many men considered their first dose of clap a *rite de passage* into manhood, by the interwar period, and certainly by the Second World War, the 'manly man' appears to have become the one who had the sense and control to take precautions against infection.[34] The bourgeois ideal of delayed gratification shifted from waiting chastely for months or years until marriage was possible, to delaying the impetuous urges of desire for a moment or two to adjust a condom or apply calomel ointment. There was also, by the Second World War, as a number of medical writers noted, a tendency for men to spurn prostitutes in favour of non-professional, though casually encountered, 'girlfriends', perceived (often misleadingly) as 'low-risk' partners. However, in certain cultural contexts, such as Wanrooij describes in Italy, prostitutes continued to be perceived as performing an important function bound up with concepts of male identity.[35]

Specific sub-groups of masculinity also featured in the particular concerns over, and provisions for, the control of VD in the armed forces in Europe. A range of chapters in this volume emphasize the impact of concerns over military health as a catalyst to debate and legislation over regulation and VD controls throughout our period, both in Europe and its colonies. Of especial interest are the different criteria which were applied in Mediterranean Catholic countries such as Spain and Italy for dealing with the health of the forces, resulting in active measures of prophylaxis which were profoundly unacceptable in the wider society.

The precise role of wartime in making VD a public issue, and in stimulating the introduction of active measures for prevention and control, is still debatable. The means of control traditionally practised in the forces might not be seen as appropriate or acceptable for a volunteer or conscript force, drawn from a rather different constituency, defending its country in a time of imminent peril. The question also arises as to the extent to which more aggressive medical policing of a threat to military health needs to be located within the more general ambience of control, regulation, and the militarization of nations at war.

VD was an important site for the intersection of medicine, sexuality and imperialism. European concepts of medical and moral danger were transferred overseas, often altering in the process. Recent historiography has demonstrated the central role played by medico-moral discourses surrounding VD in the regulation of social-sexual contacts with 'other races'. Moroever, as Levine argues, imperialist constructions of sexuality and disease formulated in the colonial context fed back into the politics of VD in the metropole. Female and non-European sexuality were conflated into fears of 'racial degeneration' and 'sexual atavism' (as witness the internal racism of the celebrated Italian criminologist, Lombroso, in his depiction of the 'born prostitute' of Southern Italy).[36]

'Social hygiene' also played a significant role in the development of emergent national and ethnic identities, both as a discourse of modernity (discarding the faults of the past) and resistance (to vices and pathologies introduced by outsiders or generated by colonialism). Thus, MacPherson, in her study of the missionary efforts of the British Social Hygiene Council in the Far East, indicates that far from being hostile to the social hygiene discourse, modernizing groups within China and elsewhere valued its potential for forging a more modern and competitive nation. Hostility often came instead from the traditional colonial authorities. However, Tuck recounts that in early-twentieth-century Uganda, fears about the spread of VD were deployed in an essentially conservative agenda by the local ruling chiefs in defence of their authority to police women and non-elite men.

While VD has been the site of intense conflicts over medical and moral strategies for combating the 'Great Scourge', these chapters suggest that there has not been a clear and constant polarity between them.[37] 'Medical' solutions such as the regulation of prostitution were frequently advanced by non-medical professionals, either in the legislature or the administration, or by a diversity of interest groups. Moreover, there was often internal dissension within the medical profession over appropriate strategies. De Vries suggests that in the Netherlands this was a generational divide, but further analysis of local case studies might well reveal that dissension reflected the varying agendas and professional ambitions of specific specialties. Medical and moral agendas became perhaps most entangled in the discourse of social hygiene. Preserving oneself from VD – either by chastity, or, as in the case of Weimar Germany or early Soviet Russia, by the responsible application of preventative measures – became the mark of the good citizen who took personal responsibility for his own sexual health and that of the nation. Yet, VD has also revealed the limitations of medical power over patterns of sexual behaviour. From the increasingly perceived inefficacy of medical regulation to the rise of antibiotic-resistance, it has mocked the claims of medicine.

There are other countries and yet other VD narratives that could have been included in this volume. For example, the voices of actual sufferers from sexually transmitted diseases (or of those policed on their account) are, if not silent, strongly muted and/or mediated by official discourses, reflecting the difficulty of accessing the experiences of victims of stigmatized ailments. Furthermore, any volume is limited by the practical constraints of length and also by the contours of existing scholarship. Nonetheless, we trust that these chapters will stimulate further interest in investigating the comparative dimensions of VD in Europe and the wider world.

NOTES

1 A. M. Brandt, *No Magic Bullet: A Social History of Venereal Diseases in the United States since 1880*, Oxford, Oxford University Press, 1985.
2 T. Rosebury, *Microbes and Morals: The Strange Story of Venereal Disease*, London, Secker & Warburg, 1972.
3 J. D. Oriel, *The Scars of Venus: A History of Venereology*, London, Springer-Verlag, 1994.
4 However, a broader picture of attitudes towards VD in nineteenth-century Britain is provided in J. Townsend, 'Private diseases in public discourse: venereal disease in Victorian society, culture and imagination', Ph.D. thesis, University of Melbourne, 2000.
5 P. McHugh, *Prostitution and Victorian Social Reform*, London, Croom Helm, 1980; F. Mort, *Dangerous Sexualities: Medico-moral Politics in England since 1830*, London, Routledge & Kegan Paul, 1987; M. Spongberg, *Feminizing Venereal Disease: The Body of the Prostitute in Nineteenth-Century Medical Discourse*, London, Macmillan, 1996; J. R.

Walkowitz, *Prostitution and Victorian Society: Women, Class and the State*, Cambridge, Cambridge University Press, 1980.

6 L. Bland, *Banishing the Beast: English Feminism and Sexual Morality, 1870–1914*, London, Penguin, 1995.

7 B. Towers, 'Health education policy, 1916–1926: Venereal disease and the prophylaxis dilemma', *Medical History*, 1980, vol. 24, pp. 70–87; S. M. Tomkins, 'Palmitate or permanganate: the venereal prophylaxis debate in Britain, 1916–1926', *Medical History*, 1993, vol. 37, pp. 382–98.

8 M. Harrison, 'The British army and the problem of venereal disease in France and Egypt during the First World War', *Medical History*, 1995, vol. 34, pp. 133–58.

9 L. A. Hall, ' "War always brings it on": War, STDs, the military, and the civil population in Britain 1850–1950', in R. Cooter, M. Harrison and S. Sturdy (eds) *Medicine and Modern Warfare*, Amsterdam/Atlanta, Rodopi, 1999, pp. 205–23; P. Levine, 'Venereal disease, prostitution, and the politics of empire: The case of British India', *Journal of the History of Sexuality*, 1994, vol. 4, pp. 579–602. For an overview of her forthcoming monograph, see her chapter in this volume.

10 See, for example, A. King, 'Venereology – a backward look', *British Journal of Venereal Diseases*, 1972, vol. 48, pp. 412–15; A. S. Wigfield, 'The emergence of the consultant venereologist', *BJVD*, 1972, vol. 48, pp. 549–52.

11 D. Evans, 'Tackling the "Hideous Scourge": The creation of the venereal disease treatment centres in early twentieth-century Britain', *Social History of Medicine*, 1992, vol. 5, pp. 413–33.

12 R. Davidson, ' " A Scourge to be firmly gripped": The campaign for VD controls in interwar Scotland', *Social History of Medicine*, 1993, vol. 6, pp. 213–35; R. Davidson, *Dangerous Liaisons: A Social History of Venereal Disease in Twentieth-Century Scotland*, Amsterdam/Atlanta, Rodopi, 2000.

13 V. Berridge and P. Strong (eds) *AIDS and Contemporary History*, Cambridge, Cambridge University Press, 1993; V. Berridge, *AIDS in the UK: The Making of Policy 1981–1994*, Oxford, Oxford University Press, 1996.

14 R. Davenport-Hines, *Sex, Death and Punishment: Attitudes to Sex and Sexuality in Britain since the Renaissance*, London, William Collins, 1990.

15 R. Davidson, 'Venereal disease, public health and social control: The Scottish experience in a comparative perspective', *Dynamis*, 1997, vol. 17, pp. 341–68.

16 B. Taithe, 'Consuming desires: female prostitutes and "customers" at the margins of crime and perversion in France and Britain, c. 1836–85', in M. L. Arnot and C. Usborne (eds) *Gender and Crime in Modern Europe*, UCL Press, 1999, pp. 151–72.

17 R. Davidson and L. Sauerteig, 'Law, medicine and morality: A comparative view of twentieth century sexually transmitted disease controls', in J. Woodward and R. Jutte (eds) *Medicine, Law and Human Rights*, Manchester, EAHM Publications, 2000. Other comparative work on Germany and England undertaken by Sauerteig includes 'Sex, medicine and morality during the First World War', in R. Cooter, M. Harrison and S. Sturdy (eds) *War, Medicine and Modernity*, Stroud, Sutton Publishing, 1998, pp. 167–88.

18 M. Lewis, *Thorns on the Rose: The History of Sexually Transmitted Diseases in Australia in International Perspective*, Canberra, Australian Government Publishing Service, 1998.

19 See, for example, L. Sauerteig, *Krankheit, Sexualität, Gesellschaft. Geschlechtskrankheiten und Gesundheitspolititk in Deutschland im 19. und frühen 20. Jahrhundert* (Supplement to *Medizin, Gesellschaft und Geschichte*, vol. 12), Stuttgart, Franz Steiner, 1999; 'Sex education in Germany from the eighteenth to the twentieth century', in F. X. Eder, L. A. Hall and G. Hekma (eds) *Sexual Cultures in Europe: Themes in Sexuality*, Manchester, Manchester University Press, 1999, pp. 9–33.

20 F. Bernstein, 'Envisioning health in revolutionary Russia: The politics of gender in sexual-enlightenment posters', *Russian Review*, 1998, vol. 57, pp. 191–217.

21 J. Forrai, 'Prostitution at the turn of the century in Budapest', in J. Forrai (ed.) *Civilization, Sexuality and Social Life in Historical Context: The Hidden Face of Urban Life*, Budapest, Semmelweiss University of Medicine Institute of the History of Medicine, 1996, pp. 55–62.

22 A. Mooij, *Out of Otherness: Characters and Narrators in the Dutch Venereal Disease Debates 1850–1990*, Amsterdam, Rodopi, 1998.

23 C. Quétel, *History of Syphilis*, Cambridge, Polity Press, 1990.

24 P. Baldwin, *Contagion and the State in Europe, 1830–1930*, Cambridge, Cambridge University Press, 1999.

25 While Sheldon Watts, *Epidemics and History: Disease, Power and Imperialism*, New Haven, Yale University Press, 1997, ch. 4, provides a useful, if selective, synopsis of the history of syphilis in Western Europe and East Asia from the fifteenth century, his treatment of comparative aspects of developments since 1870 is cursory.

26 B. Taithe, 'The rise and fall of European syphilisation: the debates on human experimentation and vaccination of syphilis, c. 1845–1870', in Eder *et al.* (eds) *Sexual Cultures in Europe*, pp. 34–57.

27 Baldwin, *Contagion and the State*, p. 483.

28 E. H. Ackerknecht, 'Anticontagionism between 1821 and 1867', *Bulletin of the History of Medicine*, 1948, vol. 22; Baldwin, *Contagion and the State*.

29 Baldwin, *Contagion and the State*, ch. 6.

30 M. Douglas, *Purity and Danger: An Analysis of the Concepts of Pollution and Taboo*, London, Routledge & Kegan Paul, 1966, p. 95.

31 Most studies have explored this dual role as a process which can be broadly characterized as a form of 'social control' or 'moral regulation'. However, for an alternative approach, see D. Evans, this volume, ch. 14.

32 See, for example, P. Bartley, *Prostitution: Prevention and Reform in England, 1860–1914*, London, Routledge, 1999; L. Mahood, *The Magdalenes: Prostitution in the Nineteenth Century*, London, Routledge, 1990.

33 L. A. Hall, *Sex, Gender and Social Change in Britain since 1880*, London, Macmillan, 2000, pp. 36–7, 93–5, 171. See also Mooij, *Out of Otherness*, for a similar demonology in the Netherlands.

34 L. A. Hall, *Hidden Anxieties: Male Sexuality 1900–1950*, Oxford, Polity Press, 1991, p. 48; B. Wanrooij, this volume, ch. 8.

35 On the long tradition within Europe of sanctioning the use of prostitutes by young men, in part as an antidote to masturbation, see Watts, *Epidemics and History*, ch. 4.

36 On Lombroso and the implications of such fears for the regulation of prostitution, see especially, B. Wanrooij, this volume, ch. 8.

37 This contrasts with much of the historiography of VD in the USA, which highlights such polarity as central in shaping the discourse surrounding VD controls. See especially, Brandt, *No Magic Bullet*; E. Fee, 'Sin vs. science: Venereal disease in Baltimore in the twentieth century', *Journal of the History of Medicine and Allied Sciences* 1988, vol. 43, pp. 141–64.

1

SYPHILIS AND PROSTITUTION

A regulatory couplet in nineteenth-century France

Andrew Aisenberg

Introduction

The attempt to write the interrelated histories of the regulation of prostitution and syphilis in modern France poses a number of paradoxes. The distinctive aspects of this regulation – the creation of officially sanctioned brothels, the inscription of prostitutes and the requirement that they submit to medical examinations for syphilis – became widely publicized and admired. So identified were these practices with the example of regulation in France that observers came to refer to them summarily as the 'French system'. For all this admiration, however, they were only infrequently emulated and adopted, and then so only in a modified form. By the end of the nineteenth century, admiration gave way to criticism. The extended and extra-legal police powers that made these regulatory efforts possible, and the exclusive focus of regulation on female prostitutes, came to be seen increasingly as incompatible with an emerging commitment to universal civil, political and (in limited cases) social rights among European nation states. Even in France, in the wake of the 1870 bloody popular massacre known as the Paris Commune, supporters of the nascent Third Republic judged the expansive police powers embodied in the regulation of prostitution and syphilis to be untenable if the Republic was to succeed. Such criticisms, however well articulated in the press and in the Chamber of Deputies, ultimately proved unpersuasive. The police regulation of prostitution remained intact in France until 1960.[1]

It is the persistence of these regulatory practices in Third Republic France, long after other European nations had rejected or significantly modified them, that has particularly preoccupied historians. That historians perceive this persistence as paradoxical is based upon certain presumptions about the principles that grounded the political system of republican France. If, as assumed by historians, the logic of democracy entails the ever-increasing inclusion of subjects in the exercise of rights, why did the Third Republic elaborate a system of social regulation that effectively excluded women prostitutes as a group from the exercise of political and social rights? For historians, the problem of this paradoxical exclusion is further highlighted by the role of science in the justifications and practices of regulating the relationship between syphilis and prostitution. For, if

15

science is based upon the sensory and rational capacities possessed by all human beings, why and how could medical understandings of syphilis define prostitutes as a social danger that effectively served to define them outside of the category of 'individual' and thereby exclude them from the enjoyment of civil, political and social rights?

Historians usually deal with these questions either by emphasizing the distance between (political and scientific) theory and (regulatory) practice, or by evoking the peculiar combination of democracy and state centralization that characterizes French republicanism.[2] Both of these strategies are inadequate for they avoid explanation and thus leave the paradox of regulation in place. My goal here is to make explanation possible by rethinking the place of science in the formulation of republican social regulation. What such a rethinking entails specifically is a nuanced consideration of the multivalent and contradictory meanings of 'rationality' that grounded the relationship between science and the regulation of prostitution and syphilis.[3]

Government officials associated their proposals and justifications for social regulation (including but not limited to the problems of prostitution and syphilis) with a vision of rationality that emphasized the human capacity of reason as the basis of knowledge, rights and sociability. In doing so, they sought to portray government intervention in social life informed by scientific research and institutions as fully adequate to the conception and practice of French republicanism. Even as they invoked the human origins of rationality, however, the nature of the regulation they sought to realize and support through rationality produced and (in turn) depended upon an understanding of individual social relations that transformed social life from an attribute of human autonomy into an object of government agency, in the process creating what Jacques Donzelot refers to as the 'invention of the social'.[4]

Examined from the perspective of the discursive operations of scientific rationality, the relationship of the intertwined regulation of syphilis and prostitution to the French legacy and practice of 'rights' becomes comprehensible, if not unproblematic. In this regulation, we see the process by which a realm of thinking about and regulating industrial social problems was articulated without reference to claims about sovereignty, avoiding an interpretation of intervention as an acknowledgement of social rights imposed by the sovereign nation on government. Such claims had been at the centre of social and political conflict that developed between an organized workers' movement and government officials (supported more often than not by industrialists) in France in the 1830s and 40s. Workers' claims sought to expose the contradictions between the Revolutionary promise of universal political equality and the emergence of widespread poverty by demonstrating how political liberty engendered and was premised upon the establishment of social distinctions. Workers offered a solution to this dilemma in the form of social rights, insisting upon the obligation of government to ensure the equal social conditions (well-remunerated work and steady employment were the two most important ones) necessary for the enjoyment of inalienable political rights. The immediate response of government to such arguments and demands, which in important ways called for the rejection of accepted notions of limited government as the basis for the possibility of political liberty, is well known: the bloody June Days of 1848. But equally significant, if less well known, is the attempt by government, through science, to fashion new ways of thinking about and regulating industrial social problems. The regulation of prostitution and syphilis is one of these.[5]

The origins of a scientific regulation of prostitution: Alexandre Parent-Duchâtelet

The earliest and most influential examination of the relationship between syphilis and prostitution was written at the height of the 'social question' in 1836 by Alexandre Parent-Duchâtelet. This study, entitled *De la prostitution dans la ville de Paris considérée sous le rapport de l'hygiène publique, de la morale et de l'administration*, served as the basis for understanding and regulating the social problem of prostitution in France and other industrializing societies. It was nothing if not rigorously scientific. Parent-Duchâtelet felt more comfortable in his preferred sites of observation, the sewer and the brothel, than in the official venues provided by the *Conseil de salubrité de la Seine* and the Academy of Moral and Political Sciences, which sponsored his investigations and which relied upon his work in advising government on policy regarding social problems. In regard to his method, Parent-Duchâtelet's refusal to define the causes of prostitution suggests the empiricist's disdain for undertaking research based upon an articulation of first principles. Indeed, at least one historian has noted the overwhelming, even exasperating, empiricism of his work, which is contrasted to the more suggestive and politically interested approach of his renowned colleague and peer, Louis-René Villermé.[6] Supposedly eschewing both conjecture and moralizing, Parent-Duchâtelet instead provides a detailed description of the different types of brothels (closed or unregistered) and prostitutes (registered or independent); the social and geographical origins of prostitutes; the array of sexual services offered to their clients; and the functioning of the dispensary, where prostitutes are checked and treated for syphilis, and its regulatory alternatives, the hospital and the prison.

However, Parent-Duchâtelet's reluctance to discuss the causes of prostitution is more than offset by his expansive statements regarding the consequences of prostitution, and it is here that the relationship of his scientific approach and the politics of the social question become manifest. In his view, disease (syphilis) is the pre-eminent consequence of prostitution; that disease 'ruins the health' of young girls in urban and industrial centres.[7] On the basis of the unassailable evidence of syphilis, Parent-Duchâtelet proceeds to describe prostitution analogically as a moral disease.[8] Indeed, throughout his analysis it is difficult to ascertain whether the disease at issue here is syphilis, prostitution, or immorality, although in the end it is the disease of working-class immorality that most interests him. Prostitution results from the 'transmission of vice' in working-class families that inhabit urban and industrial areas. Husbands and wives who live separately, young widows and widowers who take lovers on the side, and parents who drink excessively and who sleep with their children in a single bed, create a corrupting home environment and facilitate dangerous 'contacts'. Once 'inoculated' by this 'gangrene',[9] young girls abandon their families prematurely and enter the industrial work force. In factories and boarding houses where they live and work, and later in the hospitals and prisons where the consequences of their prostitution are confronted, they come into contact and/or transmit the vice of prostitution and immorality more generally. The end result, in Parent-Duchâtelet's view, is that this moral disease will spread from generation to generation, eventually affecting society as a whole. 'One of the constant laws of nature', he argues, 'is that living beings resemble those who produce them, and that generations transmit vices as well as virtues of body and mind'.[10]

This analogy of prostitution to a moral *disease* demonstrates how, in Parent-Duchâtelet's analysis, scientific and political fields are mutually constituted.[11] Syphilis is defined as the most prominent consequence of prostitution because, in turn, that disease provides a compelling basis for reconceptualizing the social problems identified with urbanization and industrialization as a consequence of working-class immorality and family life. What is at stake in this mutual definition of syphilis and prostitution is not simply the removal of industrial problems from the realm of economic analysis (poverty as the result of industrial liberty and free market practices) to a moral one (poverty as an expression of workers' irresponsibility). Rather, the relationship between syphilis and prostitution creates a new way for considering industrial social problems as moral problems. The reference to disease situates the possibilities of working-class morality and immorality outside of individual voluntarism, thus avoiding a confrontation with the contradictions of liberal discourse. Does poverty reveal the lie of the republican notion of universal liberty, which both depends upon and produces invidious social distinctions? If so, how would government resolve these problems without rejecting its commitment to protecting political and economic liberty? These questions grounded social and political conflict in the 1830s and 40s. References to syphilis avoid these questions by reorienting prostitution as a moral problem that concerns society as a whole, thus making allusions to individual liberty inappropriate and instead justifying the intervention of the state in the working-class family as an alternative.[12]

This reorientation is evident in the way Parent-Duchâtelet addresses the working-class home as part of his study of prostitution. Now associated with the causes of syphilis, the working-class dwelling is defined as a site of scientific observation rather than as a sphere whose inviolability is necessary for the fostering of the moral capacities of workers as free individuals. In the interest of knowledge, the most intimate experiences must be rendered transparent and explicable. 'I found many families still in bed together, if one can call by this name the miserable pallets upon which they were stretched out. Parents and children sleep together pell-mell, adult brothers and sisters were side-by-side in a state of total nudity.'[13] The process of investigating and understanding these causes reduces the moral relationships and influences to a set of determining conditions. In a way similar to the Cholera Commission Report on the 1832 epidemic to which he contributed, Parent-Duchâtelet considers the moral habits and influences of family members as a potential cause of disease alongside other aspects of the dwelling (toilets, filth, humidity and darkness), leading him in the process to define moral capacity *like* a space, determined rather than determining. This is best illustrated in his now famous observation that 'prostitution is as inevitable as the sewers, garbage dumps, and rubbish heaps'.[14] Once such findings are discovered, they are presented as yet another reason for intervention. The working-class dwelling, and especially the relationships and actions that define its moral potential, contains the causes of disease. As such, it constitutes a danger to society and must be regulated.

The relationship between working-class immorality and syphilis, which Parent-Duchâtelet secures by referring to both as a '*mal*', ultimately leads to an extended vision of government intervention. He characterizes that intervention as tutelary, where government will become responsible for the moral capacities that families have abdicated, an abdication made manifest in the spread of prostitution in urban and industrial centres.[15] Among the responsibilities that comprise this tutelary role, Parent-Duchâtelet includes returning unregistered prostitutes to their families, requiring the registration of those prostitutes whose families are deemed incapable of raising them, and delivering prostitutes who will not register or undergo venereal disease checks to the disciplinary complex of dispensary, hospital and prison.

Parent-Duchâtelet justifies this extended vision of government regulation by analysing it as part of government's larger responsibility for public health. This invocation of public health, which draws upon Old Regime conceptions of policing that bridged concerns about disease and morality, is strategic. Recourse to public health, which covers an array of causes of disease (both physical and moral) that endangers society, enables Parent-Duchâtelet to gloss over certain inconsistencies, and especially his shift from a focus on prostitution as a cause of syphilis to immorality as the cause of the social ill of prostitution. Now associated with disease and placed under the auspices of public health, the regulation of prostitution as a moral problem can be viewed neither as a rejection nor as a reformulation of liberty. It inhabits a separate regulatory sphere with distinct and established interests (social as opposed to individual), goals (security, health) and institutions (policing). Indeed, in Parent-Duchâtelet's view, to include the regulation of prostitution as a matter of public health is to affirm the accepted role of government in protecting the foundational status of liberty. Thus, he judges as misplaced the comments of his critics who view such regulation as a violation of liberal government's established duty to protect the enjoyment of privacy and liberty:

> How, with our present laws which protect the home and which prevent
> police agents from exceeding the limits of legality, can we reach a
> woman in her private home, who will be able to say that she is free to
> receive there her friends and acquaintances?[16]

Such protestations suggest, however, that what is at stake for Parent-
Duchâtelet in these connections between prostitution, immorality and disease is
indeed a reformulation of the possibilities of liberty. In Parent-Duchâtelet's analysis, the association between working-class immorality and the dangers of
prostitution and syphilis that lead him to advocate the tutelary functions of
government is predicated upon the assumption that workers lack the self-deter-
mining moral capacity of free individuals; indeed, in his view, it was false claims
to the contrary that account for social problems. This association between prostitution and disease secures the viability of economic and political liberty against
the problems of social inequality and social conflict (and most specifically against
the claims of workers that poverty is the inevitable and unacceptable product of
a society grounded in liberty) by writing the working class out of individualism.
Parent-Duchâtelet begins with the prostitute. She espouses freedom without duty,
which in the end is nothing more than dangerous licence. Prostitutes have
eschewed the regulatory functions of family life, they don't like to work, and even
when submitting to regulation they prefer the freer atmosphere of the general
hospital (where they can walk around, meet their lovers, and convert other
unsuspecting residents to a life of prostitution) to the prison. Syphilis, whether
prostitutes spread it or suffer from it, is proof of the dangerous consequences of
such a misplaced exercise of liberty and why it must be limited. Thus, he
concludes: 'Individual liberty is a right prostitutes cannot claim.'[17]

In this respect the physical spectre of syphilis reinforces another physical sign
of the prostitute, her sexual difference, that was often invoked in the discourse of
nineteenth-century political economy as the basis for understanding and
addressing industrial social problems through the regulation of women's moral
duties.[18] Parent-Duchâtelet generalizes the prostitute's sexual difference to
exclude the working class generally from the enjoyment of liberty. Here, he
focuses on the dangers posed by working-class male youth who take a prostitute
as a rite of passage to liberty – a danger in his view no different from the practices of the working-class prostitute: both types fill up the 'establishments
devoted to treating venereal afflictions'.[19] Parent-Duchâtelet contrasts this illusory and dangerous practice of liberty among members of the working class,
illusory and dangerous because it is detached from any sense of duty, with the
experience of the prostitute's bourgeois client. The bourgeois 'jeune homme' is
respectable and duty-bound; it is the prostitute, and not any irresponsibility on
the middle-class client's part, that puts his family's (and by extension society's)
fortune into 'danger'.[20] The freedom and duties of the young bourgeois male,
which in Parent-Duchâtelet's analysis stand for the general principle and

potential of liberty, will be realized only by placing the dangerous immorality of the working class under the auspices of government.

This vision of liberty, predicated upon the institution of government as a socializing and moralizing agent, serves as the basis for Parent-Duchâtelet's criticism of two past experiments, the pre-Napoleonic Revolutionary era and the Revolution of 1830. In a comment that expresses his intent to make his study influence the social policy of the embattled July Monarchy, Parent-Duchâtelet takes issue with the 'sophismes de légalité' supported by the Revolution of 1830.[21] In his view, both revolutions sought to realize liberty without the regulatory force of government and thus ended up creating and supporting licence. As an alternative, Parent-Duchâtelet identifies with the policing practices of enlightened absolutism in the 1770s, as well as the Napoleonic order that created the Prefecture of Police. As a result of the creation of the latter, he is happy to recognize, the 'epoch no longer exists when respect for individual liberty and the inviolability of the home were carried to the lengths of fanaticism'.[22] What he finds noteworthy here is not simply the investment of government with the authority over a range of moral issues. He also speaks appreciatively of the way in which the close association between policing and science enhanced the exercise of police authority by endowing it with discernment, making it capable of acting judiciously and effectively in sensitive matters regarding family life.[23] As an example of the productive relationship between policing and science, he praises the work of dispensary doctors who use persuasion rather than force to convince prostitutes of the need for regular syphilis checks.[24]

In the end, however, this restricted vision of liberty predicated upon government becomes difficult for Parent-Duchâtelet to uphold. If the understanding of prostitution in terms of inextricable physical and moral threats serves to exclude women prostitutes from the exercise of liberty, he cannot at times avoid thinking of them as individuals. After all, even the Napoleonic civil code invested women with basic civil rights. To avoid this problem, Parent-Duchâtelet limits his discussion of the problem of prostitution to minors, who must either be restored to their families or remain under the tutelary capacities of government, while admitting the difficulty of regulating adult prostitutes in a regime that takes seriously the paternal authority invested in husbands. But because the tutelary capacity he advocated endowed government with the moral responsibilities supposedly abdicated by parents, Parent-Duchâtelet at times expresses discomfort even with the regulation of minors, calling for 'discretion'.[25] As an example of the government's capacity for discretion and respect for individual liberty, he attempts to portray the registration and subsequent medical regulation of prostitutes as the result of a contract agreed to by them and administration.[26]

By far the most difficult obstacle for Parent-Duchâtelet to overcome is the relationship of the regulation of prostitution to the law. On the one hand, he recognizes that a regulation that defined immoral practices as a danger and sought to minimize them by placing prostitution under the supervision of government could not be guaranteed through law. Law assumes the potential moral autonomy of all subjects. The regulation of prostitution, however, not only assumes that morality (in the case of the working class) can be realized only through government, but also attempts to realize it by protecting in a limited sphere the supposedly immoral practices of prostitution.[27] For this reason, Parent-Duchâtelet advocates the continued administrative regulation of prostitution under the auspices of the Prefecture of Police. Yet, in the face of accusations of the extra-legal and thus arbitrary nature of this regulation, Parent-Duchâtelet argues that perhaps its place in a free order should be legitimized through the passage of a law. Such an aspiration left unsolved the paradox of how a regulation that defined morality as a function of government could be realized through an instrument that assumed individual moral self-determination. This paradox would become a focal point in the heated debate about the appropriateness of the regulation of prostitution that developed under the Third Republic, France's longest and most successful democratic experiment.

The Third Republic debate over prostitution

By the time the regulation of prostitution became a matter of debate for the Third Republic in the 1880s and 90s, the perception of that social problem (and social problems in general) had changed markedly. The Haussmannization of Paris, the public works transformation undertaken by Napoleon III and his prefectoral servant, Georges Haussmann, beginning in the 1850s, was intended to address the myriad problems of early urban and industrial society in Paris – disease, poverty, militancy, and the ineffectiveness of government intervention in social problems – that had been associated with the dangers of prostitution in the 1830s and 40s.[28] That experiment in urban and social planning succeeded to a remarkable extent. The tearing down of slums and the widening of boulevards made the city a healthier place; these public works projects also eliminated the spaces and chances for popular social interaction that had nurtured working-class mobilization beginning with the strikes of the 1830s and 40s and ending with the bloody 'June Days' of the Revolution of 1848. These transformations helped to integrate the marginal and working poor into the rhythms and space of modern urban social life, which increasingly came to be characterized as 'anonymous'. The public character of social life and leisure, with its cafés, café-concerts, restaurants, parks, weekend recreation in the suburbs, and boulevard amusements, provided new work and leisure opportunities for workers, culminating in what at least one historian has referred to as a cultural embourgeoisement.[29] Workers were encouraged, and appeared eager to imitate the customs and practices of the bourgeoisie. No better evidence of this imitation could be found than in the changing demand for prostitution. Workers sought out prostitutes not simply for venal sex but for the illusion of love. To that end, they favoured the street walker over the prostitute registered in the highly regulated 'maisons de tolérance', resulting in the demise of the latter institution.

But the integration of workers in urban life facilitated by Haussmannization in turn created new moral concerns that were articulated through new understand-ings about the dangers posed by prostitutes. The very forms of social life that integrated workers into urban space also, so it was argued, threatened 'to make private life public'[30] and thus put into question the continued viability of the bour-geois family and its moralizing function. Moreover, the worker's integration invalidated the image of the prostitute (and by metonymic extension, the worker) as a moral and physical species apart; in doing so, integration produced the para-doxical effect of aggravating concerns about the frailty of the (bourgeois) moral self in modern life by eliminating a well-established basis for differentiation through which moral anxieties had been displaced in the past. But integration also provided new constructions for dealing with these new moral anxieties. Now, it was the prostitute's anonymity, her apparent similarity to more established and respectable urban residents, that aroused fear. At any moment, the member of a respectable family out for a walk on the boulevards could unknowingly rub up against a prostitute whose moral and physical contamination was no less dangerous because unapparent. Not surprisingly, these hidden dangers were often transposed onto workers who, it was feared, might spread disease and immorality to unsuspecting urban residents through the rubbing (*frottement*) and '*va-et-vient*' that characterized the new city of boulevards, entertainments, and tourism.[31]

The danger of anonymous contacts came to be understood in scientific terms. This danger found its penultimate expression in the theory of latent germs. Parent-Duchâtelet's late-nineteenth-century public health successors fashioned this theory in an attempt to resolve the ambiguities in Pasteur's own laboratory-based theory of germs by taking into consideration the conditions of modern urban life in Paris that harboured, nurtured and spread germs. Here, the danger of syphilis was only one (and not even the most discussed one) of the examples of transmission by latent germs; other examples included nomads who imported typhus into Paris and spread the germ in shelters, and the Parisian working poor whose hovels contained the typhoid fever bacillus. The tuberculosis expert Grancher best described the myriad conditions of urban life that explained the experience of disease in the modern city of Paris.

> Has one reflected upon all of the direct or indirect contacts that inhabi-
> tants unknowingly suffer; the distribution of water, of milk, of bread; or
> the market, the laundry, the streetcars; or the anonymous street relations,
> the omnibus, etc., which become in times of epidemic so many sources
> of contagion. How, then, can one be surprised that, in a city like Paris,
> the inhabitants of distant neighborhoods are hit simultaneously.[32]

The relationship of science to the reassessment of the problem of prostitution helps to account for the complexity of the debate over the future of its regulation, a debate that cannot be easily demarcated between two opposing, dichotomous positions. A vocal opposition to the (administrative) police regulation of prostitution emerged in the mid-1870s.[33] That opposition comprised two points.

It took prostitution to exemplify a kind of social regulation that, because it ignored and even transgressed individual rights, contradicted the basic tenets of the French republican tradition. Criticism was directed in particular against the office responsible for the administrative regulation of prostitution, the Prefecture of Police. Here, the role of the prefecture in repressing two popular revolts in support of a social republic, the recent Paris Commune of 1870 and the Revolution of 1848, was invoked to delegitimize any place for that office in a future republican social regulation. In support of these arguments, opponents of the existing regulation of prostitution marshalled incriminating evidence, first exposed by the journalist Yves Guyot and subsequently heralded by members of the *Ligue des droits de l'homme*. That evidence revealed the inhumane treatment of prostitutes at the dispensary and of women who were mistakenly identified and arrested by police as prostitutes for the simple reason that they walked unaccompanied on the grand boulevards (at least one woman was reported to have killed herself on account of the shame resulting from her arrest for prostitution). For these critics, who presented such lurid details at sessions of the Chamber of Deputies where discussions of the police budget often turned into a debate questioning a role for the Prefecture of Police in a republican government, the police regulation of prostitution constituted nothing less than a vestige of the odious authority of the Old Regime at the heart of the Third Republic. If the Republic were to survive, so these critics argued, the police authority over prostitution would have to be dismantled in favour of a regulation protective of rights, and passed through and subject to the authority of the legislative process.

Opponents presented the police regulation of prostitution as a system that violated the rights of women, bypassed the safeguards of law, and created an inappropriate role for government in the moral lives of individuals. Their criticisms of the regulation of prostitution, however, did not extend to the scientific knowledge about the relationship between prostitution and syphilis that grounded such regulatory initiatives. They avoided such a criticism, I believe, for two interrelated yet ultimately contradictory reasons. First, they accepted the premise that scientific truth was beyond politics and thus beyond reproach. Secondly, they assumed that scientific truth ideally would work for the republican goals of freedom and progress. In doing so, they 'underread' the discursive operations of science. It was through scientific rationality that government asserted itself as a socializing and moralizing force. This lapse in criticism provided an opening in the debate for supporters of the existing regulation, many of whom served as officials at the Prefecture of Police.

In defence of the regulatory status quo, supporters cited the scientifically verifiable dangers posed by prostitution, which, as in the past, merged the physical and moral threats of syphilis. If, as a succession of police prefects and bureau chiefs argued in the 1880s and 90s, science revealed the origin and transmission of disease, then the dangers that disease posed to social order could only be regulated by police powers, as originally stated in the building blocks of republican government: the Revolutionary Municipalities Law of 1790 and the Law of

12 Messidor An VIII. In a session of the Chamber of Deputies in 1884, the police prefect Andrieux imagined the disastrous consequences that might ensue if the regulation of disease were to be removed from the authority of the police and placed in the hands of popularly elected municipal bodies:

> I suppose to take an example that happened during my administration, that an epidemic develops in an unhealthy [*malsain*] neighborhood, in the hovels where daylight hardly penetrates; what will the administration do? It will have to undertake exceptional measures, evict the tenants who occupy these buildings, burn their straw mattresses and other contaminated kitchen utensils whose presence would constitute a real danger for public health. In the interior of apartments, it will be necessary to tear off the wallpaper, replaster the walls, all things that the general interest imposes. The prefect of police has the right to do all of this, it can do it by ... the dispositions of the law of 15 and 24 August [1790]. You transfer ... not only the Conseil [d'hygiène publique] but also all that which regards the surveillance of health. Alas, ... agents will, in the event of an epidemic, enter a contaminated house, they will find a citizen at the door to whom one cannot present any law, who will refuse entry and who will exercise his right by doing so.[34]

But these advocates of the police regulation of social problems associated with the spread of disease did not rely on science to justify the accepted practice of an intermittent and repressive exercise of government that was at the basis of the Revolutionary Municipalities Laws. Rather, they summoned science as the basis for re-envisioning policing as responsible for a positive and consistent regulation of social problems. Here, in a way similar to the argument of Parent-Duchâtelet, these advocates referred to the past experience of the *Conseil d'hygiène publique*. Members of the council and police agents more generally invoked their commitment to scientific rationality which, in their view, minimized the opportunities for repressive interventions and softened those repressive interventions deemed necessary for social order. Where (as in Andrieux's statement cited above) a scientific understanding of the origin and spread of disease in urban social life could justify the maintenance of existing police powers, it was also invoked to restrain those powers in favour of positive interventions and in a way that might please republican defenders of a social order grounded in the rule of law. Thus, in the 1884 Chamber discussion, the prefectoral servant Renault praised the prefecture's new method for recording cases of contagious disease as evidence of how science limited the recourse to repressive interventions:

> Thanks to the initiative that the prefecture of police maintains in matters of hygiene for the needs of health, [it] was able to develop ten or eleven years ago a whole range of services which represent, from the viewpoint of public health and from the viewpoint of the esteem and

sympathy which the population holds for it, a considerable progress. ...
The police commissioners, in this instance, do not present themselves as
agents of repression, but as agents of protection, assistance, and relief.
It is by multiplying this kind of intervention that the function of police
will be endowed with a character which softens and tempers the
inevitable rigor of its repressive action.[35]

Undoubtedly, such invocations of science were tied to a continued commitment
to a vision of government as a necessary socializing, moral force in a democratic
republic. Here, the popular and bloody revolt of the Paris Commune cast a long
shadow, by putting into question the possibility of a truly inclusive democracy as
the basis for the Third Republic (in this regard, it is interesting to note that the
conservative first decade of the Third Republic following the Commune, known
as the 'moral order', witnessed a marked increase in the number of arrests of
unregistered prostitutes).[36] Scientific pronouncements regarding the relationship
between syphilis and prostitution served as the basis for other regulatory
proposals. A neo-regulationist position developed in the 1890s. Its supporters,
comprised mainly of doctors and hygienists associated with the Prefecture of
Police, advocated that the regulation of prostitution remain under the auspices of
the Prefecture but in a renovated form, devoid of the moralizing pretensions that
characterized past initiatives and legitimized through legislation.

Ultimately, even abolitionists could not resist the scientific pronouncements
linking prostitution and syphilis. The few moments when they acknowledged the
validity of these pronouncements led them to endorse a regulatory vision that in
other contexts they had condemned as contradicting the basic values of republican liberty and legalism. Thus, Ludovic Trarieux, the president of the *Ligue des
droits de l'homme* who fought the police regulation of prostitution, ended up
arguing in 1895:

Above all and as a matter of necessity, one must attend to dangers and stop
the propagation of wrongs [mal]. If we don't take care of this, contagion
will spread with such rapidity that perhaps the entire population would
end up being contaminated within the space of less than half a century.
The law is here above all for the defense of the social interest and, if the
mechanisms of justice cannot support it, it is necessary to look outside
those mechanisms. *I would go so far as to say that the law is to a certain extent arbitrary; there is no place for legislation where we can realize rigorous legality only at the
detriment of the sanitary condition of the nation.*[37]

The inability to separate a recognition of the validity of scientific statements
about syphilis and prostitution from a support of a police regulation of that
social problem found its ultimate irony in the legislative fate of prostitution,
which ended up proving Trarieux's prediction. As the Republic became more
securely established, its supporters grew more weary of broaching the problem

of regulating prostitution. The police regulation of prostitution continued until the 1960s, when United Nations' policy regarding prostitution led France to abandon regulation altogether.

This brief discussion of the debate concerning the regulation of prostitution is instructive, for it illuminates the complex relationship between science, regulation and republicanism in modern France. It affords a new perspective on the social question and the origins of regulation as, above all, a problem of conceptualizing human duties and bonds within the parameters of republican liberty. In modern France, regulation constituted an endeavour by government to assume the moral and socializing functions which free individuals do not possess. At the heart of this regulation, indeed what makes it seem consonant with the republican promise linking individual freedom and social order, is the discursive operation of science. Government invoked human reason, the capacity that is supposed to make human beings free and moral, as the foundation of science and thus as a legitimate basis for government intervention in a free social order. Yet the result of that relationship between government and science was to exteriorize (by objectifying) human capacities, in the end making government – and not the individual – the 'subject' of sociability in republican France.

NOTES

1 The literature is vast. Among the works I found most helpful, see A. Corbin, *Women for Hire: Prostitution and Sexuality in France After 1850*, Cambridge, Harvard University Press, 1990; J.-M. Berlière, *La police des moeurs sous la IIIère république*, Paris, Seuil, 1992; P. Baldwin, *Contagion and the State in Europe, 1830–1930*, Cambridge, Cambridge University Press, 1999; L. Engelstein, *The Keys to Happiness: Sex and the Search for Modernity in Fin-de-Siècle Russia*, Ithaca, Cornell University Press, 1992; J. Walkowitz, *Prostitution in Victorian Society: Women, Class, and State*, Cambridge, Cambridge University Press, 1980; A. M. Brandt, *No Magic Bullet: A Social History of Venereal Disease in the United States since 1880*, Oxford, Oxford University Press, 1985.

2 See especially Berlière, *La police des moeurs* and Baldwin, *Contagion*.

3 For an understanding of this conception of rationality, see A. Aisenberg, *Contagion: Disease, Government and the 'Social Question' in Nineteenth-Century France*, Stanford, Stanford University Press, 1999, Introduction.

4 J. Donzelot, *L'invention du social: Essai sur le déclin des passions politiques*, Paris, Fayard, 1984. My comments on government here draw upon Michel Foucault, especially his article 'Governmentality' in *The Foucault Effect*, edited by G. Burchell, C. Gordon and P. Miller, Chicago, University of Chicago Press, 1991, pp. 87–104.

5 This analysis of the problem of rights is developed best in G. Procacci, *Gouverner la misère: La question sociale en France, 1789–1848*, Paris, Seuil, 1993.

6 For an interpretation of Parent-Duchâtelet's empiricism, see A. F. La Berge, *Mission and Method: The Early Nineteenth-Century French Public Health Movement*, Cambridge, Cambridge University Press, 1992. Early-nineteenth-century public health interest in the sewer is addressed by A. Corbin, *The Foul and the Fragrant: Odor and the French Social Imagination*, translated by M. L. Kochan with R. Porter and C. Prendergast, Cambridge, Harvard University Press, 1990.

7 A. J. B. Parent-Duchâtelet, *De la prostitution dans la ville de Paris, considérée sous le rapport de l'hygiène, de la morale et de l'administration*, Paris, J.-B. Baillière et fils, 3rd edn, 1857, vol. I, pp. 370–1.

8 Ibid., vol. I, pp. 471, 477.

9 Ibid., vol. I, pp. 377–8.
10 Ibid., vol. I, p. 7.
11 I talk about this process in my book *Contagion*.
12 Parent-Duchâtelet, *De la prostitution*, vol. II, pp. 324–5.
13 Ibid., vol. I, p. 57.
14 Ibid., vol. II, p. 338. On the place of working-class immorality in the Cholera Commission Report, see Aisenberg, *Contagion*, pp. 21–6.
15 For a discussion of government tutelage of working-class families, see S. Schafer, *Children in Moral Danger and the Problem of Government in Third Republic France*, Princeton, Princeton University Press, 1997.
16 Parent-Duchâtelet, *De la prostitution*, vol. I, p. 480.
17 Ibid., vol. II, p. 311.
18 See J. W. Scott, "'L'ouvrière! Mot impie sordide ...". women workers in the discourse of French political economy, 1840–1860', in J. W. Scott (ed.) *Gender and the Politics of History*, New York, Columbia University Press, 1988, pp. 139–63.
19 Parent-Duchâtelet, *De la prostitution*, vol. I, p. 57.
20 Ibid., vol. II, p. 188.
21 Ibid., vol. I, p. 536.
22 Ibid., vol. II, p. 304.
23 Ibid., vol. I, p. 376.
24 Ibid., vol. II, p. 225.
25 Ibid., vol. I, p. 354.
26 Ibid., vol. I, p. 357.
27 Ibid., vol. II, p. 308.
28 Helpful works on Haussmannization include J. Gaillard, 'Assistance et urbanisme dans le Paris du Second Empire', in L. Murard and P. Zylberman, *L'haleine des faubourgs: Ville, habitat et santé au xixème siècle*, Fontenay-sous-Bois, Recherches, pp. 395–422; J. Gaillard, *Paris, la ville (1852–1870)*, Paris, Honoré Champion, 1977; A. Sutcliffe, *The Autumn of Central Paris: The Defeat of Town Planning, 1850–1870*, London: Edward Arnold, 1970; D. P. Jordan, *Transforming Paris: The Life and Labors of Baron Haussmann*, New York, Free Press, 1995; T. J. Clark, *The Painting of Modern Life: Paris in the Art of Manet and His Followers*, Princeton, Princeton University Press, 1984.
29 See Corbin, *Women for Hire*, esp. ch. 4.
30 Clark, *The Painting of Modern Life*, p. 34.
31 For an evocative analysis of these dangers, see L. Colin, *Paris: Sa topographie – son hygiène – ses maladies*, Paris, G. Masson, 1885.
32 *Annales d'hygiène publique et de médecine légale*, 3rd ser., vol. 12, 1884, p. 482. On the relationship between the theory of latent germs and urban social life, see Aisenberg, *Contagion*, esp. ch. 3.
33 A spirited analysis of this opposition can be found in Berlière, *La police des moeurs*. See also Corbin, *Women for Hire*, esp. ch. 5.
34 Archives Nationales, F⁸ 171. Chamber of Deputies, Session of 15 Jan. 1884. 'Première déliberation sur le projet de loi tendant au rattachement au budget de l'état des dépenses de la police dans la ville de Paris (extract).'
35 Archives Nationales, F⁸ 171. Chamber of Deputies, Session of 21 Jan. 1884 (extract).
36 On the rise of prostitution arrests, see Corbin, *Women for Hire*, p. 106. An account of the anxieties produced by the Commune and how they shaped scientific thought can be found in S. Barrows, *Distorting Mirrors: Visions of the Crowd in Late Nineteenth-Century France*, New Haven, Yale University Press, 1981.
37 Quoted in Berlière, *La police des moeurs*, p. 83 (italics in original).

2

PASSING THE 'BLACK JUDGEMENT'

Swedish social policy on venereal disease in the early twentieth century

Anna Lundberg

Introduction

From the late eighteenth century, fuelled by mercantilist fears of the impact of the venereal contagion upon the health and growth of its people, Swedish society attempted to contain venereal disease (VD) by combining policies of care and coercion. During the nineteenth century, patients with VD were isolated in special wards, so-called *kurhus*, established throughout the country by means of a compulsory state tax. Impoverished patients were provided for free of charge, although evidence suggests that the need for a tax to pay for such care tended to stigmatize their treatment. The *kurhus* were staffed by private physicians who also practised as state employees within the public hospitals.[1]

At the same time, wide-ranging controls on the venereally sick had been introduced. Every authority, from county governor to head of household, from physician to employer, was required to report cases of the disease to the police and provincial physician. According to a State Act passed in 1812, female workers in inns, glassblowers, journeymen and other social groups were to be specially controlled.[2] Medical care was mandatory although it was hard to keep some patients inside the clinics against their will. Significantly, while farmers were frequently discharged to harvest their crops, unmarried women who left the *kurhus* were frequently arrested and returned.[3]

Moreover, as the nineteenth century progressed, these sanitary controls were complemented by additional controls in many Swedish cities aimed at the regulation of prostitution. Women and girls who walked the streets at night could be registered as prostitutes and subjected to compulsory medical inspection. Women who exhibited deviant lifestyles and challenged the accepted feminine roles of wives and mothers were targeted because they were viewed as the main vectors of VD. The regulation of prostitution was introduced in Stockholm and in the second largest town, Gothenburg. Eleven other towns with a range of industries and a large migrant population, both male and female, also chose this strategy to contain VD during the 1870s and 1880s. Thus, as in other European countries, moral and medical pathologies became conflated within the discourse surrounding VD.[4]

In 1878, a Swedish movement, the *Federation*, was founded to fight for the repeal of the regulation of prostitution. Ulf Boëthius has described it as one of the first major women's movements in Sweden.[5] Nevertheless, the nineteenth-century debate over regulation and VD mainly took place between male members of either the *Svenska Läkaresällskapet* (Swedish Medical Association) or the *Federation*. Few women spoke about VD or prostitution in Sweden. This had a significant impact on the repeal movement, which increasingly focused on the implications of regulation for social order rather than its consequences for women. Equal rights for women did not prove an effective argument in the *Federation's* campaign within Sweden. Every proposal advanced by its representatives to repeal the regulation of prostitution and to reduce the discrimination that prostitutes suffered under Swedish law failed. Its only success was in promoting the prohibition of prophylactics, eventually implemented in 1910, in an attempt to decrease vice and immorality in Sweden.[6]

There were other reasons why repressive policies had such a lasting influence in Sweden. There was a long tradition of sanitary regulations relating to VD that accorded public health priority over civil liberties. The fact that there existed long-established precedents for the regulation of vagrants and other groups deemed a threat to public health made it easier for Swedish medical authorities to justify a similar regulation for the specific control of prostitutes; the more so as a small but highly influential group of medical experts remained committed to stringent medical and social controls.

Peter Baldwin has also emphasized that Swedish abolitionists were strongly 'influenced by Christian and moral concerns' and, in contrast to the more limited objectives of their British counterparts, strove not just for the repeal of regulation, but also for the total eradication of prostitution. Thus, he concludes that '[T]he Swedes were also strong suppressionists, refusing to allow the state to ignore prostitution and insisting that, if commercial sex were not to be outlawed altogether, at least the laws on public order should be enforced to end solicitation.'[7]

As in other European countries, the reported number of cases with VD in Sweden increased rapidly in the early years of the twentieth century, although this was in part due to the introduction of compulsory notification. In 1900, 3,681 civilian patients were diagnosed as suffering from VD. By 1918, the number of patients had increased to 24,012.[8] While case numbers increased, debates about sexuality, prostitution and VD became more heated and involved more participants than ever before. The spread of these diseases became an important issue, deeply influenced by contemporary problems such as unemployment, poor housing, alcohol and general vice. The continued use of the regulation of prostitution was the primary topic of discussion in the early decades of this century. It was perceived by some as an outdated oppression of women that did not suit contemporary Sweden. Finding a better way to contain VD became one of many challenges on the way to reforming the nation, and part of a more general contemporary quest, informed by social Darwinism, to clean up 'filth-Sweden'.[9]

A debate in 1901 between physicians working in Stockholm initiated a parliamentary committee of enquiry in 1903 on the control of VD. Its members completed their investigations and published their recommendations in 1910. They proposed to retain the regulation of *helyrkesprostituterade* – the so-called fully professional prostitute. This proposal was fiercely contested in public debate and consequently rejected by the standing committee on civil law. As a result, a further phase of debate was initiated culminating in the enactment of major legislation with the introduction of Lex Veneris on 20 June 1918. This act stipulated a mandatory obligation to notify and report cases of VD to a superior medical authority, the provision of mandatory, free medical treatment, and criminal prosecution for those risking the transmission of infection.

Hitherto, there has been little published research on the social history of VD in Scandinavia or Sweden. The notable exception is the recent wide-ranging study by Peter Baldwin of contagion and the state in Europe. In it, he emphasizes how the 'prophylactic strategies' in Sweden, which initially were generic sanitationist measures, later became the role model for German legislation, in contrast to the voluntary measures adopted in Britain.[10]

However, Swedish historians and sociologists have undertaken extensive research on contemporary social change in Sweden involving the modernization of society which might explain this distinctive role in the early twentieth century. Thus, Yvonne Hirdman and Lena Sommestad, among others, have documented the formation of 'folkhemmet'; a vision of an ideal society in which everyone could live on equal terms with access to affordable accommodation and to comprehensive educational and medical provisions.[11] Similarly, Arne Ruth has outlined the development of a modern Swedish welfare state as a model for the rest of the world, focusing on contemporary concerns of Swedish employers at the impact of labour emigration on national efficiency.

Ruth represents this quest for social and technological change as one that was perceived to be unavoidable and a moral imperative; a 'rationalistic futurism' which took the place of religion and in which 'anti-traditionalism' became, paradoxically, the dominant tradition.[12] Moreover, according to Ruth, there was a self-conscious pride among the Swedish intellectual élite that Swedish policies were distinctive in the belief that Sweden was destined to become the most progressive nation in Europe.

More specifically, Karin Johannisson and others have revealed how the health of the people became a central strand in the campaign for a cleaner and modern Sweden. While population growth remained an important issue in public debate, by the early twentieth century it was a concern with the quality of future generations that came to dominate policy-making.[13] As Johannisson illustrates, this was reflected in the passion that characterized debate surrounding health issues at the turn of the century. Issues of health and hygiene came to preoccupy a broad spectrum of Swedish professionals, including physicians, bacteriologists, biologists, politicians and 'social engineers'. In terms of the agenda of Swedish social politics, 'health and purity' were to conquer 'ignorance, disorganization, disease and filth'.[14] Health provisions were pivotal to contemporary perceptions of the welfare state and, informed by eugenic ideologies of sexual health and the family, medicine was no longer simply about curing patients but about introducing and enforcing a healthy lifestyle.[15]

It is within this context that the development of social responses to VD in Sweden after 1900 must be understood. The aim of this chapter is to analyse the impulses and constraints that shaped VD policy and the discourses that defined medical and social responses to sexually transmitted diseases. It will review the contemporary debate over prophylactic strategies and examine the final legislation that was approved by the government. It will focus in particular on early-twentieth-century discourses surrounding the regulation of prostitution as the prime strategy for containing venereal infection. Although progressive ideas heavily influenced contemporary debate, it will become apparent that many who were sick with syphilis or gonorrhoea had to pay a high price for reclaiming their health.

The Regulation Commission

Throughout Europe, in the early years of the twentieth century, major advances in medical knowledge were informing new debates over VD and prostitution. An international conference on VD in Brussels in 1901 inspired the chairman of *Svenska Läkaresällskapet*, Per Johan Wising, to hold a similar debate in Stockholm. It took place on 26 November 1901. As opening speaker, Professor Edvard Welander argued for the continued regulation of prostitution in the belief that immoral women could be held accountable for the bulk of venereal infection. In his view, women who prostituted themselves were the most dangerous and should be strictly controlled by a dedicated police force. They should not enjoy the same kind of medical treatment as other women, and they should be 'restored back into society' by means of rescue homes. However, Welander held much less repressive views about other patients with VD, for whom he advocated public sex education and less stigmatized medical care.[16]

Besides Welander, other male physicians at Stockholm hospitals and out-patient clinics participated in the debate. Magnus Möller, one of his former students, argued for the repeal of the regulation. So did Ellen Sandelin and Karolina Widerström, two female physicians who practised in Stockholm. Both of them emphasized the social disadvantages of regulation and argued for a reform of social policy with respect to VD. They stressed the need for open-mindedness, public education of adults and adolescents, out-patient-clinic care and a revision of the regulation. They found support among their colleagues. In particular, the advantage of having female physicians to care for and educate female patients was widely recognized.[17]

However, even though the majority of the participants argued for the repeal of regulation, Welander was the only professor of venereology and had long been respected as an expert in the field. None of his colleagues were yet prepared to defy him openly. Moreover, while there was a certain level of advocacy for change, there remained an overriding fear of contagion. VD was still considered such a social menace that the regulation of prostitution could not realistically be repealed until a new act had been introduced to replace it.

The more radical strands of the debate are clearly traceable in a 1903 parliamentary motion concerning VD.[18] It was submitted by two liberal members in the second chamber, Adolf Hedin and Edward Wawrinsky. Adolf Hedin was a liberal publisher and a leading figure of Swedish social-liberalism. Hedin had advocated comprehensive retirement and accident insurance for workers in 1881 and later attacked the vagrancy act for violating civil liberties. Edward Wawrinsky started his political career as a liberal and ended it as a social democrat, having also joined the peace and temperance movements.[19] Their motion proposed better availability of medical care and more effective contact tracing and public health education as a means of containing the spread of VD. It also proposed that, although prostitutes should be registered, they should only be inspected and supervised by physicians and cared for, if possible, by female physicians and nurses. In addition, the need for further financial subventions to introduce so-called rescue homes for immoral women and girls was stressed.[20] In the event, both chambers granted the motion for the formation of a governmental commission of enquiry into issues related to VD.[21]

The Commission soon became known as the *reglementerings kommitén* (Regulation Commission). As initially appointed, it was an all-male organization. Johan Wold, a rural court judge, was appointed chairman. Ivar Andersson, Senior Town's physician in Stockholm,[22] Johan Erik Johansson, a professor in physiology, and Magnus Möller, provided the medical expertise. Otto Westerberg, former secretary of the Federation, represented the abolitionist movement. Other participants were political experts or legal advisers. Carl Malmroth was a much-respected civil servant, frequently consulted by the cabinet. Bror Petrén was also a civil servant whose advice was much sought after by contemporary politicians and who was appointed consultative cabinet member to the Minister of Justice in 1911.[23] The fact that leading civil servants were appointed to the Commission is a clear indication of the importance attached to the issue by central government.

From the start, the Commission had to face several difficulties with its membership. Within a couple of months, several members ceased to participate or chose to resign. Ellen Sandelin and Hugo Tamm, former chairman of the Federation, died within a few years. Alma Sundqvist and Edvard Welander resigned soon after having been appointed. One can only speculate as to the reasons for this. Personal factors played a part but it is also possible that these members were disillusioned by the conservative ideology of the other members of the Commission. This loss of medical expertise and abolitionists inevitably affected the outcome of its investigation.

The Regulation Commission completed its proceedings in 1910. Its work was substantial and published in four separate volumes, as well as in the printed proceedings of the *Riksdag* in 1918.[24] In sum, the Commission advocated the continued regulation of professional prostitutes, increased contact tracing and mandatory medical treatment. This involved amended directives for hospitals, out-patient clinics, physicians and the *Medicinalstyrelsen* (National Board of Health). Their recommendations also involved the Penal Code. The Commission recommended that to subject others to the risk of infection be a punishable offence and that a sentence of two years of forced labour be imposed for the actual transmission of disease. They also suggested that fornication and any indecent behaviour should be punished by forced labour and imprisonment. It was a far-reaching reform that regulated not only the lives of the sick but also the professional practice of medicine.

Two of the members objected to the Commission's recommendations. Both Otto Westerberg and J. E. Johansson opposed the retention of regulation.[25] Johansson questioned the way the Commission equated professional prostitutes with male vagrants, and dissociated himself from this viewpoint. He accused the Commission of wanting to punish the women for the social scandal they created instead of concentrating on the medical issue of combating disease. On the basis of his long-term study of prostitutes in Stockholm between 1859 and 1905, Johansson argued that sentencing prostitutes to forced labour would not prevent them from carrying out their lucrative business. Nor did he believe that drawing attention to their anti-social behaviour would suffice as a deterrent. Johansson was to become one of the leading figures in the debate that followed.

1910–18: the debate

When the report of the Regulation Commission was published in 1910, it was referred to various authorities in Sweden for consideration. The *Medicinalstyrelsen*, a national body in charge of health-related issues, coordinated the response of health boards and local authorities across the country. In a statement submitted to the government in 1915, they objected to some aspects of the Regulation Commission's proceedings, believing the idea of prosecuting only one kind of prostitute to be arbitrary and impractical. It argued that the Commission had failed to fulfil all aspects of its terms of reference. It protested against the application of the vagrancy acts to prostitutes, unless they were obviously loitering. However, the *Medicinalstyrelsen* still wished to retain sanitary measures for combating the spread of VD. They argued the need for a law that would simplify the prosecution of anyone found to be communicating disease, even if the injured party chose not to bring charges.[26]

The Swedish Medical Association, *Svenska Läkaresällskapet*, was also consulted by the Cabinet on the Regulation Commission's proposals, provoking one of the longest and fiercest debates in the history of the Association. A small majority of the participating physicians agreed with the Commission and advocated the continued use of regulation. In their view, immoral female sexuality was still to blame for the bulk of venereal infections and should be controlled more stringently than other sexual behaviour. Many members attacked J. E. Johansson. Being a physiologist rather than a venereologist, Johansson was accused of underestimating the threat posed by VD. Some members accused him of leaving the country entirely unprotected against the diseases.[27]

One of his fiercest enemies was Professor Frithiof Lennmalm, a conservative neurologist who claimed to have experience of patients suffering from the neurological, spinal and cardiovascular symptoms of tertiary syphilis.[28] In a statement on 4 May 1912, Lennmalm stressed the awful suffering of innocent victims, such as wives and children. Johansson was accused by Lennmalm of only looking at the issues from a theoretical standpoint. Lennmalm viewed syphilis as 'the most difficult disease known in the history of mankind' and thought public education insufficient to protect the population. Instead, he considered that keeping as many infected prostitutes off the streets as possible was the only practical way to prevent the spread of VD, and that this necessitated state involvement in the control of those who practised vice.[29]

Another advocate of the regulation was Salomon Henschen, medical researcher specializing in diseases of the brain and a controversial and headstrong debater.[30] Henschen denied that the regulation was discriminatory or that it stigmatized women. He argued that, just as society imprisoned robbers, it should incarcerate prostitutes. Nor did he regard regulation as an affront to women, since he maintained that 'any woman that gives her body for money to the first person that pays is undeserving of respect from society'.[31] These strong opinions must have affected the members of the Association and indicate the type of conservative opposition that Johansson had to face among his colleagues.

Nevertheless, there was also significant support for Johansson and his ideas. A number of physicians no longer believed that the compulsory control of prostitutes would be the most effective measure against VD. Instead, they argued the need for education, prophylactics and contact tracing. Ulrich Müller Aspegren, who had been authorized to inspect the prostitutes in Stockholm between 1905 and 1916, Magnus Möller, Karolina Widerström, and other physicians in Stockholm, pressed for the total repeal of regulation. On the premise that men and women were going to expose themselves to contagion, irrespective of social regulations, Ulrich Müller Aspegren argued for the use of prophylactics and a more modern attitude to sexuality.[32] Meanwhile, in the course of working for the Commission, Magnus Möller had changed his mind with respect to regulation, and now viewed it as worthless for the control of gonorrhoea.[33]

Widerström argued against the use of force and for the need for humanitarian insights among physicians and Commission members. She pointed out the low wages of female workers and how this forced women to prostitute themselves in order to survive. Widerström argued that the suggested measure, to penalize prostitutes by subjecting them to forced labour, would only make them more contemptuous of society. Since voluntary rescue homes had previously proved effective, she advocated instead economic support for these institutions. Unlike many of her colleagues, Widerström considered it unnecessary for physicians to practise coercive measures against VD, on the grounds that such diseases were non-epidemic and that every adult was capable of recognizing the symptoms and seeking treatment voluntarily.[34]

Argument continued in several of the meetings of the Association in 1912. In November of that year, it voted to recommend the continued regulation of professional prostitutes. However, since the debate within the Association had been so prolonged, its statement to the *Medicinalstyrelsen* merely included every protocol from every meeting. Upset at the outcome, Karolina Widerström and J. E. Johansson took the matter to the press, expressing regret that the Association had not been able to produce meaningful advice on the issue for government policy-makers.[35] The newspaper articles caused an outrage in the *Svenska Läkaresällskapet*. Conservative members argued that debates taking place within the Association should not be aired in public.[36] In the event, the Association never did succeed in issuing a decisive statement.

Clearly, the abolitionist case still had to be made. Accordingly, J. E. Johansson published a pamphlet entitled *Prostitutionen och lösdrivarelagen* (Prostitution and the Vagrancy Act) with the help of *Svenska Föreningen för moderskydd och social reform*, an organization for the protection of mothers and social reform. Johansson argued that the Commission's proposals would subject prostitutes to an unfair and arbitrary judicial system and actually worsen their position. He considered that infected women would be sufficiently controlled by the general sanitary regulations proposed for VD without clauses specifically targeting prostitutes. Moreover, he warned that, while the regulation of professional prostitutes had hitherto been sanctioned purely by local laws, the Regulation Commission threatened to incorporate it within the Constitution. Although Johansson was certain that the regulation would eventually fall into disuse, he questioned why Swedish society would wish to prolong such an ineffective and immoral policy.[37]

Although the *Federation* had suspended its attacks on the system of regulation in 1903, in anticipation of the outcome of the Regulation Commission, it now revived its campaign. In its publication, *Reformer och skenreformer*, it welcomed the fact that the matter had been investigated and resolved. However, the *Federation* had equally strong reservations about the new proposals. In its opinion, on past experience, putting these freedom-loving women under the threat of forced labour was unlikely to prove effective. It agreed with Johansson's view that these women would be forced to accept employment merely to avoid imprisonment. However, it had no objections to mandatory medical treatment, as long as it was equally applied to both men and women.[38]

Meanwhile, the disappointment and anger felt by the Swedish women's movement at the Commission's recommendations can best be illustrated by Hilda

Sachs's book, *Den svarta domen: männens skuld och kvinnornas straff* (*The Black Judgement – Men's Guilt and Women's Punishment*).[39] Of the Commission's wish to retain the regulation of prostitution, she wrote:

> Since these measures do not interfere with those declared dangerous to the health of the people, but only those believed to be morally bad, it is clear that these are not the most scientifically useful measures but simply the legacy of a cruel and despicable punishment of sin.[40]

Sachs blamed all men for the regulation of prostitution on the grounds that most of them either visited prostitutes or tacitly supported the continuation of the system of regulated prostitution.

Other women writers who addressed the issue of VD and the statutory control of female prostitutes included Frida Stéenhof, Selma Billström and Alma Sundqvist. Frida Stéenhof, author and advocate of free love, documented the abuse of women taking place in the Bureau in 1904. She criticized Edvard Welander's views on prostitution for their bias against young women and lack of awareness of female poverty and low wages.[41] In several dramas, Frida Stéenhof presented true and equal love between spouses as the only solution to injustice and poverty. Stéenhof is considered one of the first radical feminists in Sweden[42] and probably played a significant part in initiating women's resistance to regulation.

Selma Billström described the inhumane and disrespectful treatment of women in the Bureau in Stockholm. Lecturing to women's meetings, she highlighted the role of syphilis as the cause of endless emotional stress for wives and mothers, of poor male health, and as a lethal disease in infants. Billström argued that vice and drunkenness were to blame for the spread of these diseases, and that it was wholly unfair only to regulate women. When describing the Bureau where prostitutes in Stockholm were registered, she vividly portrayed a situation where police officers maintained order while two physicians performed highly invasive physical examinations.[43]

In a pamphlet in 1913, Alma Sundqvist highlighted the fact that many women were more or less forced into prostitution because their menfolk drank and were unable to support their families. She cited, as typical, the experience of a young girl who had contracted gonorrhoea, describing the deprivation caused by her father, who was a drunkard and who demanded a large part of her meagre income for the support of his four children. As a result, she could only afford to enjoy dancing and an occasional movie by offering herself to 'familiar boys' and thus becoming registered as a prostitute. Sundqvist argued that, if this girl had had an opportunity to earn a fair wage, her life would have been a lot easier and she could have avoided becoming registered as a prostitute, and considered it an outrage to punish women instead of men for the incidence of VD in Swedish society.[44]

Women were most certainly active in the fight against the spread of VD.

Female physicians wrote several books and pamphlets in order to educate the public on sexual matters. Ellen Sandelin, Alma Sundqvist and Karolina Widerström published books with explicit information about genitals, procreation and sexually transmitted diseases.[45] However, the public discussion of sexual issues relating to VD was heavily constrained in early-twentieth-century Sweden. The discussion, sale and use of prophylactics were banned in 1910, and any books published after this date were prohibited from mentioning them.

Between 1910 and 1915, when the Commission finally submitted its recommendations and the *Medicinalstyrelsen* filed its formal response, a far-ranging debate took place in Sweden. The debate made it clear that any suggestion of continuing the regulation of prostitution would have a hard time finding acceptance in Swedish society. In 1917, two physicians, Karl Marcus and Seved Ribbing, were appointed to reconsider the suggestions recommended by the Commission. Ribbing refused to support the continued official recognition of regulated prostitution but considered coercive measures against those suffering from VD an act of humanity.[46] He returned to puritan ideals when suggesting measures to improve sexual hygiene. Thus, he stressed the importance of temperance and avoidance of salacious literature, as well as of thrift and moral education of the young in ensuring healthy sexuality. Ribbing emphasized the need for a single moral standard for men and women and the iniquity of men blaming 'seductive women' for their own immoral behaviour.[47] In his view, the model citizen would be an educated and moral person who, while acknowledging his/her sexuality, controlled it within suitable limits.

In 1917, Walter Murray, Minister of Public Administration, also submitted a report in which he reviewed the recommendations of the Regulation Commission and summarized the different opinions that had been aired over the years. Murray was hesitant about treating professional prostitutes any differently from other citizens. He argued that so-called 'professional' prostitutes only represented one-tenth of the women who prostituted themselves as a spare-time occupation. Furthermore, he maintained that regulation primarily targeted older women, who, he alleged, were immune to further contagion and therefore less dangerous to their clients. He could find no justification for keeping any remnant of the regulation within the judicial measures designed to combat VD. Nevertheless, Murray stressed the need for extensive sanitary measures against the spread of venereal infection. He suggested that sanitary inspectors should have extended powers to report misbehaving patients who were sexually promiscuous or who defaulted from treatment. He also suggested that anyone, male or female, who was arrested under the Vagrancy Act should be inspected for VD.[48] The report by Murray formed the basis for government proposals, passed by both chambers in May 1918.[49]

Contemporary debate had an obvious impact on the final version of the legislation. The proposal from the Commission, as submitted in 1910, was significantly altered to improve patient confidentiality and to lessen the threat of patients being reported immediately they defaulted from medical treatment. The regulation of prostitution *per se* was to be completely repealed. Nevertheless, in practice, the legal situation of prostitutes significantly worsened when the vagrancy laws were reactivated against them soon afterwards. Although VD policy was in some ways consistent with contemporary efforts to establish a welfare state and wider opportunities for universal medical care, this was not the case with respect to the treatment of prostitutes. Women who deviated from accepted norms of sexual behaviour were not considered equally deserving within the new society.

The outcome: Lex Veneris

When legislation was eventually passed in the form of Lex Veneris on 20 June 1918, it was markedly different from the original recommendations of the Commission. In thirty-one different paragraphs, Lex Veneris defined the venereal diseases that were to be subject to statutory controls and the means by which patients and physicians were to cooperate to contain their spread. The law was applied to patients who had been diagnosed as suffering from contagious forms of syphilis, soft chancre and gonorrhoea. Where appointed, the duty of implementing the law was devolved upon Town's physicians. Where there were several such physicians, the senior physician was held responsible. In areas where there were no such physicians, responsibility was devolved to the first provincial physician.[50] In every county, a physician was appointed *sundhetsinspektör* (sanitary inspector) and held responsible for containing the spread of contagious diseases.

Any man or woman who believed he/she had become infected with VD was obliged to subject themselves to the necessary medical treatment. The patients were also to follow certain medical stipulations in order to limit the spread of disease. All medical examinations, prescriptions and materials were free of charge, regardless of the patient's income. If the disease could be treated without hospitalization, the patient could not be forced to go to hospital. Five different categories of state-employed physicians were to provide free medical care so that patients could obtain treatment even if they resided in remote parts of the country.

Local authorities were obliged to provide medical care, and in order to ensure that they met this obligation, most provisions were publicly funded. If deemed necessary, a municipality could be forced to employ physicians specifically to care for VD patients, and if possible, one of these medical practitioners was to be female. Any town that had more than 20,000 citizens could apply for government funding to provide the necessary number of out-patient clinics. Laboratories for serological or bacteriological investigations were also to be state financed. In addition, public funding paid for travel costs incurred by provincial physicians in visiting remote communities where outbreaks of VD were suspected.

Lex Veneris also implied wide-ranging responsibilities for the individual physician. When a patient was found to be suffering from VD, the physician was obliged to inform the patient of the rules he/she was expected to obey in order to ensure effective treatment. Some patients, such as children under 15 years old, were not to be told of their disease. The physician was obliged to inform the guardian of a minor with VD, and the guardian was responsible for the contagion not being passed on to others. Marriage was prohibited for anyone who could transmit VD. It was strictly forbidden to expose anyone to the risk of being infected. If the physician found that one of his patients failed to comply with these rules, he was obliged to report this to the sanitary inspector. The sanitary inspector would then repeatedly request the patient to comply with the directives. If unsuccessful, he was entitled to enlist the help of the police in compelling the patient to receive hospital care.

Although the formal medical regulation of prostitution *per se* was excluded from Lex Veneris, it remained clear that anyone arrested for illicit behaviour according to the Penal Code could be reported to the sanitary inspector. The inspector could then require that arrested persons subject themselves to a medical inspection and, if found diseased, treatment. Any patient who refused such a request would be reported to the local Health Board. Together, the physician and the Board were entitled to ask the local police force for help in compelling the patient to undergo medical treatment.

Lex Veneris also prohibited any civil servant from spreading information arising out of its administration to any third party. Minutes, case notes and other papers were to be kept strictly confidential. Only when the transmission of VD was part of legal proceedings could its existence be divulged. Under Lex Veneris, it was also a crime for a physician to fail to report a patient to the sanitary inspector or to follow up on patients who moved away from their district. The public attorney was empowered to bring a charge of malpractice against any physician contravening these regulations and to impose a fine. It is evident that although regulation had formally ended, the sanitation measures that replaced it were in many ways equally, if not more, coercive. Purity coercion was replaced by a more medicalized form of social control.

Conclusions

This chapter has shown how social policy concerning VD was shaped in early-twentieth-century Sweden and inspired by contemporary ideas of social welfare. While, in the 1880s and 1890s, the issue of prostitution and VD had been the focus of extensive debate, it was only after the turn of the century that a new generation of physicians advanced more progressive strategies of prophylaxis and education as alternatives to regulation. These ideas caused unprecedented divisions within the Swedish medical profession, with the forces of conservatism vigorously defending the retention of regulated prostitution for women for whom 'debauchery' was the only employment.

The strategies adopted to combat VD in early-twentieth-century Sweden were primarily dictated by central government. Local government and society had relatively little say in shaping policy. Financial, medical and legal processes were imposed from above. Consistent with their employment within the state apparatus since the early seventeenth century, Swedish physicians were closely regulated by national guidelines in their treatment of VD.[51] Moreover, the thrust of state controls accorded with their own traditional conservatism regarding female sexuality. As a result, the fight against discriminatory policies concerning VD was bitter and protracted, and a new policy, Lex Veneris, was not enacted until 1918.

In important respects, Lex Veneris reflected significant shifts in Swedish society. Its enactment coincided with democratic reforms that transformed the political scene and challenged existing class and gender inequalities.[52] Lex Veneris applied wide-ranging VD controls and sanitary surveillance to all citizens and not just targeted groups in society, and significantly attracted the support of Swedish socialists. In many respects, it drew more on progressive strands of welfarism within Swedish society rather than a return to a more traditional agrarian sanitationism, as Baldwin would suggest.[53] Nonetheless, while the issue of VD had been medicalized and distanced from the regulation of public order and public morality,[54] the legal position of prostitutes had not been significantly improved. While policy-makers, such as *Medicinalstyrelsen* or the parliamentary committees, were keen to rehabilitate VD patients into the new society, by extending medical provisions and the social inclusion of the sick, this did not extend to prostitutes. Indeed, according to Tomas Söderblom, they continued to be coerced in interwar Sweden under the vagrancy laws for what was perceived to be deviant and dangerous sexuality, and their situation actually worsened. If they had no means of support other than prostitution, lived in houses of 'ill-repute', or otherwise offended public morals, they were liable to be sentenced under the laws to forced labour. Those regarded by the state as prostitutes were not among those who were to be considered suitable members of the 'new' and idealistic Swedish society.[55]

NOTES

1 For a detailed analysis of the history of VD in Sweden, see A. Lundberg, *Care and Coercion, Medical Knowledge, Social Policy and Patients with VD in Sweden 1785–1903*. Report no. 14 from the Demographic Data Base, Umeå, 1999. K. Johannisson, *Medicinens öga – sjukdom, medicin och samhälle. Historiska erfarenheter*, Värnamo, Norstedts, 1990, pp. 191–4.

2 RA, Kungliga Brev: Circulaire till samtlige landshövdingar ang. Veneriska Smittans förekommande och medel att bota densamma Örebro Slott 10 junii 1812.

3 Härnösands landsarkiv. Patient-records from the County Hospital in Härnösand, 1814–44.

4 P. Baldwin, *Contagion and the State in Europe 1830–1930*, Cambridge, Cambridge University Press, 1999, p. 371; T. Lundqvist, *Den disciplinerade dubbelmoralen*, Göteborg, SkrivCity, 1982, passim.

5 U. Boëthius, *Strindberg och kvinnofrågan till och med Giftas I*, Stockholm, Prisma, 1969, pp. 63–5.

6 Official print from the Riksdag, 1893, FK Motion no. 15. Lundqvist, *Den disciplinerade,* p. 354 and H. Levin, *Masken uti rosen nymalthusianism och födelsekontroll i Sverige 1880–1910: Propaganda och motstånd,* Stockholm, Brutus Östlings Bokförlag, 1994, p. 340.
7 Baldwin, *Contagion,* p. 390.
8 *Bidrag till Sveriges Offentliga Statistik Medicinalstyrelsens årsberättelse,* Stockholm, PA Norstedts, 1901, tab. 23b. *Sveriges Offentliga Statistik – Hälsa och sjukvård 1,* Stockholm, PA Norstedts, 1918, p. 162.
9 'Filth-Sweden' *(lortsverige)* is a frequently used expression to describe pre-1940s Sweden. It signified the antithesis of the cleaner, modern society that contemporary social engineers strove for.
10 Baldwin, *Contagion,* pp. 408, 474.
11 J. Lewis, G. Åström and Y. Hirdman (eds) *Equality, Difference and State Welfare: the Case of Labour Market and Family Policies in Sweden,* Uppsala, Maktutredningen, 1991; L. Sommestad, 'Privat eller offentlig välfärd?: ett genusperspektiv på välfärdsstaternas historiska formering', *Historisk Tidskrift,* 1994, vol. 4, pp. 602–29.
12 A. Ruth, 'The second new nation: the mythology of modern Sweden', *Daedalus,* 1984, vol. 113, no. 2, pp. 81–3, 92.
13 K. Johannisson, 'Folkhälsa. Det svenska projektet från 1900 till 2:a världskriget', *Lychnos,* 1991, Annual of the Swedish History of Science Society, Swedish Science Press, pp. 135–7.
14 Ibid., p. 141.
15 E. Palmblad and B-E. Eriksson, *Kropp och politik. Hälsoupplysning och samhällspegel,* Eslöv, Carlsson, 1995, passim; G. Carlsson and O. Arvidsson, *Kampen för folkhälsan – prevention i historia och nutid,* Uppsala, Natur och Kultur i samarbete med forskningsrådsnämnden, 1994, p. 82.
16 E. Welander, 'Huru kunna motarbeta de veneriska sjukdomarnas spridning Föredrag i Svenska Läkarsällskapet den 7 Maj såsom inledning till den af sällskapet beslutade diskussionen angående denna fråga', *Hygiea – medicinsk och pharmaceutisk månadskrift,* 1901, pp. 675–713.
17 'Föredrag i Svenska Läkaresällskapet den 26 November 1901 under diskussionen angående de veneriska sjukdomarnas sociala vådor och profylaxi', *Hygiea – medicinsk och pharmaceutisk månadskrift,* 1902, pp. 185–207.
18 Official print from the *Riksdag,* 1903. AK Motion no. 88.
19 *National Encyclopaedia,* Höganäs, Bra Böckers Bokförlag, vol. 8, 1992, p. 480; vol. 19, 1996, p. 308.
20 Official print from the *Riksdag,* 1903. AK Motion, no. 88.
21 Official print from the *Riksdag,* 1903. Skrivelse, no. 87.
22 A Town's physician was a civil servant with responsibility for all matters concerning health in the town.
23 Details on these civil servants can be found in biographical dictionaries such as *Svenskt Biografisk Lexikon,* Stockholm, Norstedts & Söner, ongoing publication, *Svenska Män och Kvinnor,* Stockholm, Albert Bonniers Bokförlag, 1955; *Nationalencyclopedia.*
24 *Bihang till Riksdagens protokoll vid lagtima Riksdagen i Stockholm, 2a saml, 2a avd 4de bandet. Underdånigt betänkande angående åtgärder för motarbetande af de smittosamma könssjukdomarnas spridning,* Stockholm, 1910.
25 Ibid., p. 12.
26 K. Leijer, 'Medicinalstyrelsens utlåtande angående reglementeringskommitténs betänkande', *Allmäna Svenska Läkaretidningen,* 1915, vol. 39, pp. 977–88.
27 *Förhandlingar vid Svenska Läkaresällskapets sammankomster,* Stockholm, 1912, p. 349.
28 H, Marcus, 'Frithiof Lennmalm', in *Hygiea – medicinsk och pharmaceutisk månadskrift,* 1924, pp. 561, 586.
29 *Förhandlingar,* 1912, pp. 349–52.

30 *Svensk biografiskt lexikon*, pp. 670–3.
31 *Förhandlingar*, 1912, pp. 353–5.
32 Ibid., pp. 188–9.
33 Ibid., 1911, pp. 511–2.
34 Ibid., 1912, pp. 25–31.
35 Dagens Nyheter, 20 and 21 November 1912.
36 *Förhandlingar*, 1912, p. 680.
37 J. E. Johansson, *Prostitutionen och lösdrivarelagen*, Stockholm, Svenska Föreningen för moderskydd och sexualreform, 1912, p. 55.
38 *Reformer och skenreformer*, Stockholm, Den Svenska Federationsavdelningens Styrelse, 1912, passim.
39 H. Sachs, *Den svarta domen: männens skuld och kvinnornas straff*, Stockholm, Wahlström & Widstrand, 1912.
40 Ibid., p. 11.
41 F. Stéenhof, *Den reglementerade prostitutionen ur feministisk synpunkt*, Stockholm, Björck & Börjesson, 1904, p. 20.
42 C. Carlsson-Wetterberg, 'Penningen, kärleken och makten Frida Stéenhofs feministiska alternativ', in U. Wikander (ed.) *Det evigt kvinnliga – en historia om förändring*, Värnamo, Tidens förlag, 1994, pp. 80, 102.
43 S. Billström, *Prostitutionsbyråns verksamhet och nytta. Inledningsföredrag af Selma Billström*, Stockholm, Emil Olssons tryckeri, 1910, pp. 3–4,10–11.
44 A. Sundqvist, *Samhället och prostitutionen*, Stockholm, Aktiebolaget Ljus, 1913, pp. 43–5.
45 E. Sandelin, *Om några smittosamma sjukdomar och deras sociala faror*, Stockholm, Wilhelm Billes Bokförlags Aktiebolag, 1902; A. Sundqvist, *Samhället och prostitutionen*, Stockholm, Aktiebolaget Ljus, 1913; K. Widerström, *Kvinnohygien*, Stockholm, P. A. Norstedt & Söners förlag, 1905.
46 S. Ribbing, *Den sexuella hygienen och några av dess etiska konsekvenser*, Stockholm, Albert Bonniers Bokförlag, 1915, pp. 213–14.
47 Ibid., pp. 254–9.
48 Official print from the *Riksdag*, 1918, proposition no 154, p. 36, pp. 41–3, 58–9.
49 K. Marcus, 'Den nya lagen angående åtgärder mot utbredning av könssjukdomar', in *Allmäna Svenska Läkartidningen*, 1918, no. 38, pp. 1,233, 1,253.
50 A provincial physician was a civil servant given responsibility for health-related matters in rural districts.
51 Similar patterns also characterize state controls and HIV/AIDS policy-making in late-twentieth-century Sweden. See B. Henriksson and H. Ytterberg, 'Sweden: The power of the moral (istic) Left', in D. I. Kirp and R. Bayer (eds) *AIDS in the Industrialized Democracies: Passions, Politics and Policies*, New Brunswick, Rutgers University Press, 1992, pp. 317–38.
52 From 1921, the Social Democrats held the majority of seats in both chambers of parliament (*Riksdag*). Women were granted the vote in 1921 and allowed to hold government posts after 1923. In addition, legislation was introduced according men and women equal legal status within marriage.
53 Baldwin's claim that Sweden 'went back to the future' in introducing Lex Veneris is therefore too simplistic and understates the more urban radical forces shaping Swedish social policy in the first half of the twentieth century.
54 Baldwin, *Contagion*, pp. 406–8; however, see also I. Millbourn, 'Prostitutionem och folkhemmet', *Historisk Tidskrift*, 1994, vol. 3, pp. 507–17.
55 T. Söderblom, *Horan och batongen. Prostitutionen och repression i folkhemmet*, Stockholm, Gidlunds Bokförlag, 1992, passim.

3

'THE SHADOW OF CONTAGION'

Gender, syphilis and the regulation of prostitution in the Netherlands, 1870–1914

Petra de Vries

Introduction

The popular view that people in the Victorian era were not supposed to express their feelings certainly does not hold true for venereal disease (VD). Like all contagious diseases that could be lethal, VD naturally inspired awe and fear, but nothing compares to the emotional responses it evoked as a sickness with sexual overtones. 'Syphilis', a term used for a variety of symptoms, was frequently described as a horrible and monstrous disease that spread its poison in darkness and in silence. It was a snake, hiding in a bed of roses. Its companion – prostitution – evoked disgust, despair, disbelief, cynicism, anger, fear, and various other feelings at the darker side of the range of human emotions. All of this had a basis in a harsh reality: the vivid descriptions in medical literature show us the suffering of those who did not survive their contacts with sin or who continued living with gruesome afflictions.

In an effort to control the real or presumed spread of VD in the nineteenth century, local and national authorities in many European countries introduced a system of sanitary inspection of prostitutes that involved the regulation of prostitution by the state. The Netherlands owed its own system of regulation to France, dating from about 1800 while the Dutch were under French rule. Military and nationalist arguments – the health of the soldier – constituted significant grounds for regulation, as was the case in the Napoleonic armies, but controlling diseases by policing prostitution was nothing new, historically speaking, and had been practised long before. After the departure of the French, sanitary supervision of prostitutes subsided somewhat until it surfaced again with renewed vigour in the mid-nineteenth century.[1] A description of the features of the Dutch system of state regulation of prostitution as it developed in the second half of the nineteenth century precedes the central questions of this chapter.

Looked at from the point of view of the prostitute, regulation operated as follows.[2] If she wanted to work in a particular town, she had to go to the police who entered her name in a register. From that point on, she was obliged to submit to a regular medical inspection of her genitals to ensure that she did not have syphilis or any other VD. If she was given a clean bill of health, this was reported in a small book, a kind of health passport. If she was discovered to be contaminated, her booklet was withheld and she was forbidden to practise her trade. From the point of view of the authorities, the system was based on two forms of power. The first was the expert opinion of a new generation of medical men; hygienists supported the system in the interests of 'public health', a new concept at the time. The second form of power consisted of a set of police regulations backed up by the local council. Hence, no national law existed, such as the better-known Contagious Diseases Acts in England that introduced regulation in certain 'designated districts'. Municipalities could decide autonomously whether or not to regulate. So some cities, about thirty-seven altogether, had sanitary regulations while others, notably Amsterdam – a city then already famous for its whores – never implemented them.[3]

Regulating diseases by police control was clearly a repressive state measure interfering with the lives of those women who were labelled as prostitutes. Although the system in the Netherlands was relatively loose compared to France, where prostitutes suffered under the infamous *police des moeurs*, the police in Dutch towns also had wide-ranging power. Policemen could pick up women from the streets, subject them to a medical examination and register them. In the port town of Rotterdam in 1877, for example, they picked up a total of 119 women from the streets and cafés and found ninety-three infected.[4] The most extreme measure the authorities could (and did) take was to lock up diseased prostitutes in a hospital until they were considered healthy again. They could be placed either in a special syphilitic hospital or in a special ward of a general hospital. If patients got any treatment at all, they were often treated with mercury, the traditional remedy against syphilis.

Regulation would perhaps have disappeared from the historical record as one of the many examples of how a powerful state ruled over its poorer citizens were it not for the rise of an international social movement against the system in the last decades of the century. Controlling VD by regulating prostitution became a 'question', an issue surrounded by intense political controversy. In the Netherlands, thousands of people from very different ideological backgrounds were mobilized to support a ban on brothels at the turn of the century. Many public debates on the sanitary inspection of prostitutes raged throughout this period among a wide range of lay people and professionals. By 1900, a vast amount of national and international literature had accumulated, a true discursive explosion of academic, social, medical, legal and political views on prostitution, VD and society. This movement, which fought against what its adherents referred to as 'the state regulation of vice', became known on the continent as *abolitionism* or the abolitionist movement. The use of these terms was intended as a reminder of black slavery. Indeed, to many of the movement's more radical advocates, prostitution was a form of 'white slavery' and regulation its legitimized form. Although the concept of white slavery contained many racist connotations, there was some truth in it as well. Prostitutes often lived in brothels as 'boarders' on a more or less permanent basis, and could easily be exploited by their madams (especially when it was a 'closed' brothel). As early as 1860, the evangelical philanthropist Ottho Heldring, founder of a network of rescue homes for 'fallen women', protested against this exploitation of prostitutes in brothels in his essay 'Does slavery still exist in the Netherlands?'[5]

At the end of the century, the regulation system broke down and was finally abandoned in the early twentieth century. This was legally reinforced by a ban on brothels in 1911, which was part of a whole set of laws, including a prohibition against the traffic in women.

At this point, it may already be clear that the regulation of prostitution is a fascinating, yet complex issue for the historian. It raises questions about the relationship between gender and sexuality, between women and the state, and between medical knowledge and political organization. It would seem that regulation did not simply appear and disappear because new and modern discoveries in bacteriology and new medical knowledge gave rise to new concepts of treating syphilis. Who infected whom was a social, if not a political, question. So, on the one hand, we must reject the idea of continuous progress of medical knowledge having a predictable social effect and try to contextualize medical opinion and discourse within a whole field of social and political forces.[6] But on the other hand, one cannot assume that political arguments and social movements alone were responsible for the disappearance of the system of sanitary inspection. So how were medical debates about VD related to the political debates about the prostitute and her shadow of contagion? In what sense did the two influence each other? Did medical knowledge bring about social changes, or did social conditions determine the range of medical options? Within the framework of these broader questions, this chapter specifically focuses on the sexual aspects and the gendered nature of regulation and anti-regulation politics. What assumptions about gender, sexuality and disease were underlying the system, how were these assumptions contested by the anti-regulationists, and what was the final outcome of this process?

The gender of syphilis

The first female doctor of medicine in the Netherlands, Aletta Jacobs, describes a scene she witnessed as a student of the University of Groningen in the 1870s:

> One day one of the professors requested me to go with him and his assistant to an annex of the hospital, where nine poorly-dressed women appeared to be awaiting our arrival. They were told in a rough voice to undress and lie down on a wooden table one after the other. Without

even touching them, both men examined their 'objects'. After a brief
consultation seven women were allowed to leave and the other two were
notified that they would have to go to the hospital. The seven women
were then led away by an insolent-looking fellow who was waiting for
them.[7]

This critical description of a medical examination under regulation is noteworthy, not only because eye-witness accounts are few and far between, but also
because Jacobs was probably the only woman ever present at such an examination in the role of doctor.[8] However, she did not fully understand what regulation
had to do with public health. While searching for information, she met with a
conspiracy of silence. Neither the professor with whom she crossed swords over
the supposed healthiness of male sexual gratification, nor other experts, were
willing to answer her questions. Librarians looked upon her with suspicion and
evaded her quest for certain titles. The silence was not broken until years later
when she was fully 'informed' about the meaning of the medical examination by
the well-known English doctor, Charles Drysdale. And indeed, the word
'informed', as she used it in her autobiography, bears the connotation of being
taught about some hidden sexual matter.[9]
    Of course this was not an isolated case involving a single female doctor. It is
obvious that the medical side of regulation was the affair of the male doctor who
knew the secrets of the female body. The gendered nature of regulation is often
commented upon by historians who point to the gross inequalities poor women
suffered when controlled by an all-male medical police.[10] Sanitary control in the
Netherlands was no exception. In fact, the particular gender arrangements of
nineteenth-century society were one of the important foundations of the system,
as epitomized by the use of diseased prostitutes in medical college classes. It
would have been impossible to show the genitals of a respectable lady in the
medical theatre for an all-male audience to inspect, but a prostitute sometimes
suffered this fate precisely because it was assumed that she had lost her true femininity and sense of shame anyway. (Perhaps to spare them and the audience an
embarrassing session, Leiden Academic Hospital repeatedly examined prostitutes 'under anaesthetics'.)[11]
    The very idea of regulation rested on the assumption that VD spread from
the body of a particular kind of woman to a man and, by inference, to his family.
There was no written theory that laid down systematically a medical model of
contagion that excluded male bodies as sources of contagion, but such a model is
evident from the theories and practices of the time. When regulation was revived
in the middle of the century, the idea of national health and social medicine was
promoted by hygienists who were concerned about cholera, drinking water and
sewage systems. New applications of statistics provided them with knowledge
about the spread of diseases, and the risks of particular social groups such as
inhabitants of poor areas. It seemed somehow logical to apply the existing model
of prevention to brothels and to other forms of prostitution. (The most famous

expert on prostitution, Dr Alexandre Parent-Duchâtelet, once compared his studies of prostitution with his studies of the Paris sewage system. In both cases, he had to stand in the excrement of society.)[12]

Prevailing attitudes about class and gender greatly supported this medical approach, as is reflected in the deep distrust of female sexuality in official documents on regulation. Up until the 1880s, an older state commission report was referred to – or perhaps actually used – as a model for regulation at the level of cities and municipalities. The members of the commission, all influential administrative authorities, argued that the sanitary inspection of prostitutes should be incorporated into the Dutch national law. This plan was never put into practice but its underlying arguments were kept alive for a long time. To highlight its point, the commission warned explicitly of the danger that emanated from different types of contaminated, lying, seductive, untrustworthy, immoral women who could ruin an innocent man. For example, the report stated that the most dangerous form of prostitution was that which entered the family in the disguise of a servant girl: 'Putting on the deceptive mask of the servant class it sneaks into the family home.' She apparently posed a threat to family harmony and integrity by transmitting her 'deadly poison' secretly to the unsuspecting men in this family.[13] The commission members observed that the 'clandestine prostitute' often succeeded in deceiving a man in order to drag him into a marriage, and this unhappy man then had 'to sacrifice the ties with his family and friends' in order to do so.[14] Fear of an unclean female body inhabited by a vicious lower-class soul was a recurring theme until at least 1900: it was not only prostitution as the main source of contamination that haunted the medical and popular literature of the time, but syphilis itself was imagined in a female body; women, not men, symbolized the connection between sexuality and death.

Statistics and the 'public' woman

The view that the prostitute's body was a main source of contamination went together with an obsession with the morality, and hence the health, of the young male. In texts and in iconography, the prototypical victim was often portrayed as a young man, blinded by passion and seduced by lewd women. The image of the male victim was also borne out by the way statistics were compiled and presented. Since prostitutes themselves were hardly ever seen as victims of VD, but at best, as intermediaries, the record of their sickness was mostly instrumental. They appeared as 'sources' in statistics. A particularly good example can be found in *Die Prostitution* by Dr Iwan Bloch, the well-known German authority on prostitution and regulation. Bloch, himself an anti-regulationist, innocently quotes as *Infektionsquellen* (sources of infection) in Mannheim in 1904 a list of female persons, referring to this information as 'an instructive statistic'. Part of his table is reproduced here.

Sources	No. of patients
waitress, barmaid	155
servant girl, cook	67
saleswoman	65
middle-class girl, daughter of the house	29
seamstress, needlewoman	27

And so the list goes on, containing all possible categories of mostly lower-class women, totalling 442 cases.[15] One cannot fail to notice that the concept of 'public health', the cornerstone of regulation and a concept that reflected significant new social approaches in medicine, was in fact loaded with masculine meanings. One of the most striking aspects of sanitary control for us today, namely, the fact that an attempt was made to control VD by the forced examination of prostitutes, and not of the men who visited them,[16] did not have its roots in a medical flaw. It was entirely in accordance with the construction of syphilis as a gendered disease.

Bloch's statistics also point us to a crucial question: who was 'a prostitute'? Or rather, what exactly was a *public* woman, and what distinguished her from other women? Looking into medical, political and legal discourses about prostitution from about 1850 to 1900, it becomes clear that the concept of prostitute itself was as much a product of state control as a reality. Police registration simply rendered a woman 'public'. Throughout the whole period, the authorities made a distinction between 'secret' and 'public' prostitution, 'secret' being the most dangerous category. The intention was to transform all 'secret' prostitution into 'public' prostitution; that is, to bring it under police supervision. By lack of any legal definition of what constituted 'a prostitute', 'secret' could theoretically be applied to any immoral woman. Police regulations in some cities spoke of prostitutes as 'all women who habitually are leading a lewd life', others were more specific, defining as prostitutes 'all those who live from prostitution'.[17]

The ideological distinction between the respectable lady and the prostitute went together with a geographical separation between them. For example, brothels were not allowed in the main streets, and they were to have non-transparent curtains. Prostitutes at public places like theatres were allowed only in areas designated by the police. They were not supposed to solicit immorally in the streets. To be defined as 'public' as opposed to 'private' meant that a person fitted into a liberal state policy that saw its remit as the public sphere. In fact, given the classical liberal paradigm about male power in the family, one may observe an interesting parallel between the power of the father and the power of the state. Just as the father controlled the sexuality of his wife and daughters, the state supervised the public woman. Prostitutes were treated in accordance with what were seen as strategies to maintain public health, public morality and public order; vague concepts that could be flexibly applied to fit particular circumstances. And once defined as 'public', the consequences could be far-reaching.

Medical truth and abolitionist politics

While medical confidence in regulation as a way of controlling VD stood almost unchallenged until about 1880, by the turn of the century the dominant discourse about regulation and prostitution had changed dramatically. If we turn our attention again for a moment to Aletta Jacobs, we see that, no longer a student, she had become a doctor, a pioneer of neo-Malthusianism and an international suffragist leader. At a public lecture in Rotterdam in 1902, she spoke with the authority of a doctor about VD, regulation and prostitution.[18] She also spoke more implicitly as 'woman' against a system she deeply detested as degrading to women, as a form of sexual exploitation, and a reflection of male sexual standards implemented by a state that denied women citizenship. Again, this was not an isolated case involving a single female doctor. Women's entry into the medical profession marked the end of an era in which women were mere objects and not subjects of medical knowledge. The development of organized feminism and its theoretical notions of sexual inequality made it possible to expose both the gendered nature of regulation and the state. The medical tide was turning against regulation as well, as was indicated by an important international conference, *Conférence internationale pour la Prophylaxie de la Syphilis et des Maladies vénériennes*, attended mainly by medical men and representatives of local authorities and national governments, held in Brussels in 1899.[19] Among the conference members the belief in the effectiveness of regulation, at least in its existing form, had been severely undermined.[20]

In her lecture, Jacobs merely reiterated the powerful arguments which anti-regulationists had already advanced in preceding decades. Abolitionism arose in the Netherlands almost directly as a result of Josephine Butler's famous 'crusade' against regulation. Her followers initially came from an evangelical-Protestant ('orthodox-Protestant') background and were related to an international movement for religious revival, the so-called Réveil. The most important male abolitionist leader, the Reverend Hendrik Pierson, was an evangelical Protestant and director of the Heldring Rescue Homes for fallen women. In 1877 he published a translation of Butler's *Une Voix dans le Désert*, which had been issued some years before as a result of her European tour among anti-regulationist sympathizers.[21] Pierson also founded the Dutch Society Against Prostitution[22] as a branch of the *Fédération Abolitionniste Internationale* in 1879, shortly after issuing *Legalized Vice*, which was more or less a programme to fight regulation and prostitution.[23] His main argument, developed in the 1880s, was that the state should not organize sin, that sanitary control was ineffective and that VD could be better prevented by closing brothels. Vice, sin and morality were among the central concepts of abolitionist thought, but we would be making a mistake if we were to dismiss the opposition to regulation as mere puritanical sentiment. Abolitionism was as complex as regulation itself. The abolitionists were a very mixed group of people, a coalition of orthodox-Protestant men and women, socialists, feminists and radical liberals. Although they were united in their political efforts to overthrow regulation and abolish prostitution, they often did so on the basis of very different agendas. Regulation reflected a liberal state policy that did not adhere to the Ten Commandments, or, alternatively, that tolerated the exploitation of women and 'the daughters of the poor'.

As the abolitionist struggle developed in the 1880s and 1890s, many arguments against regulation were put forward, but the war against the doctors was mainly fought on the basis of two sets of arguments; first, that both statistical and clinical evidence suggested that regulation was not an effective safeguard against VD, and secondly, that men should control their sexual urges. This latter argument was embedded in one of the most central political doctrines of abolitionism, which is famous for taking the female norm of chastity as a model for human behaviour in general. The first national abolitionist conference in the Netherlands in 1889 was open to all who believed in 'a single moral standard for both men and women'. Although this notion contained a whole universe of ideas about the relationship between the sexes, it also took up arms with the prevailing medical view of sexuality.

On the one hand, medical men generally thought that prostitution was something evil, that immorality should not exist, and that marriage was the appropriate place for sexual enjoyment and reproduction. On the other hand, their theoretical outlook was based on the assumption that anything other than heterosexual penetration was unnatural and/or dangerous, and, moreover, that it was not healthy, or even possible, to abstain from sexual practices altogether. Hence, they adhered to what abolitionists referred to as 'the doctrine of necessary evil'. Thus, how did the medical world respond to the abolitionist arguments?

Around 1880, Pierson, together with several allies, embarked on a lengthy debate with leading medical professors and other defenders of regulation, attacking them, among other things, for 'prostitution of science'.[24] The abolitionist attacks had a considerable impact upon members of the Dutch Medical Society,[25] who had just initiated a debate about a national law on regulation, probably in response to this challenge. Different points of view came to the fore when three consecutive committees of the Society disagreed on regulation. At least two of them had members who opposed the system. One doctor favoured prohibition of brothels as a useful strategy. He later openly supported the abolitionist point of view, declaring that it was necessary for men to control their sexual drive if social order was to be maintained, especially with regard to a father's responsibility for his offspring.[26] Another doctor opposed regulation altogether. In a much earlier publication, he had taken the position that sexual gratification was not necessary to maintain a person's physical and mental health. If the 'dormant' sexual drive was not awakened by 'singing and dancing and music and punch and naked arms and unveiled breasts', it was not difficult to resist its urge.[27] Hence, the state should not promote 'seduction'. Likewise, in a response to one of the committee reports, a doctor stated that, medically speaking, sexual abstinence was not harmful, quoting many foreign experts on the matter.[28]

Although it is probably incorrect to say that abolitionist pressure alone led doctors to think differently about male sexuality, it is undoubtedly true that it supported pre-existing moral opposition to the system. The force of the argument on male control, in itself part of a larger discourse on sexual restraint, revealed itself at many levels in the twenty years after the foundation of the Dutch Society Against Prostitution. There was virtually no opponent to regulation, including doctors (who had the almost exclusive right to speak about sexual matters), who did not hold the view that sexual abstinence was socially desirable, medically sound, or at least a personal moral victory. Significantly, books about prostitution, sexual life and sexual hygiene boomed, many of them obsessed with the need to alert young men to the risks of tasting the apple of Eve.[29]

However, not everyone shared such a viewpoint. Gillis van Overbeek de Meijer, a leading regulationist and a professor of medicine at the University of Utrecht, took the more liberal view that it was not possible to have people abstain from sex altogether. Although not an advocate of prostitution, he thought it to be the lesser evil. Prostitution, at least, was a visible enemy, whereas suppression of masturbation would only lead to 'a greater social cesspool of mutual onanists, pederasts and sapphists'.[30] Following Richard von Krafft-Ebing's famous treatise *Psychopathia Sexualis*, he pointed to the dangers of sexual abstinence in 'the abnormal' as well as to the existence of an alarming number of 'inverts' (homosexuals).[31] Van Overbeek de Meijer declared war against the abolitionist cause because it 'sowed the seeds of death and disease'.[32] He also refused publicly to support the demand for a single moral standard for both sexes. Since the 'impetus coeündi' was stronger in men than in women, he argued, they could not be considered equal in moral matters.[33]

Scientific evidence, social discourse and the male body

It is not difficult to see that the controversy surrounding male control was as much a social as a medical dispute. After all, there was only a thin line between medical opinion about abstinence and the Protestant abolitionists' view of sin. But what about 'purely' medical evidence concerning the effectiveness of controlling prostitutes? Trying to disentangle the many and complicated arguments for and against regulation, one encounters many rational 'medical' arguments, but those arguments were again deeply embedded in a social and political discourse. Statistical data seemed to provide a convincing case against regulation: statistics presented at the Brussels conference in 1899 showed that regulation did not have the desired impact on the prevalence of VD in the cities and countries involved.[34] However, 'statistical evidence' itself had been part of a political game in the preceding decades, and continued to be so after 1900. Pro- and anti-regulationists always managed to find statistical data in favour of their point of view: when brothels were closed, syphilis vanished in town A; in town B, syphilis had flourished when medical control stopped; in town C, the introduction of regulation had diminished the incidence of syphilis.[35]

Another medical argument against regulation was the danger of 'mediate contagion', or in French, 'contagion médiate'. If a woman was visited by a man with VD, the next man could be infected as well. No later examination could prevent this. This argument was often put forward by anti-regulationists as it seemed to undermine the presumed preventive capabilities of sanitary inspection. It related to another argument against the effectiveness of the system as a whole: that only women and not their customers were examined. The latter point was rejected by regulationists more than once on the grounds that, to the best of their knowledge, 'there were no men who made a living out of the professional undertaking of intercourse with women'.[36]

The reliability of the medical examination itself was also questioned. The greatest attack on the system in the Netherlands came from a highly reputable source. A former student of the famous French syphilologist, Philippe Ricord, Professor Chanfleury van IJsselstein, former medical examiner in Rotterdam, wrote a scathing brochure in 1889, entitled *Supervision of Prostitution from a Hygienic Point of View*.[37] He criticized the VD statistics on rational, medical grounds and exposed the superficial character of the medical examinations he had watched in Paris and in Brussels. On the basis of his own and more thorough research, he concluded that even the strictest medical control could not provide an effective safeguard against infection. He advised that it would be better to put a strict ban on the houses of ill-fame as well as on 'all public prostitution'. Following the publication of the brochure, abolitionists seized the opportunity to issue a separate publication, attaching an explanatory list of medical terms: *Isthmus Faucium = throat, vesiculae = vesicles*, etc. Lay people could share the insights of objective medical knowledge, or so it seemed.

Medical opinion was transformed into political statement on many other occasions. Rather, it is more appropriate to say that medical knowledge itself was intricately linked to the world outside the clinic, structured to fit particular social patterns and political discourses. A case in point was 'hereditary syphilis'. It was long known that syphilis could be transmitted in some ways to the offspring of a syphilitic parent, but from the late nineteenth century onwards the debate assumed growing importance. At the turn of the century, the well-known expert on hereditary syphilis, the French professor Alfred Fournier, distinguished the damaging effects of VD for the categories 'l'individu', 'la famille', 'l'enfant' and 'l'espèce'.[38] In other words, he argued that syphilis was threatening the nuclear family, society and the human race. The married man infected his wife, she her unborn child and thus succeeding generations. By leading to degeneracy and depopulation it even constituted a threat to the nation as an entity.[39] Undoubtedly, this view reflected the personal tragedies of infection, sickness and its congenital effects that the doctor had encountered among his patients, and Fournier was indeed very concerned about the grave medical and social consequences of syphilis. Yet, his insights, inspired as they were by the new eugenic mood and the fear of population decline, were already ideologically structured before the patient entered the surgery. As historian Alain Corbin has observed for France, it was as if doctors were translating the bourgeois fantasies of their time into scientific language. The lower classes thus transmitted to the bourgeois male, via their womenfolk, a virulent syphilis which metamorphosed into a germ fatal to the whole lineage.[40]

As medical knowledge became more widespread and was adapted by groups with a political agenda, 'hereditary syphilis' became even more part of a social discourse.[41] Orthodox Protestants in the Netherlands saw reasons to evoke the Biblical image of God 'visiting the iniquity of the fathers upon the children unto the third and fourth generation'.[42] Non-Christians also elaborated on this theme. When abolitionists embarked on a nation-wide campaign against brothels in the winter of 1902, Liberal Party member and feminist Welmoet Wijnaendts Francken-Dyserinck, a gifted speaker, demanded solidarity with idiot and lame children who suffered from the sins of their ancestors.[43] This all provided fuel for the notion of the 'innocent victim', who had been lurking for decades in the corners of medical and political debates. One archetypal victim was the inno-cent, respectable woman who was infected by a licentious husband. In particular, in the women's movement, the pure bride who suffered as a consequence of her husband's past behaviour, gained much sympathy. Of course this image of female victimization related to the real and painful experiences of women but it also took on a life of its own, given its wider implications for sexual discourse. The social image of the male victim and the contagious, wanton prostitute underwent an almost total role reversal in feminist thought, as the central source of infection became a debased, infected, married man who was not willing to control his sexual drive. Men, as Jacobs remarked, seemed not to possess the gift of reason when their passions spoke (implying that not women, but men, were closer to their 'animal' nature).[44] These views were substantiated by a report issued by the Amsterdam city council, while preparing for a vote on the prohibi-tion of brothel-keeping in 1897. On the basis of several interviews with prostitutes, the report concluded that it was mainly married men who visited the houses of ill-fame, a fact that astonished many contemporaries.[45] Thus, whereas the female body had been the main source of evil for decades, now all wrongs seemed to emanate from the male body.

As may be clear from the above examples, it was not simply a case of one-way traffic from medical insights to social definitions. It also worked the other way around. The first female gynaecologist and second female doctor in the Netherlands, Catharine van Tussenbroek, seriously criticized Alfred Fournier's famous treatment in a case of hereditary syphilis. Fournier had decided to administer mercury pills to the pregnant wife of one of his syphilitic patients. In order to preserve familial harmony the wife was not allowed to know about her husband's past. In consequence, the pills had to be given to her under false pretences, 'sous des pseudonymes honnêtes et acceptables'.[46] In the *Dutch Journal of Medicine* in 1898, van Tussenbroek pointed out that this was clearly a conspiracy between a doctor and his male patient at the expense of his wife.[47]

Her reaction shows us that by then more than just a fine crack had appeared in the invisible forces that held up the all-male view of VD.

Abolitionist victories

It is evident that sanitary control of prostitutes could only flourish in a social climate that favoured new hygienic expertise and state interference in 'public' women's lives alongside a non-interventionist approach to morality. 'Strictly medical' evidence in favour of, or against, regulation was always embedded in political and social discourse. It appears that social and political conditions largely determined which medical options were possible. But medical knowledge did in turn help to bring about social change, albeit in a direction many doctors would not have liked. Abolitionists, by placing questions about the validity of the hygienic point of view on the political agenda, strongly supported the growing dissatisfaction among medical men themselves about the effectiveness of sanitary control. This provided them in turn with medical arguments against a system that they saw as a reflection of a social order they detested. The regulation system 'organized' and 'arranged' sexuality, gender relations and sexual identities in a complicated process of control and intervention by the state. By opposing the assumptions underlying regulation the abolitionists created a platform for a debate about gender in general, leading to new concepts of masculinity and femininity, and new social norms about sexual behaviour. Moreover, by opposing the dominant liberal democratic policy with its tolerance for 'the social evil', their struggle reflected a fundamental conflict over the future of the Dutch state as a modern nation.

It is difficult to decide how important the change in medical opinion about regulation really was when it came to practical politics. Its potential to relate to many different 'social questions' at the heart of nineteenth-century society was one of the reasons why anti-regulationist politics seemed to be so successful. The sickness of the social body – sick from poverty, immorality and inequality – was seemingly reflected in the wrecked body of the prostitute as the site where human values were exchanged for money. Abolitionism, like socialism, promised at least a partial cure. From 1895 to 1905, one city after the other 'fell' into abolitionist hands, sometimes after considerable siege, since some local authorities held on to regulation as long as they could. The weakened status of pro-regulationism, the ambiguous statistical evidence, and other medical doubts about the system greatly supported the abolitionist strategy. Changes in the structure of prostitution itself may also have contributed to their success.[48] But evidence suggests that a significant number of votes against regulation in the different municipalities tended to be largely on moral and political, rather than on medical or other, grounds. This process was to a large extent facilitated by a substantial shift in Dutch politics in the same period. Politics and culture became organized along religious sectarian lines, a process known as 'pillarization', resulting in a proliferation of a Catholic and various Protestant political parties that confronted the existing liberal democratic and conservative factions.[49] An increasing number of religious voting blocs appeared both in parliament and in local councils. Male Protestant abolitionists, with their ideas about the moral character of the state, were close to the heart of this process. The prohibition of brothel-keeping in 1911 – the great abolitionist victory – was part of a set of notorious Morality Laws, several of which were inspired by an orthodox-Protestant variety of abolitionist thought. Not surprisingly, these laws are seen by historians as a victory of religious over liberal democratic state politics.[50]

Ironically, all this took place while the doctor in the laboratory uncovered more and more secrets about the disease that had plagued Europe for centuries. The discoveries by Hoffmann and Schaudinn, Wassermann, Ehrlich and others around 1900 signalled a new era of bacteriological understanding, while Salvarsan held the promise of a definite cure. When brothels were prohibited and the last strongholds of regulation collapsed, Salvarsan had just made its entry in the Netherlands.[51] Moreover, in the first decades of the twentieth century, new and somewhat less repressive approaches to the prevention of VD evolved. One would expect this to have loosened the grip of the 'sexual-abstinence solution' to the dangers of VD, but this seems not to be the case.

The ties between the medical profession and the abolitionist movement had been strengthened, at least since the Brussels conference of 1899, and the old adversaries now found a common cause in combatting VD. After the establishment of the *Union Internationale contre le Péril Vénérien*, itself an outcome of the Brussels conference, the Dutch Anti-Venereal Disease Society was founded in 1914. The Society was particularly active in giving information and building up a system of advice centres alongside the existing out-patient clinics. However, its nature was ethical-religious rather than therapeutic. The actual foundation of the Anti-Venereal Disease Society was preceded by an elaborate debate about the admissibility of prophylactics as a means of preventing VD. Eventually the chair of the Society was given to the leader of a new generation of abolitionists, Andrew de Graaf, a Protestant lawyer who was fiercely opposed to contraceptives and to neo-Malthusianism in general.[52] Protestant abolitionists in the 1890s had initiated a struggle against neo-Malthusianism, as they saw this as encouraging licentious behaviour and prostitution. Likewise, the new Society with its new chairman refrained from immoral propaganda of prophylactics. In the past abolitionism had always been informed by feminist politics and supported by neo-Malthusians, socialists and radical liberals, but now it became a bulwark of religious conservatism. It seemed as if all roads were blocked and no one was able to change the political fate of the male sexual drive.

NOTES

1 This publication is primarily based on P. de Vries, *Kuisheid voor mannen, vrijheid voor vrouwen. De reglementering en bestrijding van prostitutie in Nederland, 1850–1911*, Hilversum, Verloren, 1997 (with English summary).
2 This description is based on written police regulations, which may or may not have been enforced. Regulations and the way they were applied varied with local circum-

stances. Police power was a much debated issue, as opponents argued that it was illegal or even unconstitutional.

3 There had been an unofficial kind of regulation in the early nineteenth century. See J. F. van Slobbe, *Bijdrage tot de geschiedenis en de bestrijding der prostitutie te Amsterdam*, Amsterdam, Scheltema, 1937.

4 Dr A. P. Fokker, *Open Brief aan Ds H. Pierson. In antwoord op zijn geschrift voor eenige dagen in zake prostitutie-kwestie verschenen, tevens laatste woord*, Haarlem, Bohn, 1879.

5 O. G. Heldring, 'Is er nog slavernij in Nederland?', *De Vereeniging Christelijke Stemmen*, 1860, vol. 14, pp. 388–95, see also p. 691.

6 See also A. Mooij, *Out of Otherness: Characters and Narrators in the Dutch Venereal Disease Debates 1850–1990*, Amsterdam, Atlanta, GA, Rodopi, 1998.

7 A. H. Jacobs, *Herinneringen*, Nijmegen, SUN, 1978, p. 40, first edition, 1924.

8 Descriptions of the examination itself can be found in major sources about prostitution such as the famous work of A. J. B. Parent-Duchâtelet, *De la prostitution dans la ville de Paris, considérée sous le rapport de l'hygiène publique, de la morale en de l'administration*, Paris, Baillière, 1836 (two vols); A. Flexner, *Prostitution in Europe*, New York, Publications of the Bureau of Social Hygiene, 1919, first edition, 1914. .

9 Jacobs, *Herinneringen*, p. 182. Drysdale also took her to a place in London where 'prostitutes' were examined.

10 M. Jackson, *The* Real *Facts of Life: Feminism and the Politics of Sexuality 1850–1940*, London, Taylor & Francis, 1994; S. Kingsley Kent, *Sex and Suffrage in Britain 1860–1914*, Oxford, Princeton University Press, 1987; J. Harsin, *Policing Prostitution in Nineteenth-Century Paris*, Princeton, Princeton University Press, 1985; P. McHugh, *Prostitution and Victorian Social Reform*, London, Croom Helm, 1980; J. R. Walkowitz, *Prostitution and Victorian Society: Women, Class and the State*, Cambridge, Cambridge University Press, 1980; A. Corbin, *Les filles de noce: Misère sexuelle et prostitution aux 19e et 20e siècles*, Paris, Aubier, 1978. Related works on prostitution and social purity include S. Bell, *Reading, Writing and Rewriting the Prostitute Body*, Bloomington, Indiana University Press, 1994; L. Bland, *Banishing the Beast: English Feminism and Sexual Morality 1885–1914*, London, Penguin, 1995; B. Hobson, *Uneasy Virtue: The Politics of Prostitution and the American Reform Tradition*, New York, Basic Books, 1987; D. J. Pivar, *Purity Crusade: Sexual Morality and Social Control, 1868–1900*, Westport, Greenwood Press, 1973.

11 B. Kam, *Meretrix en Medicus: Een onderzoek naar de invloed van de geneeskundige visitatie op de handel en wandel van Zwolse publieke vrouwen tussen 1876 en 1900*, Zwolle, Geert Grote, 1983, p. 58. For France, see Parent-Duchâtelet, *De la prostitution* (1857 edition), pp. 119–20.

12 Cited by Harsin, *Policing Prostitution*, p.108; see also Parent-Duchâtelet, *De la prostitution*, I.

13 *Library of Municipal Archives Amsterdam, U 00.1626: Uittreksel uit het Verslag der Staats-Commissie, benoemd bij Koninklijk Besluit van 3 mei 1852 (Staatsblad No. 99)*, p. 2. The 'prostitute-servant' is clearly a sexual theme, indicating sexual contact with men. It may also relate to non-sexual modes of transmission of syphilis, which were still believed to exist.

14 Ibid., p. 2. It is difficult to say how influential this document was, since all regulations relating to prostitution looked similar. Many municipalities merely modified existing regulations originally drafted in the 1820s. Although the regulations of The Hague never became national law, many cities took it as a model. Some historians suggest it was not influential. See M. Bossebroek and J. H. Compagnie, *Het Mysterie van de Verdwenen Bordelen: Prostitutie in Nederland in de negentiende eeuw*, Amsterdam, Bert Bakker, 1998. Indeed, regulation never became national law, as was advised by the commission. Yet, it is clear that the report was still quoted around 1880.

15 I. Bloch, *Das Sexualleben unserer Zeit in seinen Beziehungen zur modernen Kultur*, Berlin, Louis Marcus, 1919, p. 440 (first edition 1906). Pro- and anti-regulationists usually shared the idea that prostitution was a source of contagion, but they sought different solutions.

16 Except the military. Soldiers got VD check-ups. But whatever treatment they received, they were not disciplined like prostitutes. Rather, some attempts were made to push them into 'reporting' the woman who they thought was responsible for the contagion. See De Vries, *Kuisheid voor mannen, vrijheid voor vrouwen*, p. 11.

17 De Vries, *Kuisheid voor mannen, vrijheid voor vrouwen*, p. 29.

18 A. H. Jacobs, *Nationale Vrouwenraad van Nederland. Bespreking van het Prostitutie-vraagstuk op de Openbare Vergadering te Rotterdam van 2 april 1902*, Rotterdam, Bredée, 1902.

19 Dubois-Havenith (ed.), *Conférence internationale pour la Prophylaxie de la Syphilis et des Maladies vénériennes*, Rapports préliminaires, Bruxelles, Lamartin, 1899 (vol. I), 1902 (vol. II). For an account in English, see *Preventive Hygiene. An Account of the Brussels International Conferences of 1899 and 1902*, 1909.

20 A sign of the times was that leading abolitionists were invited to the conference and its follow-up in 1902. Pro-regulationism had not disappeared, as its advocates hoped for a better system. For an abolitionist account, see *Het Maanblad Getuigen en Redden*, 1899, vol. 21, pp. 1–3, 33–4, 81–3; 1902, vol. 24, pp. 81–2.

21 J. E. Butler, *Une Voix dans le Désert*, Neuchâtel-Parijs, Sandoz, 1875; translated into Dutch as *Openbare Zedelijkheid: Een stem in de woestijn*, Amsterdam, Höveker, 1877. Evidence suggests that the text was originally published in French (as this was the international language) and translated into English many years later as *The Voice of One Crying in the Wilderness*, Bristol and London, Simpkin, 1913.

22 Nederlandsche Vereeniging tegen de Prostitutie (NVP).

23 H. Pierson, *Gewettigde Ontucht*, Arnhem, Swaan, 1878.

24 H. Pierson, *Prostitutie van de Wetenschap*, 's-Gravenhage, Beschoor, 1879.

25 Nederlandsche Maatschappij tot Bevordering der Geneeskunst, Dutch Society for the Advancement of the Art of Healing.

26 'Toespraak van J. Menno Huizinga, arts te Harlingen', in *Handelingen van het Nationaal Congres tegen de Prostitutie*, 's-Gravenhage, Beschoor, 1889, pp. 171–5. See also ibid., pp. 40–3.

27 N. B. Donkersloot, quoted in De Vries, *Kuisheid voor mannen, vrijheid voor vrouwen*, pp. 52–3.

28 A. O. H. Tellegen, quoted in De Vries, *Kuisheid voor mannen, vrijheid voor vrouwen*, pp. 53–4.

29 As a rule, women were notoriously excluded from this discourse.

30 G. van Overbeek de Meijer, 'Geneeskundig toezicht op de prostitutie', *Nederlandsch Tijdschrift voor Geneeskunde,* 1889-I, vol. 25, p. 63.

31 R. von Krafft-Ebing, *Psychopathia Sexualis, mit besonderer Berücksichtigung der conträren Sexualempfindung. Eine Medicinische-Gerichtliche Studie für Ärzte und Juristen*, Stuttgart, Ferdinand Enke, 1903 (twelfth edition, first edition, 1882); G. van Overbeek de Meijer, *De Wapenen van den heer H. Pierson, predikant te Zetten, in den strijd met zijne tegenstanders, en de kennis en het streven van de Nederlandsche Vereeniging tegen de Prostitutie*, Utrecht, Van Ditmar, 1889.

32 Van Overbeek de Meijer, *De Wapenen van den heer H. Pierson*, p. 17.

33 Van Overbeek de Meijer, 'Geneeskundig toezicht', p. 62. In his view of the male drive he relied on a German doctor W. O. Focke, but it is highly likely that Krafft-Ebing's *Psychopathia Sexualis*, was also a main source in this respect. It is noteworthy that – in an apparent effort to counteract the argument that the nature of male sexuality legitimized a double standard – Aletta Jacobs and the first female doctor in England, Elizabeth Blackwell, both suggested that the sexual drives of men and women were of equal intensity: De Vries, *Kuisheid voor mannen, vrijheid voor vrouwen*, p. 205.

34 'Rapport de M. le Professeur Dr. Augagneur' and 'Rapport de M. le Docteur A. Blaschko', in Dubois-Havenith (ed.), *Conférence internationale pour la Prophylaxie de la Syphilis*, pp. 29–71, 72–110 (see especially p. 107).

35 'Syphilis' and 'venereal disease' had similar connotations, especially in the early period of the debates on regulation when syphilis and other forms of VD were not well differentiated. A diagnosis of 'syphilis' was not always correct. Nevertheless, fears centred around 'syphilitic diseases' and not, for example, around 'gonorrhoea'.

36 *Nederlandsch Tijdschrift voor Geneeskunde*, 1879, pp. 335–6.

37 J. L. Chanfleury van IJsselstein, *Het toezicht op de prostitutie uit een hygiënisch oogpunt beschouwd*, Amsterdam, Van Rossen, 1889.

38 A. Fournier, 'Danger social de la syphilis', in Dubois-Havenith (ed.), *Conférence internationale pour la Prophylaxie de la Syphilis* (see especially p. 43).

39 Ibid., p. 43. Degeneracy was a popular theme when eugenics and evolutionary theory developed, especially in France. For the Netherlands, see Mooij, *Out of Otherness*.

40 A. Corbin, 'L'hérédosyphilis ou l'impossible rédemption. Contribution à l'histoire de l'héridité morbide', *Romantisme*, 1981, vol. 31, pp. 131–49. I am indebted to Ramón Castejón-Bolea for this reference, as well as for his information about the debates on degeneracy and population decline; see also his chapter in this book. Corbin makes the same point in A. Corbin, 'Commercial Sexuality in Nineteenth-Century France: A System of Images and Regulations', in C. Gallagher and T. Laqueur (eds) *The Making of the Modern Body. Sexuality and Society in the Nineteenth Century*, Berkeley, University of California Press, 1987, pp. 209–19.

41 Although Fournier was certainly not the only source about congenital syphilis, his work was well known in the Netherlands, even among abolitionists. His *Syphilis et Mariage* was translated as *Huwelijk en Syphilis*, Scheltema, Amsterdam, 1902, as well as an information book for 'young adult men', *Wat volwassen jongens wel eens mogen weten*, Amsterdam, Scheltema, 1903.

42 Exodus XX:5 (from: *The Holy Bible, containing the Old and New Testament*, Cambridge, British and Foreign Bible Society (about 1880)).

43 De Vries, *Kuisheid voor mannen, vrijheid voor vrouwen*, p. 235.

44 A. H. Jacobs, *Vrouwenbelangen*, Amsterdam, L. J. Veen, 1899, p. 44.

45 *Municipal Archives Amsterdam, Archief Cie van onderzoek naar de Prostitutie*, inv. nr. 1: Brief aan den Gemeenteraad 20– 1897, I; *Bijblad Maandblad Getuigen en Redden*, maart 1897.

46 C. van Tussenbroek, 'Preventieve behandeling der van den vader afkomstige heriditaire syphilis tijdens de zwangerschap' (referaat van CvT), *Nederlandsch Tijdschrift voor Geneeskunde*, 17 December 1898, II, p. 1,030.

47 Van Tussenbroek, 'Preventieve behandeling', pp. 1,028–31.

48 The 'classical' brothel declined in the second half of the nineteenth century and other, more flexible, forms of prostitution evolved. There is no definite answer as to what effect this had on regulation. See Mooij, *Out of Otherness*; Bossebroek and Compagnie, *Het Mysterie van de Verdwenen Bordelen*; de Vries, *Kuisheid voor mannen, vrijheid voor vrouwen*. I would suggest that the decline of brothels and the decline of regulation were not closely connected causally. Although the existence of brothels made the supervision of prostitutes easier than the supervision of scattered 'independent' working women, it is clear that in some countries, such as France, regulation continued in spite of the decline in brothels. In addition, the fear of the 'secret prostitute' (who was less visible and less easy to control) was always an argument in favour of regulation, rather than against it. Police regulations always explicitly included women who worked outside brothels.

49 This unique feature of Dutch politics meant that each 'pillar' in society, whether Catholic or Protestant, created its own identity in parties, unions, newspapers and, much later, in its own broadcasting stations. Around 1900 voting blocs of religious political parties appeared in local councils and in parliament. It is highly likely that their

representatives did not care at all about the medical imperfections of sanitary control. An analysis of voting behaviour in three main cities showed that all representatives from a religious political party voted against regulation and/or the ban on brothels. Liberal democrats tended to be divided on the issue. A. Lansbergen, *Het bordeelbeleid van de stedelijke overheid in Nederland, 1890–1920: een onderzoek naar motieven en besluiten omtrent het instellen van een bordeelverbod in Amsterdam, Rotterdam en Den Haag*, MA Thesis, Erasmusuniversiteit, Rotterdam, 1988 (Library of Municipal Archives, Rotterdam).

50 See, for example, S. Stuurman, *Verzuiling, kapitalisme en patriarchaat, Aspecten van de ontwikkeling van de moderne staat in Nederland*, Nijmegen, SUN, 1983.

51 For the introduction of Salvarsan, see Mooij, *Out of Otherness*.

52 For a detailed description of these developments, see Mooij, *Out of Otherness*; P. Koenders, *Tussen christelijk Réveil en seksuele revolutie, Bestrijding van zedeloosheid in Nederland, met nadruk op repressie van homoseksualiteit*, Amsterdam, Stichting beheer IISG, 1996.

4

DOCTORS, SOCIAL MEDICINE AND VD IN LATE-NINETEENTH-CENTURY AND EARLY-TWENTIETH-CENTURY SPAIN

Ramón Castejón-Bolea

Introduction

The strategies developed to confront the problem of VD in late-nineteenth-century and early-twentieth-century Spain became an important element within social medicine[1] and health administration. The so-called venereal-syphilitic diseases were, together with tuberculosis and alcoholism, the 'social diseases'[2] par excellence. The perception of these diseases, the strategies introduced to control them, and the practices which resulted, became a part of the theoretical and practical corpus of social medicine.

During the first third of the twentieth century, the corps of health officials was consolidated through the *Instrucción General de Sanidad* (General Instruction of Health, 1904) and the *Reglamentos de Sanidad Provincial y Municipal* (Provincial and Local Heath Rules, 1925–6), as the central state began to emphasize a strategy of prevention rather than episodic coping with epidemics. The establishment of this corps with its own professional dynamic directed the health system towards what was perceived as a greater rationality.[3]

VD was additionally defined by other considerations specifically arising from its predominantly sexual mode of transmission. Indeed, this understanding of its peculiar character, apart from giving the group of diseases their characteristic denomination, had strong moral connotations, since it was very frequently perceived as resulting from the transgression of sexual norms. In fact, as Roger Davidson has argued: 'Society's response to VD has been shown to be a central strand in that "whole web of discourses" that has constructed and regulated sexuality in modern society.'[4]

Although British and North American research about society's response to VD and the evolution of public health policy in relation to these diseases has been extensive,[5] this is not the case in Spanish research. Spanish historiography about VD is relatively underdeveloped, as are the related fields of the history of women and of sexuality, which would provide a necessary context.

The regulated context: prostitution and VD

One of the central features of Spanish anti-venereal policy was the existence of a system of regulated prostitution during the greater part of the nineteenth and twentieth centuries. The origins of regulationism must be sought within the Augustinian tradition, which established male fornication with women prostitutes as a lesser evil and a social necessity for the containment of potentially socially disruptive male lust. Prostitution was thus an inevitable evil, to be regulated in order to avoid excesses and to defend order (especially family order). However, after centuries of tolerance during medieval and early modern times, in the seventeenth century, during the reign of Felipe IV, regulated prostitution was prohibited.[6] This put an end to more than two centuries of regulation of brothels, and it also put an end to a lengthy period of success in the organization of venal pleasure as a real *social service* based on an ideology of the protection of family honour and of family and social order.[7] Unavoidable sexual urges, given the impossibility of men resisting the 'devil of flesh', had found a means of expression without impinging upon this order.[8] This period of closed brothels extended until the middle of the nineteenth century when regulations relating to prostitution were again issued in Spain. A new system of 'tolerated houses' was organized at a provincial and local level.

The growing concern of many European nations about VD since the late eighteenth century must be seen in the context of a new state interest in the health of their populations (especially the young and the army). This concern must also be seen in relation to pressures exerted by the military authorities who asked for the public health regulation of prostitutes. During the final third of the nineteenth century, the medical-hygienist discourse concerning the morbidity and mortality of infected individuals and the economic and demographic consequences of VD (with particular emphasis on 'forthcoming generations') was becoming more dramatic and alarmist. Thus, in 1886, a hygienist considered that 'syphilis on its own caused more damage than all the other infectious diseases together'.[9] Figures of the incidence and prevalence of VD were increasing, although their reliability was low. Indeed, in nearly all cases, foreign statistics were used due to the non-existence in Spain of reliable figures before the twentieth century. However, this discourse of the hygienists included other social concerns and anxieties. The spread of VD became an indicator of transgression of sexual norms, and the attacks that the family and the institution of marriage were enduring: 'And not only Medicine demands a fast disappearance of syphilitic diseases: it is also demanded by morality, the guardian of family peace.'[10] These concerns with the disturbance of moral and sexual order encouraged the inclusion of a moral agenda in anti-venereal strategies:

> It is advisable, thus, to embark on the regeneration of public morality
> and particularly the regeneration of men; to fight against all the
> poisonous influences that appear in customs, in fashions, in the arts, in
> literature, especially in newspaper serials and in theatre … and finally
> to make an effort towards practising the most regenerating influence,
> within the realm of domestic education and public instruction.[11]

The contemporary debate about prostitution had its first legislative outcome in
the public health commission of the Spanish parliament during the so-called
Liberal Triennium (1820–3). The *Reglamento General de Sanidad* (General
Regulation of Health) was elaborated in 1822 and its articles 386 to 398 and 447
to 454 focused directly on the regulation and punishment of prostitution.
However, this regulation was never enforced. The debate reappeared in the
medical press during the 1840s, in which positions ranging from the defence of
regulation to support for prohibitionism were expressed.[12] The latter was
defended by Pedro Felipe Monlau, the most remarkable Spanish hygienist of the
mid-nineteenth century, for whom 'Morality' and 'Hygiene' were indissoluble.[13]
This viewpoint led him to oppose any intervention with prostitution and to
promote its suppression. The regulationists, who considered prostitution to be an
incurable evil and an unhealthy industry, proposed to tolerate it while exercising
moral, police and health control over it.

The epidemiological construction of VD, locating the 'reservoir' of these
diseases within prostitutes, was common to both positions: 'All or most agree on
the fact that the real germ and breeding ground of syphilis rest on prostitution.'[14] This idea, which linked VD to prostitution and thus medical responses to
the health control of prostitutes, remained in force past the turn of the century
and persisted well into the first third of the twentieth century. As the police chief
of the Section of Hygiene in Madrid in 1900 said:

> The immoral contagion of prostitution, and the infectious contagion of
> VDs, are two correlative pathological phenomena that demand joint
> measures of preservation and sanitation. It is not possible to separate
> medical prophylaxis from social prophylaxis. The human vehicle of
> VDs is prostitution, and the real peril of this moral blight depends on
> the increase of these diseases.[15]

In practice, the Spanish regulationist system took as a model the French system,
promoted since the Restoration and developed according to the scheme designed
by Dr Alexandre Parent-Duchâtelet. In Spain, the system remained in force, save
for the republican period 1935–41, until the Franco regime officially suppressed
brothels in 1956.

Since the first regulations, in Zaragoza in 1845 and Madrid in 1847,[16] the
problem of prostitution was approached from a health and public order perspective, based on the registration of prostitutes, compulsory medical examinations

(the frequency of which depended on the specific local regulations) and compulsory hospitalization in cases of infectious disease. Between 1876 and 1899, the number of prostitutes annually registered in Madrid ranged between 1,574 and 2,000. In Barcelona there were, in 1881, 1,022 registered prostitutes; in 1884, 660 and in 1885, 688.[17] Regulation spread throughout the country due to initiatives by Provincial Governors (town councils during the period 1889–92).

Prostitutes became an object of surveillance and intervention by doctors and police. As they were considered the 'reservoir' of VD, legal discrimination against them was seen to be justified. One hygienist, put in charge of medical examinations, justified this discrimination against prostitutes on the grounds that 'showing themselves in an open way and with no restrictions, they offend morality and public modesty ... and endanger public health, disseminating infectious diseases'.[18] The association between prostitutes and VD was clear, for instance, in a draft regulation published in 1882, in which the fact of having been affected by VD was considered a decisive argument for compulsory registration.[19]

The abolitionist discourse had hardly any real presence among doctors in the nineteenth century, and its presence was also minimal within political circles. In 1877, *Public Morality. A Voice in the Desert*, by the leading British abolitionist, Josephine Butler, was translated into Spanish and that same year the republican Manuel Ruiz Zorrilla appeared as a Spanish representative at the first International Congress of the Abolitionist Federation in Geneva.[20] In 1883, a deputy of the International Abolitionist Federation, founded by Josephine Butler in 1875, came to Spain to create a local section and to request support in abolishing regulated prostitution.[21] However, until the 1920s, with the foundation of the Spanish Society of Abolitionism in Madrid in 1922 by the doctors Hernández-Sapelayo and César Juarros, this 'creed' did not begin to extend to Spain. Thereafter, the success of the abolitionist case among unions and left-wing parties, together with the growing presence of feminist organizations, led to increasing support for this viewpoint.[22]

At the end of the nineteenth century, Spain underwent a serious economic, political and social crisis. The colonial disaster of 1898 acted as a sharp shock to many elements within the nation. As Manuel Tuñón de Lara states, the idea that Spain needed a process of 'regeneration' was a common theme of Spanish commentators in the 1890s and the early years of the twentieth century.[23] The term 'regenerationism' referred generally to the attempt to modify all aspects of social life and state policy, in a modernizing direction. Modernization, as a programme, tried to adapt the patterns and current structures of Western European countries to Spanish conditions. This aim incorporated important issues of public health, in which Spain was seen to be relatively deficient.[24] Furthermore, the migratory movements and urbanization which took place during the second half of the nineteenth century, together with the social changes occurring in the last fifteen years of the nineteenth century, due to industrialization and the growth of the working class, were altering the face of Spain.[25]

The first legal manifestation of this concern with VD at the state level was enforced in March 1908, in response to a situation which, it was argued, 'produces its effect not only on the existence of the individual, but on the conservation of the race'.[26] This first central state regulation of prostitution was in fact in response to the measures put forward by the *Instrucción General de Sanidad* (General Instruction of Health), in 1904, a legal text in force until 1944, which served as a basic framework for the development of health modernization in Spain.[27] Two elements of this new development departed from previous regulations: on the one hand, the attempt to standardize hygiene regulations and the 'Special Hygiene Service' throughout the state, and on the other hand, the separation of the health from the surveillance and repressive aspects of 'Special Hygiene'. The health aspects depended on the Provincial and Local Health Boards, and the surveillance aspects depended on Provincial Governors.[28] Thus, the new Local and Provincial Health Inspectors also assumed the functions hitherto related to the medical control of prostitutes. In this way, the regulation system became integrated within public health administration.

However, many doctors criticized this law of 1908 because it did not fulfil their expectations.[29] They demanded more control over the regulated system, and the creation of public dispensaries in which the medical examinations would be undertaken only by doctors with a knowledge of venereology.[30]

Other social concerns influenced the debates about VD policy-making in early-twentieth-century Spain. Eugenic[31] and degenerationist concerns opened the VD debate to other strategies besides regulationism. Some Provincial Health Inspectors proposed an extension of compulsory medical examinations to other groups within the population. They agreed that, in addition to prostitutes, compulsory examinations and treatment should be extended to wet nurses, soldiers and sailors, imprisoned criminals, arrested beggars and regimented workers. Hygienists also demanded criminal punishment for the conscious and wilful transmission of disease and the establishment of prophylaxis stations for soldiers and sailors. Other measures proposed, markedly eugenic in character, were related to marriage: for instance, the prohibition on syphilitics getting married until they could no longer transmit their disease to their wives or offspring.[32] Some doctors asked for compulsory notification and treatment for *all* patients in 1908.[33] However, the moral programme still played a complementary role within the medical agenda on VD: as a professor of forensic medicine commented in 1908: 'There is no doubt, the task of the priest, of the teacher, of the governess, must be supported by that of the doctor.'[34]

Strategies of medical care: the hegemony of the medical model

In 1918 the *Bases para la reglamentación de la profilaxis pública de las enfermedades venereo-sifilíticas* (The basic principles for the regulation of public prophylaxis of venereal-syphilitic diseases) established a legal code which shaped the fight against VD until 1930. Under this legislation, hygienists and clinical venereologists appointed by Provincial and Local Health Inspectors gained important powers within the existing regulationist system. In June 1918, the first competitive exams for the so-called 'Doctors of Venereal Prophylaxis' (the Spanish version of the British VD Medical Officers) were announced. Six doctors in Madrid and forty-seven in Barcelona were appointed.[35]

In 1919, the first central health organization dedicated to VD, the Permanent Board against Venereal Diseases, appeared: it had only advisory functions. In 1922, it was reorganized, and an Executive Committee created. This was empowered to inspect and oversee VD services throughout the whole nation. Two years later, in 1924, it was renamed the Antivenereal Executive Committee (AEC). Now, for the first time, a central organization had budgetary powers, and the AEC became responsible for the distribution of central government funding for the struggle against VD.[36]

From the point of view of medical care, the 'Bases' of 1918 offered a legal framework for the development of accessible and free dispensaries. However, this programme, in common with other health programmes, was limited by the availability of economic resources. In 1916, the total state budget was 1,460 million pesetas, that is, the expenditure on health that year was less than 0.17 per cent of the total public expenditure. In 1920, the Ministry of the Interior allocated a mere 2.6 million pesetas to the state budget for health, an increase of 100,000 pesetas which came nowhere near catching up with the increasing inflation of this period. In 1924, the amount allocated to fight VD was only 100,000 pesetas.[37]

While the first known out-patient department for the treatment of VD was opened in 1867 in the San Juan de Dios Hospital in Madrid, and VD clinics dependent on Provincial Health Boards were founded in Barcelona and Madrid in 1919 and 1921, these catered only for prostitutes. The first dispensary which operated according to public health ideology and medical discourse about 'venereal prophylaxis' was not opened until 1924 in Madrid, during the Primo de Rivera Dictatorship (1923–9). The functions of this venereal clinic (the 'Azúa' dispensary) were explicit: 'The curative treatment of these diseases, the therapeutic sterilization of germ carriers, and the pedagogic functions'. Thus, medical treatment and preventive and educational activities (addressed both to patients and the wider public), together with issues relating to medical training, were combined in one institution.[38] The ground floor of the building was dedicated to men and the first floor to women, with separate front doors and procedures to preserve patient privacy and confidentiality.

There are no statistical time series from which to obtain an overview of the number of new cases of VD nor of the number of attendances at the clinics. Only isolated figures are available. In the second half of 1924, 4,308 women and 23,454 men attended the 'Azúa' dispensary. That year, in the other dispensary in Madrid, traditionally dedicated to the examination of prostitutes, 25,609 women and 20,884 men attended. This difference might be considered as evidence of gender inequality in the use of diagnostic and therapeutic resources; an inequality also present in Britain in the early 1900s.[39]

This programme of medical care, via out-patient dispensaries, was made possible by the availability, after 1910, of a more effective treatment for syphilis, developed by Paul Ehrlich under the name of Salvarsan or '606'. This gave rise to the idea in preventive medicine of prophylaxis by treatment. This concept was based on the notion that the best strategy in the fight against syphilis was early treatment, and that in this way the incidence of the disease might be reduced. There is considerable evidence that the fall in new cases during the second and third decades of the twentieth century in Spain could have been due to this strategy. However, it was constrained by the lack of government funds specifically allocated to clinics. In 1924, thirty dispensaries existed in Spain dependent on Provincial Health Boards, which compared unfavourably with Western European countries. In France, in 1923, almost 200 dispensaries were operating; and in Britain, in 1920, there were 190 VD treatment centres,[40] a six-to seven-fold difference in provision in relation to population numbers.

The number of VD dispensaries in Spain went on increasing during the following years. In 1928, there were fifty-six[41] although these differed markedly in the quality of their accommodation and medical facilities. For instance, in 1929, the dispensaries in Barcelona did not have their own laboratories and there was no free treatment until 1931. Besides, many dispensaries (seventeen in 1928) were still limited to providing periodic medical examinations and treatment of prostitutes. As a result, it was difficult not to associate dispensaries with prostitution, which meant that many dispensaries offering anti-venereal services to men and 'decent' women were scarcely used due to a lack of demand. In 1928, Sánchez Covisa, Professor of Dermatology and Venereology in Madrid, argued that

> In these Dispensaries the effect is limited because only one social sector
> is benefited by the immense resources at the disposal of these institu-
> tions. ... There is a section of the people who are shy, full of false
> shame, which does not allow them to attend these dispensaries and the
> specialist hospitals.[42]

However, there was a significant increase in the number of attendances by women and children at the 'Azúa' dispensary between 1924 and 1928.[43] This increasing trend in the use of VD clinics by women and children suggests that at least in some major cities efforts to attract sufferers and facilitate access to free and confidential treatment were starting to succeed. In 1931, there were seventy-three dispensaries, fifty-eight in provincial capitals and fifteen in rural districts. The establishment of the Second Republic in 1931 brought increased funding for public VD clinics, and by 1934, there were 116 dispensaries.

The medical care strategy and its new medical space, the dispensary, were supported by social reformism, both by advocates of social medicine and clinical venereologists. Indeed, this new medical space had been claimed by both groups of professionals since the turn of the century, although some clinical venereologists saw dispensaries as unfair competition for their private practice. For specialists in venereology, dispensaries provided a locus for the consolidation of their specialized knowledge, with a substantial number of patients on whom to base their practice and research. The dispensaries were also utilized as educational centres from the mid-1920s.[44]

As with other medico-social campaigns of those times (for example, those addressing tuberculosis and infant mortality), the campaign against VD exploited this new medical space of the dispensary. It was grafted onto the urban social tissue and became an instrument for the diffusion of education about hygienic practices, aimed at changing popular behaviours.[45] An important part of the propaganda against VD as well as the activities of surveillance and control by visiting nurses were conducted from the dispensary.

The tension between voluntary and coercive strategies: the triumph of social defence in the 1930s

In 1926, dermato-venereologist Lancha Fal presented his paper 'Some notes on venereal prophylaxis' to the Medical Science Academy of Cordoba. His words, written during the Primo de Rivera Dictatorship (1923–9), were: 'There are two ways of imposing a doctrine: apostolate and dictatorship … . In Spain the apostolate has obtained failure after failure, which means that a firm dictatorship is necessary to impose prophylactic measures against VD.'[46] The pathway towards more coercive VD legislation, overriding personal liberties in order to defend society, or in Lancha Fal's words, 'to provide guarantee for the future of our race, of this immortal race', was being prepared during the years of the Dictatorship.

In 1928, criminal punishment for transmission of VD was introduced in Spain with the Penal Code of the Primo de Rivera Dictatorship. Such a legal recourse was widely employed in continental Europe, in contrast to Great Britain, a variance that can probably be explained by differing sexual cultures and differing perceptions of the role of the state and its relationship to individual liberties.[47] It meant, in fact, criminalization of the transmission of VD. However, it was not easy to apply. As the clinical venereologist Bertoloty wrote in 1934, 'health crime is a fiction, and the fundamental reason is the insurmountable obstacle of obtaining evidence'. Those who defended it were probably thinking more of its deterrent effect than of its ability to reduce transmission. The rarity of accusations made during its existence, as well as the lack of unanimous medical support for this legal procedure, suggest that its viability was questionable. Thus, criminal punishment for transmission of VD never again appeared in legislation.[48]

The legal framework for the development of these coercive initiatives was the *Bases para la reorganización profiláctica de la lucha antivenérea* (Bases for the Prophylactic Reorganization of the Antivenereal Fight). They were enacted in 1930, during the intermediate government of Berenguer, following the fall of the Dictatorship. This Royal Order established compulsory treatment, in a private consulting-room or a public establishment, for all persons with VD. If patients defaulted from treatment, the doctors had to notify the health authorities. It was possible to hospitalize any patients who were a 'social peril' due to their extreme contagiousness. Patients who failed to comply with compulsory treatment could be forced to undergo examination by a doctor of the Antivenereal Official Fight and, if necessary, could be compulsorily hospitalized. Visiting nurses were responsible for discovering 'focuses of contagion' and, if possible, for persuading them to receive treatment. These nurses also had educational functions: 'to enlighten young girls and ignorant women about the danger of the disease they had been infected with': such patients could also be sent to the 'Homes for abandoned and shameful young girls'. Thus, visiting nurses combined the educational and charitable tradition of the 'visiting ladies' with specialized scientific knowledge.[49]

These 'Bases' provided for doctors to notify public health authorities of all 'contacts' voluntarily named by infected patients as being the source of their infection; so called 'conditional notification'. In this way, 'professional secrecy' was maintained. It was forbidden to treat VD by correspondence, and the advertisement of alleged 'cures' was also forbidden.

These controls were a response to pressures exerted by Provincial and Local Health Inspectors, hygienists and clinical venereologists. Prominent members of the Spanish Academy of Dermatology and Syphilography collaborated in framing the 'Bases'. In order to guarantee control and treatment of all patients, coercive measures were extended to the whole population, revealing a change in the epidemiological construction of the disease, and the acceptance of the man as a 'vector of transmission', infected from the 'reservoir' created by prostitutes (whether regulated or 'clandestine'), through whom the disease finally reached the 'innocent victims' (children and married women). These controls were an admission that regulationism had not been able to control VD, among other reasons, because it had been impotent to control 'clandestine' prostitution, a major source of infection in the eyes of many hygienists and clinical venereologists.

The regulationist model had thus reached a crisis point. In 1932, a bill for an abolitionist law was thwarted. Prominent venereologists and the famous jurist Luis Jiménez de Asúa had taken part in proceedings involving debates within the National Health Council over compulsory treatment and notification. However, the pressure on regulationism continued to increase. In May 1932, the abolitionists of Madrid, with the support of the psychiatrist César Juarros, dedicated a week to the propagation of their ideas, complaining at the slowness of the Ministry of the Interior in decreeing the abolition of regulationism. The great majority of the doctors of the Antivenereal Official Fight, at least in Madrid and the great cities, openly proclaimed themselves as abolitionists.[50] In June 1935, the decree suppressing regulationism in Spain was enacted, putting an end to a period which had commenced in the middle of the nineteenth century. The new legal framework preserved the possibility of periodical medical examinations and compulsory hospitalization when health authorities considered this to be necessary.

These coercive strategies coexisted with the development of other, voluntary, measures. By the end of the 1920s and with the arrival of the Second Republic in 1931, a voluntary approach to the VD problem enjoyed a more receptive political environment. Besides the development of the medical care programme, the diffusion of anti-venereal propaganda and sex education were promoted. The AEC declared in 1928:

> We have tried to say very clearly that the extinction of syphilis was not only a problem of science, but also of culture ... . The prophylaxis by treatment must be followed by the use of health publicity by all kinds of methods, advice, films, posters, radio talks, pamphlets, drawings, etc.[51]

With this aim in mind, in 1928 a Social and Health Propaganda Office was opened in the 'Martínez Anido' dispensary in Madrid.[52] This office, under the direction of the clinical venereologist, Julio Bravo, centralized all issues relating to anti-venereal propaganda. The Committee had been distributing anti-venereal posters since as early as 1927. These featured women soliciting men with the image of Death in the background.[53] From 1928, posters whose text and montage were the work of Julio Bravo introduced broader subjects. They did not limit themselves to warning men of the danger of frequenting prostitutes or women. The subjects of the posters aimed at inculcating male responsibility and emphasizing the obligation to take care of family, society and race. This duty was obvious in the poster 'Your Health Is Not Only Yours', where a wife and a baby, the possible innocent victims of irresponsible behaviour, were shown. The posters insisted on self-control and male continence, new values that breached the double standard of sexual morality and were fervently espoused by abolitionists and feminists.[54] Such values resonated with criticism of the use of chemical prophylaxis in the services (compulsory in the Navy since 1914).[55] The new notion was that men should be able to keep away from 'temptation', which in its turn meant a change in notions about the irresistible sexual drive of the male sex and the relationship of sexual abstention to health.

The Terrible Lesson

Part of the anti-venereal campaign was the film *The Terrible Lesson* (La Terrible Lección) shot in 1928 under the direction of Fernando Delgado, commissioned by the AEC. *The Terrible Lesson* is a fictionalized documentary. It is structured in four acts and an epilogue. The epilogue, which could be named 'Roses without thorns', is a hymn to pure, legitimate, love, free from disease. In the film, the influence of theories of social medicine, combined with the scientific and technical advances of venereology and laboratory medicine, appear clearly.

Luis, the main character of the film, succumbs to the attractions of illicit sex, embodied in casual relations with women of uncertain morality. These images reflect the construction by hygienists and clinical venereologists of 'clandestine prostitution' as the main reservoir of disease. Luis, once sick, becomes a vector of the disease and fails in his family and social duties. Thus, his punishment falls on the 'innocent victims' – his wife and his son. However, even though he pays for his wrong with his life, his wife, Lupe, and his son can count on the 'state and its organizations for combating VD' which, allied with scientific and technical weapons of medicine, restore their health and joy.

Medicine, with its vast technical resources, made the cure of the disease possible. But it was necessary to break the 'conspiracy of silence' which surrounded VD. It was here that social medicine made its proposals for health education, by endeavouring to change the relationship between parents and children: from severity and inflexibility to communication and understanding, from obscurantism to open discussion. Knowledge of the dangers associated with illicit sex became the means of avoiding the spread of these diseases. In this way, it was supposed, legitimate sexual relations – free of disease – would receive the reward they deserved.

The Terrible Lesson is an example of medical responses within a voluntarist approach to the fight against VD, which included educational measures through propaganda. However, in Spain, the enforcement of coercive measures (following the 1930 legislation) made it clear that health authorities put very little trust in such voluntary strategies. Moreover, didactic practices were resisted by the Catholic right, which had many misgivings about any sexual pedagogy established by a lay state, and continued to prefer a strategy of regulationism, with its strong base in Augustinian tradition.[56] As a result, the effects of these measures were mostly limited to certain social groups and spaces (the military, brothels, dispensaries), and the content of propaganda measures restricted mainly to warnings about the dangers of sex.[57] This served to consolidate dominant sexual morality and to stigmatize sexually active women, who continued to be considered as the 'reservoir' of disease.

NOTES

1 For a discussion of 'social medicine' within the Spanish context, see E. Rodriguez Ocaña, *La constitución de la Medicina Social como disciplina en España (1882–1923)*, Madrid, Ministerio de Sanidad y Consumo, 1987, p. 9.

2 Ibid.
3 P. Marset Campos, E. Rodriguez Ocaña and J.M. Sáez Gómez, 'La salud pública en España', in F. Martínez Navarro, J.M. Antó, P.L. Castellanos, M. Gili, P. Marset and V. Navarro, *Salud Pública*, Madrid, McGraw-Hill Interamericana, 1998, pp. 35–9.
4 R. Davidson, 'Venereal disease, public health and social control: The Scottish experience in a comparative perspective', *Dynamis*, 1997, vol. 17, pp. 341–68.
5 On the historical relationship between VD and morality, see, for example, O. Temkin, 'On the history of "Morality and Syphilis"', in O. Temkin, *The Double Face of Janus and Other Essays in the History of Medicine*, Baltimore, Johns Hopkins University Press, 1977, pp. 472–84; L. Fleck, *La génesis y el desarrollo de un hecho científico. Introducción a la teoría del estilo de pensamiento y del colectivo de pensamiento*, Madrid, Alianza Editorial, 1986, pp. 45–66. On the significance of VD and the medical and social responses that it provoked in the nineteenth and twentieth centuries, see especially, F. Mort, *Dangerous Sexualities: Medico-moral Politics in England since 1830*, London, Routledge, 1987; D. Evans, 'Tackling the "Hideous Scourge": The creation of the venereal disease treatment centres in early twentieth-century Britain', *Social History of Medicine*, 1992, vol. 5, pp. 413–33; R. Davidson, '"A scourge to be firmly gripped": The campaign for VD controls in Interwar Scotland', *Social History of Medicine*, 1993, vol. 6, pp. 213–35; R. Davidson, 'Venereal disease, sexual morality and public health in interwar Scotland', *Journal of the History of Sexuality*, 1994, vol. 5, pp. 267–93; R. Davidson, 'Searching for "Mary Glasgow": Contact tracing for sexually transmitted diseases in twentieth-century Scotland', *Social History of Medicine*, 1996, vol. 9, pp. 195–214; B.A. Towers, 'Health education policy 1916–1926: Venereal disease and the prophylaxis dilemma', *Medical History*, 1980, vol. 24, pp. 70–87; A.M. Brandt, *No Magic Bullet. A Social History of Venereal Disease in the United States Since 1880*, Oxford, Oxford University Press, 1987; E.H. Beardsley, 'Allied against sin: American and British responses to venereal disease in World War I', *Medical History*, 1976, vol. 20, pp. 189–202; E. Fee, 'Sin vs. science: Venereal disease in Baltimore in the twentieth century', *Journal of the History of Medicine and Allied Sciences*, 1988, vol. 43, pp. 141–64; J. Cassel, *The Secret Plague. Venereal Disease in Canada, 1838–1939*, Toronto, University of Toronto Press, 1987; C. Quétel, *History of Syphilis*, Cambridge, Polity Press, 1990.
6 J.-L. Guereña, 'Médicos y prostitución. Un proyecto de reglamentación de la prostitución en 1809: La "Exposición" de Antonio Cibat (1771–1811)', *Medicina e Historia*, 1998, no. 71, pp. 5–28.
7 J.-L. Guereña, 'Los orígenes del reglamentarismo en España. La policía sanitaria de las mujeres públicas (Zaragoza, 1845)', *Bulletin d'Historie Contemporaine de l'Espagne*, 1997, vol. 25, p. 39; F. Vazquez García and A. Moreno Mengíbar, *Sexo y razón. Una genealogía de la moral sexual en España (Siglos XVI–XX)*, Madrid, Akal, 1997, pp. 277–317.
8 St Augustine in *De Ordine* (II, IV, 2), and when speaking about fornication with prostitutes, had established its status as a lesser evil and social necessity. The canon lawyers and theologians of the thirteenth and fourteenth centuries had tended to excuse this extramarital behaviour, appealing to the common interest and to the principle of lesser evil. Thomas Aquinas, in *Summa Theologica* (2, 2q. 10 to 11c), following in this a principle that can be traced to Aristotle, pointed out the need for prostitutes in cities *qua mala peiora incurrantur*. Quoted in Vazquez García and Moreno Mengíbar, *Sexo y razón*, pp. 298–9.
9 E. Gelabert, *De la prostitución en sus relaciones con la Higiene, en el doble concepto de la profilaxis de la sífilis y de la reglamentación*, Barcelona, Est. Tip. de los Sucesures de N. Ramírez y C., 1886, p. 26.
10 A. Prats y Bosch, *La prostitución y la sífilis*, Barcelona, Luis Tasso, 1861, p. 9.
11 J. Viñeta-Bellaserra, *La sífilis como hecho social punible y como una de las causas de la degeneración de la raza humana*, Barcelona, La Academia, 1886, pp. 57–8.

12 For a wider discussion of the different positions on prostitution taken by Spanish hygienists throughout the nineteenth century, see, R. Castejón Bolea, 'Enfermedades venéreas en la España del último tercio del siglo XIX. Una aproximación a los fundamentos morales de la higiene pública', *Dynamis*, 1991, vol. 11, pp. 239–61; R. Castejón Bolea, 'De la Higiene de la prostitución a la lucha antivenérea: enfermedades venéreas y medicina social en España (1868–1936)', Ph.D. dissertation, University of Granada, 1995; J.-L. Guereña, 'Los orígenes de la reglamentación en la España contemporánea. De la propuesta de Carrabús (1792) al Reglamento de Madrid (1847)', *Dynamis*, 1995, vol. 15, pp. 401–41.

13 P. F. Monlau, *Elementos de higiene pública*, Barcelona, Imprenta de D. Pablo Riera, 1847, pp. 285–316.

14 R. Roselló y Olivé, 'La sífilis y la prostitución, sus relaciones; medios de prevenir sus perniciosos efectos', in *Actas de la sesión inaugural que la Real Academia de Medicina y Cirugía de Barcelona celebró en 30 de enero de 1883*, Barcelona, Imprenta de Jaime Jepús, 1883, p. 48.

15 R.G. Eslava, *La prostitución en Madrid: apuntes para un estudio sociológico*, Madrid, Vicente Rico, 1900, p. 190.

16 Guereña, 'Los orígenes del la reglamentación de la prostitución en la España contemporánea', pp. 401–41. These were followed, among others, by regulations applied in the following cities: Jerez (1855), Sevilla (1859), Alicante (1860), Santander (1862), Cádiz (1864), Valencia (1865), Barcelona (1867), Bilbao (1873), Zamora (1873), San Sebastián (1876), Avila (1881), La Coruña (1884), Granada (1884), Almería (1885), Málaga (1885), Lérida (1886), Albacete (1889), Murcia (1889), Pamplona (1889), Vigo (1889). J.-L. Guereña, 'La réglementation de la prostitution en Espagne aux XIXe–XXe siècles', in R. Carrasco (ed.) *La prostitution en Espagne de l'époque des Rois Catholiques à la IIe République*, Paris, Les Belles Lettres, 1994, pp. 307–14.

17 A. Navarro Fernández, *La prostitución en la villa de Madrid*, Madrid, Imprenta de R. Rojas, 1909, p. 113; P. Sereñana y Partagás, *La prostitución en la ciudad de Barcelona, estudiada como enfermedad social y considerada como origen de otras enfermedades dinámicas, orgánicas y morales de la población barcelonesa*, Barcelona, Imprenta de los Suc. de Ramírez y C., 1882, p. 190; C. Ronquillo, 'Un semestre de reconocimientos', *Gaceta médica catalana*, 1885, vol. 8, pp. 38–45.

18 I. de Miguel y Viguri, *Medidas de policía médica en relación con la sífilis. Discurso leído en la Academia Médica Quirúrgica española*, Madrid, Imprenta de E. Teodoro, 1877, p. 46.

19 Sereñana y Partagás, *La prostitución en la ciudad de Barcelona*, p. 232.

20 Guereña, 'La réglementation de la prostitution en Espagne', p. 239.

21 G. Scanlon, *La polémica feminista en la España contemporánea 1868–1974*, Madrid, Siglo XXI, 1976, p. 239.

22 F. Vazquez García, 'Sifilofobia y abolicionismo en Sevilla', *Bulletin d'Histoire Contemporaine de l'Espagne*, 1997, vol. 25, pp. 88–100.

23 M. Tuñón de Lara, *Medio siglo de cultura española 1885–1936*, Madrid, Tecnos, 1977, pp. 57–78.

24 E. Rodriguez Ocaña, 'The making of the Spanish public health administration during the first third of the twentieth century', *Quaderni Internazionale di Storia della Medizina Sanitaria*, 1994, vol. 3, pp. 49–65.

25 J. Nadal, *La población española (Siglos XVI a XX)*, Barcelona, Ariel, 1984, pp. 138–93.

26 R.O. de 1 de marzo de 1908, *Sanidad Nacional. Disposiciones oficiales emanadas del Ministerio de la Gobernación (Inspección General de Sanidad) durante el año 1908*, Madrid, Est. Tipográfico de V. Tordesillas, 1909, pp. 118–19.

27 Rodriguez Ocaña, 'The making of the Spanish public health administration', pp. 49–65.

28 Chapter II (Provincial Health Boards), arts 19–20; chapter V (Provincial Heath Inspectors), arts 38–9; chapter X (Provincial Health and Hygiene), arts 118–19.

29 J. de Azúa, *Reglamentación sanitaria de la prostitución. Profilaxis y terapeúticas colectivas de las enfermedades venéreas. Extracto de un informe oral, hecho ante el Real Consejo de Sanidad, en la discusión de un proyecto de Reglamento de la Sección de Higiene de la Prostitución. Junio, 1904*, Madrid, Imprenta de R. Rojas, 1905, pp. 4–22.

30 P. Blanco y Grande, *Consideraciones sobre la intervención de los Poderes Públicos en la lucha antivenérea*, Madrid, Imprenta de la Viuda de A. Alvarez, 1909, pp. 36–40.

31 R. Alvarez Peláez, 'Origen y desarrollo de la eugenesia en España', in J. M. Sánchez Ron (ed.), *Ciencia y Sociedad en España*, Madrid, EL Arquero, CSIC, pp. 179–204; R. Alvarez Peláez, 'Herencia, sexo y eugenesia', in R. Huertas, A.I. Romero and R. Alvarez (eds), *Perspectivas psiquiátricas*, Madrid, CSIC, 1987, pp. 203–18.

32 Ibid.

33 R. Mollá, 'El peligro venéreo', *Revista española de Dermatología y Sifiliografía*, 1908, vol. 10, pp. 385–92.

34 L. Lecha Martínez, *La sífilis como causa de degeneración del individuo y de la especie. Sociedad Española de Higiene*, Madrid, Imprenta de J. Sastre y C., 1908, p. 21.

35 A. Peyri, *La lluita antivenérea a Catalunya l'any 1934*, Barcelona, Tipografía S. Vives, 1934, p. 5.

36 Ministerio de la Gobernación, *Anuario de la Dirección General de Sanidad. 1924*, Madrid, Establecimiento Tipográfico Sucesor de Nieto y C., 1925, p. 164.

37 Rodriguez Ocaña, 'The making of the Spanish public health administration', pp. 49–65.

38 Ministerio de la Gobernación, *Anuario*, p. 160.

39 Evans, 'Tackling the "Hideous Scourge" ', p. 427.

40 Quétel, *History of Syphilis*, pp. 176–7; Evans, 'Tackling the "Hideous Scourge" ', p. 431.

41 Comité Ejecutivo Antivenéreo, *Algo de su labor en la lucha contra las enfermedades venéreas. Dispensarios y Sifilocomios*, Madrid, Imprenta Clásica Española, 1928, pp. 12–66.

42 J. Sánchez Covisa, 'Papel de la Universidad en la lucha antivenérea', *Ecos Españoles de Dermatología y Sifiliografía*, 1929, vol. 5, p. 580.

43 R. Bertoloty, 'La organización antivenérea en España', *Actas Dermo-Sifiliográficas*, 1931, vol. 23, pp. 530–50.

44 'Sección de noticias. Hospital de la Santa Cruz de Barcelona. Curso de ampliación y especialización de estudios. Cursillo de Dermatología y Sifiliografía, a cargo del profesor Noguer Moré', *Ecos Españoles de Dermatología y Sifiliografía*, 1925, vol. 2, p. 283. Medical courses included laboratory work and consultations at the dispensaries. The first course took place in 1923–4. Daudens Valls and Cuesta Almonacid, 'Proyecto de organización de la enseñanza, ejercicio e instituciones dermosifiliográficas de España', *Actas Dermo-Sifiliográficas*, 1934, vol. 26, pp. 891–904.

45 E. Rodriguez Ocaña and J. Molero Mesa, 'La cruzada por la salud. Las campañas sanitarias del primer tercio del siglo XX en la construcción de la cultura de la salud', in L. Montiel (ed.) *La salud en el estado del bienestar. Análisis histórico*, Madrid, Editorial Complutense, 1993, pp. 133–48.

46 R. Lancha Fal, 'Algunas orientaciones sobre sanidad antivenérea', *Ecos Españoles de Dermatología y Sifiliografía*, 1926, vol. 2, pp. 507–21.

47 G.S. Meyer, 'Criminal punishment for the transmission of sexually transmitted diseases: lessons from syphilis', *Bulletin of the History of Medicine*, 1991, no. 65, pp. 549–64.

48 R. Castejón Bolea, 'El delito de contagio venéreo: la penalización como instrumento jurídico de la lucha antivenérea', in L. Montiel and I. Porras (eds) *De la Responsabilidad Individual a la Culpabilización de la Víctima*, Aranjuez, Doce Calles, 1997, pp. 203–18. The measure had a life as short as that of the Penal Code: 1928–1932.

49 J. Bernabeu Mestre and E. Gascón Pérez, 'La visitadora sanitaria (1923–1935)', *Dynamis*, 1995, vol. 15, pp. 151–76.

50 J. Fernández de la Portilla, *La lucha antivenérea en España (Diez años de experiencia)*, Madrid, Gráfica Universal, 1930, p. 49.
51 Comité Ejecutivo Antivenéreo, *Algo de su labor en la lucha contra las enfermedades venéreas*, pp. 8–9.
52 Ibid. This office, the first known in Spain to be specifically focused on health propaganda, was probably influential in the creation in 1933, during the Second Republic, of a social hygiene and propaganda section in the General Directorate of Health.
53 Erika Bornay has synthesized these images in the equation: woman = vice = sickness = death. E. Bornay, *Las hijas de Lilith*, Madrid, Ediciones Cátedra, 1990, p. 256.
54 C. Campoamor, 'Protección social a las menores', *Ecos Españoles de Dermatología y Sifiliografía*, 1929, vol. 4, pp. 335–60. In 1929, 18,000 posters had been published and distributed.
55 From 1916, seamen who became infected through failure to carry out compulsory preventive practices were punished. J. Monmeneu, 'Profilaxis venérea y sifilítica individual', *Revista General de Marina*, 1917, vol. 25, pp. 355–68, 493–515, 611–26.
56 Vázquez García, Moreno Mengíbar, *Sexo y razón*, p. 154.
57 Ibid., p. 170.

5

'THE FATHERLAND IS IN DANGER, SAVE THE FATHERLAND!'

Venereal disease, sexuality and gender in Imperial and Weimar Germany

Lutz D. H. Sauerteig

Introduction

In the early years of the twentieth century, the spread of venereal diseases (VD) became a major concern within German public health discourses. Initial investigations into the incidence of VD seriously alarmed public health officials. According to one survey in April 1900, 1.9 per thousand of the Prussian population were being treated for VD.[1] Evidence suggested that the younger generation in the cities and the middle class were especially affected. In Berlin, the capital, about 10.0 per thousand of the population were receiving treatment for syphilis or gonorrhoea. Subsequent inquiries revealed similar or even more shocking figures. The first nationwide survey, conducted in 1919, estimated that about half a million Germans caught VD each year, representing some 8.7 per thousand of the population. However, later surveys in 1927 and 1934 suggested a slowly decreasing level of venereal infection with rates falling from a peak of 5.8 to 3.4 per thousand of the population and absolute numbers from 372,000 to 225,000 respectively.[2] These were the statistics shaping the perception of VD in society as well as in social and health policy.

The dominant strategy for combating VD in Germany up until the end of the nineteenth century had been the state regulation and control of prostitutes, introduced in Prussia at the beginning of the eighteenth century. After the foundation of the German Empire, the 1871 Penal Code allowed prostitution only if prostitutes submitted themselves to police control. Subsequently, state regulation of prostitution was extended to all of Germany. This meant that prostitutes had to register with the vice squads of the police. Although procedures were organized differently in each of the German *Länder* (states), prostitutes had to submit themselves to regular medical inspection by the vice squads and were obliged to follow strict restrictions by the police in all cities.[3] In the second half of the nine-teenth century, social purity organizations and the women's movement began to protest against state regulation of prostitution from a moral point of view. They vociferously demanded its abolition, but without any success.[4] By the end of the century, members of the medical profession who were largely in favour of the control of prostitution criticized the medical inspection of prostitutes by the vice squads as ineffective in discovering venereal infections. Indeed, at the beginning of the twentieth century, control of prostitution became increasingly difficult. On the one hand, so-called casual prostitutes (or 'amateurs') often evaded regis-tration and control by the police. As their number was believed to be increasing, and as the vice squads, especially in large cities such as Berlin or Hamburg, lacked personnel to control them, amateur prostitutes were targeted as the main source of venereal infection.[5] On the other hand, police and public health offi-cials were faced with the problem of the definition of 'prostitution'. The label 'prostitute' was extended to all those women who had sexual relations outside marriage. Finally, any employed woman who was economically independent from her father or husband – and their number clearly increased from the end of the nineteenth century both within the working class and the bourgeoisie – was to some degree suspected by the police, as well as by male venereologists and health educators, to be promiscuous or even a prostitute.[6]

In 1902, in the aftermath of the second Brussels Syphilis Congress,[7] promi-nent German venereologists such as Alfred Blaschko and Albert Neisser founded the German Society for Combating VD (*Deutsche Gesellschaft zur Bekämpfung der Geschlechtskrankheiten*). This Society succeeded in gathering together those who were interested in reforming the regulation of prostitution and willing to discuss public health strategies for combating VD. Subsequently, the Society developed into an influential pressure group that made contacts not only with the public health bureaucracy and with members of the different political camps in German society – namely Conservatives, Socialists, and Liberals – but also with the women's movement and social purity organizations.[8]

In the years before the outbreak of the First World War, prostitution and the spread of VD became a major topic in public health and social policy discourses. The wild, hectic pace of urban life, the spread of prostitution and unleashed sexuality were assumed to be major reasons for the spread of VD. By the end of the nineteenth century, VD had become a metaphor for the moral decline of a German society heading towards physical and cultural degeneration. Connected to this moral panic, social causes such as the prevalent alcoholism of the working class, their deplorable housing conditions in the urban and industrial regions of Germany, and also the delayed marriages in the upper classes, were named as factors fostering the spread of VD. Together with continuously declining birthrates, high VD rates that were expected to increase even further were perceived as threatening not only the nation and Germany's military strength but also the future of the 'race'. Thus, at the beginning of the twentieth century, VD became a leading issue exposing health policy to the agenda of racial and social hygienists.[9] At the foundation meeting of the German Society for Combating VD in Berlin on 19 October 1902, the senior medical officer in Prussia, Martin Kirchner, declared that the 'Fatherland is in danger, save the fatherland!'[10]

After nearly thirty years of debates on how to control the spread of VD, the German parliament (*Reichstag*) finally passed the Act for Combating VD (*Reichsgesetz zur Bekämpfung der Geschlechtskrankheiten*) in 1927.[11] This chapter examines the main topics raised in these debates and analyses them from two perspectives: on the one hand, the question of sexual morality and gender relations in health policy, and on the other, the question of the relative importance of governmental intervention and individual freedom.

As will be seen, there were strong mutual influences between health policy and notions of sexual morality and sexual behaviour. For an analytical purpose, two general approaches can be distinguished. One can be identified as the moralistic approach; the other as the pragmatic approach characterized by a more scientific and medical attitude towards VD.[12] In the moralistic approach, VD and the fear of infection were used to enforce a middle-class morality of sexual self-control and pre-marital abstinence, as well as faithfulness within marriage. Therefore, moralists opposed any policy which might diminish the fear of infection, arguing that this would destabilize moral norms and society. This was assumed to be of even greater importance in a time of dwindling religious faith in society when religion seemed to be losing its power to prevent people from behaving immorally.[13] Hence, moralists rated morality higher than the health of the individual. Pragmatists, on the other hand, were convinced that only a medical approach could stop the spread of VD. Their aim was to educate the public so that people would behave according to a medical scientific rationale. In the interest of the family, the state, the nation and the race, the individual should realize a personal obligation to lead a healthy life.

The second crucial question in health policy was the clash between the citizen's freedom and the interest of society and the nation. Where should the line be drawn? In contrast to England, where the sexual and corporeal liberty of the individual citizen in the conduct of his/her body was strongly defended, the development in Germany pointed in the opposite direction.[14] The increasing influence of racial hygienists made public health policy value the right of the nation and race to be protected against the spread of venereal infection more highly than the freedom of the individual. Resistance against this development was only marginal and thus had no chance of success.

Venereal disease, sexual morality and gender

Around 1900, the perception of VD in Germany began to change fundamentally from a moralistic to a more pragmatic attitude. In the nineteenth century, VD had been perceived as shameful diseases that were contracted in non-marital sexual relationships (i.e. with prostitutes) and were thus seen as the consequence of wickedness or immorality and treated as a personal problem of the infected. Only innocent victims, such as children and spouses who had been infected by their sinful father or husband, were exempted from moral condemnation. Men often concealed their infection in order to escape moral censure. Moreover, such was the stigma associated with the disease that within the medical profession, as in England,[15] it was even debated as to whether an infected wife should be informed of her disease because of the likely repercussions for marital harmony.

Yet, infected persons not only avoided consulting a venereologist, to escape moral stigmatization men often concealed their infection because this implied a confession of immoral behaviour. The long-lasting treatment of syphilis and gonorrhoea was also expensive and thus could be afforded only by upper- and middle-class patients. The introduction of compulsory health insurance legislation in 1883 changed this situation but only to some degree. Both the health insurance and disability insurance legislation considered VD as self-inflicted diseases. To protect insured workers from misuse of their mutual funds, they restricted the benefits in cases of venereal infection. Insured VD patients had the right to medical treatment financed by their insurance scheme but sick payment was withheld. Sick payment, however, was essential as it not only secured the sick worker's family at least some income but also represented the only means to finance hospital treatment. Therefore, without the support of sick payment, most VD patients could only be treated as out-patients. This was criticized by many venereologists who considered hospital treatment essential, especially where protracted syphilis therapy was required.[16]

However, it was not only financial constraints that kept VD patients from going to hospital. Many hospitals refused to accept VD patients for moral reasons. Consequently a shortage of hospital beds prevailed. Moreover, those hospitals which did accept VD patients imposed rigid restrictions on them; for example, not allowing them to walk in the hospital garden or to see visitors. VD wards were frequently located in the oldest parts of hospitals, with barred windows and little light and fresh air. In many hospitals, VD patients were more or less kept like prisoners.[17]

After 1900, the perception of VD patients as being personally responsible for their infection began to alter. Increasingly, VD was considered to be a medical as well as a social problem to be solved by public health policy. For example, the reform of the health insurance legislation in 1903 can be seen as a first major step in the direction of a more pragmatic attitude towards VD. After heated debates in parliament, Social Democrats and Liberals enforced this reform against fierce resistance from the Catholic Centre Party and the Conservatives. Social Democrats and Liberals successfully argued from the standpoint of social hygiene that VD constituted a major threat to society. As a result, legislation was passed which ensured that VD patients were entitled to the same benefits as all other members of health insurance schemes. A venereal infection was no longer perceived as self-inflicted but had become a medical and social problem. The result of the 1903 reform was twofold. On the one hand, the financial situation of VD patients improved considerably. On the other hand, VD patients were now controlled by the medical regime to a much higher degree. As members of the health insurance system, VD patients were obliged to avoid any risk of infection and, if infected, had to consult an approved specialist immediately.[18]

The trend towards medicalizing VD is also illustrated by the gradually changing conditions of VD patients in hospitals. Although VD patients were still not treated like other patients, protests from doctors, from the Society for Combating VD, and from the patients themselves led to some improvements. The aim was to remove all conditions that formally stigmatized VD patients, thus rendering infected persons more willing to undergo treatment in hospitals. The protest against the deplorable and dreadful conditions in VD wards culminated in the summer of 1893 when some socialist doctors, amongst them Alfred Blaschko, organized a boycott of the leading German teaching hospital, the *Königliche Charité* in Berlin. Several Berlin health insurance schemes joined the boycott and stopped sending patients to the *Charité*. Consequently, the *Charité*'s income was considerably reduced and the hospital deprived of patients on whom they depended for medical teaching. The boycott was successful and in 1897 Prussia started an extensive rebuilding programme.[19] In-patient treatment for the venereally infected was not only considered to be important for medical reasons but also for the better control of patients. A problem that arose especially with these in-patients was how to deal with them when they had to undergo protracted VD treatment in hospital. Programmes were proposed to occupy and educate them. Women were provided with some vocational training to divert them from prostitution.[20] Both aspects, improving treatment conditions and intensifying the control of VD patients, were, therefore, closely intertwined.[21]

The changing attitudes towards VD were perhaps even more evident in public debates. After 1900, the symptoms and treatment of syphilis and gonorrhoea became the subject not only of parliamentary debates. They were also discussed in public health meetings and exhibitions, in special lectures for workers, soldiers, students, and even for pupils at school, thus targeting dangerous sexuality among those groups of urban youth who were believed to be sexually most active.[22] Women as well as men were included in these health education campaigns, especially those of the working class (factory workers, maids, etc.), but also the bourgeoisie.[23]

Moreover, VD also became a topic in theatre plays such as Eugène Brieux's *Les Avariés* (Damaged Goods) which was translated into German in 1903 under the title *Die Schiffbrüchigen*.[24] The Society for Combating VD organized reading evenings of Brieux's play and later, after they got permission from the police, theatre performances in several German cities. In 1917, the first VD film, *Es werde Licht!* (Let There be Light!), also produced with the support of the Society for Combating VD, was shown in one of the huge Berlin cinemas. The great success of *Es werde Licht!* was the start for numerous further film productions, some of them, however, only using the pretext of health education to present films which were regarded as pornographic.[25] In addition, later in the 1920s, radio talks dealt with VD as a topic. The aim of these public health campaigns was to inform people on the symptoms, epidemiology and treatment of VD. However, the discourse surrounding VD was not limited to the medical aspect. It addressed issues of appropriate sexual behaviour, sex education and prostitution. It was hoped to achieve a deterrent effect by showing the horrible symptoms of syphilis and gonorrhoea. Health educators wanted the promiscuous to become aware of the risk they were running by having sexual relations outside marriage and by leading an immoral life. Hence, the underlying intention of the VD campaigns was to promote the picture of the healthy citizen abstaining from dangerous sexuality and obeying the moral norms of self-control and self-restraint.[26]

The public health exhibitions, especially the VD pavilion at the International Hygiene Exhibition in Dresden in 1911, as well as theatre and film performances, attracted vast audiences. This remarkable public interest in VD was not only due to enthusiasm for medical and public health education. Many visitors to VD exhibitions and films were also attracted because of the sensational and voyeuristic aspects. They were curious to see hyper-realistic wax models of diseased organs, especially as even wax models of genitals were on display. Sometimes, wax models and film sequences were so realistic that some visitors fainted. VD films were always suspected of being pornographic and therefore controlled by film censorship. Often whole sequences had to be cut, or films were exhibited only under certain restrictions; for example, only in the presence of a physician or in different versions for male and female audiences.[27]

At the beginning of the twentieth century, the success of VD treatment was still limited. The Salvarsan (arsphenamine) therapy introduced by Paul Ehrlich in 1910 had constituted a real breakthrough in the treatment of syphilis but still remained difficult and dangerous.[28] An effective therapy for gonorrhoea with sulphonamide only became available after the mid-1930s. Hence, there were only two alternatives: either to abstain from sexual intercourse and to remain chaste, or to use prophylactics such as condoms and disinfectant solutions. The debate over prophylaxis clearly reveals the contrast between the moralistic and pragmatic approaches to VD policy.[29] Furthermore, it illustrates that any decision which affected the disciplinary impact of the fear of venereal infection also had important consequences for society as a whole.

The moralists, including representatives of the Catholic and Protestant churches, social purity organizations, the conservative wing of the women's movement as well as some medical practitioners, saw the spread of pornography, birth control and homosexuality, the increasing divorce rates, and, last but not least, VD, as clear indicators of the degeneration of society. For them, chastity and early marriage were the only strategy to avoid venereal infection. Since the nineteenth century, the conservative wing of the women's movement had criticized the double moral standard. From a moralistic standpoint, they persistently demanded an equally high moral standard of chastity for both women and men.[30] In general, the moralists propagated a religious and moral renewal of society and opposed any measures which would remove the fear of venereal infection because this fear would act as a deterrent. Thus, the fear of infection became a major bedrock in their battle against the dissolution of social order and morality. If religious faith could no longer prevent people from immoral behaviour, then at least the fear of VD would force them to remain chaste. Paula Mueller-Ortfried, the president of the conservative *Deutsch-evangelischer Frauenbund* (German-Evangelical Women's Alliance), argued in 1915 that 'Who sins has also to bear the risks of sin.'[31] Thus, in the final analysis, moralists rated morality more highly than the health of the individual.

Other health educators – mainly venereologists, but also members of the radical wing of the women's movement – criticized this strategy as ineffective in combating VD. Their approach, influenced by medico-scientific reasoning, was more pragmatic. Although venereologists such as Alfred Blaschko also considered chastity as probably the safest route to avoid infection, they did not believe that the majority could and would follow the moralistic strategy and abstain from sexual relations outside marriage. Therefore, pragmatists recommended informing the public about prophylactics. Every man who had non-marital sex should, they argued, have the moral duty to use preventatives in order to fulfil his responsibility towards family, state, nation and race. Hence, prophylaxis only aimed at protecting men, not women. Even in the case of prostitution, the prophylaxis strategy centred on the protection of the male client and not of the prostitute herself. Thus, one could argue that this strategy reinforced the double moral standard. Although it meant accepting extra-marital sexual contacts, women were still expected to have sexual relations only within marriage, and those women who did not comply with this moral standard were still labelled as prostitutes.

This was an issue on which the radical wing of the women's movement, namely Helene Stöcker and her *Bund für Mutterschutz* (League for the Protection of Mothers), departed from other pragmatists. They fought for a reform of prevailing gender relations and, in contrast to the conservative wing of the women's movement, propounded a *Neue Ethik* (New Ethic) with equal sexual rights for men and women. Helene Stöcker wanted to free women of any moral restriction. The provocative slogan of the *Neue Ethik* was free love outside marriage for both sexes. However, Helene Stöcker's *Neue Ethik* remained marginalized within the women's movement, where the moralistic attitude dominated the discourse on sexuality. Moreover, most of the other pragmatists would also have strongly rejected Stöcker's *Neue Ethik*. Nonetheless, Stöcker at least forced the women's movement to reflect upon and discuss openly questions of gender relations and sexuality.[32]

Although the protest of the moralists was vociferously expressed and backed by influential Protestant and Catholic church leaders, it could not halt the gradually but fundamentally changing norms shaping sexual morality. This became evident during the First World War. Although the distribution of chemical prophylactics or condoms remained problematic, the German military educated soldiers and officers in using prophylactics and thus contributed to their popularization.[33] In the Weimar Republic, the medico-scientific approach dominated VD policy even more. This indicated a more pragmatic and rational attitude towards VD as the decision to inform the public on preventatives meant that the moralistic policy of deterrence was rejected as being ineffective. The 1927 VD Act removed any remaining restrictions on the sale of prophylactics.[34] Thereafter, chemical disinfectants and condoms could be purchased from vending machines in the public toilets of larger railway stations, bars and cafés in most German cities. In 1932, there were about 1,300 such vending machines installed in public toilets.[35] Approximately 1,000 organizations supporting the sex reform movement distributed free prophylactics to their members.[36] Although the National Socialist Regime later tried to restrict the sale of prophylactics from vending machines, they did not forbid the use of prophylactics in general. Soldiers and members of the SS, for example, were provided with condoms throughout the Second World War, despite the shortage of rubber.[37]

The medicalization of the VD problem in German health policy also had repercussions for the control of prostitution. The 1927 Act for Combating VD abolished state regulation of prostitution and replaced it by medical controls. All persons, whatever their gender, who were suspected of having promiscuous sexual relations could be forced to undergo medical inspection.[38] In fact, it was primarily women who were placed under this form of medical control. The consequences of medicalizing prostitution thus remained ambivalent. On the one hand, prostitutes were released from the humiliating practice of police control. Whereas, in the nineteenth century, prostitution had been solely a moral issue, it was now redefined in medical terms as an issue of social hygiene. On the other hand, this was another step towards stricter medical control of society and towards the healthy citizen.[39]

To sum up, after the turn of the century, VD control had become an issue for health policy and social hygiene. VD patients were no longer duly punished sinners but patients who needed medical treatment both in their own interests and in the interests of society, the nation and the race.

Venereal disease, law and medical control

The other central issue which surfaced around 1900 was how society and the state should react to venereally infected persons who were not willing to comply with their medical treatment, or who remained sexually active and therefore threatened others with the risk of infection. These debates raised fundamental and contentious issues relating to the use of legal compulsion for the purposes of disease control. The basic dilemma was how, within legislation, to balance the interests of public health and the liberty of the individual.[40]

Different strategies to secure stricter surveillance of VD patients were discussed. One strand of the debate was whether there should be compulsory notification of VD cases and a legal obligation on the infected to undergo qualified medical treatment, even against their will. This implied that VD would be treated in law in similar fashion to other infectious diseases such as smallpox or cholera. The main argument in favour of notification was that only by reporting VD cases could proper treatment be assured for those who refused to comply with medical advice, and who thus posed a risk to society and the nation. Those who opposed notification were convinced that this would undermine the confidentiality between the doctor and the patient. Furthermore, it was argued that compulsory notification would lead to concealment of infection and encourage patients to resort to unqualified lay-healers.[41]

In Prussia, compulsory notification for syphilis was first introduced by the 1835 Public Health Act in the aftermath of the Napoleonic wars. However, most medical practitioners virtually ignored this provision.[42] The question of effective infectious diseases legislation only resurfaced after a devastating cholera epidemic had swept through the harbour-town of Hamburg in 1892.[43] In 1900, an Imperial Act introduced compulsory notification for certain infectious diseases.[44] Along with their struggle for abolition of the state regulation of prostitution, members of the German women's movement were strongly in favour of including VD in this Act. They argued that, by introducing general compulsory notification, not only the prostitute but also the male client who posed a threat to the health of other women would have to be notified. However, many within the medical profession and public health administration rejected this idea as a threat to confidentiality and VD was excluded from this act.[45]

Likewise, proposals to introduce penal legislation against persons with VD who exposed their sexual partners to the risk of infection did not succeed, although they were advocated not only by the Catholic Centre Party but also by prominent individuals such as the Berlin penologist, Franz von Liszt, and the Breslau venereologist, Albert Neisser.[46] Legal experts considered the existing regulations of the German Penal Law to be sufficient. Under the Penal Law, the deliberate and wilful communication of any infectious disease was already indictable as an assault. However, it was very difficult to prove this in a case of VD. Thus, cases in which a person was sentenced to imprisonment were exceptional. New reform plans were intended not only to penalize the transmission of VD but also the exposure to a possible risk of infection. Hence, it would have been unnecessary to prove that an infection with VD really had taken place or that the victim had been infected only by the accused.[47]

The emergency situation of the First World War with its enormous toll of lives, especially of the younger generations, the still falling birth rate, and the soaring number of VD cases among soldiers, fostered a greater willingness to introduce more radical steps towards combating VD. Accordingly, the main argument supporting compulsory VD controls and for restricting the citizen's freedom became population policy and racial hygiene. Under emergency legislation of 1918, a person could be convicted of assault when exposing a sexual partner to venereal infection. The maximum penalty was three years of imprisonment.[48] Although this paragraph was gender neutral, this legislation mostly affected women. In the 1920s, an average of about 650 people per year, 75 per cent of whom were women, were convicted under this legislation. The maximum penalty, however, was never imposed; the majority were sentenced to less than three months' imprisonment.[49]

During the First World War, the president of the Imperial Social Insurance Office (*Reichsversicherungsamt*), Paul Kaufmann, became one of the most influential proponents of compulsory notification. He suggested that, following their discharge from the military, all venereally infected soldiers should be reported to the Social Insurance Boards (*Landesversicherungsanstalten*) for supervision of further treatment. As soon as compulsory notification for soldiers had been accepted by the military and proved to be a successful strategy, Kaufmann was sure – although he never admitted it in public – that notification could easily be extended to the civilian population. The women's movement also petitioned for the introduction of compulsory notification as they now feared that infected soldiers would transmit VD to their female partners at home. Thus, during the War, a broad alliance, which was joined by the Protestant churches and social purity organizations, demanded stricter control of the venereally infected. The military, however, opposed any procedure which would merely have targeted soldiers and not the civilian population. Therefore, notification for soldiers remained voluntary and hence only rarely implemented.[50]

Another step towards stricter control of VD patients was the foundation of VD Advice Centres (*Beratungsstellen für Geschlechtskranke*). In 1916, 93 Advice Centres existed and their number increased to 185 in 1922. Although many of them were closed during the inflation of 1923/4, most Advice Centres reopened again later; and their number rose to 187 in 1926 and to 264 in 1931. These Advice Centres provided free medical counsel and diagnosis to everybody. Because of strong opposition from physicians' organizations, especially from the so-called Hartmannbund, an organization founded in 1900 to promote the economic interests of practitioners, no treatment was provided. Instead, patients had to be referred to local VD specialists.[51] However, in special cases, the Advice Centres covered the costs of treatment and even reimbursed travel expenses and loss of earnings. Most of the Advice Centres were financed by the Social Insurance Boards of the German *Länder*.

Besides giving advice and organizing VD education campaigns, the most important task of the Advice Centres was to control VD patients. Venereologists reported their VD cases and if the patient (male or female) discontinued treatment, the Advice Centres sent letters to remind the patient to attend. With the 1918 Decree for Combating VD, the Advice Centres were even allowed to implement compulsory treatment. Although the majority of the patients went to the Centres because they had been reported by their practitioner, hospital, health insurance scheme, or by the military administration, about 30 to 40 per cent came voluntarily. Thus, the Advice Centres had a twofold function. On the one hand, they became a new element within the expanding social welfare system of the Weimar Republic. On the other hand, they played an important role in establishing a comprehensive system to control VD patients, both male and female. Soon, medical practitioners accepted the Advice Centres as means for expanding their medical control. Thus, the Advice Centres connected the local function of health care with the central function of health control.[52]

However, the legal power of the Advice Centres to implement compulsory treatment remained limited. This situation only changed with the 1927 Act for Combating VD. It required everyone infected with VD to undergo treatment by a duly qualified practitioner. Medical practitioners were now compelled to notify health authorities of any patient who failed to comply with their treatment regimes, defaulted from treatment, or continued to endanger public health by remaining sexually active. Health authorities could then commit these patients for further treatment to locked wards of hospitals, using a police force if necessary.[53] The VD Act thus functioned as a substitute for the nineteenth-century state regulation of prostitution. The vice squads of the police were abolished, at least officially, and their role (but sometimes their personnel as well) was taken over by the local health administration. Now it was no longer only the prostitute who was under medical control but also her male customer. There was, however, no overwhelming consensus in favour of general compulsory notification for VD. Many medical practitioners strongly advised against such proposals as they were afraid that this might undermine the fundamental principle of confidentiality.[54]

The 1927 VD Act, which is still in force today, albeit with some modifications,[55] was a critical point in the German tradition of state intervention in VD control. After intense debates about the relationship of personal liberty to public health controls, a decision in favour of the public interest had been made. This policy was supported by the Society for Combating VD as well as by influential public health administrators such as Paul Kaufmann, President of the Imperial Social Insurance Office. Since the outbreak of war, Kaufmann had argued in favour of 'a permanent control of VD patients'.[56] In 1923, the venereologist and Chairman of the Society for Combating VD, Joseph Jadassohn, declared in the *Reichstag* that 'Personal rights stop where they compete with the welfare of the public.'[57] There was a broad party consensus in the *Reichstag* that VD patients had a responsibility towards the family and to the future of the state and the race to seek qualified medical treatment when infected. This was the basic argument used to emphasize the state's right to enforce medical treatment of VD patients.

It was even planned to introduce compulsory medical certificates to stop venereally infected persons from marrying. Since the turn of the century, marriage as the place for procreation had attracted the interest of racial hygienists and medical practitioners who argued for special health legislation to protect marriage.[58] However, their plans to introduce compulsory medical certificates did not succeed. Since 1921, those wanting to marry merely had to obtain an official leaflet from the registrar informing them of the importance of the health status of their future partner and advising infected persons to abstain from marriage. But they were not officially prohibited from marrying. In 1927, however, they were legally bound by the VD Act to inform their future spouses of a former venereal infection.[59] This was significant because it now gave the spouses legal grounds to sue if their infected partners had failed to fulfil this requirement. Yet, a venereal infection as such was still not sufficient grounds for a divorce. In divorce cases, a venereal infection of one partner which occurred after marriage could only be used as proof of infidelity. In such a case, however, physicians were not allowed to give evidence. They were only allowed to break the principle of confidentiality in cases in which they could prevent further transmission of infection; for example, from the infected patient to the spouse. But even then, doctors seem to have been reluctant to do so.[60] It was the National Socialist regime which in 1935 introduced compulsory medical certificates to be shown to the registrar before marriage. In cases of hereditary diseases, mental diseases, or infectious diseases, the couple were not allowed to marry. However, because of shortage of personnel and organizational problems, this regulation was barely implemented. Only when the registrar had reasonable grounds for suspicion was a medical certificate required as a condition for marriage.[61]

Conclusion

German VD policy in the late nineteenth and early twentieth centuries can be characterized as being both pragmatic and interventionist. On the one hand, there was a clear shift from a health policy dominated by moral considerations during the nineteenth century towards a pragmatic approach from the turn of the century onwards. Taboos surrounding VD were removed, restrictions on the social insurance legislation abolished and broad health education campaigns started. As a result, information on VD became increasingly available to the public, even to school-leavers. Patients got free access to more modernized treatment facilities and prophylactics were much more easily obtainable for the public. Hence, one could argue that fear of infection and, in the case of condoms, fear of pregnancy, both of which had been closely related to sexuality, had been at least partially reduced.

On the other hand, the 1927 VD Act considerably extended medical control over sexual behaviour and amplified the power of the medical profession to regulate their patients. The nineteenth-century police regulation of prostitution was replaced by medical control of both the prostitute and the client, operated by qualified practitioners and health authorities. VD patients were now legally obliged to seek treatment by properly qualified practitioners. Thus, the 1927 VD Act also regulated patients' choice of treatment regimes. Lay healers were no longer allowed to treat VD. Hence, in the course of the early twentieth century, the right of the individual citizen to decide what happened to his/her body, should it become infected, was severely restricted.[62]

However, the VD Act also limited state intervention in health policy. Compulsory treatment was only legal when VD was in an infectious stage. Consequently, VD patients could only be forced to undergo treatment until the risk of infecting others had disappeared. More significantly from today's perspective of bioethics, patients retained the legal right to refuse any therapy that might threaten their life, as could be the case with Salvarsan or mercury therapies.

Beyond these dichotomies of moralism versus pragmatism and of state intervention versus individual freedom, German VD policy also reflects the traditional gender relations. Whereas strategies to control VD patients mainly aimed at the dangerous sexuality of women, strategies for prevention of infection were supposed to reduce men's risk of contracting VD. Again, although the VD Act introduced strict health controls for both men and women, it was primarily women who were sentenced under this legislation. Thus, the picture of German VD policy in the late nineteenth and the early twentieth centuries remains ambivalent. There was less moral but more medically motivated control of VD, but the double moral standard persisted. It was men, not women, who profited from prophylactic strategies and public health policy designed to contain the spread of VD.

NOTES

1 A. Guttstadt, 'Die Verbreitung der venerischen Krankheiten in Preußen, sowie die Maßnahmen zur Bekämpfung dieser Krankheiten', *Zeitschrift des königlich-preußischen statistischen Bureaus*, 1901, supplement 20. On the results and statistical problems of VD surveys in Germany, L. Sauerteig, *Krankheit, Sexualität, Gesellschaft. Geschlechtskrankheiten und Gesundheitspolitik in Deutschland im 19. und frühen 20. Jahrhundert*, Stuttgart, Franz-Steiner, 1999, pp. 68–82; H. Haustein, 'Statistik der Geschlechtskrankheiten', in J. Jadassohn (ed.) *Handbuch der Haut- und Geschlechtskrankheiten*, vol. 22, Berlin, Springer, 1927, pp. 238–1,033.

2 F. W. Wedel, 'Die Ergebnisse der Reichserhebung der Geschlechtskranken im November/Dezember 1919', *Medizinalstatistische Mitteilungen aus dem Reichsgesundheitsamte*, 1925, vol. 22, pp. 63–81; Dornedden, 'Endgültiges Ergebnis der Reichszählung der Geschlechtskranken 1927', *Reichsgesundheitsblatt*, 1928, supplement 3, pp. 579–642; Dornedden, Baland, 'Reichszählung der Geschlechtskranken 1934', *Reichsgesundheitsblatt*, 1935, supplement 1, pp. 1–36.

3 On prostitution in Germany, see S. Krafft, *Zucht und Unzucht. Prostitution und Sittenpolizei im München der Jahrhundertwende*, München, Hugendubel, 1996; F. W. Stallberg, *Eine Stadt und die (Un-)Sittlichkeit. 100 Jahre Prostitutionsüberwachung in Dortmund*, Dortmund, Projekt-Verlag, 1992; N. R. Reagin, '"A true woman can take care of herself". The debate over prostitution in Hanover, 1906', *Central European History*, 1991, vol. 24, pp. 347–80; L. Abrams, 'Prostitutes in Imperial Germany 1870–1918. Working girls or social outcasts', in R. J. Evans (ed.) *The German Underworld. Deviants and Outcasts in German History*, London and New York, Routledge, 1988, pp. 189–209; R. Schulte, *Sperrbezirke. Tugendhaftigkeit und Prostitution in der bürgerlichen Welt*, Frankfurt, Syndikat, 1979, second edition, 1984; R. J. Evans, 'Prostitution, state and society in Imperial Germany', *Past and Present*, 1976, vol. 70, pp. 106–29.

4 See Sauerteig, *Krankheit, Sexualität, Gesellschaft*, 1999, pp. 57–62; L. Sauerteig, 'Frauenemanzipation und Sittlichkeit. Die Rezeption des englischen Abolitionismus in Deutschland', in R. Muhs, J. Paulmann and W. Steinmetz (eds) *Aneignung und Abwehr. Interkultureller Transfer zwischen Deutschland und Großbritannien im 19. Jahrhundert*, Bodenheim, Philo, 1998, pp. 159–97; A. T. Allen, 'Feminism, venereal diseases, and the state in Germany, 1890–1918', *Journal of the History of Sexuality*, 1993, vol. 4, pp. 27–50.
5 See Evans, 'Prostitution', 1976; Alfred Urban, *Staat und Prostitution in Hamburg vom Beginn der Reglementierung bis zur Aufhebung der Kasernierung (1807–1922)*, Hamburg, diss. jur. 1925, published 1927, pp. 111–25.
6 A. Blaschko and W. Fischer, 'Einfluß der sozialen Lage auf die Geschlechtskrankheiten', in M. Mosse and G. Tugendreich (eds) *Krankheit und Soziale Lage*, München, J.F. Lehmanns, 1913, p. 509. See Sauerteig, *Krankheit, Sexualität, Gesellschaft*, pp. 48–9, 390–1; K. Walser, 'Prostitutionsverdacht und Geschlechterforschung. Das Beispiel der Dienstmädchen um 1900', *Geschichte und Gesellschaft*, 1985, vol. 11, pp. 99–111.
7 On the two conferences on prostitution and syphilis in Brussels, see Sauerteig, *Krankheit, Sexualiät, Gesellschaft*, pp. 62–8; see also P. de Vries, this volume, ch. 3.
8 On the history of the German Society for Combating VD, see Sauerteig, *Krankheit, Sexualität, Gesellschaft*, pp. 89–125.
9 Sauerteig, *Krankheit, Sexualität, Gesellschaft*, pp. 44–52. On the impact of racial hygiene on German politics, see P. Weindling, *Health, Race and German Politics between National Unification and Nazism, 1870–1945*, Cambridge, Cambridge University Press, 1989; P. Weingart, J. Kroll and K. Bayertz, *Rasse, Blut und Gene. Geschichte der Eugenik und Rassenhygiene in Deutschland*, Frankfurt/M., Suhrkamp, 1988.
10 Quoted by Anna Pappritz in her report in *Soziale Praxis*, 12, 1902/03, p. 106.
11 'Reichsgesetz zur Bekämpfung der Geschlechtskrankheiten', 22 February 1927, *Reichsgesetzblatt*, 1927, part I, no. 9; H. Haustein, 'The German Federal Law for Combating Venereal Diseases', *Health & Empire*, New Series, 1927, vol. 2, pp. 89–99.
12 The construction of these two ideal types was inspired by Max Weber's ideal types of social behaviour. See M. Weber, *Wirtschaft und Gesellschaft. Grundriß der verstehenden Soziologie*, revised edition, ed. by J. Winckelmann, Tübingen, Mohr, 5th edition, 1976, pp. 12–13; M. Weber, 'Die "Objektivität" sozialwissenschaftlicher und sozialpolitischer Erkenntnis' (first published in 1904), in Max Weber *Gesammelte Aufsätze zur Wissenschaftslehre*, ed. J. Winckelmann, Tübingen, Mohr, 7th edition, 1988, pp. 146–214, especially pp. 190–209; M. Weber *Basic Concepts in Sociology*, translated by H. P. Secher, New York, Philosophical Library, 1962.
13 See R. Bessel, *Germany after the First World War*, Oxford, Clarendon Press, 1993, pp. 220–53; C. Usborne, *The Politics of the Body in Weimar Germany. Women's Reproductive Rights and Duties*, Basingstoke, Macmillan, 1992, pp. 69–101.
14 See R. Davidson and L. Sauerteig, 'Law, medicine and morality: A comparative view of twentieth-century sexually transmitted disease controls', in J. Woodward and R. Jütte (eds), *Coping with Sickness: Medicine, Law and Human Rights*, Sheffield, EAHMH Publications, 2000.
15 See L. Hall, this volume, ch. 7
16 Sauerteig, *Krankheit, Sexualität, Gesellschaft*, pp. 141–5.
17 Ibid., pp. 126–9; A. Blaschko, 'Hygiene der Geschlechtskrankheiten', in A. Gärtner (ed.) *Weyls Handbuch der Hygiene*, vol. 8, Leipzig, Barth, second edition, 1918–22, p. 412; A. Moll, *Ärztliche Ethik. Die Pflichten des Arztes in allen Beziehungen seiner Thätigkeit*, Stuttgart, Enke, 1902, p. 184.
18 Sauerteig, *Krankheit, Sexualität, Gesellschaft*, pp. 145–57.
19 See E. Bernstein (ed.) *Die Geschichte der Berliner Arbeiter-Bewegung. Ein Kapitel zur Geschichte der deutschen Sozialdemokratie*, vol. 3, Berlin, Vorwärts, 1910, pp. 383–9; A. Labisch, 'Das

Krankenhaus in der Gesundheitspolitik der deutschen Sozialdemokratie vor dem Ersten Weltkrieg', *Medizinische Soziologie. Jahrbuch*, 1981, vol. 1, pp. 131–5.

20 F. Nagelschmidt, 'Beschäftigung von Geschlechtskranken in Krankenhäusern', *Zeitschrift für Bekämpfung der Geschlechtskrankheiten*, 1909/10, vol. 10, pp. 177–91.

21 Sauerteig, *Krankheit, Sexualität, Gesellschaft*, pp. 129–33 and 136–8.

22 Blaschko and Fischer, 'Einfluß der sozialen Lage', pp. 524–5. See Sauerteig, *Krankheit, Sexualität, Gesellschaft*, pp. 49–50. On sex education in Germany, see L. Sauerteig, 'Sex education in Germany from the eighteenth to the twentieth century', in F. X. Eder, L. A. Hall and G. Hekma (eds) *Sexual Cultures in Europe: Themes in Sexuality*, Manchester and New York, Manchester University Press, 1999, pp. 9–33.

23 Blaschko and Fischer, 'Einfluß der sozialen Lage', p. 509. See Sauerteig, *Krankheit, Sexualität, Gesellschaft*, pp. 48–9, 390–1; Walser, 'Prostitutionsverdacht'.

24 E. Brieux, *Die Schiffbrüchigen (Les Avariés). Ein Theaterstück in drei Akten*, translated by M. Schann, Berlin and Köln, Albert Ahn, 1903.

25 The boom in (semi-)pornographic films after the First World War ended with the reintroduction of film censorship in 1919/20; see the 'Lichtspielgesetz', 12 May 1920, *Reichsgesetzblatt*, 1920, p. 953; K. Petersen, *Zensur in der Weimarer Republik*, Stuttgart and Weimar, Metzler, 1995, pp. 31–40, 50–5, 247–9.

26 Sauerteig, *Krankheit, Sexualität, Gesellschaft*, pp. 187–227.

27 Ibid., pp. 217–24; L. Sauerteig, 'Lust und Abschreckung: Moulagen in der Geschlechtskrankheitenaufklärung', *Medizin, Gesellschaft und Geschichte*, 1992, vol. 11, pp. 89–105; L. Jordanova, *Sexual Visions. Images of Gender and Medicine between the Eighteenth and Twentieth Centuries*, New York, Harvester Wheatsheaf, 1989, pp. 43–65; T. Schnalke, *Diseases in Wax. The History of the Medical Moulage*, Berlin, Quintessence, 1995.

28 L. Sauerteig, 'Salvarsan und der "Aärztliche Polizeistaat". Syphilistherapie im Streit zwischen Ärzten, pharmazautischer Industrie, Gesundheitsverwaltung und Naturheilverbänden (1910–1927); in M. Dinges (ed.) *Medizinkritische Bewegungen im Deutschen Reich (ca. 1870–ca. 1933)*, Stuttgart, Franz Steiner, 1996, pp. 161–200.

29 For a more detailed analysis, see L. Sauerteig, 'Moralismus versus Pragmatismus: Die Kontroverse um Schutzmittel gegen Geschlechtskrankheiten zu Beginn des 20. Jahrhunderts im deutsch-englischen Vergleich', in M. Dinges and T. Schlich (eds) *Neue Wege in der Seuchengeschichte*, Stuttgart, Franz Steiner, 1995, pp. 207–47.

30 On the position of the different wings of the German women's movement in the debate on VD, see Allen, 'Feminism'. On the German women's movement, see B. Greven-Aschoff, *Die bürgerliche Frauenbewegung in Deutschland 1894–1933*, Göttingen, Vandenhoeck & Ruprecht, 1981; R. J. Evans, *The Feminist Movement in Germany, 1894 – 1933*, London, Sage, 1976.

31 Archive of the Diakonisches Werk der Evangelischen Kirche in Deutschland, Berlin, CA 94: meeting of the Central Committee of the *Innere Mission* (Home Mission), 9 November 1915, p. 47.

32 On the *Bund für Mutterschutz*, founded in 1905, see A. T. Allen, *Feminism and Motherhood in Germany, 1800–1914*, New Brunswick, NJ, Rutgers University Press, 1991, pp. 173–205; T. Wobbe, *Gleichheit und Differenz. Politische Strategien von Frauenrechtlerinnen um die Jahrhundertwende*, Frankfurt/M. and New York, Campus, 1989, pp. 99–130; B. Nowacki, *Der Bund für Mutterschutz (1905–1933)*, Husum, Matthiesen, 1983.

33 L. Sauerteig, 'Sex, medicine and morality during the First World War', in R. Cooter, M. Harrison and S. Sturdy (eds) *War, Medicine and Modernity*, Stroud, Sutton, 1998, pp. 167–88.

34 'Reichsgesetz zur Bekämpfung der Geschlechtskrankheiten', 22 February 1927, *Reichsgesetzblatt*, 1927, part I, no. 9; see Sauerteig, *Krankheit, Sexualität, Gesellschaft*, pp. 302–16.

35 H. Röschmann, 'Zwei Stimmen zur Schutzmittelfrage', *Mitteilungen der Deutschen Gesellschaft zur Bekämpfung der Geschlechtskrankheiten*, 1932, vol. 30, p. 177; Geheimes Staatsarchiv, Preußischer Kulturbesitz, Rep 76, VIIIB/3828, p. 319.
36 A. Grossmann, *Reforming Sex. The German Movement for Birth Control and Abortion Reform, 1920–1950*, Oxford, Oxford University Press, 1995, pp. 31–5, 46–70; K. von Soden, *Die Sexualberatungsstellen der Weimarer Republik 1919–1933*, Berlin, Hentrich, 1988, pp. 9–12, 64–90; H. Lehfeld, 'Die Laienorganisationen für Geburtenregelung', *Archiv für Bevölkerungspolitik, Sexualethik und Familienkunde*, 1932, vol. 2, pp. 63–87.
37 See F. Seidler, *Prostitution, Homosexualität, Selbstverstümmelung. Probleme der deutschen Sanitätsführung1939–1945*,Neckargemünd,Vowinckel,1977,pp.107–16,156–7,160–90.
38 'Reichsgesetz zur Bekämpfung der Geschlechtskrankheiten', 22 February 1927, *Reichsgesetzblatt*, 1927, part I, no. 9.
39 For a more detailed treatment, see Sauerteig, *Krankheit, Sexualität, Gesellschaft*, pp. 380–420.
40 Davidson and Sauerteig, 'Law, medicine and morality'.
41 Sauerteig, *Krankheit, Sexualität, Gesellschaft*, pp. 322–5.
42 'Regulativ über die sanitätspolizeilichen Vorschriften der am häufigsten vorkommenden Krankheiten', 8 April 1835, paragraph 65, in F. L. Augustin, *Die Königlich preußische Medicinalverfassung, oder vollständige Darstellung aller, das Medicinalwesen und die medicinische Polizei in den Königlich Preußischen Staaten betreffenden Gesetze, Verordnungen und Einrichtungen*, vol. 4, Potsdam and Berlin, Horvarth, 1838, pp. 978–80.
43 See R. J. Evans, *Death in Hamburg. Society and Politics in the Cholera-Years 1830–1910*, Oxford, Clarendon Press, 1987.
44 'Gesetz zur Bekämpfung der gemeingefährlichen Krankheiten', 30 June 1900, *Reichsgesetzblatt*, 1900.
45 Sauerteig, *Krankheit, Sexualität, Gesellschaft*, pp. 319–22, 325–7.
46 Motion of the Centre Party to amend paragraph 327a of the Imperial Penal Law, *Stenographische Berichte über die Verhandlungen des Deutschen Reichstags*, vol. 172, no. 31, p. 180; F. von Liszt, 'Der strafrechtliche Schutz gegen Gesundheitsgefährdung durch Geschlechtskranke. Gutachten', *Zeitschrift für Bekämpfung der Geschlechtskrankheiten*, 1903, vol. 1, pp. 1–25; A. Neisser, *Die Geschlechtskrankheiten und ihre Bekämpfung. Vorschläge und Forderungen für Ärzte und Soziologen*, Berlin, Springer, 1916, pp. 128–30.
47 See Sauerteig, *Krankheit, Sexualität, Gesellschaft*, pp. 361–5.
48 'Verordnung zur Bekämpfung der Geschlechtskrankheiten', 11 December 1918, *Reichsgesetzblatt*, 1918, no. 184, pp. 1,431–2. A similar regulation was also included in the Imperial Act for Combating VD of 1927, 'Reichsgesetz zur Bekämpfung der Geschlechtskrankheiten', 22 February 1927, *Reichsgesetzblatt*, 1927, part I, no. 9.
49 Report of the 10th Parliamentary Committee on Population, *Verhandlungen des Deutschen Reichstags*, vol. 411, no. 2,714, pp. 11–12; K. Pohlen, 'Kriminalstatistik betr. das RGBG', *Mitteilungen der Deutschen Gesellschaft zur Bekämpfung der Geschlechtskrankheiten*, 1933, vol. 31, pp. 88–96. See Sauerteig, *Krankheit, Sexualität, Gesellschaft*, pp. 365–8.
50 Sauerteig, *Krankheit, Sexualität, Gesellschaft*, pp. 328–42.
51 The Berlin VD Advice Centres were an exception.
52 For further details, see Sauerteig, *Krankheit, Sexualität, Gesellschaft*, pp. 166–86.
53 'Reichsgesetz zur Bekämpfung der Geschlechtskrankheiten', 22 February 1927, *Reichsgesetzblatt*, 1927, part I, no. 9.
54 Sauerteig, *Krankheit, Sexualität, Gesellschaft*, pp. 342–3, 400–8, 419–20.
55 'Gesetz zur Bekämpfung der Geschlechtskrankheiten', 23 July 1953, *Bundesgesetzblatt*, 1953, part I, p. 700.
56 Bundesarchiv Berlin, 15.01/11870, p. 229; P. Kaufmann, 'Geschlechtskrankheiten und Arbeiterversicherung. Die neuen Beratungsstellen für Geschlechtskranke', *Berliner Volkszeitung*, no. 169, 2 April 1917.
57 365th meeting, 14 June 1923, *Verhandlungen des Deutschen Reichstages*, vol. 360, col. 11,354.

58 H. Senator and S. Kaminer (eds) *Krankheiten und Ehe. Darstellung der Beziehungen zwischen Gesundheitsstörungen und Ehegemeinschaft*, Leipzig, Lehmann, 1904, second edition, 1916; Neisser, *Geschlechtskrankheiten*, pp. 144–77; see G. Czarnowski, *Das kontrollierte Paar. Ehe- und Sexualpolitik im Nationalsozialismus*, Weinheim, Studien-Verlag, 1991, pp. 38–42.
59 'Reichsgesetz zur Bekämpfung der Geschlechtskrankheiten', *Reichsgesetzblatt*, 1927, vol. I, no. 9, p. 62, §6. See Sauerteig, *Krankheit, Sexualität, Gesellschaft*, pp. 369–80.
60 See Sauerteig, *Krankheit, Sexualität, Gesellschaft*, pp. 323–4, 370.
61 Czarnowski, *Kontrollierte Paar*, Weindling, *Health*, pp. 531–2; Weingart, Kroll, Bayertz, *Rasse*, pp. 513–18; R. Proctor, *Racial Hygiene. Medicine Under the Nazis*, Cambridge/Mass. and London, Harvard University Press, 1988, pp. 136–41.
62 Sauerteig, *Krankheit, Sexualität, Gesellschaft*, pp. 421–36.

6

VISIONS OF SEXUAL HEALTH
AND ILLNESS IN
REVOLUTIONARY RUSSIA

Frances Bernstein

Like its Western allies and opponents, Imperial Russia had its own venereal crisis to contend with during the tumultuous years of the First World War. Here too observers noted a dramatic increase in disease rates among soldiers both in the rear and at the front. This was traced variously to the failures of the state policy of prostitute regulation and medical-police control; to the infiltration of barracks by 'clandestines' posing as laundresses and maids; or, in the paranoid assessment of the military high command's chief of staff for the southwestern front, to the intentional introduction of syphilitic women among the troops, supposedly masterminded by a wealthy German-Jewish cabal.[1] But whereas their military and civilian counterparts abroad had the authority and the resources to adopt a variety of measures against the spread of disease, Russian health officials could do little but note these trends and fear for the consequences of this, as well as the many other epidemics raging at the time; in addition to VD, typhus, cholera, scurvy, smallpox, malaria and famine were rampant among the civilian population as well as at the front, and the situation continued to deteriorate throughout the Civil War.[2] The country, of course, had even bigger problems at the time, and it was therefore only after the removal of the tsar and two revolutions that medical officials attached to the public health ministry of the new Soviet state were in a position to turn their attention to these matters.

Shortly after the People's Commissariat of Public Health (*Narkomzdrav*) was founded in July of 1918, it initiated a widespread programme of 'sanitary enlightenment' (*sanitarnoe prosveshchenie*) or popular health and hygiene education. Like political agitational-propaganda, which was employed at this time to galvanize the masses in defence of the Revolution against internal and external adversaries,[3] sanitary enlightenment developed rapidly during the first years of Soviet power as a weapon against the country's other enemies: disease, sickness, and, by extension, the phenomenon that doctors considered to be their root cause: the Russian population's ignorance of even the most basic principles of hygiene. In the realm of sexual health, the need for popular enlightenment was considered to be particularly urgent, due to both pre-revolutionary restrictions on sex education (with public discussions of sexuality hindered by the tsarist police, state censors, and the Orthodox church) and the continued rise in VD rates during the first decade of Soviet rule. Such concerns prompted the development of an entire subfield of sanitary propaganda, known as sexual enlightenment, which emphasized disease prevention through the advocacy of abstinence, fidelity and the avoidance of prostitutes.[4]

This chapter focuses on one particularly invaluable and effective forum for spreading such information about sexual health among the population: the public health poster. Specifically, it examines a series of sexual-enlightenment posters used in the campaign against VD in order to explore what the idea of health, and in particular sexual health, signified in the context of revolutionary Russia. Since a healthy population was deemed essential for the successful realization of socialism, physical health was never far removed from political well-being. Not only did disease and poor hygiene endanger the working masses; there were also categories of people (disease carriers, the morally suspect) whose very existence or actions appeared to threaten the health of the regime. Enlightenment posters specified the types of health-conduct which *Narkomzdrav* desired of the population.[5] Conversely, posters also depicted behaviours, and by extension people, condemned for being 'unhealthy'. While historical analyses of Soviet Russia in the 1920s often emphasize the population's ideological, party and labour obligations, this chapter urges a broader definition of societal duty by considering the health obligations, and in particular the sexual-health responsibilities, for citizenship in the new state.[6] In portraying the requirements for health and the experience of sickness in gender-specific terms, posters demonstrated that being a healthy citizen meant different things for men and women. This study thus sheds light on the contribution of public health to the formulation of the idealized 'New Soviet Woman and Man', and the employment of a medical-scientific discourse to legitimize gender difference in the new 'republic of equals'.

Those familiar with the anti-VD/prostitution visual propaganda disseminated in such countries as the United States, Great Britain and France during the First and Second World Wars will perhaps be struck by certain similarities between those images and the ones reproduced here.[7] The centrality of gender to the representation of good and bad health is common to both, as is the figure of the dangerous single woman. Such similarities are not in themselves surprising; as in the West, gender in the early Soviet state served as a vehicle through which to articulate and manage the country's anxieties over modernity. What is perhaps more interesting is how images that at first glance seem so alike can be invested with such diverse and culturally specific meanings, the product of very different historical processes and contexts. The politics of class that inform the depiction of the prostitute in American posters, for instance, are quite distinct from those that shape the image of her Russian counterpart in this supposedly classless society. Hence the present study's focus on the specifically Russian meaning behind such apparently familiar images.

Popular health education was not new to Russia in 1918; many socially committed physicians had attempted to spread sanitary information among 'the people' in the second half of the nineteenth century. However, the scope of hygiene education remained limited due to the continued suspicion of the censors and the regime, especially after the widespread support of doctors for political reform in 1905. It declined still further during the First World War, when doctors directed their energy into other channels. In the area of sexual health, the obstacles to such educational endeavours were even more formidable. Although the need for sex education was widely discussed in medical and peda-gogical literature by the end of the century, censorship laws prohibited doctors from conducting public discussions on the topic. Educators were only permitted to lecture from previously approved texts which, according to one source, dated from twenty to thirty years earlier. Lectures also had to be delivered in police presence, to ensure that the speaker did not deviate from the written material. In such instances, the police would stop the talk and break up the gathering; neither extemporaneous elaborations nor even answers to audience questions were permitted.[8] Not surprisingly, also prohibited were the mass education campaigns proposed by advocates seeking to end the state regulation of prostitution.[9] In place since the 1840s, the system was abolished only after the February Revolution of 1917.

The fundamentally different position of health education after the Revolution reflected both the state's recognition of the importance of sanitary measures, hygiene and education to its primary mission to remake society, and the vast amount of time and energy *Narkomzdrav* spent on its prophylactic approach to health, stressing disease prevention rather than the treatment of pre-existing illnesses.[10] Soon after its founding, the Commissariat created a Department of Sanitary Enlightenment, which oversaw the establishment of regional sections throughout the country and the training of doctors in the methodology of sani-tary enlightenment.[11] It convened congresses, designed museum exhibitions and published scholarly journals, lecture outlines and teaching aids, as well as dissem-inating a wide range of popular educational materials. The kind of images shown in this chapter would have been produced at the request of, and in close cooperation with, the Commissariat's Department for the Struggle against Venereal Disease, or one of the regional enlightenment divisions or institutes, or by the enlightenment departments attached to individual VD institutes or commissions, all following *Narkomzdrav* models.[12]

The goal of sanitary enlightenment was to preserve health and prevent disease, thereby preparing people to manage their own physical and psycholog-ical well-being independently. 'Consciousness' – that marker of Marxist political maturity – figured prominently here as well: a healthy worker was automatically a conscious one, and to attain 'consciousness', one had to make every aspect of one's life healthy. One also had to be able to recognize those dangers and imped-iments in the way of good health. As one educator put it: 'If you know your enemy well, and you know from which side he's preparing to attack you, then it is easier; it is obvious, not only how to defend yourself, but how to defeat him.'[13]

Posters represented an especially suitable method for reaching the public and identifying its enemies and its allies.[14] They could be produced inexpensively, and could penetrate areas of the country which would not have their own doctors or sanitary personnel for years to come. Especially in the first half of the decade, when this was most often the case, the health posters that hung in marriage registration bureaus, worker and student clubs and cafeterias, to name but a few locations, were potentially the only continual contact people had with Soviet medicine. Sanitary-enlightenment posters arrived on the scene soon after the appearance of revolutionary, political posters in the second half of 1918, mobilizing the population in a different but no less crucial way to defend the new state. The goal of health-education posters, like political posters, was to convey information in a simple, uncomplicated manner, ensuring comprehensibility whether or not viewers were literate or took the time to read the minimal, accompanying text.[15] Through the repetition of immediately decipherable images and simplistic juxtapositions of good and evil, hero and foe, sanitary posters utilized the forms of visual representation that would be familiar to Russians – the icon, the *lubok* (the peasant broadsheet), and the political poster – guaranteeing that their audience would already know how to 'read' them.[16] Such previous exposure to political posters as well as icons helped prepare viewers to look at images of health through a similar moral framework.[17]

The vivid image depicted in Figure 1 adheres closely to these objectives. Dating from the early 1920s, this anti-syphilis poster follows the representational tradition of the religious icon, depicting a distinctly Soviet vision of heaven and hell, the trinity and the Madonna and child. To help viewers identify the poster's moral dichotomy, there is an overt spatial separation of good from bad, under-lined by the very different use of crosses. The poster vividly contrasts the red cross, that icon of modern healing, with the religious cross, which literally crushes those who refuse to take their health into their own hands, and thus signifies what happens to people who put their faith in religion as opposed to science. Yet these buried figures are not enemies; neither the disease nor the person(s) responsible for its transmission are pictured. Instead they are victims, of the illness itself and of their own ignorance: an ignorance which explains why people would not treat syphilis, as well as why they would continue to look to religion for their salvation.

Despite the absence of enemies, the poster is not lacking in heroes. At the centre stands Soviet medicine, represented by a male doctor in a white coat, usually, as here, wearing glasses to connote intelligence and perspicacity. Completing the trinity, to the doctor's right and left are two figures which would be immediately recognizable to viewers: the male proletarian and the Red Army man. These two, who literally look to the doctor in the middle, are actively

Figure 1 'We will cure syphilis'

Note: Translation of the original captions: In the very beginning of the disease syphilis is cured quickly. Neglected syphilis is cured slowly through accurate treatment. The consequences of untreated syphilis: craziness, paralysis, deformity, stillborn children, idiot children.

engaged in the fight to make life healthy, and, it seems, comprise the 'we' of the title. Indeed, the worker literally takes his health into his own hands by clasping the hand of the physician. The woman on the right, not much larger in size than the children on the left, is the passive recipient of health, which will be fought for by the active cooperation of the triumvirate in the middle. While the woman is included in the paradise featured at the top (perhaps because of her status as mother), her downturned head reinforces her subordinate standing and her lack of consciousness, since she, like the children, does not visually acknowledge the authority of Soviet medicine.

Readers familiar with the VD posters produced somewhat later in the decade (see below) might be surprised at the extent to which this poster is desexualized in view of the subject-matter and of the poster's intended recipients. As the images make clear (the clean-shaven face and clothing of the man, the bare head of the woman), the poster was designed to engage an urban audience, and syphilis in the cities was considered to be a sexually transmitted disease. Using an interpretative model for distinguishing between the forms of VD inherited from their pre-revolutionary counterparts, Soviet doctors distinguished between a sexual variety, found in the cities, and a supposedly non-sexual variety found among the peasantry, believed to be transmitted through the sharing of common dishes and utensils, close quarters and poor hygiene.[18] This apparent discrepancy can be explained by the fact that this poster is not concerned with either the prevention of sexual diseases or with the identification of a specific agent of infection, themes which would be addressed in posters in the coming years. Instead, it invokes the by now familiar revolutionary and heroic images of the proletarian and soldier, in order to encourage these urban viewers to seek out treatment for pre-existing conditions. Produced at a time when the country was just beginning to recover from mass epidemics of the Civil War period, the poster focuses on the need to eradicate the disease rather than on the risky behaviours associated with its transmission.

In many of the posters reproduced here, as well as in sanitary-enlightenment posters more generally, women occupy a distinctly marginal position. Men are depicted far more frequently and more often serve as the posters' subject. The male image becomes both normative and neutral: his health needs and problems can stand for anyone's. Women, on the other hand, can only portray women's particular health issues. This assumption of a male subject is not peculiar to health posters; historians have linked the predominance of the male form in political posters to the perception of the October Revolution as a male event by those who designed and commissioned its symbols.[19] In similar fashion did sanitary-enlightenment posters depict health as a 'male event', and, consequently, naturalize the concept of maleness. The reason for this lies in the way knowledge, and especially consciousness, are gendered within these posters. Because men were considered to be more conscious, eager and capable of making their lives healthy, health posters (other than those expressly designated for female viewers, such as posters illustrating breastfeeding techniques) were either implicitly or explicitly coded to appeal to men. Men's education took precedence; once properly informed, they would, in theory, pass this new knowledge on to women.

Neither the male orientation of sex education posters nor the messages they conveyed about gender and sexual behaviour were limited to those dealing with the subject of VD. In Figure 2 the woman shown in the bottom left corner is no longer a passive recipient of the health fought for by men, but now represents a direct danger to male health and a symbolic political threat as well. The physical culture movement of the 1920s, a major component of the 'fight for a healthy lifestyle' (the central mobilizing slogan of the Commissariat's public health campaigns in the 1920s), was addressed specifically at young people, and especially young men. One of the primary motives of interesting youth in physical culture was to keep them from engaging in such dangerous, non-collective behaviours as masturbation and premarital sex.[20] Thus the ornamental woman in the bottom left corner functions as the sexualized symbol of the individualism which is represented by Otto the weight lifter, in sharp contrast with the communal ideal depicted on the right.[21]

Women, it appears, have no place in the Soviet world featured on the right; they are not a part of the collective, the proletariat, or the class and, moreover, escape the burdens shouldered by those who protect the health of their country. Able to keep the dandy from his tennis match, the woman might prove just as capable of distracting a young man from the important work of defending his homeland or the Revolution, a threat underlined by her association with the bourgeoisie, and, even more significantly, fascism, most likely its Italian variant (Germans here are depicted and mocked for their interest in and fascination with record-breaking and sport superstars). Given the physical-culture movement's orientation towards sexual abstinence, the anti-sex subtext of this poster becomes clearer. The depiction of Soviet society as an all-male world suggests less the exclusion of real women from the physical-culture movement or from the working class than the symbolism of woman *as* sexuality in the visual language of these posters. Having sublimated their sexual energy through exercise, the men have no need for that particular amusement, nor for the consequent threat to collectivism this woman represents.

If the young, conscious male proletarian characterizes the symbolic ideal of masculinity and health to which all men should aspire, symbolic representations of women in health posters are primarily negative. Two of the most vivid threats to the health of men during the 1920s are illustrated by female images: the prostitute in the city, and the old woman folk-healer in the countryside. These two dangerous women are pictured in Figure 3. At the centre an industrial worker (whose face is flushed either from the heat of the machinery or as a sign of his poor health) grips the lever which will determine his fate.

This poster was also intended for use as a board game. Players begin at square number 1, which proclaims 'To make labour and lifestyle healthy is the pledge of victory over social diseases.' The first to make a complete circle (indeed, a revolution) and return to this point wins. Depicted in the spaces along

Figure 2 'Physical culture. The weapon of the class struggle'

Source: (Moscow, 1927; print run: 7,000)

Note: Translation of the original captions: What bourgeois sport gives: the training of fascists, individualism, professionalism and recordbreaking. What Soviet physical culture gives: the training of the Red fighting man, collectivism, 'massism' and the 'making healthy' of the class. Physical culture – an amusement for the bourgeoisie, a necessity for the proletariat.

Figure 3   'Board game: toward a healthy lifestyle'

Source: (Rostov-na-Donu, late 1920s; compilers K. Lapin and A. Berliand)

Note: Translation of the original captions: In left wheel: 'The making healthy of labour and daily life is the concern of workers themselves.' In right wheel: 'Through the making healthy of labour and lifestyle to the victory over social diseases.'

the way are both good health behaviours and those which lead to illness. A player landing on a square with a red circle, signalling a bad health choice, must move to the square indicated by the other number in the box, where the correct practice is illustrated or could be learned (at a medical clinic, for instance).

Space 34 shows a smiling woman in red, tapping a man on the shoulder in front of a beer hall. The red in the woman's cheeks is from rouge, not the arduous work of the proletarian or a signal of bad health. And yet, returning to Square 12, we learn that her attractive exterior is misleading, as well as threatening. This space features a microscope allowing viewers to 'see', through technology, the spirochaete which causes syphilis. Square 12 in turn directs players back to 3, which shows a VD clinic, and hence reveals the ultimate significance of the woman's touch. The man here is presented as the innocent actor in this transaction, easily corrupted by the prostitute's predatory sexuality.

The connection established between the transmission of syphilis and the sexually dangerous woman is strikingly different from earlier approaches to the disease in visual propaganda, as in Figure 1. In that poster, ignorance was blamed for preventing sufferers from seeking treatment. After the introduction of the New Economic Policy (NEP) in 1921, which brought to Russian society a partial return to a market economy and widespread economic instability, a more identifiable agent, and enemy, was needed. The result was a dramatic shift in the depiction of sexually transmitted diseases. The prostitute, widely drawn upon during the 1920s to personify this reviled economic policy,[22] assumed the role of the easily identifiable human transmitter, becoming the most evocative visual image of the source of VD in sanitary-enlightenment posters. It should be stressed that this figure, who bears more than a passing resemblance to the diseased 'good-time girls' of Western First World War health posters, was new to the Russian context in the 1920s. The previous lack of such visual images was presumably due to the tsarist proscriptions on sex education mentioned above, even though the prostitute had long been a military and medical concern as well as a prominent symbol in pre-revolutionary literature. Moreover, this NEP-era image of the sexually dangerous woman was not limited to health education, but was pervasive in the popular culture of the period.[23]

In square 37 we find the same man, perhaps after his encounter with the woman in red, turning for help to the folk-healer. Square 27 reveals the only possible consequence of this meeting, a cross-covered graveyard which, like Figure 1, links religion with a death caused by ignorance.[24]

That the poster is about the experience of, requirements for, and dangers to the health of men is underlined by the worker in the centre and the overwhelming presence of males; the masculine orientation is apparent even if no attention is paid to the text or if the viewer is illiterate. Other than the two dangerous females, women appear cleaning rooms (squares 6 and 28), with backs turned (8), or in silhouette, accompanying a groom to the marriage bureau (19). The industrial setting, frequent depiction of male proletarians, and the scenes of women engaged in domestic tasks underscore another important feature of the way these posters represent this health campaign. While offering positive images of men both at work and in everyday life, the representations of women at remunerated work are decidedly negative, as either sex-worker or folk-healer. Significantly, as unwanted remnants of a hated and unhealthy past, both occupations had to be eliminated before the new society could be made healthy. The dichotomy between positive male and negative. female occupations accentuates the relationship between female health and the realm of private life, and the apparent dependence of male health on the restriction of women to this sphere.

The game also depicts two other social diseases which threaten the health of our worker: tuberculosis and alcoholism. Alcohol is represented inanimately, through the presence of a bottle (22, 31, 32) or by association with the prostitute standing in front of a bar (34). The link between prostitution and alcohol consumption – that is, the view that drinking led men to prostitutes – is developed in Figure 4. While in the previous poster women who do not pose a threat to men's health are turned away from viewers, here only the prostitutes gaze directly at the spectator. The face of the man at the top is hidden by shadow; those in the circle at the centre are in profile, looking at the prostitutes across a table littered with bottles. In contrast, the knowing and direct glances of the women are paired with the graphic depiction of the disease for which they are responsible. A microscope is no longer needed to see the evidence of the prostitute's sexual pathology, although the inclusion of the pie chart, with its hard data, underscores the 'scientificity' and legitimacy of these graphic drawings.

Moreover, the presentation of the genitals in the primary stage of syphilis is consistent with the formula for depicting sexual organs in evidence throughout sex-education materials during this period. Healthy genitals are never shown; biological functions and the internal structure of the organs are presented in cross sections or in diagrammatic form. Showing the genitals covered with sores and papules may aid viewers in recognizing the presence of VD and thus encourage them to get help, but it also functions as a scare tactic, to warn men in the most vivid way possible to avoid bars, drinking and the company of prostitutes.

In some posters, text and drawing seem to carry conflicting messages. In the anti-prostitution poster shown as Figure 5, the 'us' in the title are summoned to join the heroic, larger-than-life proletarian in 'helping' such fallen women, regardless of whether or not they desire this assistance. The poster's text and background image refer to the 'official' explanation for the phenomenon of prostitution, which was seen as a consequence of the mass unemployment, labour shortages and exploitation associated with NEP. As a result of this socio-economic explanation, *Narkomzdrav* officially waged its battle against prostitution, not the prostitute, who, according to its standpoint, could not be held responsible for her actions. The text and background illustration affirm the state's commitment to assist these women by providing hostels for the homeless, treatment in venereal clinics and placement in special labour clinics which combined these

Figure 4 'Syphilis'

Source: (Penzensk, 1923; print run: 3,000)

Note: Translation of the original captions: In cities, industrial centres and in factory settlements syphilis is primarily passed through prostitution, connected to carousing and drunkenness. Drunken café, restaurant and bar-goers look for entertainment with prostitutes. Drunkenness is a loyal fellow traveller of the spread of the syphilis infection.

Figure 5 'Let us intensify the fight with prostitution, the shameful legacy of capitalism'

Note: Translation of the original captions: Let us help girls and women receive qualifications. Let us expand the building of boarding houses and workshops for unemployed, clinics and venereal dispensaries. Let us strike at debauchers!

two functions, where women also learned an industrial trade and received an education.[25]

The foreground image, however, is far less generous or sympathetic. While the behaviour of both the man and woman qualify them as debauchers, the man, with a shocked look on his face, is treated as a misbehaving, naive child snatched safely away from the seductive woman, who is the sole object of the proletarian's wrathful gaze. Pointed towards the institutions which have been built to help her, the woman stands defiantly, hand on hip. At the same time as her clothing and cigarette mark her as a prostitute (or a 'Nepwoman', with whom she is symbolically associated through her attire, overt sexuality and association with money), she is also linked with the capitalist past, making her doubly unwelcome.[26]

In the visual language of these posters, the concept of touch plays a role of considerable importance, vividly conveying ideas about authority, control and agency. Figure 1 displayed the healing, knowing touch of the physician, who confers both health and the correct knowledge onto the proletarian. The loss of control as the body succumbs to disease and the corrupting knowledge associated with deviant sexuality are embodied in the contagious touch of the prostitute (Figure 3).[27] In this anti-prostitution poster we encounter a third kind of touch. The arm which prevents the man from becoming the prostitute's latest victim by snatching him back into a safe, sunlit industrial world represents the intervention of the state and its partner, conscious (male) society. While the poster concludes by promising to strike at all debauchers, it is significant that the proletarian does not touch the prostitute because of her potential for contamination.

Over the course of the 1920s the iconography of the prostitute – her attire, carriage and proximity to the beer hall – was repeated so frequently in health posters that eventually she would have become instantly recognizable to spectators. In Figure 6, therefore, as with the board game, a visual short-cut is possible; the word prostitute is no longer necessary in order to identify her occupation. Including both the left- and right-hand scenes leaves no doubt as to which figure is the victim of syphilis, and which its agent. Moreover, the poster progresses from the assumption that the prostitute is the one carrying the disease to the representation of her *as* the disease: she embodies the syphilis which should at all costs be avoided. Thus the exhortation to 'Beware of Syphilis' also admonishes those who viewed the poster to beware of this woman. In Figure 4, viewers were presented with a graphic illustration of the genitals in the first stage of syphilis. This poster depicts the end result of the disease, a fate perhaps worse than death: syphilis of the brain and spinal cord. In representing the experience of syphilis in one of its most advanced forms, the poster portrays the suffering of the entire man (as opposed to just the genitals) as a result of contact with the prostitute.

Equated with disease in the last poster, the prostitute is equated with all women in Figure 7. By engaging in casual sex, all women become figurative prostitutes, since the danger posed to men's health by sexual contact with them is

Figure 6 'Syphilis is one of the most frequent reasons for illnesses of the brain and spinal cord. Beware of Syphilis!'

Figure 7 'Casual sex: the main source of the spread of venereal disease'
Source: (Moscow; print run: 10,000)

the same. Like the women in the other posters, she is well fed, smoking a cigarette, with one hand provocatively on her hip. Indeed the plump healthiness of these women would have been one of the most damning visual marks against them. The era of NEP was, after all, a time of mass female unemployment and hunger, where substantial numbers of women turned to prostitution as their sole means of survival. At odds with the prevailing (and official) socio-economic explanation of the phenomenon, this depiction of the well-fed prostitute once again aligns her with the kept 'Nepwomen' and their usurer boyfriends, not to be pitied but reviled for her very plumpness.[28] In this case, her illness – in the form of a sore on her upper lip – is easily visible to the audience, if not to the man, and the moment of contagion is foreshadowed by the touch of their cigarettes and the passing of the flame. Another equally crucial marker of the danger this woman represents is the very fact of her being outside, on the boulevard, in the dark.

Analysis thus far has focused primarily on the masculine orientation of these posters – the use of male subjects and the way posters appealed to male viewers. Yet obviously women also saw these posters, which conveyed information relevant to them as well. Posters urged men to fight actively in order to attain and maintain good health. The message imparted to urban women as well as men was that, to a great extent, women's health depended upon the space which they occupied, and consequently, their behaviour within that space. At the same time that men were cautioned about the kinds of women (and behaviours) to avoid on the boulevard, women were warned to avoid the boulevard itself; in these posters only prostitutes, or women who should be identified as prostitutes, ventured out in public at night. To preserve their reputation, and hence their health, women were instructed never to stray far from home. And yet the danger was not just a question of transgressing acceptable boundaries but also of appearing in those locations alone. A single woman on the street at night became automatically suspect.[29]

Figure 8, which followed 7 in a *Narkomzdrav* series on VD, introduces the second victim of the illness, and the third symbolic feminine image in sex-education posters. Having contracted syphilis from the prostitute in the last poster, the same man passes the infection to his innocent and trusting spouse. The presence of the disease is unknown to the woman, who only sees the romance reflected by the silhouette; viewers, however, witness his evil intent, portrayed by his horrible face and contaminating hand. The man's awareness of his contagion is underlined by the reference to Article 150 of the Russian Republic's Criminal Code, introduced in 1926, which held a person criminally liable for consciously spreading VD.[30] Unable to snatch the man away before he is contaminated by the prostitute, now the hand that reaches for him is the punishing arm of the law.

Viewed on its own, Figure 8 presents man as the source of danger and corruption. Yet it should be kept in mind that this poster was part of a series which was meant to be shown together. Thus even in posters which focused on

109

Figure 8 'Article 150 severely punishes those who infect another with venereal disease'

Source. (Moscow; print run: 10,000)

male culpability, the prostitute as the origin of sexually transmitted VD was a constant point of reference. Nonetheless, such severe representations of men – as monstrous and knowingly evil – remained the exception in sex-education posters. Far more frequently, as in Figure 9, posters expressed the idea that VD was contracted by men due to ignorance and susceptibility to the twin seductions of dangerous sexuality and alcohol.

In this anti-gonorrhoea poster, which directly addresses a male viewer, extramarital sex and VD are explicitly equated with prostitution, a contention supported by the scientific data contained in the bar graphs and statistics. And yet, according to a number of statistical studies undertaken during these years, the spread of infection by prostitutes was claimed to be statistically insignificant.[31] If educators themselves subscribed to this interpretation, how is the prevalence of this image in health posters to be understood? Possible clues to this answer can be found in Figure 9, in which the unsuspecting wife and the diseased prostitute (accompanied by the ubiquitous cigarette and alcohol) are presented as functional opposites, negative images of each other. The women are dressed in almost identical clothing; only the hats are slightly different, and the

Figure 9   'By entering into an extramarital sexual relationship you endanger the health of your family'

Source: (Moscow)

colours of the coats and their fur trim have been reversed. The man is dressed identically in both drawings, suggesting a short lapse of time between the two scenes.

The depiction of these two women as functional opposites reinforces their sexual and moral difference. In sexual-enlightenment posters, only two options of sexual behaviour are made available to women. A woman can either opt for the passive sexuality of the wife or, as initiator or active participant, be marked as a prostitute whose sexual deviance is linked to disease and the market. She is either the innocent victim of disease resulting from sex which had been initiated by a man or a contagious and predatory actor.

Because of their active role in sexual encounters, prostitutes are not considered to be 'real' women: those who passively endure both sex and contagion. Similarly, 'normal' female sexuality inevitably leads to reproduction, and the positive depiction of women as sexual participants is restricted only to those posters which also contain or refer to healthy offspring. This link between a more passive female sexuality and reproduction is reinforced by illustrating the prostitute as the sole example of women engaged in non-procreative sex. As these posters suggest, the pathology represented by the prostitute derives as much from her engagement in recreational sex as from her capacity to spread disease. Yet it is solely in relation to the prostitute that the practice of non-reproductive sex is acknowledged. Sex-education posters promote a vision of compulsory heterosexuality, where the single possible form of infidelity involves a man cheating on his wife, the lone potential source of contagion to a man is a dangerous woman, and the only way a disease might pass from one woman to another is through an adulterous husband.

Health posters' presentation of the two alternatives of female sexuality provides a behavioural blueprint for both male and female spectators. While male behaviour is held responsible for introducing VD into the family, eradicating the illness itself ultimately depends upon the conduct of women; the only way to prevent the spread of disease is to ensure that women choose the second sexual option. In these posters, sexually aggressive women – as prostitutes – inevitably deprive themselves of the rewards of family and motherhood; women's reputation and fate require that they remain sexually passive. Depicting women as either sexual aggressors or innocents also provides men with a simplistic formula to help them make sexual and life choices: a man's health and ultimately the health of his family depend upon the sexual behaviour (and implied morality) of the partner he chooses. Yet, significantly, his right to make that choice, to be a sexual agent and sexually active, is never questioned.

Whereas previous posters primarily reflected an urban milieu, Figure 10 also embraces the context of the countryside. 'The Paths of Sexuality' exhibits the three alternatives of sexual behaviour available to the worker/peasant who stands in the upper-left corner. He may progress immediately from healthy work, through political and sanitary enlightenment, to the wedding bureau, resulting in a healthy marriage, happy family and viable descendants. However, if he makes

Figure 10　'The paths of sexuality – the straight path goes toward health, the crooked
paths lead to illnesses'

the first mistake by becoming entangled with a prostitute (note the bottle of
vodka in his back pocket), he can then visit a doctor, be treated and enlightened
and eventually arrive at the marriage bureau and his waiting bride.

Yet should our worker/peasant choose the crooked path, his fate takes a
dramatic turn for the worse. Treatment by a folk-healer will eventually lead to
either infertility, unhealthy offspring, stillborn children or the last stop (before
death) of the syphilitic: the psychiatric hospital. Because this poster portrays the
experience of village life, several examples of non-sexual syphilis are also
included: spreading and/or contracting the disease by eating from a common
bowl, sharing tools at work and kissing religious artifacts such as icons and the
cross.

In the sharply gendered world of these posters, with their separate spheres
and distinct sexual roles, the experience of illness is also portrayed differently for
men and women. Representative of men's suffering is the syphilitic in Figure 11,
remarkably similar to the one featured in 6: his sickness is depicted as an end in
itself, a tragedy on its own terms (reinforced by the drawing of the diseased sex
organ). Women's illness, on the other hand, is always linked to maternity, either
by their inability to conceive, or by the presence of congenitally ill children. The
emotional appeal is directed instead at the sickness of the child, as in Figure 9,

113

Figure 11   'Only a physician can diagnose an illness and determine the proper treatment'
Source: (Moscow; print run: 10,000)

and especially the degeneration of the family. A single woman, as symbolic or actual prostitute, is never shown suffering from VD, just passing it to men.

The image of woman as mother, surrounded by healthy children, is accompanied in this poster by a second positive and maternal female figure: the nurse or medical assistant to the doctor. Just as the healing touch of the physician at the centre is opposed to the corrupting touch of the priest, the nurse or midwife serves as a counterpoint to the negative image of the folk-healer. More frequently, however, posters contrast the female folk-healer and the male doctor; in sanitary-enlightenment posters the nurse or female medical assistant never appears independently, as does the male physician, to characterize Soviet medicine. In Figure 11, for example, the doctor steps in to bar the folk-healer's access to the sick man, his arm shielding the patient from a form of physical contact which would be as harmful as the contagious touch of the prostitute.

Depicting folk healing as female and modern health care – represented by the authoritative figure in white – as male posits a dichotomy between the two in terms which would be immediately understandable to viewers, who may not grasp the difference between the jars and herbs of the peasant healer and the pills and vials of the doctor. Similarly, the medication or therapies used to treat disease are never shown independently of the physician; since only he knows how to use them it is his personal authority which symbolizes the power of *Narkomzdrav* and modern healing. The female medical assistant, lacking this command of knowledge and hence the power it confers, cannot represent Soviet medicine in the same way. Women never appear in these posters alone; they are always accompanied by another woman, another man or children.[32] While the male form in health posters can stand alone to represent a single man, a class, or an entire society, the female image lacks this capability. Women's meaning is constituted in relation to the other details and figures which accompany them in each drawing: they may represent a behaviour or disease which should be avoided, or a population in need of education and direction.[33]

Sexual-enlightenment posters communicate the limits that were placed on woman's requirements for health citizenship, and consequently on her participation in civil society. Woman's health depended upon her observance of boundaries, by remaining in her proper place and sphere; her well-being was ensured by staying off the boulevard, near to her home and children and ceding the central role of healer to men.

The educators who designed and disseminated these posters believed that they were in the midst of a health emergency. This chapter has argued that men were sought out first in health-education posters because in this crisis atmosphere it was assumed that they were both more conscious and more committed to making the country healthy. In thinking about the types of behaviours being advocated to both women and men, it is important to keep in mind the principal role health posters played in constituting reality. By the mid-1920s, whether or not women's political equality had been achieved (as officially proclaimed), their participation in the public sphere was an indisputable fact. Part of the way doctors appealed to men was by representing a world in which men's status was central and unthreatened, in which good health meant the exclusion of women from the boulevards and public spaces and the removal from society of sexual illness, now coded as female.

One last point needs to be made with regard to the function of posters as constitutive of reality. Even as doctors commissioned and designed sanitary-enlightenment posters during the 1920s, the composition of Soviet medicine was gradually changing, as increasing numbers of women entered the profession.[34] Perhaps images such as the posters featured in this chapter served as a palliative to doctors as well; by placing physicians at the centre of Soviet medicine, and hinting at the potentially disruptive and irrepressible nature of female sexuality, these images reinforced the unassailable authority of male doctors in matters of Soviet health.[35]

This chapter has sought to illuminate the particularly Russian context behind images of sexual illness in early Soviet health propaganda. In addition to the explanations offered above, the images featured in these posters differ from their Western counterparts in one other crucial respect. Whereas the sexually dangerous woman became a staple of Western health propaganda, recycled for use during subsequent wars and other 'health emergencies', her Russian counterpart was far more ephemeral. Indeed, the sexual-enlightenment campaign of the 1920s represents the only time in the history of the Soviet Union that sexual illness – in the guise of the dangerous woman – was depicted visually in public health materials. At the end of 1931, with the consolidation of the Stalinist state, the entire field of sexual enlightenment suddenly disappeared. When health concerns were subordinated to the goals of production during the Five Year Plans, an educational programme whose origins lay in an implicit connection between sex and disease ceased to be an acceptable topic for public discussion. Prostitution, long linked in Marxist-Leninist theory to the inequities of bourgeois society, was declared 'solved' at this time and women caught engaging in this now non-existent occupation were sent to labour camps for re-education. This blackout held even when limited sex education was reintroduced during the 1940s to check the high rates of VD associated with the Second World War. Identifying a sexual enemy who could be safely vilified without implicating the sexual behaviour of the population as a whole proved impossible in a country where the prostitute no longer officially existed. Her re-emergence would have to wait until the final, crumbling days of the Soviet empire, when this dangerous sexual predator reappeared in visual propaganda to illustrate yet again the anxieties of Russian society in crisis.

NOTES

All posters featured here are from the Archive of the Scientific-Research Central Medical Museum, Moscow. I acknowledge with gratitude the museum staff's help in obtaining access and in reproducing the images, and in particular wish to thank Mikhail Poddubnyi for his assistance and enthusiasm for the project. An earlier version of this chapter appeared in *Russian Review*, 1998, vol. 57, pp. 191–217.

1 L. Bernstein, *Sonia's Daughters: Prostitutes and Their Regulation in Imperial Russia*, Berkeley, University of California Press, 1995, p. 294.
2 On the epidemics of these years, see J. Hutchinson, *Politics and Public Health in Revolutionary Russia, 1890–1918*, Baltimore, Johns Hopkins University Press, 1990, p. 193; and A. J. Haines, *Health Work in Soviet Russia*, New York, 1928, ch. 11.
3 P. Kenez, *The Birth of the Propaganda State: Soviet Methods of Mass Mobilization, 1917–1929*, Cambridge, Cambridge University Press, 1985.
4 On the history of sexual enlightenment in Soviet Russia see my ' "What everyone should know about sex": Gender, sexual enlightenment, and the politics of health in Revolutionary Russia, 1918–1931', Ph.D. diss., Columbia University, 1998.
5 On health posters designed to teach the skills necessary for motherhood, see E. Waters, 'Childcare posters and the modernisation of motherhood', *Sbornik: Study Group on the Russian Revolution*, 1987, vol. 13, pp. 65–93. For a contemporary account, see 'Vystavka po okhrane materninstva vo Dvortse Truda', *Iskusstvo i Promyshlennost'*, 1924, vol. 2, pp. 47–52.
6 Citizenship is defined here as membership in the new body politic. The definition is from E. Wood's 'Citizenship and gender in post-Revolutionary Soviet Russia: Women workers as the sharp eyes and tender hearts of the New Republic', unpublished paper. For other analyses of the concept of membership in the new state, see E. Kimerling, 'Civil rights and social policy in Soviet Russia, 1918–1936', *Russian Review*, 1982, vol. 41, pp. 24–46; and S. Fitzpatrick, 'Ascribing class: The construction of social identity in Soviet Russia', *Journal of Modern History*, December 1993, vol. 41, pp. 745–70. On the idea of health obligations in another historical context, see A. Labisch, 'Doctors, workers and the scientific cosmology of the industrial world: The social construction of "health" and the "homo hygienicus" ', *Journal of Contemporary History*, 1985, vol. 20, pp. 599–615.
7 See for instance A. M. Brandt, *No Magic Bullet: A Social History of Venereal Disease in the United States since 1880*, New York, Oxford University Press, 1987; and S. Gilman, *Sexuality, An Illustrated History: Representing the Sexual in Medicine and Culture from the Middle Ages to the Age of AIDS*, New York, John Wiley & Sons, 1989, ch. 11.
8 L. Engelstein, *The Keys to Happiness: Sex and the Search for Modernity in Fin-de-siècle Russia*, Ithaca, Cornell University Press, 1992, p. 200; and V. M. Bronner, 'Iazyk faktov', *Venerologiia i dermatologiia*, 1927, vol. 10, pp. 895–6.
9 Bernstein, *Sonia's Daughters*, pp. 294, 308.
10 On the founding and organization of *Narkomzdrav*, see Hutchinson, *Politics and Public Health in Revolutionary Russia*; S. Gross Solomon and J. F. Hutchinson (eds) *Health and Society in Revolutionary Russia*, Bloomington, Indiana University Press, 1990. On the prophylactic orientation of Soviet medicine, see M. I. Barsukov, *Velikaia Oktiabrskaia sotsialisticheskaia revoliutsiia i organizatsiia sovetskogo zdravookhraneniia*, Moscow, 1951; A. I. Nesterenko, *Kak byl obrazovan Narodnyi komissariat zdravookhraneniia RSFSR: Iz istorii Sovetskogo zdravookhraneniia*, Moscow, 1965.
11 Bernstein, ' "What everyone should know" ', ch. 3.
12 Ibid., ch. 1.
13 I. M. Katsenelenbogen, 'Zadachi sovetskoi meditsiny', in *Sanitarno-prosvetitel'naia rabota v izbe-chital'ne*, Leningrad, 1925, p. 9.
14 K. V. Lapin, 'Var'irovanie form v muzeino-vystavochnom dele po sanitarnomu prosveshcheniiu', *Teoriia i praktika sanitarnogo prosveshcheniia*, ed. S. N. Volkonskaia and F. Iu. Berman, 4th edn, Moscow, 1928, p. 114.
15 L. O. Kanevskii, 'Osnovnye momenty organizatsii sovremennoi gorodskoi museino-vystavochnoi raboty po sanitarnomu prosveshcheniiu', *Teoriia i praktika*, 2nd edn, Moscow, 1926, p. 113.

16 Steven White has distinguished four native sources for the Bolshevik political poster: the *lubok*; Russian satirical journals; commercial posters; and icons. See his *The Bolshevik Poster*, New Haven, Yale University Press, 1988.

17 It bears emphasizing that this process of differentiation and hierarchization was not limited to the category of gender during the 1920s. Such binaries (class, ethnicity, geography and so on) were a central feature of life during these years, and played a crucial role in the articulation of Soviet identities.

18 On the distinction between sexual and non-sexual syphilis in the 1920s, see S. Gross Solomon, 'Innocence and sexuality in Soviet medical discourse', in R. Marsh (ed.) *Women in Russia and Ukraine*, Cambridge, Cambridge University Press, 1996, pp. 121–30; and Solomon, 'The Soviet-German syphilis expedition to Buriat Mongolia, 1928: scientific research on national minorities', *Slavic Review*, 1993, vol. 52, pp. 204–32; Engelstein, *The Keys to Happiness*, ch. 5.

19 E. Waters, 'The female form in Soviet political iconography, 1917–1932', in B. Evans Clements, B. Alpern Engel and C. D. Worobec (eds) *Russia's Women: Accommodation, Resistance, Transformation*, Berkeley, University of California Press, 1991, pp. 227, 232.

20 I examine the physical culture movement in ' "What everyone should know about sex" ', ch. 5.

21 On the opposition to individualism and competition in early Soviet sports, see J. Riordan, *Sport in Soviet Society: The Development of Sport and Physical Education in Russia and the USSR*, Cambridge, Cambridge University Press, 1977.

22 E. Wood, 'Prostitution unbound: Representations of sexual and political anxieties in postrevolutionary Russia', in J. T. Costlow, S. Sandler and J. Vowles (eds) *Sexuality and the Body in Russian Culture*, Stanford, Stanford University Press, 1993, pp. 124–35.

23 See the discussion in E. Naiman, *Sex in Public: The Incarnation of Early Soviet Ideology*, Princeton, Princeton University Press, 1997.

24 As Nancy Frieden has shown, the vilification of folk medicine to promote 'modern' medicine was employed by pre-revolutionary health educators as well. See her 'Child care: medical reform in a traditionalist culture', in D. L. Ransel (ed.) *The Family in Imperial Russia*, Urbana, University of Illinois Press, 1978, p. 242.

25 F. Halle, *Women in Soviet Russia*, New York, Viking Press, 1933, pp. 235–6.

26 The 'Nepwoman' (*Nepmanka*) was the symbolic female companion to the 'Nepman', the gluttonous, depraved private 'businessman'/trader who personified NEP.

27 On the concept of touch, see Gilman, *Sexuality*.

28 For a fascinating analysis of the ideological threat posed by the well-fed Nepwoman see Naiman, *Sex in Public*.

29 J. R. Walkowitz has astutely analysed the relationship between female independence, sexual danger, public space and public order in *City of Dreadful Delight: Narratives of Sexual Danger in Late-Victorian London*, Chicago, University of Chicago Press, 1992. See also G. Pollock, *Vision and Difference: Femininity, Feminism, and the Histories of Art*, London and New York, Routledge, 1988, ch. 3.

30 For the text of Article 150 and the history of anti-VD legislation see I. Ia. Bychkov and N. S. Isaev, *Ugolovnaia otvetstvennost' za zarazhenie venericheskoi bolezni st. 150 ugolovnogo kodeksa*, Moscow, 1931.

31 N. A. Semashko, 'Meropriiatiia Narkomzdrava po lichnoi profilaktike', in V. F. Zelenin (ed.) *Polovoi vopros v svete nauchnogo znaniia*, Moscow, 1926, p. 327.

32 Other kinds of posters also lack single female images. See Waters, 'The female form in Soviet political iconography'; V. E. Bonnell, 'The representation of women in early Soviet political art', *Russian Review*, 1991, vol. 50, pp. 267–88. The situation changes in the early 1930s in relation to collectivization and the industrialization agenda of the Five Year Plans.

33 On similar issues of visual syntax in political posters, see Bonnell, 'The iconography of the worker in Soviet political art', in L. H. Siegelbaum and R. Grigor Suny (eds)

118

Making Workers Soviet: Power, Class, and Identity, Ithaca, Cornell University Press, 1994, p. 352.

34 Kate Sara Schecter, 'Professionals in post-revolutionary regimes: A case study of Soviet doctors', Ph.D. diss., Columbia University, 1992.

35 The conflicts resulting from the entrance of women into previously male medical and health-care professions have been addressed in a number of different historical and geographical settings. See, for instance, M. Poovey, ' "Scenes of an indelicate character": The medical "treatment" of Victorian women', in C. Gallagher and T. Laqueur (eds) *The Making of the Modern Body: Sexuality and Society in the Nineteenth Century*, Berkeley, University of California Press, 1987, pp. 137–68; O. Moscucci, *The Science of Woman: Gynaecology and Gender in England, 1800–1929*, Cambridge, Cambridge University Press, 1990.

7

VENEREAL DISEASES AND SOCIETY IN BRITAIN, FROM THE CONTAGIOUS DISEASES ACTS TO THE NATIONAL HEALTH SERVICE

Lesley A. Hall

In mid-nineteenth-century Britain, characteristic squeamishness towards manifestations of sexuality assumed that venereal diseases were too disgusting a subject for discussion, with consequent reluctance to recognize them as a problem. No general system for regulating prostitution which could incorporate medical policing existed – prostitution in Britain was not based on brothels (although there were offences defined in law as 'brothel-keeping'), around which it was easiest to base regulation.

'Undeserving' patients (male and female) with venereal diseases were rejected by most voluntary hospitals and neglected within the poor law system, and friendly societies usually refused to pay sickness benefits to subscribers with these 'self-inflicted' ailments.[1] Venereology was not taught in the undergraduate medical syllabus. The financial rewards of private practice could be considerable, but practitioners tended to shrink from the associated stigma of quackery.[2] Through 'shame', or misguided by advertisements or misleading recommendations, sufferers of all social classes attempted self-treatment or resorted to quacks. These included: 'chemists, qualified and (more frequently) unqualified, and herbalists' and other 'so-called specialists in venereal diseases ... entirely ignorant of medicine'.[3] Folk myths persisted: the most noxious of these was that these afflictions could be cured by intercourse with a virgin, a superstition still current well into the twentieth century.[4]

On the other hand, a strong feminist discourse on the causes and remedies for prostitution endeavoured to shift the blame for the dissemination of venereal diseases away from a group they considered unjustly victimized. This gained much of its force from the campaign against the Contagious Diseases Acts (1864, 1866, 1869) which has been extensively discussed by historians. Initially passed late at night in a thinly attended House of Commons, these Acts, aimed at ameliorating the serious inroads made by venereal diseases in the armed forces, were inspired by European regulationist systems. They were regarded at the time as giving the sexual double standard the force of law by instituting compulsory inspection of women alleged to be prostitutes in certain designated garrison and naval towns. This provision was aimed specifically at maintaining in fighting health a group in itself often stigmatized, consisting almost entirely of unmarried men drawn from the lower social classes.

The statement made in the course of the 1871 Royal Commission on the Contagious Diseases Acts that

> there is no comparison to be made between prostitutes and the men who consort with them. With the one sex the offence is committed as a matter of gain; with the other it is an irregular indulgence of a natural impulse[5]

was not an uncontested monolithic belief, any more than Sir Samuel Solly's earlier claim that syphilis 'was intended as punishment for our sins and we should not interfere in the matter'.[6] Almost as soon as the Acts were passed there was considerable opposition, including outrage among middle-class women already active in other campaigns to improve what they perceived to be the degraded social position of women. Objections came also from men, not only middle-class civil libertarians and moral reformers, but working-class men agitating against a measure which bore almost exclusively upon women of the lower classes.

However, the struggle was not a straightforward contest between the medical profession on the one hand, and middle-class feminist activists and their allies on the other. There was a difference between the popular perception of a 'medical' solution to the problem and what members of the medical profession actually thought. For example, John Simon, Medical Officer to the Privy Council, did not think the Acts were a good example of sanitary legislation. It could be argued that they represented an already dated concept of public health as cleaning up nuisances, rather than the more nuanced model of prevention which was emerging, and demonstrated a lag between popular ideas and medical developments. The group of doctors who actively opposed the Acts has not been much explored – this included the interesting alliance of the freethinking Malthusian radical Drysdales and the extremely anti-Malthusian C. H. F. Routh.

The campaign accustomed women to engaging with subjects ladies were supposed to know nothing about, linking on to a longer tradition of prostitute rescue. Under the charismatic leadership of Josephine Butler, the Ladies' National Association for the Repeal of the Contagious Diseases Acts mounted a forceful critique of the assumptions about male sexuality and female culpability which underlay the Acts. This developed into a broader concern about questions of sexual morality, the state, and society, evolving into a wider social purity movement by the 1880s. After much agitation, the CD Acts were suspended in

1883 and repealed in 1886.[7] Peter Baldwin has drawn attention to the relative ease with which this one group of central government acts was annulled (passed by parliament and repealed by the same body), contrasting it with the densely entangled complexity of local and central systems which institutionalized regula-tion in most areas of continental Europe.[8]

By the 1890s, doctors, lawyers and many others were aware of syphilis as a looming problem. Courts of law increasingly defined the matrimonial transmission of venereal disease as cruelty and thus grounds for separation or divorce. But the idea that women should be informed of the potential risks before marriage was still abhorrent to most men in positions of medical or legal power, and doctors, in the interests of preserving domestic harmony, were seldom explicit with married women suffering from mysterious maladies.

Some writers were articulating the problem to a wider public. Syphilis provided a potent metaphor in several 'New Woman' novels (Sarah Grand's *The Heavenly Twins*, 1893, Emma Brooke's *A Superfluous Woman*, 1894, and the short stories of 'George Egerton') for the dangers to which women were exposed when pursuing the conventionally desirable marriages which they were told should be their prime aim. It symbolized the moral difference between knowing, even corrupt and tainted men, and the 'innocent' women they married, and all the perils from which young girls were shielded through a policy of keeping them deliberately ignorant. Yet syphilis blighted not only the women's own lives but their children's.[9]

By the 1890s, alliances were shifting, with a new informal consortium of individuals and groups concerned about the problem, including military and public health doctors as well as social purity and rescue workers, attempting to engender official action. In 1896, concerned members of the medical profession and workers in allied philanthropic fields came together, drawing up a memorial in 1897 asking for the appointment of a Royal Commission to investigate the prevalence and effect of venereal diseases in the United Kingdom: individuals working at close quarters with the problem believed that they were far more widespread than commonly imagined. 'Suggested Terms of Reference for Enquiry re Venereal Diseases' were composed in 1898 by a Colonel Long (presumably Charles W. Long MP, retired Colonel in the Royal Artillery, who tried to get parliament to set up a VD enquiry in 1905).[10] These were: to ascertain 'how great the evil is', and what arrangements already existed, prior to devising means to prevent or limit the spread of these diseases. In 1898, a meeting which included representatives of eight rescue associations, ninety-six women engaged in social work, seventy-two men of all classes and fifty-two members of the medical profession passed a resolution in support of the Memorial, which was presented to the Prime Minister, Lord Salisbury, in 1899. No action was taken: Salisbury considered that 'public opinion was not sufficiently informed and enlightened'. This view was possibly influenced by fears of a revival of the Contagious Diseases Acts in an extended form, following the recent furore over the reintroduction of the CD Acts in India, a belief that the problem was in decline, and an idea that anyway they should be fought on moral and religious grounds.[11]

There are questions about how cohesive this group was. Possibly the appointment of an official enquiry was the only point that could be agreed on, although most, if not all, were opposed to the reintroduction of the Contagious Diseases Acts and desired the inclusion of men in any scheme, on grounds of both justice and efficacy. All emphasized protecting the innocent and checking the spread of these diseases. There was frequent emphasis at this period on the unjust burden being placed upon the innocent: 'the innocent' meaning wives and children of ('guilty') infected men; also those who acquired the disease through sharing a cup or an innocent social kiss with a sufferer, and medical and nursing personnel who contracted the diseases in the course of treating the diseased. The 'guilty' sufferer by the turn of the century was far more often perceived as male, conveying disease to his innocent family, as opposed to a contaminated prostitute infecting healthy young male bodies. Two distinct strands can be discerned in this growing concern and activity over venereal diseases in Britain during the first decade of the twentieth century. There was a predominantly feminist concern to publicize the problem of 'secret diseases', whereas other campaigners were more interested in putting pressure on the appropriate governmental authorities to 'do something' (without much success in actually generating official action).

There was growing international concern: strong resolutions, proposed by the British Medical Association, were passed at the Brussels International Medical Congress in September 1899 calling for a full enquiry into the causes and prevalence of VD. The issue became increasingly part of anxieties not just about individual health but national well-being. The Interdepartmental Committee on Physical Deterioration, 1904, recommended in its report appointing a Commission of Enquiry into the prevalence and effects of syphilis. Political upheavals thwarted attempts to present another Memorial to the Prime Minister promoting a Royal Commission.[12]

In the new century, women's arguments against the double moral standard could be presented as an issue with repercussions for the nation and the 'race'. Across the whole range of the suffrage movement, women spoke out with the facts of medicine, science and sociology to show how men's insistence on their need for extra-marital sex was ruining the nation. Louisa Martindale, of the non-militant London Women's Suffrage Society led by Millicent Garrett Fawcett, brought the authority of a doctor as well as a suffragist to her work *Under the Surface*, 1908. The Society, under whose auspices it was published, was subjected to attacks in parliament alleging that the book was 'injurious to morals', giving it unexpected publicity.[13] Martindale argued that venereal diseases originated from prostitution, caused by the existing male-dominated social system. The solution was 'THE EMANCIPATION OF WOMEN'.[14] Cicely Hamilton, actress, writer and member of the Women's Freedom League, in her polemic *Marriage as a Trade*, 1909, argued that the perils of venereal infection were 'sedulously concealed', yet 'If marriage is a trade we ought to know its risks'.[15] The subject was also alluded to in the various women's suffrage journals.[16]

The name most often associated with an attack on men as lust-driven predators festering with disease is that of Christabel Pankhurst, who in *The Great Scourge*, 1913, promoted 'Votes for women, and chastity for men' as the panacea for the diseases vitiating the nation's fitness. She defended the militant suffrage campaign and its destruction of property 'by the retort that men have destroyed, and are destroying, the health and life of women in the pursuit of vice', and claimed that the vast majority of men had one or another form of venereal disease.[17]

The subject of VD was, therefore, gradually being more talked about: Pankhurst did not single-handedly breach a monolithic conspiracy of silence but was an extremist contributor to a thriving debate. The subject was of increasing concern to doctors, public health workers (including the growing numbers of women employed in this area), welfare workers, philanthropists and reformers. There were continuing attempts to engender government action, if only an investigation. In 1911, the Royal Commission on the Poor Laws recommended that the powers of detention already applicable to other contagious diseases should be extended to the venereally infectious. However, a Memorial urging more widespread action by the Local Government Board, while sympathetically received by the President of the Board, was 'duly pigeon-holed': while the Board did institute an official inquiry, this was undertaken by Dr R. W. Johnstone 'in the midst of other official duties'.[18]

In 1913, with an International Congress due to meet, and without waiting for Johnstone's report, Sir Malcolm Morris and others, having decided that approaching politicians and government departments was an exercise in futility, concluded that

> the only way to get a chance of obtaining a full inquiry was to startle and impress the 'man in the street' in order that public pressure should be brought to bear on the Government, so that, yielding to panic and clamour, that should be granted which was denied to reason, evidence and argument.

A 'plain unvarnished statement of the facts' was published in the *Morning Post* over many well-known names as well as those of nearly every doctor with an official position. 'These tactics succeeded to perfection': the matter was openly discussed by the press, and agitation for an inquiry spread even to those who had once opposed the idea. The International Congress passed strong resolutions on the subject, and when parliament next rose, the Prime Minister announced the appointment of a Royal Commission.[19] While this direct appeal to public opinion clearly drew on the experience and activities of women suffragists, arguably it was necessary that this should be undertaken by distinguished male leaders of the medical profession on the front page of the *Morning Post* before the government would take notice. The concerned individuals and groups whose lengthy agitation had finally achieved the long-standing aim of a Royal Commission, formalized themselves into the National Council for Combatting Venereal Diseases in November 1914, to continue public propaganda and educational measures.[20]

What also stimulated action was the availability of the Wassermann Test (already instrumental in indicating the extent of the problem) and the introduction of Salvarsan, which enabled more reliable diagnosis and treatment. 'Science' did have an impact (in spite of contemporaneous vigorous campaigns for the eradication of tuberculosis, there was no equivalent 'magic bullet', and TB was only eradicated by a combination of improving living standards and antibiotic therapy).

Ironically, shortly after this long campaign had finally achieved action by the government, the First World War broke out, bringing the problem of VD forcibly to the fore. Facilities in the forces were better developed than in civil life (the first British trials of Salvarsan were undertaken by Lt-Col. L. W. Harrison at the military hospital in Rochester Row[21]). However, the system was placed under considerable stress by the outbreak of war. Although rates of admission per 1,000 per annum of all troops actually declined by over two-thirds between 1911 and 1916 (followed by a slight rise), an absolutely larger number of men was involved, and once conscription was introduced the question became particularly sensitive. 400,000 cases of venereal disease were treated in the course of the war, gonorrhoea comprising 66 per cent of the total and syphilis about a quarter. There was a considerable differential between the proportions of cases among British troops and those from the Dominions.[22]

Means of reducing the prevalence of venereal diseases among the troops varied. Exhortations to sexual continence, most famously Lord Kitchener's address to the British Expeditionary Force, were sometimes employed. The National Council for Combatting Venereal Diseases undertook the provision and training of special lecturers: exhortations, given a medical rather than a purely moral basis, may have had some effect. Particularly in France, reliance was placed on the traditional 'maisons tolerées', i.e. licensed brothels, closed in response to public opinion in 1918.[23] There was no simple dichotomy between a traditional military agenda of control and new medico-moral models. The beliefs of individuals, institutionalized practices, external pressures from local conditions or allies or social purity groups at home, had a complex influence on the measures taken in specific circumstances.[24] What actually constituted the most effective approach remained debatable. The policies pursued by the British appeared 'laissez-faire', even haphazardly ad hoc. American and Dominion forces placed reliance upon prophylactic packs, containing preventives and equipment for self-disinfection, and some British medical officers vigorously demanded the adoption of this new model.[25] Measures were tending to focus more on the man, for example with early treatment in ablution areas as soon as possible after exposure, even when control of prostitution was part of the package.[26] However, in 1918, a Regulation under the Defence of the Realm Act (DORA 40D) providing for the remanding for examination of any woman suspected to be a source of infection to members of the forces, aroused enormous opposition as reinstating the CD Acts under the guise of wartime necessity.[27]

Meanwhile, the Royal Commission, chaired by Lord Sydenham, spent several years hearing copious evidence on the prevalence of venereal disease and the provisions for its diagnosis and treatment, as well as recommendations as to how to combat the 'terrible peril to our Imperial race'. Only a few years after Edward VII had asked whether it was necessary to have women on the Royal Commission on Marriage and Divorce, three were appointed to this Commission on an even murkier topic. All were very distinguished, respectable, and well on in years: Mary Scharlieb, one of the first British women to qualify in medicine, by then a very eminent practitioner, Mrs E. M. Burgwin, an Inspector of the Feebleminded, and Louise Creighton, of the National Vigilance Association, widow of a bishop. A significant number of women gave evidence; in fact the first non-official witness called was Dr Helen Wilson of the Association for Moral and Social Hygiene (daughter of Henry Wilson MP, ally of Josephine Butler).

In 1916, the Commission produced its final report. The necessary structures for implementing the Wassermann Test and Salvarsan treatment were lacking: few hospitals routinely undertook Wassermann Tests and poor law and public health authorities lagged even further.[28] Salvarsan being a very new therapeutic agent, there were controversies as to how, and by whom, it should be administered. Medical practitioners were 'to a large extent unfamiliar with the newer methods of diagnosis and treatment, and ... failed to appreciate the importance of these diseases'.[29] The Commission insisted:

> It is of the utmost importance that this institutional treatment should be available for the whole community and should be so organized that persons affected by the disease should have no hesitation in taking advantage of the facilities.[30]

It was essential to get away from the old stigmatizing and punitive attitudes to sufferers, or ideas of 'innocent' and 'guilty'. The Royal Commission, in the interest of public health rather than human rights, advocated no distinction between the sexes, between 'good' and 'bad' women, or between the classes in tackling the problem.

This was extremely widespread: an estimated figure of as many as 10 per cent of the urban population had syphilis and an even greater proportion gonorrhoea, and the diseases appeared to be proportionately much more common among men than women. However, as the Commission pointed out, accurate figures were very hard to come by, although the probability was that VD was far more prevalent than official statistics, for example of causes of death, would indicate.[31]

The Commission's recommendations were implemented in 1916 through Local Government Board Regulations under existing public health legislation, and the Public Health (Venereal Diseases) Act of 1917. A nationwide system, free, voluntary, and confidential, aimed at bringing sufferers and adequate expert treatment together. Administration of Salvarsan was restricted to authorized trained doctors, and the purveying of purported remedies by any but qualified doctors criminalized.[32] Attempts to make the communication of venereal disease a crime, however, failed.[33]

The agitation for the Royal Commission and the production of its recommendations were the outcome of the alliance between a number of interest groups with rather different agendas – public health doctors, social purity reformers, eugenists and feminists – who were nonetheless able to find common ground in the need for an investigation and seizing the opportunity offered by Salvarsan to eradicate a national peril. The significance of the agency of particular individuals should not be underestimated. Arthur Newsholme at the Local Government Board had been concerned over the venereal disease problem for some considerable time, while envisaging the scheme of which he was substantially the architect, as an exemplar of new public health administration and a flagship for the potential of state medicine.[34] Colonel Lawrence Harrison brought the benefit of his military experience in the treatment of venereal diseases. Sybil Gotto (later Neville-Rolfe) had dedicated herself from an early age to the problem of eradicating these diseases and continued to do so for several decades.[35] Dr Helen Wilson combined the authority of a doctor with the abolitionist fervour of her background in dealing with the issue. Even before the setting up of the Royal Commission she had investigated existing treatment facilities as well as putting pressure on the Local Government Board.[36]

However, such a united front was inherently unstable. Behind the immediate desiderata on which all could agree, there were conflicts over means and about the way forward. Growing discussion of the previously taboo subject focused not merely on providing treatment, but on prevention, with some wanting to go even further than providing efficacious remedies for the already diseased. The National Council for Combatting Venereal Diseases, which received funding from the Ministry of Health for the purposes of education and propaganda, was reluctant to advocate prophylaxis, on the grounds that it encouraged immorality, although it considered that provisions for early treatment were desirable – this line was also politically acceptable to the Ministry. Considerable and heated debate spilt over from medical journals into the lay press, and led to the formation of a Society for the Prevention of Venereal Disease. 'Preventionists' argued for wider dissemination of information about prophylactic self-disinfection (rather than condoms[37]), and for chemists to be allowed to sell the relevant substances (illegal under the 1917 Venereal Diseases Act). Some historians have regarded the SPVD as a force of modernity battling the forces of obscurantism, but while the radical feminist Stella Browne praised prevention as 'free from the hideous barefaced sex-injustice involved in "regulation"', Dr Hugh Wansey Bayly, the Secretary of the SPVD, was an anti-feminist and proto-fascist with a strong adherence to the sexual double standard, who admitted that the SPVD's 'Directions to Women' were aimed at prostitutes.[38]

Lord Trevethin's Committee of Enquiry on Venereal Disease in 1923 failed to come down firmly on either side or produce a viable compromise. It reported that individuals could not be obstructed from obtaining means of disinfection and suggested that chemists might be permitted to sell disinfectants in 'a form approved and with instructions for use approved by some competent authority', as they were already allowed to sell condoms. But for chemists to advertize this service, or for more general facilities for disinfection to be provided, was deemed inadvisable. The Committee also considered that prevention might be mentioned by doctors to (male) patients in VD clinics. However, they placed greater reliance on extending existing provisions for treatment, increased public knowledge, and improved attention to diagnosing and treating pregnant women and babies, basically advocating continuation of the *status quo*. This enabled the government to leave the situation unchanged.[39] The SPVD never achieved the NCCVD's favoured position, given Ministry refusal to entertain the potentially contentious topic of prophylaxis.

The feared explosion of venereal infections in the aftermath of the War did not occur. VD was responding to the recently implemented measures and also declining because, although many more men had been exposed to infection during the War, 'never was there a period ... when those infected received treatment as satisfactory and complete'.[40] The effect on the reported incidence of venereal diseases of a voluntary non-compulsory system providing free, confidential and expert treatment rapidly became apparent. In spite of the low esteem, even stigma, associated with the care of venereal diseases, the system was extensively patronized by those suffering from them, or fearing they did. As early as 1919 over one million patients were seen in a year within the new clinic system, and although attendances increased between 1920 and 1923 (1,488,514 to 1,605,617), and improvements in recognition and recording would have tended to inflate the figures, numbers of actual cases fell significantly: syphilis by nearly 50 per cent, and gonorrhoea by nearly a quarter.[41] By 1924, deaths registered as due to syphilis revealed a dramatic reduction since 1918.[42] While the medical and official picture of the efficacy of the fight against syphilis was rosy, the increased amount of propaganda may have created unprecedented anxieties among the general population: presumably the growing attendance at clinics reflected a rise in the 'worried well' as well as the diseased. The clinic system was seen to be working and the prophylaxis debate died down. By 1925, 193 clinics had been established: funded 75 per cent from central government sources, they formed part of local public health administration, and the number of patients using them suggests confidence in the guarantee of confidentiality. The great majority of known syphilis cases were treated through clinics rather than private practice.[43] In 1932, H. Wansey Bayly complained that 'The venereal specialist sees ruin staring him in the face, as ... more and more patients go to clinics who do not properly belong to the hospital class'.[44]

'Fusion' between the SPVD and the NCCVD was discussed during 1924, the latter conceding that the sale of disinfectants with suitable instructions by chemists was a desirable element in the battle against venereal diseases, providing that commercial exploitation could be avoided. Amalgamation only narrowly failed to take place the following year.[45] The NCCVD moved into broader issues of social hygiene and sex education as the 1920s drew on, changing its name to the British Social Hygiene Council in 1925. It undertook various programmes of education and propaganda and was particularly up to date in its exploitation of cinema as a means of disseminating its message, although often drawing on old-fashioned melodramatic tropes.[46] As a result of the Local Government Act, 1929, it lost the generous block grant which had supported its activities throughout the 1920s. Responsibility for quota payments to the Council was devolved to the local authorities, themselves under pressure to economize during the 1930s: some did not pay at all, while others paid less than the required capitation fee. This seriously affected the BSHC's ability to carry out a full programme of activities.[47]

Meanwhile, there were suggestions that lifestyle changes – though not necessarily the high standard of chastity promoted by the BSHC – had caused the decline in numbers of infections. Some authorities claimed that this was the epidemiological consequence of

> an entirely new social code ... allow[ing] intercourse between the sexes
> to occur without the attendant circumstances of dirt, shame and
> furtiveness, and without entailing social disability.[48]

While few venereologists would have gone this far, there was certainly a widespread perception during the interwar years that 'prostitution ... becomes promiscuity', supported by the argument that chancroid, associated with professional prostitution, was dying out.[49] It was also suggested (on somewhat anecdotal evidence) that while an older generation regarded 'prostitutes as the only "fair game". ... Young men tend to deny having had anything to do with a prostitute, regarding it as a slight on their attractions.'[50] This apparent change varied by social group: the great majority of cases in the mercantile marine, as might be expected in a mobile population, were the result of mercenary transactions.[51]

In 1925, with the country covered by a network of public treatment centres, the new and articulate professional group employed in them formed the Medical Society for the Study of Venereal Diseases.[52] In spite of the apparently generous provision of clinics, the medical officers working in them deplored the conditions under which they worked and the ways in which the spirit and even the letter of the system were being breached. They had the traditional lowly status of 'pox doctors', in spite of the newly scientific status which diagnostic and therapeutic developments had added to their role. They complained that 'in our relations with colleagues and laity we are often considered to be outcasts', and 'often ignored until [colleagues] wish to get rid of unpopular patients'. Specialists in related departments were often unwilling to be associated with venereologist colleagues. Venereal departments were allocated to 'unhygienic cellars, or inconvenient corners of hospitals', lacking laboratory facilities, and with often very inadequate privacy for consultation, even though the venereal department could boast of curing the majority of its patients.[53] Appointments committees were wont to appoint doctors lacking in any qualification, except, possibly, experience as an army medical officer. Excessive segregation and disinfection measures were imposed upon VD patients and the areas they frequented, and there could be opposition and a 'sanctimonious attitude of mind' among nursing staff, while male VD nursing orderlies were not admitted to the State Register.[54]

In 1937, with the introduction of sulphonamides, 'it was commonly said that venereology would soon cease to exist as a special subject'. A drug therapy which did not demand the instrumental skills previously required for the treatment of gonorrhoea sent numerous patients back to private practitioners, although emergence of resistant strains soon became apparent.[55] The number of early cases of syphilis seen in clinics in 1939 was under 5,000, a decline of over 45 per cent since 1931; there had been a slight peak in the early 1930s due to economic recession and mass unemployment. Congenital syphilis showed steady decline, probably due to efforts in ante-natal clinics, although these varied widely by locality.[56] The most radical breakthrough, however, was the discovery of penicillin, which had the major advantage that treatment did not have to be continued for a lengthy period. It was not generally introduced however until 1944; even then there was prejudice against its use in venereal disease, and syphilis came sixth on the priority list, except in cases resistant to usual treatments.[57]

While possibly it was the case that by the time of the outbreak of the Second World War, as some argued, 'men's morals are better; they are more responsible and their relations with women are less sordid than in the old days', and 'crude prostitution is falling into disuse in the better walks of life',[58] prostitution was still rife, as almoners and social workers found when tracing contacts. Women pursuing promiscuous liaisons though not a full-time career of prostitution were often either supplementing their income or acquiring gifts in kind. It was alleged that the 'older prostitute has a more professional attitude towards disease and will, if warned of possible infection, attend for examination or treatment' unlike feckless younger women who did not regard prostitution as a career.[59]

As in 1914, the outbreak of war saw an almost immediate upsurge in the number of infections. Within the armed forces

> Venereal disease was found to be the most difficult of all diseases to
> control owing to the restrictions imposed on preventive measures by
> public opinion and to the manner in which it was contracted.[60]

Information was supposed to be disseminated to all servicemen about the risks
involved and the provisions available but 'many denied ever having had a lecture
on the subject'. There was little advance planning, and inadequate facilities for
prevention or treatment.[61] Various measures were introduced: condoms were
issued and educational films acquired from the USA, lectures given and poster
campaigns initiated. Antibiotics enabled rapid treatment, sometimes not even
involving hospitalization.[62]

The home front was also affected by the rising VD rate. The Ministry of
Health transferred responsibility for venereal education and propaganda from
the British Social Hygiene Council to the Central Council for Health Education,
signifying commitment to a preventive medical rather than a moral approach
(though many of the previous attitudes persisted). A joint Ministry/CCHE
campaign to increase public awareness of the diseases and treatment facilities
began in 1942.[63] Powerful taboos still operated: advertisements in the press and
radio broadcasts made some inroads but initial hardhitting copy employing
common vernacular terms such as 'pox' and 'clap' was vitiated by what *The
Lancet* considered to be the 'mistaken sense of delicacy' if not downright prudery,
of newspaper proprietors.[64]

A torrent of correspondence from the general public requested further information,[65] and the unusual step was taken of commissioning an investigation into
the efficacy of the campaign by the pioneering social survey organization, Mass
Observation. Mass Observers approached members of the general public in the
street and questioned them on the advertisements and attitudes more generally
to the control of venereal diseases during 1942–3. They discovered 'great willingness' among the public to know more, and even 'active desire' for greater
openness, although some respondents considered the whole subject 'dirty',
'nasty', even 'horrible'. Responses provide a rich trove of popular beliefs and
attitudes, and prove how very diverse these were. There was a persistent assumption among many that the main source of infection was the prostitute and that
the disease could be controlled by regular examinations and licensed houses:

> you must tackle the source of it – the woman with the germs. Why were
> the troops free from venereal disease in the last war? Because women
> had to have a doctor's certificate once a week.

Not everyone saw the prostitute as central: several comments blamed traditionally suspect groups such as 'soldiers and ATS' or 'blinking foreigners' (especially
Americans) as well as 'little cheap loose-living girls'. While the diseases were
often located in particular, stigmatized bodies and recommendations made for
'an order forbidding people having the disease to mix with other people', others

131

saw them as miasmatically pervasive and only to be avoided by 'great cleanliness' and caution about using public lavatories. More humane and 'modern' suggestions were the use of some form of inoculation, and media campaigns of education and propaganda, reflecting experience of other public health initiatives.[66]

Defence of the Realm Regulation 33B followed more traditional methods of control. Gender-neutral in intention, given the furore over Regulation 40D in the First World War, this required notification of contacts named by more than one infected person. Even so, it bore more heavily upon women – during its first six months 64 women had been informed upon and only two men.[67] Although, epidemiologically, prostitutes were still the greater risk,[68] it was pervasively assumed that professionals knew 'how to take care of themselves',[69] and the 'easy amateur' was seen by medical opinion as the major reservoir of disease. Men, though tending to eschew prostitutes, were reckless with casually met girlfriends, with whom they least expected infection. Even 'girls of good repute, who would no doubt later become mothers' were contributing to VD statistics.[70] But in spite of the persistence of the view that 'the female carrier is the reservoir of infection' the male partners in the transaction were becoming increasingly visible; for example, as irresponsible defaulters who failed to complete courses of treatment, or men who were too drunk to recall their partner, and bore increasing blame.[71] Consorting with prostitutes and becoming venereally infected were no longer seen as marks of manhood. By the late 1940s, male venereal disease patients were increasingly depicted as neurotic or inadequate (though some die-hards still claimed they were 'fighting soldiers of the finest type'),[72] and Lt-Col. T. A. Ratcliffe correlated good morale in a military unit with a low VD incidence.[73] Thus, from a manly concomitant of militarism, sexually transmitted diseases had become a mark of failure.

Little thought was given to venereal diseases when setting up the National Health Service, even though numbers of infections peaked in 1946, indeed a Statutory Instrument to reinstate the confidentiality requirement established in 1917 had to be hastily issued.[74] However, incidence declined steadily as 'new and effective remedies became increasingly available' through the comprehensive service consolidated by the introduction of the NHS in 1948, run locally by regional hospital boards and boards of governors. By the early 1950s it was assumed that venereal infections were 'These Dying Diseases', with a consequent retreat to the traditional reluctance to think about these diseases with their connotations of illicit sexuality, and a resurgence of medical indifference and administrative neglect.[75]

NOTES

1 *Departmental Committee on Sickness Benefit Claims under the National Insurance Act* Cd. 7687, London, HMSO, 1914, §§134–41; *Royal Commission on Venereal Diseases, Final Report* Cd.

8189, London, HMSO, 1916, §§134, 137–8; T. J. Wyke, 'The Manchester and Salford Lock Hospital, 1818–1917', *Medical History*, 1979, vol. 19, pp. 73–86.

2 M. Adler, 'The terrible peril: a historical perspective on the venereal diseases', *British Medical Journal (BMJ)*, 1980, vol. 2, pp. 202–11; L. W. Harrison, 'Those were the days! or random notes on then and now in VD', *Bulletin of the Institute of Technicians in Venereology*, [n. d. ?1950s], pp. 1–7.

3 Local Government Board, *Report as to the Practice of Medicine and Surgery by Unqualified Persons in the United Kingdom* Cd. 5422, London, HMSO, 1910, p. 15; *Royal Commission on VD, Final Report*, §188, §133.

4 *Royal Commission on VD, First Report: Appendix: Minutes of Evidence (1913–1914)* Cd. 7475, London, HMSO, 1914, §2,822.

5 *Royal Commission upon the Administration and Operation of the Contagious Diseases Acts: Volume I: The Report* C. 408, London, HMSO, 1871, §60.

6 *Report of the Committee Appointed to Enquire into the Pathology and Treatment of Venereal Disease, with the View to Diminish its Injurious Effects on the Men of the Army and Navy* Cd. 4031, London, HMSO, 1868, Minutes of Evidence, Q. 3898.

7 D. Dunsford, 'Principle versus expediency: a rejoinder to F. B. Smith', *Social History of Medicine*, 1992, vol. 5, pp. 503–13; P. McHugh, *Prostitution and Victorian Social Reform*, London, Croom Helm, 1980; F. Mort, *Dangerous Sexualities: Medico-moral Politics in Britain since 1830*, London, Routledge & Kegan Paul, 1987, pp. 174–6; F. B. Smith, 'The Contagious Diseases Acts reconsidered', "Unprincipled expediency": a comment on Deborah Dunsford's paper', *Social History of Medicine*, 1990, vol. 3, pp. 197–215; 1992, vol. 5, pp. 515–16; J. R. Walkowitz, *Prostitution and Victorian Society: Women, Class and the State*, Cambridge, Cambridge University Press, 1980.

8 P. Baldwin, *Contagion and the State in Europe, 1830–1930*, Cambridge, Cambridge University Press, 1999, p. 509.

9 E. Showalter, *A Literature of Their Own: British Women Novelists from Brontë to Lessing*, London, Virago, 1982, pp. 210–14.

10 R. Davenport-Hines, *Sex, Death and Punishment: Attitudes to Sex and Sexuality in Britain since the Renaissance*, London, Collins, 1990, p. 211.

11 E. B. Turner, 'The history of the fight against venereal disease', *Science Progress*, 1916–1917, vol. 11, pp. 83–8; Association for Moral and Social Hygiene (AMSH), 'Venereal diseases', File 1 (Box 311), Fawcett Library, London, Guildhall University.

12 Turner, 'The history of the fight against venereal disease'.

13 *The State and Sexual Morality*, London, George Allen & Unwin Ltd, 1920, p. 8.

14 L. Martindale, *Under the Surface*, London, London Women's Suffrage Society, 1908.

15 C. Hamilton, *Marriage as a Trade*, London, Chapman & Hall, 1909, pp. 54–5.

16 L. Garner, *Stepping Stones to Women's Liberty: Feminist Ideas in the Women's Suffrage Movement*, London, Heinemann, 1984, pp. 21–2, 38–40.

17 C. Pankhurst, *The Great Scourge and How to End It*, London, E. Pankhurst, 1913.

18 *Public Health*, 1913, vol. 25, p. 51.

19 Turner, 'The history of the fight against venereal disease'.

20 National Council for Combatting Venereal Disease Provisional Executive Committee minutes, 24 Nov. 1914, British Social Hygiene Council archives, Archives and Manuscripts, Wellcome Library for the History and Understanding of Medicine, CMAC: SA/BSH/A.2/1. *British Journal of Venereal Diseases* ('Combatting' is the spelling used in the original name.)

21 L. W. Harrison, 'Ehrlich *versus* syphilis, as it appeared to L. W. Harrison', *BJVD*, 1954, vol. 30, pp. 2–6.

22 *History of the Great War Based on Official Documents; Medical Services: Diseases of the War*, London, HMSO, 1923, p. 118.

23 B. Towers, 'Health education policy, 1916–1926: venereal disease and the prophylaxis dilemma', *Medical History*, 1980, vol. 24, pp. 70–87.

24 M. Harrison, 'The British Army and the problem of venereal disease in France and Egypt during the First World War', *Medical History*, 1995, vol. 34, pp. 133–58.

25 Sir B. Donkin, 'The fight against venereal infection'; Sir F. Champneys, 'The fight against venereal infection: a reply to Sir Bryan Donkin'; Donkin, 'The fight against venereal infection: a rejoinder'; Champneys, 'The fight against venereal infection: a further reply to Sir Bryan Donkin', *The Nineteenth Century*, 1917, vol. 82, pp. 580–95, 1,044–54; 1918, vol. 83, pp. 184–90, 611–18. There was also considerable correspondence on this topic in the *BMJ* during 1919 and 1920.

26 L. A. Hall, ' "War always brings it on": War, STDs, the military, and the civilian population in Britain, 1850–1950', in R. Cooter, M. Harrison and S. Sturdy (eds) *Medicine and Modern Warfare*, Amsterdam, Rodopi, 1999, pp. 205–23.

27 AMSH, 'Venereal diseases', file 2 (Box 311).

28 *Royal Commission on VD: Final Report*, §136.

29 Ibid., §143.

30 Ibid., §144.

31 Ibid., §§10–11.

32 'Venereal diseases: state provision for their diagnosis and treatment'; 'Medical notes in parliament: The Venereal Diseases Bill', *BMJ*, 1916, vol. 2, p. 111; 1917, vol. 1, p. 557.

33 'Criminal Law Amendment and Sexual Offences Bills', *The Shield: Journal of the Association for Moral and Social Hygiene*, 1918–1920, 3rd Series, vol. 2, p. 5.

34 J. M. Eyler, *Sir Arthur Newsholme and State Medicine, 1885–1935*, Cambridge, Cambridge University Press, 1997, pp. 277–94.

35 S. Neville-Rolfe, *Social Biology and Welfare*, London, George Allen & Unwin Ltd, 1949, 'Autobiographical Note', pp. 11–48.

36 *Royal Commission on VD: First Report: Minutes of Evidence* Cd. 7474, London, HMSO, 1914, §§5,288–693.

37 Norah March (of the SPVD) to Alison Neilans of the Association for Moral and Social Hygiene, 21 Dec 1921, AMSH, 'Venereal diseases', file 2 (Box 311).

38 AMSH, 'Venereal diseases', file 2 (Box 311); H. Wansey Bayly, *Triple Challenge, or War, Whirligigs and Windmills ... A Doctor's Memoirs of the Years 1914 to 1929*, London, Hutchinson, 1935; Stella Browne to Janet Carson, 11 July 1920, British Sexology Society archives, 'Misc', Harry Ransom Center; S. M. Tomkins, 'Palmitate or permanganate: the venereal prophylaxis debate in Britain, 1916–1926', *Medical History*, 1993, vol. 37, pp. 382–98.

39 Ministry of Health, *Report of the Committee of Enquiry on Venereal Disease*, London, HMSO, 1923.

40 Sir A. Newsholme, 'The decline in registered mortality from syphilis in England. To what is it due?', *Journal of Social Hygiene*, 1926, vol. 12, pp. 514–23.

41 W. M. Chambers, 'Prostitution and venereal disease', *BJVD*, 1926, vol. 2, pp. 68–75.

42 Newsholme, 'The decline in registered mortality from syphilis'.

43 P. L. Adams, 'Health of the state: British and American public health policies in the Depression and World War II', unpublished dissertation for the Doctorate of Social Welfare, University of California–Berkeley, 1979, pp. 326–67.

44 *The Lancet*, 1932, vol. 1, p. 1,229.

45 Extraordinary General Meeting of the NCCVD, 14 May 1924, 20 June 1924; Executive Committee meeting, 19 Jan. 1925: SA/BSH/A.1/3, A.2/8.

46 T. Boon, 'Films and the contestation of public health in interwar Britain', unpublished Ph.D. thesis, University of London, 1999, pp. 133–75.

47 Ministry of Health file 'British Social Hygiene Council', MH53/1328, Public Record Office.

48 F. G. Crookshank, 'Medico-legal problems in relation to venereal disease', *BJVD*, 1926, vol. 2, pp. 36–58.

49 J. H. Stokes, 'The future of syphilis', *BJVD*, 1928, vol. 4, pp. 274–89.
50 G. L. M. McElligott, 'The venereal history: truth or fiction?', *BJVD*, 1932, vol. 8, pp. 292–7.
51 H. M. Hanschell, 'The problem of venereal disease in the merchant marine' and A. O. Ross, 'The problem of the treatment of venereal disease in the mercantile marine', with discussion, *BJVD*, 1929, vol. 5, pp. 202–28.
52 Presidential Address by Dr W. S. Fox, *BJVD*, 1926, vol. 2, pp. 59–64.
53 R. Lees, 'VD – Some random reflections of a venereologist', *BJVD*, 1950, vol. 26, pp. 157–63.
54 C. Mills, 'Collaboration between the venereal disease and other departments'; I. N. Orpwood Price and J. A. Burgess, 'Is a new deal in the control of venereal disease necessary?' (2 papers and discussion), *BJVD*, 1934, vol. 10, pp. 233–48; 1944, vol. 20, pp. 19–30.
55 A. King, 'These dying diseases: venereology in decline?', *The Lancet*, 1958, vol. 1, pp. 651–7; Sir W. Dalrymple-Champneys, 'The epidemiological control of venereal disease', *BJVD*, 1947, vol. 23, pp. 101–8; 'Scotland versus VD', *The Lancet*, 1944, vol. 1, p. 668; R. Lees, 'Venereal diseases in the armed forces overseas (1)', D. J. Campbell, 'Venereal diseases in the armed forces overseas (2)', *BJVD*, 1946, vol. 22, pp. 149–58, 158–68; F. A. E. Crew (ed.) *History of the Second World War: United Kingdom Medical Series; The Army Medical Services: Administration II*, London, HMSO, 1955, p. 236.
56 L. W. Harrison, contribution to discussion of Dalrymple–Champneys, 'The epidemiological control of VD'; Burgess, 'Is there a new deal in the control of venereal disease?'.
57 Campbell, 'Venereal diseases in the armed forces overseas (2)'; *History of the Second World War ... The Army Medical Services: Administration II*, p. 238.
58 *The Shield*, 1938, 5th series, vol. 6/3, p. 125; D. White, 'The basis of a new moral appeal', *The Shield*, 1939, 5th series, vol. 7/1, pp. 1–4.
59 H. M. Johns, 'Contact tracing', and M. A. Wailes, 'Contact tracing and the prostitute', both in *BJVD*, 1945, vol. 21, pp. 15–21.
60 *History of the Second World War ... The Army Medical Services: Administration II*, pp. 231–2.
61 Lees, 'Venereal diseases in the armed forces overseas'.
62 *History of the Second World War ... The Army Medical Services: Administration II*, p. 234.
63 R. Sutherland, 'Some individual and social factors in venereal disease', *BJVD*, 1950, vol, 26, pp. 1–15.
64 'Venereal disease publicity', *The Lancet*, 1943, vol. 1, p. 276.
65 Sutherland, 'Some individual and social factors'.
66 Mass Observation, 'Venereal disease survey 1942–1943', Tom Harrisson – Mass Observation Archives, University of Sussex, A.9 Box 1.
67 *The Lancet*, 1944, vol. 1, p. 167.
68 Col. J. E. Gordon, 'The control of venereal disease: an epidemiological approach', *The Lancet*, 1944, vol. 2, pp. 711–15.
69 Wailes, 'Contact tracing and the prostitute'.
70 Lt-Col. T. A. Ratcliffe, 'Psychiatric and allied aspects of the problem of venereal disease in the Army', *Journal of the Royal Army Medical Corps*, 1947, vol. 89, pp. 122–31; 'Parliament: From the Press Gallery: Debate on venereal disease', *The Lancet*, 1942, vol. 2, p. 738.
71 'Legislative control of venereal disease', *The Lancet*, 1944, vol. 2, pp. 17–18; 'The social background of venereal disease: a report on an experiment in contact tracing and an investigation into social conditions: Tyneside experimental scheme in venereal disease control, October 1943 to March 1944', *BJVD*, 1945, vol. 21, pp. 26–34; 'Compulsory methods and the treatment of venereal diseases', *The Shield*, 1942, 5th series, vol. 9/2, pp. 55–8.

72 Maj. G. O. Watts and Maj. R. A. Wilson, 'A study of personality factors among venereal disease patients', *Canadian Medical Association Journal*, 1945, vol. 53, pp. 119–22; E. D. Wittkower, 'The psychological aspects of venereal disease', *BJVD*, 1948, vol. 24, pp. 59–67.
73 Ratcliffe, 'Psychiatric and allied aspects of the problem of venereal disease'.
74 Statutory Instruments: 1948 no 2517: The National Health Service (Venereal Diseases) Regulations, 1948.
75 King, 'These dying diseases'.

8

'THE THORNS OF LOVE'

Sexuality, syphilis and social control in modern Italy

Bruno P. F. Wanrooij

Since the discovery of the sexual transmission of syphilis, the social history of what today are called 'sexually transmitted diseases' in Italy has been so closely related to attempts to regulate prostitution that it is almost impossible to distinguish them. In the public debate the transmission of syphilis through non-sexual forms of direct contact – most importantly between nurslings and wet nurses – received much less attention. Writing in the first decade of the twentieth century, Iwan Bloch stated that the solution of the so-called sexual question was in the equation 'no more prostitution, no more venereal diseases'.[1] However, the importance of the debate about regulated prostitution goes beyond issues of health: it created opportunities for men and women to discuss sexual matters in public. Yet, at the same time, the overhanging threat of disease and death set the tone for a negative and pessimistic vision of sex. The notions of disease, contagion and infection made it virtually impossible to avoid the moralistic approach already so common in the earlier religious discourse about the sixth commandment. The new struggle against venereal diseases (VD) thus provided the conceptual framework for discussions of the role of sexuality in Italian society. In the debate, the incidence of VD was often used as a yardstick for the more general state of the nation, and warnings against the dangers of revolutionary movements and ideas were phrased in a terminology derived from medical discourse.

Closely linked with the prominent place which syphilis occupied in social imagination was the attempt by members of the medical profession to increase their prestige and achieve social and political status through their exclusive access to the knowledge and technology necessary to guarantee the health of the nation. The strategies used in this context by medical doctors – the creation of a monopoly position for experts, the defence of traditional science against whoever dared to challenge its basic assumptions, and the attempt to depoliticize decisions – all contributed to a profound change in the social role and prestige of (medical) science.

The introduction by Prime Minister Cavour of a system of prostitution in brothels, motivated by venereologist Casimiro Sperino's perception of the need to check the diffusion of VD in the army, and to guarantee the health of the Italian people, marks the beginning of a debate which was to last until 1958, and maybe even longer. The regulation of prostitution which was introduced on 15 February 1860 followed the 'Instructions regarding prostitution' elaborated by Sperino, which had become law in the kingdom of Piedmont-Sardinia in 1855. The Cavour Regulation was extended to all the regions which in the following years were annexed to the new Italian kingdom. Thus, by 1870, when unification was completed, the Regulation was applied to the entire Italian territory.

The rules, which were clearly inspired by the Belgian experience, aimed at concentrating prostitution in closed houses, and at limiting, as much as possible, the freedom of movement of the women who were registered as prostitutes, either because they had applied for registration or because they had been forced to register as prostitutes by public authorities, as often happened to women accused of being clandestine prostitutes. The regulation was motivated by the desire to stop the apparent increase in the number of cases of syphilis: every two weeks prostitutes were obliged to undergo a medical examination. In case of infection medical treatment in a venereal hospital was mandatory.[2]

Before the extension of the Piedmont legislation to the rest of Italy, the legal situation of prostitution in the various pre-unification Italian states varied from tolerance to prohibition, as in the papal states. Prohibitionism, however, was not strictly applied in Rome. Only after public complaints would the police intervene and send diseased prostitutes to the hospital of San Giacomo for mandatory treatment. Nevertheless, according to Felix Jacquot, a military surgeon with the French troops stationed in Rome, the incidence of syphilis was lower in Rome than in France. His explanation for this difference was that the sexual life of the Romans was more moderate, and that the number of prostitutes was lower.[3] In Sicily, a decree of the viceroy published in 1823 established compulsory medical checks and treatment for prostitutes but was never fully applied.[4]

Following the Cavour legislation, an 1862 governmental decree created venereal hospitals for the treatment of prostitutes with VD. A new regulation issued in 1871 introduced some reforms but did not alter the characteristics of the hospitals as places of incarceration. The women, who were essentially locked up, were obliged to work and were not allowed to have contacts with the outside world without permission of the director. They were subject to strict discipline and in the case of any infraction of the rules, risked punishments such as the reduction of food rations. Close links existed between venereal hospitals and asylums. Young women who, after having been sent to an asylum by their parents or by public authorities, refused to accept the discipline of the asylum could be punished by incarceration in a hospital. On the other hand, transferral to an asylum could be the reward for young women in venereal hospitals who behaved well.

The main goal of the asylums, or 'conservatories', was to save the honour of girls who, because of their poverty, family conditions or personal characteristics, were considered to be 'at risk'. Admission often followed illegitimate sexual relations, and a significant proportion of these girls had VD.[5] The activities of the asylums were motivated, above all, by charity and the moral obligation to rescue poor girls. Catholic influence explains the great number of activities in this field and the favour with which they were looked upon by the government.[6] While trying to rescue girls from a future as prostitutes, the asylums also played a role in maintaining public order. The police often would send to the asylums victims of sexual violence or girls suspected of immoral behaviour.

Notwithstanding the philanthropic inspiration, the regime which all inmates of the asylums underwent was severe; based on work, prayer, discipline and obedi-ence. According to the educators, even the victims of sexual violence had to be re-educated. They were convinced that the loss of sexual purity was sufficient to undermine the capacity of a minor to resist future sexual advances. As the 'value' of a woman was based on the 'possession' of honour, it did not matter very much whether the sexual acts had been extorted or consensual. Sex itself was seen as a form of perversion and its effects could be compared to contagion: 'Perversion is implicit in the act. The seeds of evil thrown by the corruptor will flower in the mind of the minor who doesn't have the capacity to stop this from happening.'[7]

The introduction of regulated prostitution has to be set against the back-ground of a growing differentiation of gender roles. In the second half of the nineteenth century, a process of urbanization started in Italy. Young men, espe-cially, became extremely mobile, but also many young women moved to the cities to find jobs as domestic servants or in industry. In 1913, women outnumbered men among the immigrants who flocked to Milan, escaping from the dire condi-tions of life in the rural areas.[8] This greater mobility had contrasting consequences for women, who gained greater freedom, but often also lost the support of the traditional family network. As they could no longer count on family and community pressure to convince young men to take up family respon-sibilities, it was more difficult for women to find stable partners. Moreover, the fact that they were now held more directly responsible for their acts was used to justify repressive measures against all those who violated social norms. Attempts were made to force single mothers to take care of their children rather than abandoning them, and police forces replaced parental control by arresting young women on the streets during the night without valid reason or chaperonage. At the same time these developments were also affecting prostitution not only by creating the conditions for increased supply and demand, but also by preparing the stage for punitive actions.[9]

Many medical doctors emphasized the problems of young men who, after having reached physical maturity, had to delay marriage for social and economic reasons. They claimed that, as it was impossible for the majority to live up to the ideal of chastity, only a system of regulated prostitution could provide young men with the necessary safe outlet for their sexual desires, and help them to avoid both masturbation and the seduction of 'honest' girls.[10] Visits to brothels were seen as less socially disruptive than non-mercenary sexual relations because the latter might disregard class differences and interfere with marriage strategies.

Most of these doctors did not consider the possibility that young women also had sexual needs, and often simply denied the existence of female sexual desires.

Science also legitimated regulated prostitution in another way. According to positivist scientists like Cesare Lombroso, prostitution was the 'biological destiny' of a minority of women who shared certain physical and psychological characteristics: precocity combined with sexual frigidity and, above all, a form of 'moral insanity' which caused these women to abandon female modesty.[11] Theoretically, Lombroso was convinced that the characteristics of 'natural born prostitutes' could be found in all social classes, albeit under different disguises. In his studies of the aetiology of crime, however, it becomes clear he considered their incidence higher among young lower-class women from the South.[12] By highlighting the biological origins of women's recourse to prostitution, medical and anthropological theories tended to eliminate 'sentimentalism' in judging the conditions of prostitutes' lives, and to eradicate remaining male feelings of guilt.[13]

The introduction of regulated prostitution should also be placed in the framework of the middle classes' and upper classes' growing fear of the lower classes, who no longer seemed to be willing to uphold the basic values of traditional society: property, work and the family. Regulation served as a metaphor for the separation of the most dangerous elements of the lower classes from those who could be rehabilitated, and for the need to put those who refused to obey the rules under administrative and sanitary control.[14] More concretely, the law discriminated above all against prostitutes, who were deprived of their civil rights and forced to subject themselves to medical inspections. Even more importantly, police registration forced lower-class women, who occasionally used prostitution as a temporary solution for their economic problems, to become full-time prostitutes, and made a return to 'normal' life difficult. The regulation also hit women in general, whose freedom of movement was limited as a result of police activities under which all women risked being arrested and subjected to humiliating medical examinations.[15] Moreover, regulation targeted the poor as potentially dangerous, and intervened accordingly. The prostitutes, almost exclusively poor women, were placed under sanitary and police control, and similar measures, including compulsory medical inspection, were applied to poor men like conscript soldiers, criminals and vagabonds.

The Italian workers' movement perceived prostitution as a form of exploitation of the proletariat, and occasionally acknowledged the common interests of workers and prostitutes. In the case of general strikes, the workers who had crossed their arms in the attempt to force their employers to give in, would invite prostitutes to 'cross their legs'.[16] This feeling of solidarity with their 'unfortunate sisters' was particularly strong among the anarchists and the more radical sectors of the workers' movement, who were not afraid to identify with outsiders, and used tales about the horrors of sexual exploitation and of VD to enhance feelings of class hatred.[17]

The introduction of the Cavour legislation met with strong opposition from the more radical and democratic forces in Italian society, which looked to the United Kingdom as an example. Josephine Butler had already met Giuseppe Mazzini and Aurelio Saffi, the leaders of the Italian democratic opposition in exile, in Oxford in the 1850s. Later, Anna Maria Mozzoni had informed her that in Italy the system of regulation had caused an increase in the number of clandestine prostitutes and of cases of VD.[18] In 1875, Butler visited Italy, and gave speeches in cities such as Milan, Florence and Naples. Her efforts led to the creation of an Italian section of the international abolitionist movement, which saw the participation of men and women like Giuseppe Nathan, Aurelio Saffi and his wife Georgina Crawford, Jessie White Mario, Agostino Bertani and Anna Maria Mozzoni. Although Bertani was himself a member of the medical profession, the abolitionists were critical of the role played by medical doctors, and accused them of contributing to the diffusion of vice by inspecting the prostitutes and certifying their health conditions:

> It would be absurd to think [argued Ernesto Nathan, brother of Giuseppe] that without Regulation young people would take a vow of chastity and like St. Anthony would start to fight the passions and the seductions of the flesh, but it is as absurd to deny that the official sanctions and the so-called sanitary provisions represent a passport without which many would not surrender to the first stimuli of passion.[19]

While the abolitionists of course agreed about the need to eliminate state regulation, they were less united in proposing alternatives, and some thought of prohibitionism as an alternative way to prevent the diffusion of VD. Initially, the abolitionists were not very successful, partly because most activists belonged to a cosmopolitan elite with strong international links but limited contacts with the lower classes and the Catholic majority of Italy. It was therefore relatively easy for the Minister of the Interior, Agostino Depretis, to disregard their protests when, in 1880, he increased taxation on brothels.

Depretis' decision had the unforeseen effect of reinforcing opposition to regulation. In order to make their opinions about prostitution better known, the abolitionists created their own journal *La coscienza pubblica*. The growing capacity of the abolitionists to influence public opinion forced the government in 1883 to accept the creation of a parliamentary commission of enquiry. Two years later the commission, which had among its members both Bertani and the venereologist Celso Pellizzari, published its conclusions: regulation as such should be abolished, and sanitary control and police control should target brothels, not prostitutes. The government postponed the discussion of these proposals, which represented a major victory for the abolitionists, but in 1888 was forced to introduce new rules abolishing the forced medical treatment of prostitutes with VD, and improving their living conditions.[20] The new measures were severely criticized by venereologists, who cited statistics indicating a rapid growth in the incidence of VD, with an increase among conscript soldiers from 5.91 per cent in 1883 to 10.23 per cent in 1889. The victory of the abolitionists, in any event, was shortlived. In 1891, Giovanni Nicotera, Minister of the Interior, promulgated a new regulation reinforcing police and sanitary control.

Moralistic arguments played an important role in the discourse of the abolitionists, who often refused to recognize that prostitution could be a choice for poor women to whom the labour market offered scarce and not particularly attractive alternatives. The opposition to regulated prostitution often seemed inspired above all by a refusal to accept what was considered state certification of vice. However, in this case moralism was closely connected with ideas of social justice. The more feminist-oriented abolitionists were keen to emphasize the need for female solidarity and saw the abolition of regulated prostitution as part of a more ample programme including the improvement of the conditions of female workers, better education for women, and female suffrage.[21]

Socially progressive arguments became less important when Catholics joined the abolitionist movement. Especially with the emergence of the anti-white slavery campaign, the abolitionists invested most of their energy in fighting immorality, rather than in trying to do something about poverty, which according to most observers was the real cause of prostitution. Those in favour of regulation normally preferred to use the prestige and apparent objectivity of science to counter the arguments forwarded by the abolitionists about the offence against the rights and liberties of prostitutes, and of women more generally.

The discourse about VD was inspired by the desire to protect national health, but its social and political meaning goes beyond this practical issue, and is connected with the tendency to describe the functioning of society in terms of human biology. Building on this metaphor, Luigi Luciani emphasized in his inaugural lecture at the University of Siena in 1880 that there was a close parallel between physiology and the social sciences. In this organic view of society, any action disrupting the established order resembled a disease threatening the healthy body of society.[22] Critics of contemporary society would likewise compare modern vices to syphilis, and complain that this disease gained victims above all among young people, who were more incautious and inexperienced.[23]

Similar interpretations of the similarities between the human body and human society convinced numerous members of the medical profession to become active in politics. Two medical doctors became head of the government in the years after unification (Luigi Carlo Farini and Giovanni Lanza), and many others contributed to political decisions as ministers or members of parliament.[24] The aspiration of medical doctors to increase their social prestige, to inspire laws, and to educate and guide the nation was not accepted without debate. Especially among the clergy, many refused to believe that a proper and healthy code of behaviour could exist without religion.[25] To try and cure VD was useless if no attempt was made to eliminate the cause:

Who are the medical doctors? The priests of science. And who perverts young people by claiming that vice is necessary to maintain health? It's them. And then they cure syphilis with special attention.

If only a small part of the efforts made to heal syphilis would be put into the elimination of vice, today syphilis would no longer exist. Instead, all efforts aim not at extirpating vice, but at favouring it, by making its consequences innocuous.[26]

According to Father Gemelli, rector of the Catholic University of the Sacred Heart, the efforts to moralize young people by giving them information about VD achieved little success. The lectures about the danger of VD which the famous physiologist Pio Foà gave at the beginning of the century obtained the opposite effect. Students would walk out of the room, and persuade their friends to accompany them to a nearby brothel to 'examine whether the fruits of sexual life were indeed so bitter'.[27] Many years later, the author of a popular booklet about VD warned young men who made fun of the infections and considered them the beginning of their career as Latin lovers, that these were 'serious, long-lasting, painful, and tedious' diseases.[28]

Fear of VD was thus seldom sufficient to convince young men to adopt a more austere life-style, and there is some evidence that VD was considered part of a certain view of masculinity. Convinced that a sex outlet was necessary, fathers would accompany their sons to brothels, teaching them that if they wanted to be real men, they had to accept the risk of VD.[29] The early-twentieth-century artists of the futurist movement, as always keen on provocation, subscribed to this attitude:

Gonorrhoea – I can't deny it – is annoying, it hurts and it's slightly embarrassing, yet – due to the funny mechanisms of morality – it is also what makes a man really a man [...] To be forced to treat our most delicate parts roughly, to clean yourself like a rusty rifle, the frankness of touching yourself like a surgeon, all this gives a new *aplomb* to a man, and eliminates for ever the down of boyhood.[30]

It is likely that this attitude, which contrasted sharply with the terror which syphilis especially had inspired in the past, was at least in part influenced by a new optimism about the efficiency of medical treatment after Schaudin's discovery, in 1905, of the role of *Treponema pallidum*, and even more so after Ehrlich's subsequent discovery of a more efficient cure of syphilis with Salvarsan 606, which was soon produced by three major pharmaceutical firms in Italy. The new medicine permitted a rapid recovery from primary and secondary lesions, but had no effect on tertiary meningoencephalitic lesions. During the Great War, Julius Werner Jauregg's experiments enabled more successful medical treatment in these cases also.[31]

The Great War and its consequences – the mobilization of women for work in industry and their escape from family control, the concentration of large masses of young men in Northern Italy, the rapid increase in wealth, and the crisis of traditional morality – contributed to a rapid increase in the number of cases of VD.[32] Initially, the problem did not attract much attention and no special measures of prevention were taken. The situation changed, however, when it became evident that diseases could undermine the morale of the troops and make them less fit for warfare. In May 1916, the Ministry of the Interior issued new rules regarding prostitution which implied a return to mandatory medical inspection, and prescribed isolation and compulsory treatment for prostitutes with VD. In order to protect the health of soldiers, Ferdinando De Napoli urged military doctors to be as rigorous as possible while inspecting prostitutes. Moreover, he proposed to subject soldiers to medical and hygienic treatment immediately before and after visits to brothels.[33] The more perspicacious observers, however, realized that regulations could do little to stop the important social and economic changes in society which were at the basis of the problem. Moreover, they admitted that regulation affected only a minority of prostitutes anyway, because, especially in the big cities, many women refused to apply for police registration and worked as clandestine prostitutes.

The creation of brothels for soldiers provoked the protests of moralists according to whom the measures favoured vice, and spread prostitution and VD to villages where hitherto they had been unknown. Rodolfo Bettazzi, president of the Italian League for Public Decency, complained that the increase of VD could not be stopped by handing out 'booklets exclusively about hygiene (disgustingly cold and materialistic), full of advice about how to avoid disease while having contacts with mercenary women'.[34]

In the years following the Great War, the movement in favour of sexual liberation became more important in Italy. An alternative view of prostitution emerged, no longer inspired by moral condemnation or by health considerations, but supposedly more rational. The futurist writer, Italo Tavolato, published a eulogy in praise of prostitution. Prostitutes, he said, rather than being victims, gave free rein to their natural instincts, and nothing – religion, morality or higher wages – would convince them to change.[35] According to Gustavo Punzo the condemnation of prostitution made sense only in the framework of a more general condemnation of sexuality. Recognizing that sexual relations were important for physical and mental health, one could only say that, from a theoretical point of view, the activities of prostitutes were necessary, healthy and moral. What made prostitution in reality immoral was not sex, but its commercial exploitation in closed houses with bad hygienic conditions, contagious diseases, and the obligation of women to accept any number of clients. Although Punzo claimed to be a feminist, his defence of female sexual liberation seems to have been inspired above all by the desire to find willing partners for the growing number of single, sexually active men.[36]

The Italian 'roaring twenties' ended in 1922 with the rise to power of the fascists, who inaugurated policies aiming at a general return to order and to the traditional gender hierarchy in the family. The role of the male breadwinner as head of the family was reinforced, and efforts were made to limit the role of women to that of wives, mothers and housekeepers. Female emancipation was condemned as the 'extension to women of a materialistic and hedonistic mentality'.[37] In this context of a return to law and order, the legislation regarding prostitution also became more rigorous: the availability of more effective medical treatment in fact did not change the repressive attitude of public authorities with regard to prostitution. New legislation regarding 'the prophylaxis of venereal diseases and syphilis' was introduced by Mussolini in 1923. The so-called Mussolini Regulation, which according to Furio Travagli represented 'one of the first measures of a sound moral and demographic fascist policy',[38] expressed an authoritarian approach to the problem of VD. Prostitutes were not formally obliged to accept medical checks, but if they refused they would be considered infected, and be obliged to undergo medical treatment. Later legislation reintroduced compulsory examinations.[39] Prostitutes who continued to work after having received a certificate testifying the presence of infectious disease could be forcibly removed to a venereal clinic. Article 4 of the Mussolini Regulation called for the creation of special clinics for the prophylaxis and free treatment of VD. Gender discrimination continued to exist as hospitalization was reserved for women, whereas men would be cured preferably through out-patient treatment.

The abolitionist movement almost disappeared during the era of fascism, and a more prosaic approach to the problems of prostitution became common. Contacts with prostitutes were considered normal for young men, but efforts were made to avoid these contacts leading to contagion with VD, above all because this could have a negative influence on the fertility rate. Popular publications instructed males how to avoid contagion during visits to brothels. One suggested inspecting the prostitute carefully, applying vaseline or, even better, using a condom, and, after the sexual act, washing carefully, urinating and applying special ointments, like the one developed by Metchnikoff.[40] Proposals modelled on the distribution of quinine in areas infested with malaria were made for the free distribution of the Metchnikoff ointment. Another booklet, published on behalf of the city council of Genoa, recommended sexual continence as the best way to avoid VD. Should this be impossible, then the advice was to make sexual contact as brief as possible.[41]

The activities of Italian venereologists, who in 1923 joined an International Union against Venereal Disease founded in France in December 1922 and presided over by Professor Bayet, obtained the support of Benito Mussolini. The leader of the Italian government gave legal recognition to the Italian Institute of Hygiene, Social Security and Assistance, and expressed to its president Ettore Levi his confidence that hygienic education could be the right antidote to the diffusion of VD.[42]

Under fascism, medical practitioners were able to exploit the social prestige enjoyed by science since the nineteenth century to dictate solutions to problems which went well beyond their professional competence. According to Pietro Babina, Freud's 'pan-sexual' vision of a society saturated with sexuality had become reality as a result of erotic literature, movies, theatre, advertising, etc. Environmental conditions in the big cities were conducive to the untimely arousal of unhealthy sexual instincts in young people.[43] Giovanni Franceschini also compared the 'fever of the senses' dominating the life of urban dwellers negatively with the 'innocence of the fields'.[44] In these cases, medical doctors used the fear of a wider diffusion of VD, presented as a logical outcome of the moral conditions of the cities, to legitimate the fascist opposition against geographical mobility, and to sustain the fight against urbanization.[45]

In his handbook of social medicine, Travagli elaborated a general plan to defeat VD characterized by a complete disregard of privacy and personal freedom, and invoking a combination of moral, police and sanitary control. Like his colleagues, Travagli's point of departure was the idea that the struggle against VD should be part of a campaign of moralization, including a return to the sober life-style and traditional values of country life, and opposition to neo-Malthusianism.[46] More concretely he proposed a rigorous application of the laws regarding the obligation on medical doctors to notify syphilis, free treatment for men in venereal hospitals, the institution of a prenuptial certificate, and the creation of a personal document certifying sanitary conditions. An intention to promote the professional interests of venereologists probably inspired his request to oblige all students of medicine to take courses in dermosyphilopathy, and was certainly also behind the proposal to prohibit all publicity for cures of VD which had not been approved by medical science.

In fact, the exclusive competence of medical science to treat VD was not recognized by all. The nineteenth-century Sicilian anthropologist Giovanni Pitré reported the popular belief that it was possible to heal gonorrhoea by deflowering a virgin. This belief, also found in other parts of Europe, was not limited to backward Sicily. In Northern Italy, men with syphilis would rape small boys or girls convinced that transmitting the disease would bring about cure.[47] Even in the 1960s this idea, often leading to the sexual abuse of minors, had not disappeared.[48]

The availability of new, more efficient, cures in the years immediately after the Second World War created a more optimistic view about the possibility of rooting out VD, which remained a major problem only in certain areas, like Naples, where clandestine prostitution had increased enormously, and hygienic conditions were awful. It now seemed possible to eliminate the problem once and for all if only the right measures could be taken: that is, sexual and hygienic education, easy access to medical treatment, and, possibly, compulsory premarital medical examinations including the Wassermann Test.[49] Vincenzo Pezzeri proposed to authorize medical doctors working for insurance companies to apply the test to all those who depended on the companies' out-patient departments for medical assistance.[50]

Optimism about the decline of VD, and a growing awareness of women's rights, were some of the reasons behind the renewed opposition to the fascist legislation on regulated prostitution, which had survived fascism itself. In 1948, Lina Merlin (1887–1979), a socialist member of parliament, proposed a bill for the abolition of closed houses. Anticipating the approval of the bill, as from 1948 the Ministry of the Interior no longer issued authorizations for the opening of brothels. During the following decade the number of brothels diminished from 717 to 543. Merlin's bill, however, was not approved until 1958, because it met with the opposition of brothel-keepers, who organized themselves into the *Associazione Gerenti Autorizzati*. The Association financed campaigns in the newspapers against the 'Salvation Army mentality' of Lina Merlin, and accused her of disregarding male privileges. Protests were expressed also by the national association of venereologists, who argued that the abolition of mandatory medical checks on prostitutes would lead to a rapid increase of syphilis and other venereal diseases. During their Fifth National Congress the venereologists criticized in particular the fact that Merlin not only wanted to abolish brothel prostitution, but also wanted to do away with compulsory medical examinations and treatment.[51] In addition, they argued that the abolition of regulated prostitution, if it ever took place, should be gradual, and be prepared for by a lengthy period of education of the masses. Traditional arguments about the male need for a sexual outlet were probably behind the warning that the abolition of brothels would lead to an increase of sexual crimes. The conclusion of venereologist Italo Levi-Luxardo was clear:

> Personal freedom, ethical and social reasons, morality and philosophy, those are all nice words, but they cannot and should not prevail over more concrete considerations of enormous social importance like those connected with the prophylaxis of venereal diseases.[52]

The group of abolitionists was internally divided because for most Catholic moralists abolition was part of a more complex effort towards moralization, including measures against premarital sex, adultery and contraception.[53] By forcing men to adopt the same high moral standards as they imposed upon women, these Catholics wanted to reconstruct the moral grounds of male superiority. These ideas were in clear contrast with the views of Lina Merlin, who saw the abolition of regulated prostitution as part of an attempt to eliminate social wrongs and to redress the inequalities between the sexes and the social classes. Merlin herself, nevertheless, shared some of the more moralistic views of the leftist tradition: she cited with admiration Lenin's words about the need for self-discipline, and expressed the hope that sport and country life would be able to keep young people away from the vices of the city.

The main cause of the delay in the abolition of regulated prostitution, however, was neither the opposition of brothel-keepers, nor the internal divisions of the abolitionists, but the silent opposition of the overwhelmingly male members of parliament, who simply refused to put the issue on the agenda.

Even after the abolition of closed houses, many authors continued to look back at the times of brothel prostitution with a nostalgic attitude, and shared the feelings expressed by one of Italy's most well-known journalists, a few years before the approval of the new legislation. According to Indro Montanelli, closed houses were necessary as a sexual outlet for young men, who, through contacts with prostitutes, could learn how to make love without preoccupations and unnecessary timidity.[54] Not a few women shared these ideas, and were convinced that occasional visits to brothels were less dangerous for the stability of their family, than a more serious extramarital affair.[55]

This tolerant attitude explains why, until the 1960s, many men were introduced to heterosexuality through contacts with prostitutes: 25 per cent of the men born in the years 1913–32 had their first complete sexual relations with prostitutes. Moreover, the percentage was still 21 for the generation born between 1933 and 1942, which reached adulthood when the debate about organized prostitution was raging in parliament and in the press. Twenty years later the percentage had diminished to 13.[56]

Opposing the idea that contacts with prostitutes were a form of sexual education, Lina Merlin saw male sexual initiation in brothels as the main cause of the incapacity of many husbands to recognize the sexual needs of their wives. She refused to accept the argument that the abolition of regulated prostitution would lead to an increase of VD. Above all, she argued, it was unjust that only the prostitutes were held responsible, whereas the sexual act implied the participation of at least two persons. If mandatory medical checks were supposed to be useful, why not extend them to males? After all, in many cases husbands transmitted VD to their wives.

In a speech to the Senate on 12 October 1949,[57] Lina Merlin cited statistics attesting that in 23 (sic) per cent of cases of VD, visits to a brothel were the cause of contamination, while prostitution outside closed houses counted for a further 37.2 per cent. Extramarital sexual relations explained 12.4 per cent of cases, whereas in 2.3 per cent of cases the source of contagion was the marriage partner. Hereditary syphilis counted for 2.8 per cent. Finally, in 21.7 per cent of the cases of VD the reasons for contagion were unknown. According to Merlin, the high incidence of VD, rather than indicating the need for regulated prostitution, proved that the system had no preventive value, and only served to give prostitutes and their clients a false impression of security. With prostitutes serving up to one hundred clients per day, medical checks could hardly be expected to be an efficient safeguard against infection.

Merlin was aware of the impossibility of eliminating prostitution altogether, and her project aimed above all at abolishing the role of the state in the organization of prostitution, and at restoring the civil rights of prostitutes. As for the struggle against VD, she proposed to increase the funds for free and confidential medical treatment, and to try and change the mentality which saw VD as 'shameful'. If they could only be convinced that VD was not different from other social diseases, patients would voluntarily accept medical assistance.

Merlin's bill, which was finally approved in 1958 with 385 votes in favour and 158 votes against (from the right), aimed at the emancipation of prostitutes rather than at the elimination of prostitution, and therefore punished only persons involved in procuring and in the exploitation of prostitution. Those who organized prostitution now ran the major legal risks, while the prostitutes themselves had not much to fear as long as they did not offend decency or public order. Contrary to her expectations, only a small minority of prostitutes profited from the passing of the Merlin bill to abandon prostitution, and most prostitutes turned to street-walking. Illegal brothels employed only prostitutes who could guarantee a high income, and who did not represent special risks because they were minors or drug addicts.

The approval of the bill proposed by Lina Merlin should be understood in the context of a decline of the incidence of VD made possible by the availability of penicillin. Notwithstanding the success of the new therapy, only a few months after the irrevocable end of regulation the National Association of the Inspectors of Dermosyphilopathy proclaimed a rapid increase in VD, and two years later the Minister of Health declared that the incidence of syphilis had doubled since the abolition of closed houses, and had tripled since the pre-war years. According to Lorenzo Cioglia, the availability of more efficient therapies would not be sufficient to stop this increase which was connected with important changes in society, such as greater social and geographical mobility, and more frequent contacts between young men and women.[58]

Even Catholic moralists like Piero Pajardi used the need to protect public health as an excuse to ask for a partial reintroduction of the registration of prostitutes. He suggested that respect for the independence and personal rights of the prostitute should now be combined with mandatory medical checks in order to protect both the women themselves and their clients.[59] Similar ideas were voiced in parliament, where already in 1959 proposals were put forward to punish the exploitation of prostitution more severely, and to reintroduce compulsory medical checks for women working as prostitutes. Attempts were also made to make prostitution as such more difficult, for instance by making the rules against soliciting more severe.

The official statistics regarding VD do not seem to justify these requests. Psychoanalyst, Cesare L. Musatti, was therefore probably right in writing that the abolition of organized prostitution worried most male opponents not because of a possible increase in cases of VD, but because it touched some of the more profound aspects of the male gender identity.[60] Giovanni Comisso expressed the opposite fear that moralists were trying to use the statistics about VD in order to repress all expressions of sexuality, except relations between married people aiming at procreation.[61]

While for almost a hundred years the regulation of prostitution by mandatory medical examinations of prostitutes had been considered the most important weapon against the diffusion of VD, there had been other measures as well. In

1870, the obligation to notify health authorities of infectious diseases was introduced together with more specific laws regarding VD. In 1888, the clinics for the mandatory treatment of infected prostitutes were reorganized and transformed into specialized clinics for the free treatment of contagious venereal diseases. New legislation, approved in 1901, defined syphilis, gonorrhoea and chancroid as 'venereal diseases'. Legal courts would now accept that the infection of a woman by her syphilitic husband was a valid ground for separation.[62]

Under fascism a new crime was introduced with the 1930 penal code. Article 554 punished persons who knowingly transmitted syphilis or gonorrhoea with imprisonment from one to three years. It is likely that the law was meant to be applied above all against prostitutes and not against their clients. Husbands who infected their wives probably did not run many risks because prosecution took place only in cases when a complaint was filed. Venereologists were aware that the law would not be very effective, but they nevertheless appreciated its intimidating tone.[63] However, the connection which was constantly made between VD and immorality, and the confusion between the moral and the sanitary aspects of the problem, continued to pose major problems for an efficient programme of health care. Fascism confirmed its authoritarian intentions when proposals were forwarded to oblige medical doctors to notify all cases of VD, to oblige the patients to subject themselves to medical treatment, and to prohibit marriage until complete recovery.[64] A similar approach, which branded all those who had VD as vicious, and labelled VD itself as 'secret' and 'shameful', could only have a negative influence on the patients' willingness to seek medical assistance. The punitive attitude towards patients with VD was also evident in the attitude of mutual aid organizations providing health insurance, which in cases of VD refused to pay for medical treatment, or paid only part of it.[65] Only a few authors tried to counter this tendency by stating that VD was the result of contagion, and had no necessary link with vices of any kind.[66]

While reaffirming the principle of free treatment, Law 837 of 1956 and successive laws updated existing legislation and established a list of four diseases (syphilis, gonorrhoea, chancroid and lymphogranuloma venereum) for which there was an obligation to notify sanitary authorities. Similar obligations existed in cases of abortion and sterilization. The 1956 law tried to anticipate the abolition of regulated prostitution by introducing the obligation for all those suffering from VD (men and women) to obtain a cure, and offering, if necessary, free treatment. It failed, however, in its objectives, because medical doctors refused to divulge information about their clients, and because there were no sanctions for those who refused medical treatment, since the medical doctors responsible for the health system at the level of the province could order medical treatment, but had no means of enforcing it.[67] The 1956 law, which is still valid today, like all other official documents, refers to 'venereal diseases'; the broader term of sexually transmitted diseases (STDs) has not yet found full acceptance in Italy.

In 1972, responsibility for the diagnosis and treatment of VD was transferred to regional governments. The result was a growing differentiation in the treatment and operational conditions of various VD centres, with important differ-ences both between and within regions. Today, the precise incidence of VD is unknown not only because the legal obligation to report relates to only a few of the sexually transmitted diseases, but also because medical specialists tend to disregard this obligation. The Higher Institute for Health (*Istituto Superiore della Sanità – ISS*) has estimated that, if all cases were reported, the figures would be at least 100–150 per cent higher. In an attempt to improve data collection, in September 1991, a national VD surveillance agency was created which receives information from about 48 VD clinics. Its aim is not to register the total number of cases, but rather to monitor developments and to gather the data necessary for a better assessment of VD.[68]

The obligation to notify cases of VD was never fully respected, especially in the case of clients paying for medical treatment. Another method of prophylaxis, premarital medical examinations, never became a legal obligation, nor did it ever enter social custom. Already, in 1919, Ferdinando De Napoli had proposed making a medical check-up mandatory for men who intended to get married, and had pointed out that for 80 per cent of married women with VD, their husband was the source of contagion.[69] Especially in the fascist period, when the incidence of syphilis was estimated at 1.2 per cent of the population, many medical doctors demanded the introduction of a mandatory premarital exami-nation. Brides, so they said, were tolerant about the premarital sexual experiences of their future husbands, but they wanted to be certain that their spouse would not transmit VD to them. Premarital medical examination could eliminate this risk.[70] The fascist regime was expected to set aside considerations of individual liberty:

> According to fascist doctrine freedom is an outdated idea: we are nothing, the Nation is everything. The supreme interest of this 'Right of the Nation' towers over individual interests, and eliminates them if they damage the community, and especially if they are a threat to the race, undermining its physical and moral strength.[71]

The proposal, however, failed to convince Mussolini, who objected that limits to the freedom of marriage could have negative results for the fascist family policies aiming at a rapid increase of the population.[72]

The idea of using compulsory premarital medical visits as a check on the diffusion of VD re-emerged once more during the discussion over the abolition of regulated prostitution. The attitude of the Catholic Church was one of the main obstacles to the introduction of the obligation to produce a medical certifi-cate before getting married. The Fourth Congress of Catholic Medical Doctors, which took place in Rome in 1949, pronounced itself against any form of state intervention limiting the individual freedom to decide about marriage. No form of obligation was accepted, but young people were encouraged to have a medical check before getting married. Whatever the outcome of that visit, it should not limit individual rights.[73]

Such opinions were extremely important given the fact that Roman Catholicism was the state religion in Italy until 1984, a position which granted the church a great influence on all decisions regarding marriage, family and sexuality. It comes therefore as no surprise that, when in 1952 the Commission of Hygiene and Health of the Italian Senate approved a proposal to introduce the obligation of a medical examination for intending spouses, it followed the guidelines set out at the 1949 congress. The proposal specified that the result of the examination should not restrict the freedom of marriage. Moreover, in order to protect privacy, the certificate would only attest to the examination and not contain any medical information.[74] Not even this moderate proposal ever obtained legal status.

A century of organized prostitution left clear traces in Italian gender relations and continued to influence attitudes towards sexuality even after the abolition of closed houses. For a long time the use of condoms continued to be identified with prostitution. The legislation prohibiting the sale and use of contraceptives introduced by the fascists in the 1930s had not affected the production of condoms because they were deemed necessary as a protection against VD. The Hatù factory, which had been built in 1922, could therefore continue to produce condoms, but was obliged to focus on their use as a protection against VD, as the product name underlined (*Ha*bemus *Tu*torem). During the fascist period the Italian army would put this 'small object which could serve for protection when off duty' at the disposal of conscript soldiers.[75] The result of this identification of the use of condoms with prostitution, however, was that 'honest' women would often consider the use of condoms offensive.[76]

This explains in part the increase in the number of illegitimate births during fascism, when dire economic conditions made the creation of new households difficult. Moreover, as some observers have noticed, it is likely that difficult access to contraception, combined with the desire to avoid pregnancy and VD, convinced many young people to prefer sexual contacts which excluded penetration.[77] It should be remembered, however, that 'petting' had a bad reputation because it contrasted with the myths surrounding virility. Moreover, most sexologists condemned 'petting', because they feared that this practice would replace 'normal' sexual relations. Furthermore, 'petting' was deplored because it expressed a 'utilitarian' approach to sexuality, aiming at 'maximizing profits and minimizing risks'.[78]

Even after the fall of fascism, many continued to identify the use of condoms with immorality,[79] and notwithstanding repeated attempts by lay and leftist parties in parliament to abolish the fascist law against propaganda in favour of birth control, the prohibition remained in force until 1971. Only then did the Constitutional Court rule that the legislation, based on the fascist principle according to which 'the number means power', conflicted with the principles laid down in the Constitution. The verdict acknowledged that the defence of public decency could not justify the existence of a specific law regarding birth control, and rewarded the efforts of organizations such as the AIED (Italian Association for Demographic Education), founded in 1956 with the aims of defending the principles and practice of a voluntary and conscious limitation of the number of children.[80]

One of the consequences of the prohibition on public discussion of the various methods of birth control was the low level of information about sexuality and birth control which still characterized Italy in the 1970s.[81] A more long-term consequence was the widespread negative attitude about the use of condoms which persists today notwithstanding the necessity of promoting safe sex practices. Paradoxically, many Catholics find the use of condoms as a protection against sexually transmitted diseases unacceptable because of their potential use for contraception. In 1993, an anti-AIDS campaign in high schools was blocked because it endorsed the use of condoms, and in 1997 the installation of condom dispensers in high schools in Turin and Milan caused a major outcry in the conservative press. According to the Association of Catholic Parents, installing a condom dispenser in secondary schools would encourage forms of behaviour which were dangerous. Medical studies, it was added, had shown that the use of condoms offered no real protection against the risk of AIDS. Chastity was the only solution. More recently, private and public television networks have agreed not to broadcast publicity for condoms during prime time.

The generally negative attitude towards condoms is reflected also in the sexual behaviour of young Italians, who now seem to be well aware of the health risks connected with unprotected sexual relations, but nevertheless often refuse to use condoms for safe sex purposes. The main reasons for this refusal are the impression that use of condoms can diminish sexual pleasure, the idea that buying condoms publicizes private and intimate affairs, and the feeling that the use of a condom will ruin the romantic atmosphere especially with new partners. In addition, the idea that VD is transmitted almost exclusively by prostitutes is still widespread.[82]

The abolition of regulated prostitution in 1958 signalled a period of crisis for the medical profession. Not only did venereologists lose jobs in the public administration, but, more seriously, the social role of medical science itself was challenged. During the 1970s, the gay movement, the feminist movement, and the movement in favour of sexual liberation all contested the exclusive right of the medical profession to approve or condemn sexual behaviours. More generally, feminists criticized the male characteristics of medical science, and called for a rediscovery of female medicine.[83]

The conflict between the gay movement and the medical profession was particularly violent. Homosexuality had been 'rediscovered' in the 1960s, when venereologists warned that the diffusion of syphilis among homosexuals could become a serious concern.[84] Trustworthy statistics about a presumed increase of the number of homosexuals and about the supposedly recent diffusion of homosexuality among the working classes were lacking, but observers felt nevertheless sure that 'these are, in any case, extremely serious developments, not only because homosexuality denies the biological fundamentals and moral principles of sexuality, but also because of the dangerous consequences of this malpractice for the diffusion of venereal diseases'.[85] In the light of these observations it is surprising that, even as late as the early 1970s, venereologists reported popular beliefs according to which VD could not be transmitted through homosexual relations.[86]

Homosexuality soon occupied an important place in medical debate. During a conference on 'homosexual pathology' which took place in Rome in May 1963, Giacomo Santori claimed that homosexuals were 'abnormal' because their sexual choice contrasted with the 'anatomic, physiological, instinctive, rational and social integration between male and female' characterizing 'normal' human sexuality. For this reason homosexuality could not be considered a simple variation of normal human behaviour, however high its incidence might be, and the treatment of homosexuality was to be considered one of the responsibilities of medical science.[87]

Paul Chauchard phrased his opinion about homosexuality in terms which derived directly from the phraseology of the venereologists: 'Inversion is contagious and can attack normal persons. The serious problem of the commercial exploitation of the needs of homosexuals makes it necessary to introduce legal measures against inversion.'[88] It is important to note that these theories could easily be interpreted as support for the attempts by politicians, such as the Social Democratic member of Parliament Bruno Romano, to introduce legislation against homosexuals, on the grounds that they could 'contaminate' young people.

In the early 1980s, the suspicion that AIDS had been 'invented' by medical science to stop the growing social acceptance of homosexuality made the gay movement hesitant to undertake action. Soon, however, the movement launched 'safe sex' information campaigns which greatly contributed to reducing risks. Notwithstanding this success, moralists and religious groups continued to oppose campaigns against AIDS which tried to safeguard the right to sexual pleasure.

In more general terms, as already mentioned, the long debate about prostitution and VD set the tone for the discussion about sexuality. Both the threat of VD and that of unwanted pregnancy were used to convince single women of the necessity of defending their virginity, an important form of symbolic capital in traditional Italian society.[89] The risks of VD and the concepts of contagion and disease were also used to denounce the dangers of mixing social classes, for instance in dance-halls.[90]

After the war, the experience of other countries, where a wider diffusion of condoms had offset, at least in part, the possible risks of more liberal sexual mores, was ignored in favour of an interpretation of sexuality characterized by a double standard which placed the responsibility for upholding morality almost exclusively on women, and offered men the alternative of a visit to brothels.[91] Thus, in the absence of adequate protection, the threat of contagion with VD may well have contributed to delaying changes in public morality and gender relations.

NOTES

1 I. Bloch, *La vita sessuale dei nostri tempi nei suoi rapporti con la civiltà moderna*, Torino, STEN, 1921 (1910), pp. 242–3. See also A. Cherubini, 'Sifilide e prostituzione', in A. Cherubini and F. Vannozzi, *Previdenza di malattia e malattie sociali dall'Unità alla Prima Guerra Mondiale*, Roma, Istituto italiano di medicina sociale, 1990, p. 180. Cf. about the conditions of wetnursing D. I. Kertzer, 'Syphilis, foundlings, and wetnurses in nineteenth-century Italy', *Journal of Social History*, 1999, vol. 32, n. 3, pp. 589–602.

2 'De la prostitution dans la ville de Turin', in A. J.-B. Parent-Duchâtelet, *De la prostitution dans la ville de Paris considerée sous le rapport de l'hygiène publique, de la morale et de l'administration*, Paris, J.-B. Baillière et fils, 1857 (Troisième édition complétée par des documents nouveaux et des notes), vol. II, pp. 872–87.

3 F. Jacquot, 'De la prostitution dans la ville de Rome', in Parent-Duchâtelet, *De la prostitution dans la ville de Paris*, pp. 848–71.

4 A. Cutrera, *Storia della prostituzione in Sicilia. Monografia storico-giuridica*, Palermo, ESA, 1971 (1901); G. Fiume, 'Le patenti di infamia. Morale sessuale e igiene sociale nella Sicilia dell'Ottocento', *Memoria. Rivista di storia delle donne*, 1986, n. 2, pp. 71–89.

5 Rossana (pseud. of Z. Centa Tartarini), *Sotto la ferula. Dolore, povertà, degenerazione muliebre*, Torino, Bocca, 1911. See Cherubini, 'Sifilide', pp. 180–1.

6 S. J. Woolf, 'The poor and how to relieve them: the Restoration debate on poverty in Italy and Europe', in J. Davis and P. Ginsborg (eds) *Society and Politics in the Age of the Risorgimento. Essays in Honour of Denis Mack Smith*, Cambridge, Cambridge University Press, 1991, pp. 49–69. On asylums see A. Groppi, *I conservatori della virtù. Donne recluse nella Roma dei papi*, Roma-Bari, Laterza, 1994; L. Guidi, *L'onore in pericolo. Carità e reclusione femminile nell'Ottocento napoletano*, Napoli, Liguori, 1991.

7 A. Segre, 'La corruzione di minorenne (art. 335 Cod. Pen.)', in *Scritti giuridici dedicati ed offerti a G.P. Chironi nel XXXIII anno del suo insegnamento*, Torino, Bocca, 1915, vol. II, pp. 159–82; A. Buttafuoco, *Le Mariuccine. Storia di un'istituzione laica: l'Asilo Mariuccia*, Milano, Franco Angeli, 1985, pp. 173–5.

8 M. Palazzi, 'Le molte migrazioni delle donne. Cambiamenti di stato civile e partenze per lavoro in Italia fra Otto e Novecento', in D. Corsi (ed.) *Altrove. Viaggi di donne dall'antichità al Novecento*, Roma, Viella, 1999, pp. 79–109; M. Palazzi, *Donne sole. Storia dell'altra faccia dell'Italia tra antico regime e società contemporanea*, Milano, Bruno Mondadori, 1997.

9 M. Gibson, *Prostitution and the State in Italy 1860–1915*, New Brunswick/London, Rutgers University Press, 1986, pp. 99–100. On marriage strategies in Rome see M. Pelaja, *Matrimonio e sessualità a Rome nell'Ottocento*, Roma-Bari, Laterza, 1994.

10 For a general discussion of chastity see S. Fajrajzen, *L'astinenza sessuale. Dal punto di vista clinico, psicologico, fisiologico, etico e morale*, Torino, Bocca, 1952.

11 C. Lombroso and G. Ferrero, *La donna delinquente, la prostituta e la donna normale*, Torino, Bocca, 1923 (1893), pp. 365–75; M. Gibson, 'The female offender and the Italian school of criminal anthropology', *Journal of European Studies. Literature and Ideas from the Renaissance to the Present*, 1982, pp. 155–65, and '"On the insensitivity of women". Science and the woman question in Liberal Italy, 1890–1910', *Journal of Modern Italy*, 1990, vol. 2, n. 2, pp. 12–41; R. Villa, *Il deviante e i suoi segni. Lombroso e la nascita dell'antropologia criminale*, Milano, Franco Angeli, 1985; B. Wanrooij, '"La carne vedova". Immagini della sessualità femminile', *Belfagor*, 1987, vol. 42, n. 4, pp. 454–66.

12 M. Gibson, 'Biology or environment? Race and Southern "deviancy" in the writings of Italian criminologists, 1880–1920', in J. Schneider (ed.) *Italy's 'Southern Question'. Orientalism in One Country*, Oxford/New York, Berg, 1998, pp. 99–116.

13 A. Zerboglio, 'Sulla prostituzione', *L'anomalo*, 1891, vol. 3, n. 2, pp. 38–46. According to Primo Ferrari, author of a popular publication about VD, the opponents of regulation suffered from sentimentalism, and failed to understand that regulation was the

155

only way to limit contagion and protect morality. See P. Ferrari, *Prostituzione e sifilide*, Milano, Vallardi, 1891.

14 G. Gattei, 'Controllo di classi pericolose. La prima regolamentazione prostituzionale unitaria (1860–1888)', in M. L. Betri and A. Gigli Marchetti (eds) *Salute e classi lavoratrici in Italia*, Milano, Franco Angeli, 1982, pp. 763–5; Gibson, *Prostitution and the State*, pp. 176–7.

15 For the application of the Cavour Regulation see M. Gibson, 'Medici e poliziotti. Il regolamento Cavour', *Memoria. Rivista di storia delle donne*, 1986, n. 2, pp. 90–100.

16 R. Michels, *La morale sessuale*, Milano, Bocca, 1949 (1912), pp. 112–13.

17 E. G. B., *La prostituta*, Vicenza, Gio. Battista Eugerio, 1890.

18 M. Schwegman, *Feminisme als boetedoening. Biografie van de Italiaanse schrijfster en feministe Gualberta Alaide Beccari (1842–1906)*, 's-Gravenhage, Nijgh & van Ditmar Universitair, 1989, pp. 163–4. For a portrait of Josephine Butler, see the ironic notes in the posthumously published novel of the journalist, lawyer and politician, Giovanni Faldella, *Donna Folgore*, Milano, Adelphi, 1974, pp. 218–19. The novel was written in 1906–9.

19 E. Nathan, *Le diobolarie e lo Stato. Quadro di costumi regolamentati*, Roma, Forzani, 1887, p. 42; C. Antonini and M. Buscarini, 'La regolamentazione della prostituzione nell'Italia postunitaria', *Rivista di storia contemporanea*, 1985, vol. 14, n. 1, pp. 83–114.

20 Cf. G. Tammeo, *La prostituzione. Saggio di statistica morale*, Torino, Roux, 1890, pp. 40–5; L. Fiaux, *La police des moeurs en France et dans les principaux pays de l'Europe*, Paris, E. Dentu, 1888, pp. 630–3. For a negative judgement about the measures introduced in 1888, see A. Costa, *I farabutti. Nuovo libro in difesa della morale*, Milano, Libr. M. d'Azeglio, 1891, pp. 10–15.

21 J. White Mario, 'All'opera tutti', *La coscienza pubblica*, 1882, vol. 1, ns 3–4, pp. 35–8. Jessie White was aware that, for the poor, prostitution was 'a job like any other, with nothing special about it; a job which even allowed women to be good mothers', J. White Mario, *La miseria a Napoli*, Firenze, Le Monnier, 1877, p. 48. See also Rina Macrelli, *L'indegna schiavitù. Anna Maria Mozzoni e la lotta contro la prostituzione di Stato*, Roma, Editori Riuniti, 1981.

22 L. Luciani, *La fisiologia e la scienza sociale. Discorso inaugurale per la riapertura della R. Università di Siena (nell'anno accademico 1880–1881)*, Siena, Tip. sordo-muti di L. Lazzeri, 1880.

23 G. Guggino, *Dell'impurità e dei mezzi per vincerla. Studi*, Torino, Marietti, 1908, pp. 7–8.

24 G. Cosmacini, *Storia della medicina e della sanità in Italia. Dalla peste europea alla guerra mondiale 1348–1918*, Roma-Bari, Laterza, 1987, pp. 394–5.

25 G. Arrò-Carroccio, *I giovani e le nuove condizioni d'Italia*, Firenze, M. Cellini, 1871, pp. 276–81.

26 M. Bernabei, *Educazione del sesso*, Milano, Albrighi & Segati, 1933, pp. 80–1.

27 A. Gemelli, *La tua vita sessuale. Lettera ad uno studente universitario*, Milano, Vita e pensiero, 1948, pp. 11–17; P. Foà, *Sull'igiene fisica e morale della gioventù*, Roma, Leonardo da Vinci, 1923.

28 R. Palmer, *L'inferno del sesso (malattie veneree: notizie storiche e cliniche)*, Bologna, Nettuno Omnia, 1966, p. 4.

29 E. Lombardo Pellegrino, *L'amore nel diritto*, Messina, Tip. dell'Epoca, 1893, pp. 27–8.

30 E. Settimelli, *Nuovo modo d'amare*, Rocca S. Casciano, Cappelli, 1918, pp. 92–3.

31 Giorgio Cosmacini, *Medicina e sanità in Italia nel ventesimo secolo. Dalla 'Spagnola' alla 2ª guerra mondiale*, Roma-Bari, Laterza, 1989, pp. 40–9.

32 V. Montesano, *La lotta contro le malattie veneree*, Roma, Leonardo Da Vinci, 1922, pp. 18–21.

33 F. De Napoli, *Guerra e problema sessuale*, Bologna, Tip. Gamberini e Parmeggiani, 1915, pp. 3–5; G. Casalini, *L'igiene dell'amore sessuale. Pagine dedicate agli uomini*, Roma, M. Carra e C. di L. Bellini 1921 (second completely revised edition), pp. 11–20.

34 R. Bettazzi, 'Per il bene del nostro esercito', *Vita nova*, 1917, vol. 7, ns 1–4, pp. 11–13; B. Wanrooij, *Storia del pudore. La questione sessuale in Italia 1860–1940*, Venezia, Marsilio, 1990, pp. 44–59.

35 I. Tavolato, 'Elogio della prostituzione', in *I processi al futurismo per oltraggio al pudore*, with a conclusion by B. Corra and E. Settimelli, Rocca S. Casciano, Cappelli, 1918, pp. 119–29.

36 G. Punzo, *Riabilitazione della donna. Valori sessuali*, Catanzaro, La Giovine Calabria, 1919, pp. 89–94. Similar ideas had been expressed twenty years earlier by Mario Morasso; see M. Morasso, *Uomini e idee del domani. L'egoarchia*, Torino, Bocca, 1898, pp. 287–8.

37 For a systematic programme for a complete return to a male-dominated order in family and gender relations, see F. E. Loffredo, *Politica della famiglia*, Milano, Bompiani, 1938. The book had the honour of a preface by the powerful Minister of Education, Giuseppe Bottai.

38 F. Travagli, 'Malattie sessuali', in C. Coruzzi and F. Travagli (eds) *Trattato di medicina sociale*, Milano, Wassermann, 1938, vol. 2, p. 460.

39 R.D. 18 giugno 1931, n. 733. *Approvazione del testo unico di pubblica sicurezza*, Art. 205.

40 *Le malattie sociali, l'alcoolismo, la sifilide, la tuberculosi*, Torino, Tip. A. Eusebio, 1928.

41 *Istruzioni popolari sulle malattie veneree*, Genova, Tip. filli Pagani, 1921.

42 'Dopo tre anni...verso la meta', *Difesa sociale*, 1923, vol. 2, n. 12, pp. 1–9.

43 P. Babina, *L'amore e il sesso*, Milano, Istituto di propaganda libraria, 1940, pp. 17–18.

44 G. Franceschini, *Vita sessuale. Fisiologia ed etica*, Milano, Hoepli, 1941 (1933), pp. 2–3, 94–5.

45 B. Mussolini, 'Sfollare le città', *Il Popolo d'Italia*, 22 Nov. 1928; B. Wanrooij, 'Mobilitazione, modernizzazione, tradizione', in G. Sabbatucci and V. Vidotto (eds) *Storia d'Italia*, vol. 4, *Guerre e fascismo*, Roma-Bari, Laterza, 1997, pp. 408–10.

46 Travagli, 'Malattie sessuali', pp. 493–4.

47 G. Pitré, *Medicina popolare siciliana*, Firenze, Barbèra, 1949, p.141. The same observations can be found in the reports of the parliamentary commission which in the 1880s investigated the conditions of agriculture; see A. Damiani, 'Relazione sulla I circoscrizione', in *Atti della Giunta per la inchiesta agraria*, vol. 13, n. 1, Roma, Forzani, 1884, p. 33; see also A. La Cara, *La base organica dei pervertimenti sessuali e la loro profilassi sociale*, Torino, Bocca, 1924 (1902), pp. 25–6; A. Dalla Volta, 'Superstizione e criminalità sessuale', *Rassegna di studi sessuali, demografia ed eugenica*, 1929, vol. 9, n. 4, pp. 157–66; Buttafuoco, *Le Mariuccine*, pp. 122–3.

48 A. Tozzi, *Frigidità, sterilità, impotenza*, Torino, MEB, 1964, pp. 14–15.

49 I. Levi-Luxardo, 'Le malattie veneree. Problema medico sociale', *Difesa sociale*, 1948–9, p. 17.

50 V. Pezzeri, 'L'assistenza diretta ambulatoriale nell'assicurazione malattie. Sua importanza medico-sociale', *Difesa sociale*, 1947–8, pp. 33–47.

51 'V Convegno nazionale dell'Associazione ispettori dermosifilografi', *Difesa sociale*, 1954, vol. 33, n. 1, pp. 207–9.

52 I. Levi-Luxardo, 'Relazione', in *La piaga sociale della prostituzione*, Roma, Istituto nazionale di medicina sociale, 1950, part 1, *Atti del 2° convegno della Società di medicina sociale per lo studio del problema della prostituzione. Roma, 22–23 aprile 1950*, p. 82.

53 L. Scremin, *La prostituzione e la morale*, Milano, Istituto di propaganda libraria, 1949, p. 21.

54 I. Montanelli, 'Addio Wanda' (1956), in Id., *I libelli*, Milano, Rizzoli, 1975, pp. 282–3; P. Bianchi, *Le signorine d'Avignone. Studi di costume sull'Italia di ieri*, Milano, Ferro, 1967; G. Vergani, *Giovanotti, in camera. Due secoli di marchette*, Milano, Baldini & Castoldi, 1995; C. Augias and M. Antonetto (eds) *Quelle signorine*, Milano, TEA, 1996 (1980).

55 A. Garofalo, *L'italiana in Italia*, Bari, Laterza, 1956, pp. 91–3.

56 M. Castiglioni and G. Dalla Zuanna, 'L'inizio delle relazioni sessuali', in M. Barbagli and C. Saraceno (eds) *Lo stato delle famiglie in Italia*, Bologna, Il Mulino, 1997, p. 77. The information gathered by Gabriella Parca, who interviewed 1,018 men in the early 1960s, seems to confirm this situation. For 20 per cent of the men, premarital sexual relations were limited to contacts with prostitutes, while 51 per cent admitted having had contacts both with prostitutes and other women; see G. Parca, *I sultani. Mentalità e comportamento del maschio italiano*, Milano, Rizzoli, 1965, pp. 61–71.

57 Now in L. Merlin, *La mia vita*, E. Marinucci, ed., Firenze, Giunti Barbèra, 1989, pp. 123–66. The 23 per cent of cases of VD attributed to visits to brothels should read 23.6 per cent.

58 L. Cioglia, 'Osservazioni e proposte in tema di profilassi antivenerea e di controllo della prostituzione', *Difesa sociale*, 1961, vol. 40, n. 1, pp. 15–53.

59 P. Pajardi, 'Perché diventa sempre più necessario rivedere la legge Merlin', *Avvenire*, 21 Aug. 1969.

60 C. L. Musatti, 'Prefazione', in H. Greenberg, *Le ragazze squillo*, Milano, Bompiani, 1959, pp. xiv–v.

61 G. Comisso, 'Carne da prigione', *Il Mondo*, 14 April 1959.

62 See the verdict of the Tribunale di Palermo of 8 October 1904 quoted in *Lo Stato civile Italiano*, 1905, vol. 5, n. 1, p. 15.

63 L. Maggiore, 'Per la difesa della stirpe. La politica sanitaria del regime', *Difesa sociale*, 1931, vol. 10, n. 9, p. 426.

64 F. Mariani, *Il volto dell'amore. Per la formazione morale della nuova gioventù d'Italia*, Siena, Combattenti, 1926.

65 A. Mieli, 'Sempre la lotta contro le malattie veneree e il regolamento dei tranvieri municipali romani', *Rassegna di studi sessuali*, 1921, vol. 1, n. 6, p. 331; C. Pogliano, 'Aldo Mieli, storico della scienza (1879–1950)', *Belfagor*, 1983, vol. 38, n. 5, pp. 537–57.

66 *L'amore senza freccia. Malattie sessuali, prevenzione e cura – La sterilità e sua guarigione – Neomalthusianismo, limitazione volontaria della prole – Libitogenia, arte di avere figli maschi e femmine a volontà – Eugenetica, arte di avere figli belli*, Milano, Ist. Hermes, s.a.

67 Gian Paolo Meucci in E. Polli and C. Bettinelli (eds) *Prostituzione e società*, Milano, AMCI – Sezione di Milano, 1976, pp. 76–81; F. Donato di Migliardo, *Della prostituzione. Osservazioni de iure condito e de iure condendo. Ricerca dei clienti per la strada. Esercizio del meretricio nella propria abitazione. Malattie veneree*, Torino, Quartara, 1961, pp. 21–3.

68 M. Giuliani and B. Suligoi, 'La sorveglianza in Italia delle malattie sessualmente trasmesse', in M. Dolivo *et al.*, *Malattie sessualmente trasmesse*, Milano-Parigi, Masson, 1994, pp. 245–55.

69 F. De Napoli, *La donna e l'abolizionismo. In tema di profilassi antivenerea e di politica sanitaria*, Milano, 1920.

70 G. Mariani, 'L'importanza sociale della profilassi e terapia nella sterilità da malattie intersessuali', in F. Bocchetti (ed.) *I problemi della maternità e dell'infanzia. Atti dei congressi scientifici*, vol. IX, *I doveri del medico nella politica demografica del regime fascista*, Roma, Fed. it. naz. fasc. contro la tuberculosi, 1941, pp. 117–51.

71 See Umberto Gabbi's remarks about Giuseppe Baffico, 'Della visita prematrimoniale', *Archivio fascista di medicina politica*, 1927, vol. 1, n. 3, pp. 151–5.

72 See P. Capasso, 'Il certificato prematrimoniale', *Rassegna di studi sessuali e di eugenica*, 1924, vol. 4, n. 3, pp. 176–85.

73 P. Castelli, *Il fidanzamento*, Milano, Istituto La Casa, 1956, pp. 333–4.

74 N. Santero, 'La medicina sociale profilattica di domani', *Difesa sociale*, 1953, vol. 32, n. 1, pp. 7–14.

75 F. Barberi, *Sotto le armi. Diario 1929–1930*, Roma, Cadmo, 1988, p. 37.

76 A. L. Berth, *Vita sessuale prematrimoniale*, Milano, De Vecchi, 1962, pp. 90–1.

77 N. Brunori, *Maschilità e femminilità nella condotta umana*, Firenze, Sansoni, 1952, pp. 201–2.

78 C. Risé, *Rapporto sul comportamento sessuale dei giovani in Italia*, Milano, Sugar, 1966, pp. 228–36.
79 H. A. Bowman, *Il matrimonio moderno*, Milano, Longanesi, 1951, pp. 498–9.
80 See V. Olivetti (ed.) *Il controllo delle nascite*, Milano/Roma, Avanti!, 1957; L. Caldwell, *Italian Family Matters. Women, Politics and Legal Reform*, London, Macmillan, 1991.
81 See M. Livi Bacci, *A History of Italian Fertility during the last Two Centuries*, Princeton, Princeton University Press, 1977.
82 C. Buzzi, *Giovani, affettività, sessualità. L'amore tra i giovani in una indagine IARD*, Bologna, Il Mulino, 1998, pp. 115–35.
83 C. Jourdan, *Insieme contro. Esperienze dei consultori femministi*, Milano, La Salamandra, 1976, pp. 9–10.
84 G. B. Contini and V. Musumeci, *Aspetti attuali del problema profilattico e terapeutico della sifilide*, Torino, Minerva Medica, 1963, pp. 95–6.
85 C. Gerin, P. Fucci and M. Angelini Rota, *Aspetti medico-sociali della prostituzione con particolare riferimento alle attuali norme di legge*, Roma, Istituto italiano di medicina sociale, 1964, p. 17.
86 G. A. Passetti, *Venere pericolosa*, Firenze, La Meridiana, 1971.
87 G. Santori, 'Introduzione', in *Aspetti patogenici dell'omosessualità. Atti del convegno, Roma 11–12 maggio 1963*, Torino, Minerva Medica, 1963, pp. 7–16.
88 P. Chauchard, 'Les invertis peuvent-ils être normaux?', in *Aspetti patogenici*, pp. 17–19.
89 J. Schneider, 'Of vigilance and virgins. Honor, shame, and access to resources in Mediterranean societies', *Ethnology*, 1971, vol. 10, pp. 1–24; L. Guidi, 'Onore e pericolo. Il valore di una donna secondo il sistema di carità napoletano dell'Ottocento', in G. Fiume (ed.), *Onore e storia nelle società mediterranee*, Palermo, La Luna, 1989, pp. 165–80.
90 R. Calabrese, 'Degenerazione sessuale e vendita di carne bianca', *La ginecologia moderna*, 1910, vol. 3, n. 4, pp. 182–5; O. Belsito Prini, 'Necessità della difesa contro le malattie sessuali', *Rassegna di studi sessuali e di eugenica*, 1926, vol. 6, n. 4, pp. 309–11.
91 J. Brown, *Educazione sessuale moderna*, Milano, Paris, 1952, pp. 7–15. According to Catholic moralists, young women were wrong in trying to obtain equal rights by adapting to the male norm of sexual freedom rather than by demanding that men obey the rules of chastity; S. Di Francesco, *Armonia coniugale. Rilievi, considerazioni e consigli di un ginecologo*, Milano, Istituto La Casa, 1956, pp. 129–31.

9

PUBLIC HEALTH, VENEREAL DISEASE AND COLONIAL MEDICINE IN THE LATER NINETEENTH CENTURY

Philippa Levine

The intent of this chapter is to examine a meaningful and interesting disjunction in nineteenth-century 'health talk'. While venereologists in the mid- and late-nineteenth century were more than comfortable operating within the vocabulary of public health, sanitationists and public health professionals routinely avoided references to venereal disease (VD) in their writings and their speeches. Acknowledged as a health problem of some magnitude, there was throughout the nineteenth century much discussion of the best way to manage the venereals. The notorious Contagious Diseases (CD) Acts were, of course, the best known of the policies adopted for controlling VD over the course of the century. Venereal specialists mostly favoured the legislation, claiming the Acts as an important and far-sighted public health measure. Yet the main figures in public health continued to avoid the topic of VD whenever possible.

This tension itself would make an interesting enough point of debate, but the picture can be further complicated and enriched by focusing attention on Britain's colonies. The CD system in place in almost all of Britain's imperial possessions is worth consideration for a host of reasons. Colonial CD legislation tended to be more thoroughgoing than its domestic counterparts, it often pre-dated domestic legislation, and frequently reached more of the civil population than was ever the case in Britain, where the three Acts of 1864, 1866 and 1869 were limited to garrison towns and seaports.

CD legislation, while widespread, was always controversial. In the nineteenth century, it was also a critical prop of British imperial rule. With their emphasis on regular examination and medical detention, the laws in this arena assumed a direct relationship between sexual activity and efficient disease transmission. While the medical reading of the debate was invariably overlain with presumptions about the inevitable and dangerous outcome of promiscuity, its moral portion was encoded within a new and increasingly technical vocabulary of medical expertise. And since medicine was a male enclave and prostitution an allegedly female occupation, we cannot divorce these issues from considerations of gender.

Domestic sanitary reform seldom included much in the way of VD policy. While regulationists claimed their intent as sanitary and in the interests of the newly fashionable idea of public health, CD enactments were kept largely separate from other sanitary reforms. While learned and detailed discussions of and blueprints for drainage and sewage, bath and wash-house regulation, vaccination, food and drink adulteration and nuisance-abatement became the bread-and-butter of the sanitary reform movement, the control of VD was rarely a topic discussed publicly by sanitary policy-makers.[1] Even Sir John Simon, whose initiatives included support of the domestic CD Acts, failed to include them in his survey of the achievements of the sanitary lobby for 'national sanitary purposes'.[2] More than any other disease group, the venereals were, of course, twinned with long-standing moral and religious considerations of sexual behaviour. Alongside the more obvious ways in which those connections raised questions around culpability and behaviour, they also hampered what it was possible to say about such diseases, certainly in the public arena.

VDs were in many ways unlike the other medical and sanitation issues which formed the bulk of public health attention in the nineteenth and early twentieth centuries. One of the difficulties in knowing how to assess their relationship to the public health movement stems from the differing 'reads' on public health offered by contemporary commentators. For Deborah Lupton and Catherine Waldby, it is the 'social' rather than the individual body which is the focal point for public health.[3] Conversely, however, Lara Marks and Michael Worboys argue that public health in the nineteenth century came to focus increasingly on the individual.[4] The attention to and interpretation of STDs, both then and now, combined these two otherwise oppositional approaches, since surveillance was both of the body as an individual infective entity and of sexual behaviour understood as collective in its implications, affecting the social as much as – if not more than – the individual body.[5]

Public health was squarely aligned with a faith in scientific rationalism, claiming a dispassionate neutrality and insisting that germs knew barriers neither of class nor race.[6] The emphasis on empirically knowable 'risk populations' lent medicine the vocabulary necessary to mask prejudice as science in the identification of those risk populations. And of course, the CD system was precisely about the triumph of identifying such groups – women, poor or colonized, and said to spread VD by their promiscuous sexual contact. Yet, despite the seemingly rationalist language in which this one-sided system of examining vendors but not clients was cast, there was never a moment when STDs were not capable of eliciting an emotive response. Though Lupton claims that '[f]or public health, the utilitarian imperative rules', that cannot hold true in the case of VD.[7] When one considers the locus of blame, the frequently punitive nature of treatment, or the attitude to venereological training in medical schools, the unease about a 'moral' disease group is never far from the surface. And, too, the category of risk was more complex than it would later become, for the CD system rested on a distinction between those 'at risk' – the soldiers who needed protection – and those who constituted the actual risk – the women registered as prostitutes. Risk was neither simple nor descriptive; it distinguished between an active agent and a passive receptor.

British sanitationist literature of the mid-nineteenth century is emblematic of a curious melding of scientific rationalism and moral stricture. Yet VDs as a target of public health strategy were not integrated into discussions of sewage, water supply or vaccination. Indeed, though the CD Acts were often touted as a public health measure in Britain, they were introduced to parliament in the early hours of the morning and pushed through the legislative channels, as their detractors claimed, by stealth. Miles Ogborn argues that the attention to health rather than prostitution allowed the domestic acts to be seen as neither legitimizing 'vice' nor overstepping governmental boundaries by poaching on the philanthropic turf of 'rescue'.[8] This reading was, of course, vociferously challenged by the Acts' opponents, notably in the late 1870s. But in British colonial settings, these sentiments were not part of the necessary legitimation of controversial laws. The regulationist policies enshrined in colonial Contagious Diseases ordinances and acts were actively and openly supported alike by government, the medical establishment and the military. Their emphasis on prostitution rather than disease was, I would argue, central to the understanding colonists brought to bear on the need for such legislation.

By the mid-1860s, the consolidation of this regulatory system within a broader national-imperial policy was apparent. By 1870, CD laws were in place in more than a dozen of Britain's colonies, in treaty ports where the British had commercial and naval interests, and in the United Kingdom. A few colonies were exempted. Mauritius and the nearby Seychelles, acquired by the British as a result of the Napoleonic Wars, are never mentioned in the CD literature, though Mauritius was certainly invited to pass an ordinance.[9] The legislation also seems to have by-passed such early African settlements as The Gambia, Sierra Leone and the Gold Coast, presumably because their European populations numbered only in the hundreds. British Honduras, British Guiana and the Falkland Islands all escaped CD regulation. But a wide range of colonies *were* affected, from the plantation economies of the Caribbean to the white settler colonies of the southern hemisphere, from the European and Europeanized colonies of the Mediterranean and North America to the cluster of Asian colonies sprawled around the Indian and Pacific Oceans. What binds these colonial ordinances and acts together is that *everywhere*, without exception, they differed – and usually radically – from the domestic British acts.

The idea of CD laws as public health imperatives was certainly not wholly abandoned in colonial contexts. In India, the official representation of the 1864 Cantonment Act (directed at the military cantonments established by the British, and the first of two major CD measures in India in the 1860s) was that it 'has for its object the protection of public health'.[10] Hong Kong's Colonial Surgeon, Dr Murray, argued in 1869 that the founding principle of the colony's CD ordinance was simple: its 'sole object' was 'restricting the extent of contagion, and curing the disease'.[11] In Queensland, parliamentary supporters of the law likewise insisted that the proposed measure was medical, not moral; its sponsors promoted the measure explicitly as one of public health.[12]

But colonial administrators were keenly aware of and wedded to the need for distinctive imperial versions of CD legislation, even while they stressed the primacy of medical principles. They frequently argued that to apply a model intended for a Western nation would be folly in the circumstances of the East. Not surprisingly, such thinking did not apply in white settler environments where there was rather a tendency for parliamentarians to adopt a self-congratulatory sense of having improved on the British version of the laws. In non-white colonies, however, the question of why an English-style law would be futile under Eastern conditions was a common and much-rehearsed theme. A Colonial Office administrator, writing of the Hong Kong law in the 1870s, pointed out 'that the circumstances of Hong Kong are widely different from those of England'. His evidence was an unsubstantiated claim that three-quarters of the colony's Chinese women were engaged in the sex trade.[13] Preposterous claims such as this, though, were a crucial element in establishing difference, as was an insistence on the need to adjust laws to local conditions. Indeed, Lord Ripon, who became India's Governor-General in 1880, thought Indian CD enactments akin more to the continental European than the British system. The system, he said, 'goes far beyond the English law and introduces a system of registration, not only of prostitutes, but of brothel-keepers, which the framers of the English measure thought extremely objectionable'.[14] Such marked differences have considerable significance for our understanding of the public health dimension of the colonial enterprise.

In Chinese-populated colonies such as Hong Kong and the Straits Settlements, proponents of the CD system, ignoring contradictory claims that the goals were purely medical, routinely insisted that the ordinances were enacted as much to protect women from the brutalities of Chinese sexual slavery as they were to keep soldiers free of infection. Such representations stressed a humanitarian protectionism alongside medical necessity. In the 1890s, when the compulsory genital examinations of women were outlawed by imperial diktat, these colonies were permitted to maintain brothel registration as a means of protecting women from unscrupulous managers.

Equally powerful, however, was the insistence in the colonial context that the dirtiness of the setting made legislation both more urgent and necessarily more intrusive. Hong Kong's Colonial Surgeon reporting in 1879 on his visits to the colony's brothels did not hide his horror at the greasiness and filth he claimed to encounter. 'I've a pretty good stomach and don't stick at trifles, but I found the inspection of these places acted as a very unpleasant emetic.'[15] Medical officers in the colonies frequently complained that registered women and their premises were unclean. More generally, the prostitute, as a vessel for many men's semen, was associated with filth. VDs were not only marked on the body but were passed via those forms of bodily contact most policed by moralists and hygienists alike. Tropical climates were seen as likely breeding grounds for infection and contagion, and they were regarded, too, as inflaming the passions and negating caution and reason. These were vital elements, of course, in the reading of VD as a measure of promiscuity, as of the reading of the tropics as less civilized and less seemly. Though the moral theme ran through much of medical reasoning at this time (despite those ever-present claims to neutrality!), it was nowhere more prominent than in considerations of VD, for while hygiene and personal culpability could enter into readings of other illnesses, their overwhelming association with sexuality elevated the VDs to a separate status in the medico-moral universe. And the invariable reading of a sensual East meant that while all of these sentiments were alive in the domestic arena too, they framed the colonial more decidedly.

A number of historians have noted recently this close colonial association between hygiene and morals. Timothy Burke points out how cleanliness became a marker of civilization in colonial Zimbabwe,[16] and Anne McClintock has traced what she calls the 'soap saga' as a 'God-given sign of Britain's evolutionary superiority'.[17] The growing association between cleanliness and femininity fuelled by Victorian readings of the domestic lent added meaning to the sanitary issues around prostitution and disease. Prostitutes, by their trade, mocked the idea of women as guardians of the sanitized and sanctified hearth. Their rejection of domesticated womanhood alongside their potential role in purveying disease brought together complex associations between race, sex, hygiene and femininity. Hygiene became another means by which racial difference – and its effects upon sexual difference – was made visible.

It was not that dirt – whether cast in an older environmentalist frame or through the lens of germ theory – was not part of public health discourse in Britain. It was, of course, as critical in that setting as in the colonies. But the Hong Kong surgeon's disgust at the brothel could not be replicated in the home context. While he could, and loudly did, call for greater surveillance of the local brothels, that strategy necessitated an official recognition of houses of prostitution. In the British CD Acts, that was simply not possible, for to inspect brothels would also mean to acknowledge their legitimacy. Had the CD Acts proceeded in that direction, it would have been a lot tougher to maintain the claim that they dealt solely with health issues. Legitimacy and respectability were too closely entwined in British claims around law and liberty for such an association to be risked. In the colonies, however, where the ordinances spoke to so considerable a variety of other issues, the brothel could be legally recognized, even if public disclaimers of regret needed to accompany its formal registration.

I see these differences as fundamentally racial in their application. Dirty women, the inhabitants of the greasy brothels, were, after all, also racially marked women. Much of the justification for the particular modes of regulation which were feasible in the colonies stemmed from a racial reading of VD and its effects on, and origins in, lesser but more sexualized peoples. When the Southern African colony of Natal tried to pass a CD law in 1890, the Colonial Office stepped in to prevent its promulgation, since the system was then being wound down throughout the colonies. But the justification for the law given by Natal's governor to the Colonial Secretary is worth repeating as an index of this long-standing medicalized racialization. 'These diseases were more or less common in the country districts, principally among the native and coolie Indian population ... [the] vast number of barbarous, or semi-barbarous, people of native race ... are ignorant of the danger ... incapable of taking precautions against it ... and ... are peculiarly exposed to the evil results of its contagion.'[18]

In multi-ethnic but predominantly white Queensland, the racial issue actually helped keep the CD system in place long after crown colonies and protectorates had been forced to abandon it. The Queensland CD Act came under attack in 1886 by feminists and their allies. In the Legislative Assembly, it was racial arguments which helped sway politicians in favour of maintaining the Act. The Premier informed the Assembly that 'nearly half of the black population of Australia has perished from [syphilis], and ... there are many islands in the Pacific now where scarcely a man, woman, or child is free from it'.[19] It was a stunning feat of exaggeration, although VD rates among Australian aboriginals did run high.[20] But the spectre of black infection, and the prospect of its trans-ference to a white population, were effective political tools. The Queensland CD Act of 1868 survived the attack, and remained on the statute books well into the twentieth century. The bitter irony of this tale is worth noting, for while aborig-inal VD rates were a useful political weapon in debate, the Queensland CD Act was never applied to the indigenous population.

In the colonies, the registers in which public health and VD could be articu-lated thus operated differently. This contrast between Britain 'at home' and overseas offers an interesting medium in which to think about the politics of public health. Medical care in the colonies was aimed primarily at the British military and at resident colonists; it was already and always in this respect more oriented towards a preventive and protective mode than its domestic counter-part. Veena Oldenburg, among others, has eloquently shown how much greater efforts at sanitation in India were in areas of British residence.[21] Vijay Prasad and Dane Kennedy have pointed out the considerable inequalities in sanitary service to Indian and to British sections of towns, cantonments and hill stations. In most colonies indigenes had little access to Western medical care; there were mission hospitals, a few government dispensaries, and some civil hospitals but there was neither uniform policy nor much funding for these enterprises.[22] Local peoples had few illusions that medical offerings were intended to benefit anyone other than those who ruled them.

But for indigenous women under the surveillance of the CD system, there was gratuitous treatment albeit of a coercive kind, and after the abandonment of regulation in the 1890s, free treatment remained available on a voluntary basis.[23]

It is worth contrasting the long and steady history of the colonial lock hospital both with the piecemeal provision of colonial health care more generally and with the history of domestic lock hospitals. Lock hospitals in Britain had always found it difficult to secure funding, but in the colonies their provision (never generous, always contentious) was considered a budgetary staple.[24] There were endless spats about whether women should be charged fees which would form the basis of lock hospital income, and there was sporadic resentment from municipal governments over the expectation that they would donate monies for these purposes, but lock hospitals were considered integral to colonial health care.

Equally, their long and relatively stable history contrasts strikingly with the crisis management which largely defined other arenas of colonial health care.[25] Colonial governments responded to outbreaks of plague or cholera, especially when they threatened to affect the white soldiery, but basic provisions for more mundane or for preventive health care beyond the white minority were non-existent. The brothel was one of the few institutions associated with locals where an active sanitation programme was even attempted. In Fyzabad cantonment in India's North-West Provinces, special accommodations for the business of sex were arranged to ensure that 'in every room ... a permanent brickwork stand has been erected, the height of a man's hips, and on this stand the basin is kept ever ready with water. Soap is always present, and a towel is kept on a nail close by.'[26] In the Straits Settlements and the Federated Malay States, after the formal CD system was abolished, enterprising colonial doctors established medical clubs to which brothel-keepers could send their workers for treatment in exchange for a weekly subscription.[27]

But beyond sex work, arrangements such as these are significant largely by their absence. Though conditions would, by British lights, seem to make the case for effective public health more pressing, there were sound Victorian-style reasons for the lack of interest. The officer commanding British troops at Hong Kong, for example, thought the locals more tolerant of filth: '[T]he streets are so narrow and the houses so badly constructed and ventilated, that it would be impossible to make the buildings healthy, or habitable, except for Chinese.'[28] And at the Straits, a government committee concluded that miserable conditions were immaterial: 'It does not appear ... that the general health of the inmates suffers materially from these causes.'[29]

It was perhaps this alleged immunity (a product, presumably, of environmentalist readings of disease transmission) that encouraged the assumption that VDs acquired in the tropics were more virulent, long-lasting and damaging – at least to Europeans – than domestic versions. Describing syphilitic men returning to Britain from India, a Surgeon-Major at Netley military hospital came close to suggesting that VD effected the transformation of Englishmen into unhealthy and unmanly Easterners. The unfortunate sufferer, he claimed, came off the troop ship 'utterly broken down in health, hardly able to crawl, covered with scabs and sores, with the foul odour of the disease about them, objects of disgust and loathing to themselves and all around them'.[30] Clinicians and social commentators alike talked up venereal afflictions as more insidious in their damage than other afflictions, silently stalking the unwary and rendering something more lasting than mere death – long-term inter-generational consequences. VDs, and most especially syphilis, became a locus of blame in the discourse of sickness and health, an originary moment of ill health passed on to the innocent as well as the unwary, and, it was implied, exacerbated by the ghost of inter-racial contact. In the New South Wales Legislative Assembly in 1875, a local politician anxious (unsuccessfully, as it turned out) to introduce CD legislation into the colony, proclaimed the 'known fact that most of the diseases to which the human frame was liable were attributable to' VD.[31] An international congress on hygiene and demography in London in 1891 heard that the fevers European soldiers experienced in India were often 'much aggravated by the syphilitic taint' or were themselves 'purely syphilitic'.[32] An Indian military surgeon made the same argument later in the decade, speaking of how 'many local diseases have their origin in or are so marked by venereal entanglement'.[33] These were ideas of long standing, and linked race and environment to disease in myriad ways.

Tellingly, many of those who campaigned to make VD a visible health issue had ties to the military. While neither VD nor colonial CD policies were, in fact, ever exclusively military, it was on soldiers' health that much of the debate turned, a factor that drives home the critical point that understanding racial politics necessarily involves acknowledging whiteness as ideology. The yoking of VD to military concerns had the effect of placing a martial state centre stage. Soldiers were, of course, an imperial necessity. Moreover, the military reforms of the mid-nineteenth century which introduced shorter and shorter periods of service rested on an assumption that soldiers would return to heterosexual family life in Britain. Their post-soldierly duties in propagating the race meant that their freedom from constitutional disease became a deeply gendered metaphor for the health of the race and of the nation. John Gamble and F. B. Smith have both argued that the domestic CD Acts were necessary and humane laws serving the essential purpose of protecting military efficiency.[34] That women with soldier and sailor clients were thus solely liable to surveillance and detention is, for them, the unfortunate by-product of a degraded occupation and status, the women a pawn in the larger game of imperial defence. It is the same argument generated certainly in colonial circles at the time of the legislation, for though public debate was often crafted around sanitary issues, internal debate – and that seized by abolitionists – re-cast the Acts as centring not on urgent health issues so much as on the control of women, and more especially of women disadvantaged by the twin problems of poverty and stigmatization. Throughout the colonies, medical and police memoranda, lock hospital reports and internal policy discussion documents concentrated less on the public health aspects of the law than on the practical control of prostitution. The intemperance of rank-and-file soldiers or the wisdom of examining them as well as the women surfaced occasionally for desultory discussion, but the focus was primarily on managing prostitute women.

It is, then, despite the pious claims of the age, difficult to represent the system of regulation enshrined in colonial CD law as purely concerned with issues of health and sanitation. Mary Poovey has argued that, in the mid-nineteenth century, prostitution was treated differently and separably from other issues linked to female sexuality. While she sees questions around childbirth and contraception as largely medically conceived at this juncture, prostitution – primarily because of the fear of syphilis – was 'transformed ... into a social problem of such magnitude that by the 1840s this kind of female sexual behaviour was being discussed in forms as various as newspapers, highbrow quarterlies, novels, and "scientific" treatises on VD and sanitation'.[35] By the late 1850s, these medical and social issues had begun palpably to coalesce, driven by the vocabulary of the clinician. By the later years of the century, as social purity campaigns as well as medical interest brought VD increasingly into the political spotlight, this medico-social connection was the norm.

The persistent yoking of venereal infection to other sicknesses and to ultimate decay served as a link between venereology and what we might think of as the 'dramatic' end of the medical mainstream, dealing with the most serious, the most debilitating, and the most tenacious of health problems. Sanitary reformers, as we have seen, gave the topic a wide berth but the gravity of these illnesses allowed those involved in VD campaigns to wield the language of public health and sanitation to considerable effect. Regulationists thus routinely presented CD measures as a wing of sanitary reform or public health even while most sanitarians were silent on the topic. W. M. Frazer notes this discrepancy in a survey of English public health published in 1950; municipal health authorities 'scarcely mentioned' that VDs were 'taking each year a heavy toll of the population, both in lives and health'.[36]

It is worth recalling in this tension-filled context how fully the 'landscape of Victorian Britain' was an 'imperial culture' in which attempts to separate domestic from imperial considerations fail to recognize their intertwined histories.[37] Elizabeth Van Heyningen's argument that the CD Acts were 'pre-eminently imperial legislation' concerned principally with the security of the empire certainly alerts us to the colonial questions at the heart of CD policy.[38] In the 1860s, when venereal outbreaks among British soldiery returning from overseas were impossible to ignore and military VD rates were rising in almost all of Britain's garrisons, the topic acquired a good deal of urgency.[39] Recent changes in the administration of India and the accompanying substantial increase in soldiers stationed there were frequently the focal points of these concerns. The Army Sanitary Commission rather sadly confessed that 'the marked increase of VD coincident with the great accession of European troops in 1858 is worthy of note'.[40] The Herbert Commission, reporting on sanitary conditions in the army in India to the Commons in 1863, found venereal cases accounted for 20 to 25 per cent of the total number of men hospitalized.[41] For the Hong Kong garrison, the *Lancet* recalled the pre-ordinance days before 1858 when VDs 'were among the most common causes of unfitness for duty'.[42]

In the wake of the 1857 Mutiny, at the time of the 1865 revolt in Jamaica, and with the problems of the Crimea still stingingly familiar, Britain's military prowess looked 'glaringly deficient' in the era of CD enactment.[43] Though VD was a significant problem in almost all armies, military VD rates were higher in the British than in any of the continental armies, and just after the Mutiny in 1859 the infection rates for British troops in India rose to a staggering 359 per 1,000 of hospital admissions.[44] These alarming figures may have added to the perceived need for a more elaborate regulation system for India. In any event, in a period of growing imperial prowess the condition of the army was clearly a necessary complement to the maintenance and indeed extension of colonial rule, and it is to this connection that Van Heyningen's reading of the CD Act in the Cape Colony draws attention. Britain's overseas and domestic military needs were seen, in many respects, as co-terminous with Britain's burgeoning role as an imperial power. Military doctors, moreover, were among the pioneers of new medical techniques, and while indigenous peoples seldom benefited very greatly from new medical developments, the differing conditions offered by colonial politics, climates and relations gave different meaning to public health in settings beyond island Britain. VD, always a source of multiple anxieties and invariably the topic most shunned by reformers in the domestic arena, demonstrates in its conflicting messages and in the jumbled policies applied to it in the name of good sanitary management, the distance we must still travel to understand in its entirety the complex politics of nineteenth-century public health.

NOTES

1 See, for example, A. P. Stewart and E. Jenkins, *The Medical and Legal Aspects of Sanitary Reform*, London, R. Hardwicke, 1867, and H. W. Rumsey, *Laws Affecting the Public Health in England*, London, n.p., 1870. Rumsey notes in his single paragraph on syphilis (p. 9) that it is a disease 'no less formidable than smallpox' but discusses the implications of this no further.

2 J. Simon, *English Sanitary Institutions Reviewed in Their Course of Development, and in Some of their Political and Social Relations*, London, Cassell, 1890, p. 345.

3 D. Lupton, *Medicine as Culture: Illness, Disease and the Body in Western Societies*, London, Sage, 1994, p. 31; C. Waldby, *AIDS and the Body Politic: Biomedicine and Sexual Difference*, London, Routledge, 1996, p. 95.

4 L. Marks and M. Worboys, 'Introduction', in L. Marks and M. Worboys (eds) *Migrants, Minorities and Health. Historical and Contemporary Studies*, London, Routledge, 1997, pp. 8–9.

5 The venereals were not quite unique in this respect for, in the nineteenth century, masturbation occupied a similarly disturbing place in the medical lexicon. See A. Hunt, 'The great masturbation panic and the discourses of moral regulation in nineteenth and early twentieth century Britain', *Journal of the History of Sexuality*, 1998, vol. 8, pp. 575–615.

6 V. Gamble, 'The Provident Hospital Project: An experiment in race relations and medical education', *Bulletin of the History of Medicine*, 1991, vol. 65, p. 457; A. Kraut, 'Silent travelers: germs, genes and American efficiency, 1890–1924', *Social Science History*, 1988, vol. 12, pp. 377–94.

7 Lupton, *Medicine as Culture*, p. 32.

8 M. Ogborn, 'Law and discipline in nineteenth century English state formation: The Contagious Diseases Acts of 1864, 1866 and 1869', *Journal of Historical Sociology*, 1993, vol. 6, pp. 37–8.

9 S. Amos, *A Comparative Survey of Laws in Force for the Prohibition, Regulation and Licensing of Vice in England and Other Countries*, London, Stevens & Son, 1877, p. 407.

10 *Annual Report on the Lock Hospitals of the Madras Presidency for the Year 1877*, Madras, Government Press, 1878, p. 11. V/24/2287, Oriental and India Office Collection (OIOC), British Library (BL), London.

11 Colonial Office Papers, CO 129/296 (4718), Public Record Office (PRO), London.

12 Queensland, *Parliamentary Debates*, Second Series, 1868, VI, 16 January 1868, pp. 853–5, esp. Hon. W. Wood. B. A. Smithurst points out that the bill's sponsors saw the legislation as public health ('Historic and epidemiologic review of venereal disease in Queensland', unpublished MD thesis, University of Queensland, 1981, vol. I, p. 69).

13 CO129/184 (6690), Memo of C. P. Lucas to F. Meade, 6 May 1879, PRO.

14 Add. Ms. 43,574, Ripon Papers, LXXXIV, Diary No. 111, Minute, 21 October 1880, f. 470, 1880, BL.

15 *Annual Report of the Colonial Surgeon, 1879*, n.d., n.p., p. 66^v, CO131/11, PRO.

16 I follow Timothy Burke in using the post-independence name of Southern Rhodesia, Zimbabwe.

17 T. Burke, *Lifebuoy Men, Lux Women: Commodification, Consumption, and Cleanliness in Modern Zimbabwe*, Durham, NC, Duke University Press, 1996, pp. 31–2; A. McClintock, *Imperial Leather: Race, Gender and Sexuality in the Colonial Context*, New York, Routledge, 1995, pp. 207–8. See, too, J. and J. Comaroff, 'Home-Made hegemony: Modernity, domesticity and colonialism in South Africa', in K. Tranberg Hansen (ed.) *African Encounters with Domesticity*, Brunswick, NJ, Rutgers University Press, 1992, esp. p. 280.

18 *British Parliamentary Papers (PP)*, House of Commons [HC], 1894 (147), C. B. H. Mitchell to Lord Knutsford, 28 July 1890.

19 Queensland, *Debates of the Legislative Assembly*, Fourth Session of the Ninth Parliament, 1886, vol. L, 1 October 1886, Brisbane, James C. Beal, Government Printer, 1886, p. 1,052.

20 Aboriginal VD rates for this period were notoriously inaccurate.

21 V. T. Oldenburg, *The Making of Colonial Lucknow 1856–1877*, Princeton, Princeton University Press, 1984, pp. 104–5. See too J. B. Harrison, 'Allahabad. A sanitary history', in K. Ballhatchet and J. Harrison (eds) *The City in South Asia: Pre-modern and Modern*, London and Dublin, Curzon Press/Atlantic Highlands, NJ, Humanities Press, 1980, pp. 166–95; D. Kennedy, *The Magic Mountains: Hill Stations and the British Raj*, Berkeley, University of California Press, 1996, p. 191; V. Prasad, 'Native dirt/imperial ordure: The cholera of 1832 and the morbid resolutions of modernity', *Journal of Historical Sociology*, 1994, vol. 7, pp. 243–60.

22 K. N. Panikkar, 'Indigenous medicine and cultural hegemony. A study of the revitalization movement in Keralam', *Studies in History*, 1992, vol. 8, pp. 228–9.

23 Coercion and voluntarism are relative terms in this instance, and this paragraph represents a severe over-simplification. See my forthcoming book, *Prostitution, Race and Politics: Policing Venereal Disease in the British Empire, 1860–1918*, for more detailed attention to this issue.

24 J. Bettley, 'Post voluptatem misericordia: The rise and fall of the London Lock Hospital', *London Journal*, 1984, vol. 10, pp. 167–75; H. F. B. Compston, *The Magdalen Hospital: The Story of A Great Charity*, London, Society for the Promotion of Christian Knowledge, 1917; L. E. Merians, 'The London Lock Hospital and the Lock Asylum for Women', in L. E. Merians (ed.) *The Secret Malady. Venereal Disease in Eighteenth-Century Britain and France*, Lexington, University of Kentucky Press, 1997, pp. 128–45.

25 D. Arnold, 'Smallpox and colonial medicine in nineteenth-century India', in D. Arnold (ed.) *Imperial Medicine and Indigenous Societies*, Manchester, Manchester

University Press, 1988, pp. 45–65; M. Harrison, *Public Health in British India. Anglo-Indian Preventive Medicine 1859–1914*, Cambridge, Cambridge University Press, 1994; L. Doyal and I. Pennell, 'Pox Britannica: Health, medicine and underdevelopment', *Race and Class*, 1976, vol. 18, pp. 155–72; M. Lyons, *Colonial Disease: A Social History of Sleeping Sickness in Northern Zaire 1900–1904*, Cambridge, Cambridge University Press, 1992; M. Vaughan, *Curing Their Ills: Colonial Power and African Illness*, Stanford, CA, Stanford University Press, 1991.

26 *Fourth Annual Report on the Working of the Lock-Hospitals in the North-West Provinces and Oudh for the Year 1877*, Allahabad, n.p., 1878, p. 96, V/24/2290, OIOC.

27 J. G. Butcher, *The British in Malaya 1880–1941: The Social History of A European Community in Colonial South-East Asia*, Kuala Lumpur, Oxford University Press, 1979, p. 199; L. Manderson, 'Migration, prostitution and medical surveillance in early twentieth-century Malaya', in Marks and Worboys (eds) *Migrants, Minorities and Health*, pp. 62–3; B. O'Keefe, 'Sexually transmitted diseases in Malaysia: A history', in M. Lewis, S. Bamber and M. Waugh (eds) *Sex, Disease, and Society: A Comparative History of Sexually Transmitted Diseases and HIV/AIDS in Asia and the Pacific*, Westport, CT, Greenwood Press, 1997, p. 161.

28 Minute of General Officer Commanding, Hong Kong, 26 Jan. 1874, CO131/11, PRO.

29 *Report of the Committee appointed to Enquire into the Working of Ordinance XXII of 1879, commonly called the Contagious Diseases Ordinance*, April 1877, CO273/91 (6629), PRO.

30 *PP*, HC, 1897, C.-8379, *Report of A Departmental Committee*, p. 30, appendix II, Surgeon-Major H. R. Whitehead, 21 August 1896.

31 *Report of Proceedings in New South Wales Legislative Assembly, Sydney Morning Herald*, 8 December 1875, p. 4, Mr Farnell).

32 *Transactions of the Seventh International Congress of Hygiene and Demography*, vol. 11, *Indian Hygiene and Demography*, London, Eyre & Spottiswoode, 1892, p. 65.

33 W. Hill-Climo, 'The British soldier in India and enthetic diseases', *United Services Magazine*, 1896–7, vol. 15, n.s., p. 375.

34 J. G. Gamble, 'The origins, administration and impact of the Contagious Diseases Acts from a military perspective', unpublished Ph.D. dissertation, University of Southern Mississippi, 1983; F. B. Smith, 'The Contagious Diseases Acts reconsidered', *Social History of Medicine*, 1990, vol. 3, pp. 197–215.

35 M. Poovey, 'Speaking of the body. Mid-Victorian constructions of female desire', in M. Jacobus, E. Fox Keller and S. Shuttleworth (eds) *Body/Politics: Women and the Discourses of Science*, New York, Routledge, 1990, p. 30.

36 W. M. Frazer, *A History of English Public Health 1834–1939*, London, Baillière, Tindall & Cox, 1950, p. 336.

37 A. Burton, 'Recapturing *Jane Eyre*: Reflections on historicizing the colonial encounter in Victorian Britain', *Radical History Review*, 1996, vol. 64, p. 60.

38 E. B. Van Heyningen, 'The social evil in the Cape Colony 1868–1902: Prostitution and the Contagious Diseases Acts', *Journal of Southern African Studies*, 1984, vol. 10, p. 173.

39 A. R. Skelley, *The Victorian Army at Home: The Recruitment and Terms and Conditions of the British Regular 1859–1899*, London, Croom Helm, 1977, p. 53.

40 *Report on Measures Adopted for Sanitary Improvements in India during the Year 1868*, London, HMSO, 1869, p. 54. V/24/3675, OIOC.

41 *PP*, HC, 1863 (3184), XIX, *Report of the Commissioners Appointed to Enquire into the Sanitary State of the Army in India*, p. 126. K. de Bevoise finds a similar situation in the Philippines; in 1898 the army sick report showed about 25 per cent of all cases as venereal: 'A history of sexually transmitted diseases and HIV/AIDS in the Philippines', in Lewis, Bamber and Waugh (eds) *Sex, Disease, and Society*, p. 119.

42 'Contagious Diseases in China', *The Lancet*, 14 November 1868, p. 645.

43 F. Harcourt, 'Disraeli's imperialism, 1866–1868: A question of timing', *Historical Journal*, 1980, vol. 23, p. 95.

44 P. D. Curtin, *Death by Migration: Europe's Encounter with the Tropical World in the Nineteenth Century*, Cambridge, Cambridge University Press, 1989, p. 156; Officers of the Royal Army Medical Corps, *A Manual of Venereal Diseases*, London, Oxford Medical Publications/Henry Frowde/Hodder & Stoughton, 1907, pp. 1–3; D. Arnold, 'Sexually transmitted diseases in nineteenth and twentieth century India', *Genitourinary Medicine*, 1993, vol. 69, p. 3.

10

HEALTH AND EMPIRE

Britain's national campaign to combat venereal diseases in Shanghai, Hong Kong and Singapore

Kerrie L. MacPherson

Introduction

At the close of the First World War, Britain's National Council for Combatting Venereal Diseases (NCCVD) launched an imperial campaign of enlightenment and education on sex and sexually transmitted diseases that extended to crown colonies and protectorates like Hong Kong or Singapore, as well as the British-influenced treaty port of Shanghai. This was clear proof, according to *The Lancet*, 'that the Empire is beginning to realize the need of tackling with vigour the whole question of venereal diseases'.[1] To that end, a Far Eastern Commission was formed, led by Mrs C. Neville-Rolfe, OBE and Dr R. Hallam, to enquire into the conditions affecting the prevention and cure of VD. Although the Commission was under the auspices of the Ministry of Health, the Colonial and Foreign Offices, and the Treasury, it was strictly an educational and voluntary body.[2]

Yet, historians of British colonial medicine and public health policy often conflate colonialism with coercion; that is, the application of universal or standardized policy to different colonies without regard to the cultural or historical singularities of the 'colonized'. Furthermore, medicine and public health policy as it developed in the West is viewed as hegemonic or imperialist, 'colonizing the body', thereby precluding any understanding or appreciation of other medical systems or practice encountered during Western colonial expansionism. Important studies of imperial medicine such as David Arnold's on nineteenth-century India, Lenore Manderson's study of colonial Malaya, or more recently, Brenda Yeoh's environmental study of Singapore, focus on what they see as a critical example of a more generalizing process that exposes the 'role of knowledge in the service of state power'.[3]

Modern scholarship of imperial histories has underscored this view by rescuing the 'subaltern voices', highlighting the resistance of the 'other', locked in a struggle of unequal power relations, to surveillance or control. Pier M. Larson, in his study of Malagasy Christianity in the nineteenth century, argues that while these 'neo-Foucauldian studies of imperial discourse' stress 'the role of knowledge in the service of state power', they sell short the 'intellectual resilience' of the so-called 'colonized minds'. Moreover, Larson shows in his own study that those who contested 'hegemonic interpretations and practices of Christianity' in highland Madagascar were not the Malagasy peasants, but the British missionaries themselves. In her study of plague epidemics and British colonial medicine in Cape Town and Hong Kong, Molly Sutphen raised similar questions in her analysis of the debates that emerged among colonial doctors and administrators, faced with the realities of local environments and cultures, over the effectiveness of 'tried and true anti-plague measures'.[4]

What these studies suggest is the very real limitations of 'knowledge' or state power, let alone human agency, even if demonstrably intrusive and coercive at any given point in time. They also suggest that these analyses tend to be formulaic and use historical evidence only insofar as it confirms what has already been assumed. As Bridget Towers has argued in her study of British health education policy on the prophylaxis of VD after the First World War, the policy debates cannot be merely understood as a simplistic division between 'moralists and medics'. In her view there was 'a far more complicated division of interests involved', and we may add, particularly so in colonial outposts of Empire.[5]

If we examine the historical processes that marked the inter-war period, it is much more problematic to conflate colonialism with coercion for several reasons. The first 'uncontestable' process was the ineluctable movement against the continuation of the regulation of prostitution as a control system for VD. Repeal of the Contagious Diseases Acts in 1886 in Britain (following their suspension in 1883), and the subsequent repeal of the CD legislation in her colonies, ended a VD control system that had begun in 1864. Similar measures in Europe and North America had also proved inefficacious, given that the prevalence of VD and its 'physical and moral menace to civilization' continued only moderately abated. Indeed, at the International Conference for the Prophylaxis of Venereal Disease held in Brussels in 1899, venereal experts manifested a shift of emphasis to moral and medical education for control.[6] During the First World War, experience gained by various military authorities in their attempts to prevent the spread of VD, along with medical and scientific advances in the understanding of the aetiology of, and the biological consequences of, untreated VD, resulted in better diagnostic techniques, more effective treatments, clearer classifications and better reportage for statistical purposes. These developments transformed the nature of preventive health care. They coincided with another historical process that can be loosely described as a broadening concept of public health reflecting social and political movements transforming the colonial state's relations not only to the individual but also to the publics that it served. For it was no longer necessary to wait for major medical or public health initiatives to be launched almost exclusively by the colonizers. This would manifest itself in the expansion of political participation, and new institutions reflecting an increase in local representation; women's rights and education; as well as serious debates over the efficacy of self-government, as a prelude to decolonization.

We will test these conceptualizations by looking at a little-studied imperial campaign and its impact on formulating public health policy in colonial and what have been called 'semi-colonial' settings in the Far East.[7] Any examination of the history of prevention and treatment of VD in Shanghai, Hong Kong and Singapore will reflect the intersection of colonial (or foreign) influences and Chinese culture. Of course, all three were international seaports, which besides their mercantile commerce often served as major ports of call for foreign troops and navies, and higher rates of VD chiefly attributable to prostitution were accepted as inevitable, and theoretically preventable. Attempts to control VD by state medicine in the nineteenth century in all three ports, principally by the application of Britain's Contagious Diseases Acts (and the establishment of lock hospitals), and their subsequent failure and repeal, have been studied elsewhere.[8] What these studies reveal is the variation in application of the Acts in the face of local conditions as well as the divergent positions taken within these communities in the subsequent controversies that they inspired.

The reasons for the high incidence of VD in the local communities were complex and directly related to Chinese customs and attitudes towards women and their place in society.[9] Prostitutes, identified as a chief source for the spread of VD, entered the profession either voluntarily (to raise money for their families or to pay off debts), or were bought, falsely adopted, or kidnapped as children and trained in various accomplishments suited to the life by 'pocket mothers' (brothel-keepers, who were usually women and former prostitutes themselves), or mortgaged or sold by husbands and families. Poverty was regarded as the prevailing incentive for the widespread trafficking and commerce in women and girls.[10] However, they were not the only source of infection. The pervasive system of concubinage (to ensure a male heir to carry on the duties of the lineage) in the wealthier classes contributed to the spread of VD. These women were drawn from two sources: daughters of the poor sold as 'secondary wives' and sometimes suffering from hereditary syphilis, and professional prostitutes or courtesans 'frequently suffering from previously contracted syphilis'.[11] There were also the beinu or mui tsai (literally 'female slave' or bond servants who were children sold into domestic and sometimes sexual servitude), and the 'protected women', mistresses of foreigners who occupied an anomalous position in society, neither concubine nor prostitute, but unique to Singapore, Hong Kong and China's treaty ports. In sum, Chinese prostitution was viewed as 'essentially a bargain for money and based on a national system of female slavery, polygamy and mui tsai'.[12] Furthermore, the Chinese had a highly developed medical culture which differed radically from and often conflicted with the evolving science of medicine in the West.[13] Focusing on race, sex (and gender) and disease, we will examine how colonial realities shaped public health policy.

The National Council for Combatting Venereal Diseases

The NCCVD was established in 1914 during the sittings of a Royal Commission on Venereal Diseases set up in 1913, chaired by Lord Sydenham of Combe, who became the NCCVD's first president. The Royal Commission's final report, issued in 1916, became the basis for a national scheme for the prevention and treatment of VD. The Commission advocated two major shifts in approach to amelioration and control as applied to the civil population. The first was nation-wide free and confidential treatment: by 1921, under Article III of the Public Health (Venereal Diseases) Regulations, 1916, over 176 recognized treatment centres (for both men and women) were provided by County and County Borough Councils in hospitals and other institutions, with funding from central government, under the supervision of the Ministry of Health. The second was comprehensive propaganda and education 'as to the dangers and effects of these diseases, and as to the necessity for early and skilled treatment': this was coordi-nated centrally by the NCCVD, with the support of the Ministry and government funding.[14]

   Although the NCCVD was responsible for the campaign of public enlighten-ment, they faced competition from a rival voluntary body, the Society for the Prevention of Venereal Diseases (SPVD), chaired by Lord Willoughby de Broke. The SPVD criticized the official policy 'of exhorting the public to be chaste and advising them to consult a doctor when infected', a campaign which they claimed had not succeeded in preventing the spread of VD. The SPVD advo-cated instead a policy of 'self-disinfection', a system tried in the military during the Great War, by issuing disinfectant 'packets' and instructions, prepared under the auspices of the Society for distribution to the civil population. In their view, such early preventative measures would both reduce the rate of infection and the costs of government-funded VD clinics, this latter point being particularly persuasive with ratepayers.[15] These proposals would have required an amend-ment to the Venereal Diseases Act, 1917, which made it an offence for any non-qualified medical practitioner, such as a chemist, to treat, advise, prescribe, or advertise, in connection with the treatment of VD 'for reward direct or indirect'.[16]

   The NCCVD was quick to respond to the SPVD. They pointed out that 'such simple measures' had only mixed success in both the Australian and American armies and had not reduced the incidence of VD, although military discipline should have obviated problems faced by laxity in application of the prescribed treatment among the civil population. Evidence marshalled from one London clinic in a three-month period showed that one-fourth of the people who had taken 'precautions' along the lines advocated by the Society became infected, largely as a result of being intoxicated at the time. Thus, medical opinion was divided over the efficacy of 'self-disinfection' when left to individual proficiency.

   There were other divisions. Control or abolition of VD had vital social and political dimensions arising from an intersection of public morals and public

health. The NCCVD was convinced that broadcasting knowledge of self-treatment might encourage 'persons running the risk of infection who would
otherwise avoid that risk, and thus to increase the spread of disease'. This argument was reminiscent of that deployed during the campaign against the
Contagious Diseases Acts in the previous century concerning the sense of false
security given to clients of medically inspected and regulated brothels. The
NCCVD was particularly critical of the SPVD for its insensitivity to the effects
of their propaganda, 'spreading its leaflets broadcast and putting up its posters
for every boy and girl to read'.[17]

Despite the differences in policy between the two over preferred methods of
prophylaxis and their implications for public funding, a controversy eventually
extending throughout the Empire (though not without 'third party' efforts to
bring about a '*modus vivendi*'), the two bodies shared common ground.[18] Both
concurred that the best way to avoid VD was to abstain from promiscuous sexual
acts, that a continuous policy of public 'enlightenment' on sex and the biological
consequences of untreated VD was imperative, and that early treatment, by
qualified medical personnel, would diminish that risk. They also agreed, in the
words of *The Lancet*, that '[w]e cannot hope to stamp out venereal diseases in this
country if there is not a concerted and world-wide alliance of effort against
them'.[19]

The Far Eastern Commission

To the NCCVD, these 'organized campaigns of misrepresentation' by the SPVD
were merely goads to more action in pursuit of their goals. By 1919, overseas
branches were established in South Africa (1917), Bombay (1918), Tasmania
(1918), Canada and West Africa (1919), and the National Council made efforts
to extend the campaign to the crown colonies and protectorates under British
rule. 'You will see that the Empire', observed Lord Sydenham from the chair of
the fifth annual meeting of the National Council, 'has gradually been covered by
organizations, which will do most valuable spade-work in assisting our great
object.'[20] These efforts paid off. The Treasury agreed to fund two small commissions to the eastern and western group of colonies, enough to support a medical
man ('pathologist, clinician and speaker'), a woman ('not necessarily medical'),
and a clerk. An advertisement was placed in *The Lancet* and the *British Medical
Journal* for a suitable medical candidate, though it was clear that the 'woman'
would be the General Secretary of the National Council, Mrs C. Neville-Rolfe.[21]
Sybil Neville-Rolfe, an effective speaker and social activist, began her career in
'rescue work' among women and children. She was a founder of the Eugenics
Education Society, which had petitioned the government in 1912 to set up a
Royal Commission on Venereal Diseases, and the organizer of the women's
section of War Savings. Mrs Neville-Rolfe, whose special interest was conditions
affecting the health of women and children, would be a formidable force in
carrying the message of the NCCVD to the colonies.[22]

177

The medical commissioner chosen on the recommendation of the Ministry of Health was Dr Rupert Hallam, the medical officer in charge of the VD clinic at the Royal Infirmary, Sheffield, who was not the Council's first choice. He had only a 'theoretical' knowledge of the Wassermann technique (which he promised to familiarize himself with), and was not used to addressing lay audiences, but this deficiency was soon remedied by practical experience.[23] Dr Hallam, Mrs Neville-Rolfe as the educational commissioner, and Miss E. O. Grant, acting as secretary, constituted the Far Eastern Commission to visit Hong Kong, Shanghai, Singapore and Colombo.[24]

Their terms of reference were: to consult with colonial governments as to the local steps that could be taken as to the prevention and cure of VD; to discuss all constructive means to develop a complete scheme of treatment and prevention; and to report to the NCCVD on the local conditions as to VD in each colony.

Shanghai

Shanghai was not a colony, but a city divided into three independent jurisdictions – the Chinese city, the International Settlements administered by their independently created Shanghai Municipal Council, and the French Concession with its Conseil Municipal, though the foreign-controlled areas were overwhelmingly populated by Chinese. The scheme to include Shanghai (and other treaty ports frequented by British seamen) in their colonial visits was raised by members of the NCCVD in discussions held with the Foreign Office. A representative of the consular service considered that, although a visit to Shanghai would be 'desirable', as it was a large international seaport and probably ranked as the fifth largest city in the world by 1920, there was no need to visit other treaty ports where British influence and interests were less apparent. Understandably, given their zeal, the NCCVD delegation was not totally convinced of his arguments. Nonetheless, they pressed the Foreign Office to wire the British minister in Shanghai to enquire whether the Shanghai Municipal Council would welcome the Far Eastern Commission after their visit to Hong Kong.[25] The Shanghai Municipal Council agreed to 'afford every assistance in our power to the Commission'. The National Council forwarded the Hong Kong programme and requested advice as how to adapt it to make it suitable to local conditions in Shanghai. As it transpired, Shanghai was their first port of call due to logistical problems, and after their scheduled visits to major Canadian cities and Japan they sailed to Shanghai arriving on 14 December 1920.[26]

The Shanghai Municipal Council was caught in a vice. The Council was under considerable pressure from ratepayers, social activists, moral welfare committees, medical personnel, and indeed the entire polyglot community to act on the recommendations of the special report on *Vice Conditions in Shanghai* prepared following a resolution passed at the ratepayers' meeting of 1919. The report raked over the seamier side of communal life, especially the need to check what was described as 'commercialized vice'. Although religion and morality were central to all decisions regarding the role of prostitution and VD, the message was forthright: the dangers of continued acceptance of such diseases bordered on official irresponsibility.[27]

The Special Vice Committee (including two women) made sixteen recommendations to the Municipal Council, the foremost being that 'brothels be eliminated'. Other recommendations covered laws to prohibit indecent advertisements, street soliciting, 'brothel wine licences', and further provision for treatment of VD (but the cessation of examination of prostitutes by the health department). Better reportage of VD statistics was also proposed, with public funds to be withdrawn for non-compliance, increased public grants to institutions such as the Door of Hope for rehabilitation of prostitutes, and a conference of 'all educational authorities in Shanghai and neighbourhood' for investigating the advisability and methods of teaching social hygiene in schools.[28]

The Municipal Council, perhaps with reference to the earlier failed experiment in state medicine (a locally adapted and partial version of Britain's Contagious Diseases Acts), cautiously endorsed most recommendations except those aimed at eliminating brothels (as these would just move a short distance out of the Settlements' jurisdiction and therefore be uncontrolled), although licensing of brothels was considered as a compromise position. However, the Special Vice Committee, incensed by the inaction of their elected representatives, brought their report and recommendations to a public vote which was carried at the April meeting of the ratepayers. The municipal order was duly published and all brothels, foreign or Chinese, were required to take out a licence on or before 30 June 1920. Furthermore, in a phased process of elimination (a system used previously to close opium dens and shops), it was decided that a lottery would be conducted whereby one-fifth of the brothel licences would be withdrawn annually until all were withdrawn. The licences drawn for closure would be published in the press and the *Municipal Gazette*, and the brothel owners notified by the police. Immediately, protests were lodged by the Chinese Chamber of Commerce, Chinese restaurants and food shops and even by the 'singing girls' (*su nu* or entertainers) of the Settlements. They particularly objected to the indiscriminate application of the regulations to all brothels without classification, especially to the first-class houses, which were, according to custom, 'houses of entertainment'. Their protests were based on the reality that considerable revenue was generated by these houses and their ancillary activities. In the case of the 'singing girls', they did not consider themselves to be prostitutes (though this was an open secret). The Municipal Council replied that 'whilst the Council did not concur with the whole of recommendations made ... it had, as a consequence of the Ratepayers' Resolution, no option but to adopt them'. The so-called 'Sing Song houses' were exempt if they were '*bona fide* conducted as such', and not in fact as brothels.[29]

The beleaguered Municipal Council, recognizing that 'opinions from a great distance commanded respect in Shanghai', eagerly awaited the arrival of the

Commission and turned the responsibility for the visit over to the Moral Welfare Committee to organize a suitable venue. An 'Advisory Committee' was formed with members who had served on the Special Vice Committee. A full programme of public meetings, lectures and conferences was drawn up (including translators) and well over twenty-two institutions and societies were visited. Verbatim accounts of the public lectures were published in the local press.[30] Mrs Neville-Rolfe was singled out for high praise and was eulogized for her special appeal to reach out to women and children in order to create a society 'where there is no wreckage and where venereal disease is non-existent'. 'Shanghai's only remark is', opined *Millard's Review*, an American-owned journal in Shanghai, '[h]ats off to the English suffragist!'[31] This admiration was reciprocated by the commissioners in the shape of a lengthy and detailed report with comprehensive recommendations to the Shanghai Municipal Council.[32]

Although the Health Committee generally endorsed the views of the Commission – the importance of prevention, diagnosis (including laboratory work) and treatment of VD – they concluded that the proposal to give medical and hospital treatment to all persons afflicted 'entirely at public expense ... was impracticable'. The issue of free treatment was regarded as a 'crushing burden on the ratepayers' and one which would 'produce comparatively infinitesimal results on the vast mass of population, reinforced as this is, by continued daily contact with the rest of China'. The independently governed Shanghai International Settlement 'was so situated with respect to the rest of China' that the prevention and treatment of VD necessitated conformity to wider realities.[33] In the meantime, the SMC began a campaign of 'public enlightenment', purchasing the remaining literature, posters, and slides from the Commission, and the municipal secretary offered to serve 'as if he was a branch officer of the National Council'.[34]

Yet, the future success of any educational campaign to eliminate VD was partly prefigured by the changes, social and political, that became manifest in the gradual transformation of China since the revolution of 1911 from a traditional polity to a republican and modern state. The 'new society' envisaged by a more revolutionary generation was conditioned by the need for a 'new people' (*xin min*), that included an equal role and status for women. Thus, the goals of the NCCVD intersected with elements of Chinese reformism, predicated on nationalist pride, that viewed VD and prostitution as threatening the viability of the Chinese race. Whether advocating the abolition or regulation of brothels, Chinese reformers of all persuasions embraced biological and sex education in the schools, and modern medical treatment of VD.[35]

Hong Kong

Fortified by their success in Shanghai, the commissioners faced a cold reception in Hong Kong when they arrived on 20 December 1920. They had been warned before they left England that the Governor, Sir Reginald Stubbs, would not welcome their visit. At their first meeting he informed them that neither the government nor the medical establishment wanted them. Furthermore, he was 'specially dubious of the advisability of a woman speaking on the subject of Venereal Diseases in the Colony', and he did not want Lady Stubbs 'to identify herself in any way with the work of the Commission' (the commissioners would never meet her).[36] No preparations were made for their visit and initially any assistance asked for by the commissioners was declined. However, there was support for the educational aims of the Commission, chiefly from the British Navy, the Chamber of Commerce, several legislative councillors and the Catholic Bishop. The Governor relented and allowed a 'small private conference' with representatives of the army, navy, Chamber of Commerce, government departments, religious leaders, seamen's and women's organizations, while the Chinese were to be approached through the Secretary of Chinese Affairs.[37]

The situation in Hong Kong was somewhat unusual, as one of the first administrative acts after the occupation of the island in 1841 was to guarantee that the Chinese population would be governed 'according to the laws, customs and usages of the Chinese'. Colonial governments, anxious to secure local support for their regime, perpetuated this situation even if those customs, like concubinage, *mui tsai*, or the traffic in women and girls, ran counter to progressive ideas of a civil society (whether in Britain or, by 1912, in the Republic of China). Interestingly, the Governor's resistance stemmed from his view that Chinese opinion was adamantly opposed to raising the subject at all, and he brusquely instructed the commissioners on local affairs: 'We are a small community in the midst of the Chinese. The infection comes from the Chinese. We cannot do anything without the Chinese. Any attempt at education will meet with the most determined opposition. Chinese parents will not hear of their children being taught such matters.' Furthermore, he objected to the advertisement of free treatment of VD on the grounds that '[t]he younger generation are much upset by the revolution. The present lessening of morality among the younger generation is causing great anxiety among the older generation.' Finally, if the commissioners were advocating Western medicine over Chinese, it was doomed from the outset 'as a Chinaman who desires treatment will ... nine times out of ten, go to a native Chinese doctor' who would 'strongly resent your calling him a quack'.[38] Driving his point home, the Governor informed the commissioners that two Chinese-appointed members of the legislative council, Mr Lau Chupak (representing the 'old Chinese') and Mr Ho Fook (representing the 'wealthy Eurasian group'), had refused to meet the commissioners.[39]

The commissioners reacted by moving quickly to secure the support of these prominent members of the Chinese community through the intermediaries of Mr Ho's son-in-law, and Mr Lau's manager, who were persuaded to present the aims of the Commission to these respective gentlemen. To the commissioners' surprise, the two legislative councillors reported that they 'had never been seriously asked' to meet with the commissioners, and furthermore they were advised not to 'waste their time', particularly 'as there was a woman mixed up in it'. To the contrary, the legislators were fully supportive of the goals of the Commission and convened a special meeting with the Chinese Chamber of Commerce who passed a unanimous resolution in support of their aims, which they conveyed to the Governor.[40]

The American YMCA was also allowed to arrange a meeting but only postal invitations were allowed because the Governor had censored the Press, a situation that the Press happily alluded to, probably to the embarrassment of the government.[41] Despite the Governor's dire predictions, 'at a 24 hour notice ... an audience of over 450 Chinese attended' to the satisfaction of the commissioners. Yet they felt that the 'atmosphere of taboo round the subject was ... very injurious to the work ... and prevented a clean public health attitude towards the problem'.[42]

The commissioners were perhaps justifiably critical of Hong Kong after their visit to Shanghai where a municipal enquiry into local vice conditions resulted in important recommendations regarding communal public health. By contrast, in their opinion, despite British rule, the public health of Hong Kong was 'in its infancy'. The government medical department came under direct attack for not making a serious attempt to improve the standard of health of the 'native population'. Mrs Neville-Rolfe was particularly incensed that there was no attempt made to enlighten Chinese women as to the effects of untreated VD on their health and their children's well-being. Public health was also complicated by the 'competition between Eastern and Western medicine', allowing patients to choose which form of treatment they wanted in private charitable hospitals under government 'supervision' such as the Kwong Wah or the Tung Wah. Both hospitals were criticized for being 'dirty and ill-equipped'. Furthermore, as a rule, these hospitals debarred cases of VD, only admitting patients suffering from the later stages of infections. The Po Leung Kuk was also visited and its good work as a refuge for Chinese girls (kidnapped or abandoned) was impugned by allegations by its former medical officer that it was being used as a recruiting ground for cheap supplementary wives by members of the Committee. The medical profession was seen as obstructing the abolition of licensed brothels because of their lucrative 'contract practice' in issuing certificates of freedom of infection, and fears that free medical treatment would reduce the volume of their practice. Finally, the education department, which would be responsible for carrying the hygiene campaign into the schools, was faulted as a 'lax organization' with 'no direct control over the schools' and no 'definite standard for the teachers'.[43] The import of the commissioners' message was clear. The key to prevention was in education and public enlightenment regardless of sex, age or ethnic background.

By the time they presented him with their final recommendations, the Governor's opposition to the campaign was largely tempered by the crystallization of a 'strong body of support' in the community for their work. He agreed to open a port clinic (for the merchant marine), and to make provisions for free diagnosis and treatment. He also sanctioned a careful campaign of 'public

enlightenment' (as in Shanghai, the government purchased the NCCVD literature), though he opposed the creation of a semi-official body to oversee the
work. However, he opted for retaining the *status quo* in supporting the licensed
brothel, as preferable to 'scattered clandestine prostitution'. Neville-Rolfe,
acknowledging the difficulties of the task in Hong Kong where 'western customs
were superimposed on eastern', nonetheless maintained '[t]here was ample
evidence that enlightened Chinese opinion was in favour of the policy of the
National Council'. This decision would embroil Governor Stubbs in a continuing acrimonious debate with the Colonial Office and the NCCVD.[44] By 1922,
due to years of agitation and debate in Hong Kong and Britain, the abolition of
the *mui tsai* system was settled, although the ordinance of 1923 was not enforced
with any rigour until the Guangdong provincial government abolished the
system of 'slavery' in 1927.[45] By 1934, the licensed brothel was phased out, but
concubinage remained legal until 1970.

Singapore

Sailing into Singapore, the administrative centre of the Straits Settlements, on
17 January 1921, the commissioners were unaware that the campaign in Hong
Kong had influenced their reception. To their annoyance, the Governor and his
wife, Sir Lawrence and Lady Guillemard, were away in the Federated Malay
States and would not receive them until three days before their visit ended. Their
scheduled preliminary conference was cancelled, and only on the last day of
their visit was an official conference convened by the Governor. The 'disadvantages of this', they claimed, made it difficult for them 'to reach many of the
representative persons whose assistance and co-operation we required'.
Furthermore, the acting Governor, Sir William Murison (the Colonial Secretary),
candidly informed them that Governor Stubbs had advised Guillemard not to
receive them. They were assured, however, that, 'after careful consideration',
Governor Guillemard would indeed meet with them and allow an open public
forum for their campaign, neither censoring the Press (as had been done in
Hong Kong), nor obstructing their visit.[46]

Similar to the situation in Shanghai, the commissioners found themselves
faced with a local 'venereal disease controversy'. It had erupted in the previous
year among the local medical fraternity, and the Protestant bishop and other
laymen, over the formation of a Federated Malay States Branch of the Society
for the Prevention of Venereal Diseases. Not wishing to exacerbate a local issue
that would clearly hamper their educative mission (considering the controversy
in Britain between the NCCVD and the SPVD over their respective policies
towards the prophylaxis of VD), the President of the Malaya Branch, Dr
Rattray (also President of the Medical Association), was contacted immediately
in order that they might explain their position and secure the Society's support.
To their relief, the commissioners found the 'elements of difference in policy so
apparent at home were not acute under Eastern conditions'; namely that

'[s]elf-disinfection for the illiterate was recognized by the [Malaya branch]
Society for the Prevention of Venereal Diseases as quite impracticable'.[47]
Effective preventive medicine in the hands of government authorities was
anxiously sought by the local branch. What this meant later became clear. The
commissioners found to their dismay that there was an appreciable reservoir of
support in the medical community (including the Principal Medical Officer), the
Attorney-General, and the non-official members of the Legislative Council for
reintroducing the Contagious Diseases Acts. Not wishing to 'jeopardize the
future of the free treatment scheme', the commissioners avoided as much as
possible the issue of the suppression of brothels and the compulsory medical
examination of prostitutes. In addition, they laid the accumulated evidence
before the medical community and the Governor on the uselessness of the state
regulation of prostitution as a public health measure.[48]

Contrary to local opinion, the commissioners thought that the situation as
regards prostitution was not as 'undesirable' as in Hong Kong, although it was
more complicated in view of the ethnic divisions within the Straits Settlements.
Of the half a million people in the Straits Settlements, less than ten thousand
were Europeans; 400,000 or 78 per cent were Chinese (mostly of the labouring
classes); 11 per cent were Malays; 8 per cent Indian; 1.5 per cent Eurasian and
the remaining 1.5 per cent were Japanese, Arabs, Thais, and Filipinos. European
prostitutes had been banished and their brothels closed and the Japanese consul
had taken similar steps with his own nationals engaged in the trade. Malay prostitutes were located in the poorer section of town and did not work in brothels.
According to their informants the most numerous prostitutes were Chinese.
Approximately 500 Chinese women (underestimated) worked in brothels located
in the 'most frequented part of town' exclusively for a Chinese clientele. As in
Shanghai and Hong Kong, 'Europeans [were] not admitted owing to the
strength of Chinese opinion'. Although the government did not license brothels,
they were recognized and allowed to remain as long as they 'were decently
conducted'. Clandestine prostitution was widespread, mainly involving Eurasian
women, but beyond government interference. Caught between the impractica-
bility of immediately abolishing brothels, and unwilling to countenance them
through licensing as in Hong Kong, the Governor opted for the *status quo* for the
time being and was firmly against the reintroduction of the Contagious Diseases
Acts.[49]

The negative communications from Hong Kong also gave rise to 'considerable uneasiness, especially with reference to the Chinese population'. As in Hong
Kong, this 'unease' had a dual provenance. On the one hand, it alluded to the
well-established Chinese trafficking in women and girls throughout southeast
Asia, principally from Guangdong province, for the purposes of prostitution.
Singapore was an important and profitable link in a chain of human commodi-
ties; a situation tolerated as the majority of Chinese immigrants in Singapore
were male labourers who could not afford the 'bride price' or bring their wives
from China to Singapore.[50] On the other hand, it alluded to segments of the

Chinese community who knew the evils of the system but were unwilling simply to equate it with other social customs, such as concubinage, or *mui tsai*. As in Hong Kong, prominent members of the Chinese community had established the Po Leung Kuk, a charitable institution under government supervision to end the kidnapping of young girls and to provide a refuge for those who were 'ill-treated, under-age or abandoned'. The commissioners who visited the institution were 'much struck with the difference between its excellent and efficient management and the Po Leung Kuk in Hong Kong'.[51]

Through the good advice of Legislative Councillor, Dr Lim Boon Keng (an active participant in the local VD controversy), an introduction was secured with the president of the Chinese Chamber of Commerce who had heard of the Hong Kong meeting. The commissioners 'fortunately' were able to allay any disquiet by providing him with 'full accounts from the Hong Kong Chinese press', which he was able to use 'as the basis for local propaganda in the Chinese press'. Interestingly, the leading English language newspaper, *The Straits Times*, though under no censorship or objection from the government as was the case in Hong Kong, was initially 'very opposed' to the visit of the Commission, a view they communicated to their readership. A meeting was arranged with the Chinese Chamber resulting in a 'unanimous resolution in favour of the policy of free treatment and public enlightenment with reference to venereal disease'.[52]

The Commission's programme was largely fulfilled. They visited every medical institution, prominent social organization, and a range of military, religious or charitable institutions and distributed literature and educational films. In addition to the general recommendations made to every port they visited, they made additional recommendations to Governor Guillemard. They proposed that a joint scheme for the provision of facilities for free diagnosis and treatment of VD be coordinated between Singapore and the Federated Malay States; that a venereal specialist be added to the staff of the principal medical officer; that a special clinic for residents in the centre of town (this referred to the Chinese population) be provided in addition to those in outlying hospitals; that a medical woman should be in charge of the clinics for women and supervise educational propaganda; that public enlightenment among all sections of the population be coordinated with the medical services in cooperation with the (newly established) Federated Malay States Council for Combatting Venereal Disease (affiliated with the NCCVD); and finally, that the government should appoint a trained and qualified woman to assist the Protector of Chinese with reference to all questions affecting the care of women and girls. In contrast to Hong Kong, the Governor and Lady Guillemard supported the founding of a local branch of the NCCVD and volunteered to act as joint presidents of the council, and the honorary secretary of the local branch of the SPVD acted as joint secretary for both organizations.[53] Furthermore, the visit of the NCCVD prompted the most comprehensive report on VD in Singapore, a harrowing account of local conditions that Guillemard published to the embarrassment of the Colonial Office.[54]

Conclusion

The Far Eastern Commission of the NCCVD continued to agitate for their general goals, above all, free treatment and confidentiality for all persons infected with VD, as well as promoting specific recommendations reflecting the local conditions of each city that they visited. A measure of their success was that in each place, free international port clinics were planned or opened by May 1921, although the Commission's request that their reports be published in the form of a parliamentary white paper was declined.[55] The NCCVD, renamed the British Social Hygiene Council in 1925, continued to agitate for reform through their journal, *Health and Empire*, as well as supporting imperial conferences for sharing medical intelligence.

What if anything did this imperial campaign accomplish? Clearly the NCCVD had laid the basis for what has become the accepted approach for the prevention and treatment of VD and established the importance of sex and biological education for the general public. It was recognized that the possible elimination or more effective control of these diseases was not only an international problem but an imperial one, in which education, not coercion, could bridge the impasse of gender, age, ethnic background (race), and cultural and environmental differences. The campaign also signalled that haphazard provisions for, or even neglect of, public health and preventative health care by the British government and their colonial representatives were no longer acceptable. One of the most important revelations of the Far Eastern Commission (and the Western Commission) was the deficiencies of the colonial medical service, in failing to provide non-gendered and non-racial medical care, in its lack of knowledge of new diagnostic techniques and treatments, as well as the inadequate training of doctors and nurses responsible for health care delivery. In part, this was in recognition that the state faced real limitations in its power to effect changes, however salutary, when local environments and cultures intersected with the social and political dimensions of public health.

NOTES

1 *The Lancet*, 21 Jan. 1922, p. 140.
2 I wish to thank the Contemporary Medical Archives Centre, Wellcome Library for the History and Understanding of Medicine, for showing me every courtesy and allowing me access to their archival holdings on the NCCVD, listed by Lesley Hall.
3 D. Arnold, *Colonizing the Body: State Medicine and Epidemic Diseases in Nineteenth-Century India*, Berkeley, University of California Press, 1993; D. Arnold, 'Sex, state and society: sexually transmitted diseases and HIV/AIDS in modern India', in M. Lewis *et al.* (eds) *Sex, Disease, and Society: A Comparative History of Sexually Transmitted Diseases and HIV/AIDS in Asia and the Pacific*, Westport, Greenwood Press, 1997, pp. 19–36; L. Manderson, *Sickness and the State: Health and Illness in Colonial Malaya, 1970–1940*, Cambridge, Cambridge University Press, 1996; L. Manderson *et al.* (eds) *Sites of Desire, Economies of Pleasure: Sexualities in Asia and the Pacific*, Chicago, University of Chicago Press, 1997; B. Yeoh, *Contesting Space: Power Relations and the Urban Built Environment in Colonial Singapore*, Kuala Lumpur, Oxford University Press, 1996; B.

Yeoh, 'Sexually transmitted diseases in late nineteenth- and twentieth-century Singapore', in Lewis *et al.*, *Sex, Disease, and Society*, pp. 177–202.

4 P. Larson, ' "Capacities and modes of thinking": Intellectual engagements and subaltern hegemony in the early history of Malagasy Christianity', *American Historical Review*, 1997, vol. 102, no. 4, pp. 969–1,002; M. Sutphen, 'Cookie-cutter epidemics? The Colonial Office and the plague epidemics in Cape Town and Hong Kong, 1901–1902', London, Institute of Commonwealth Studies, University of London, 1992.

5 B. Towers, 'Health education policy, 1916–1926: Venereal diseases and the prophylaxis dilemma', *Medical History*, 1980, vol. 24, pp. 70–87.

6 Dr Barthelémy, 'La conférence internationale pour la prophylaxie de malades vénériennes', *Revue de médecine légale*, 1900, vol. 8, pp. 41–8; *British Medical Journal*, 9 Sept. 1899, pp. 676–8.

7 Very little has been written about the Far Eastern Commission of the NCCVD. However, for Hong Kong, see N. Miners, *Hong Kong under Imperial Rule, 1912–1941*, Hong Kong, Oxford University Press, 1987, pp. 198–9; K. MacPherson, 'Conspiracy of silence: A history of sexually transmitted diseases and HIV/AIDS in Hong Kong', in Lewis *et al.*, *Sex, Disease, and Society*, pp. 97–9. For Shanghai, see C. Henriot, 'Medicine, VD and prostitution in pre-revolutionary China', *Social History of Medicine*, 1992, vol. 5, p. 114.

8 On Shanghai's experiment with state medicine and its lock hospital inspired by the British CD acts, see K. MacPherson, *A Wilderness of Marshes: The Origins of Public Health in Shanghai, 1843–1893*, New York, Oxford University Press, 1987, pp. 213–58. For Hong Kong, see Miners, *Hong Kong under Imperial Rule*, pp. 191–3; K. MacPherson, '*Caveat emptor!* Attempts to control the venereals in nineteenth century Hong Kong', in L. Bryder *et al.* (eds) *New Countries and Old Medicine*, Auckland, The Auckland Medical Historical Society and Pyramid Press, 1995, pp. 72–8; for Singapore, see J. Warren, *Ah Ku and Karayuki-San: Prostitution in Singapore, 1870–1940*, Singapore, Oxford University Press, 1993, pp. 122–52.

9 In the inter-war period, recognizing the limitations of the statistical records, the incidence of VD in China was estimated to range from a low of 5 per cent of the general population to a high of 50 or 60 per cent (L. T. Wu, 'Problem of venereal diseases in China', *China Medical Journal*, 1927, vol. 41, no. 1, pp. 28–36). In Hong Kong from 1919 to 1924, the incidence of VD was 1.5 to 3.2 per cent of all admissions to hospital. However, a survey of ten police stations in the New Territories showed an annual incidence of 43.5 per cent of the force (H. Macfarlane and G. E. Aubrey, 'Venereal diseases among the natives of Hong Kong', *The Caduceus*, 1922, vol. 1, no. 1, pp. 22–7). In Singapore from 1919 to 1922, the incidence of VD based on statistics from twelve major medical practices showed a 50 to 80 per cent infection rate amongst males. More alarming was the report that one in four of all Chinese children born in Singapore was syphilitic (Warren, *Ah Ku and Karayuki-San*, pp. 170–1).

10 The most comprehensive examination of prostitution in nineteenth-century Hong Kong is: *Report of the Commissioners to Enquire into the Working of the 'Contagious Diseases Ordinance, 1867'*, Hong Kong, Noronha, 1879, commissioned by the Governor, Sir John Pope Hennessy, who was bitterly opposed to the Acts and the system of regulation of prostitution resulting from them. According to interviews conducted by the Commission, a Chinese medical practitioner, Mr Pang, testified that only 25 per cent of the Chinese women in Hong Kong were not prostitutes. If he was correct, out of an adult female population of approximately 24,000, 18,000 were prostitutes as of 1878. The first police magistrate, Charles May (who allegedly owned brothels in Lyndhurst Terrace), put the figure higher. *Report of the Commissioners*, p. 31. For the twentieth century, see the rather impressionistic works of Wu Hao, *Fengyue tangxi* (Brothels of Tangxi), Hong Kong, Boyi chuban jituan youxian gongsi, 1989 and

Xiangjiang fengchen shi (History of prostitution in Hong Kong), Hong Kong, Boyi chuban jituan youxian gongsi, 1990. For Singapore, see Warren, *Ah Ku and Karayuki-San*. For both colonies, see the voluminous *Contagious Diseases Ordinances (Colonies). Copies of Correspondence or Extracts therefrom, Relating to the Repeal of Contagious Diseases Ordinance and Regulations, in the Crown Colonies, H.C. 242*, London, Colonial Office, 1890. For two excellent recent studies that cover the attempts to regulate prostitution in Shanghai in the nineteenth and twentieth centuries, see C. Henriot, *Belles de Shanghai: Prostitution et Sexualité en Chine aux XIXe–XXe Siècles*, Paris, CNRS Editions, 1997, pp. 301–86; and G. Hershatter, *Dangerous Pleasures: Prostitution and Modernity in Twentieth Century Shanghai*, Berkeley, University of California Press, 1997, pp. 226–303. For a critical and comprehensive review of recent studies of prostitution, see T. Gilfoyle, 'Prostitutes in history: from parables of pornography to metaphors of modernity', *American Historical Review*, 1999, vol. 104, no. 1, pp. 117–41.

11 Macfarlane and Aubrey, 'Venereal diseases among the natives of Hong Kong', pp. 22–7.

12 *Report of the Commissioners to Enquire into the Working of the 'Contagious Diseases Ordinance, 1867'*, p. 5.

13 Quan Hansheng, 'Qingmo xiyang yixue chuanru shiguoren soqidi taidu' (Late Qing attitudes towards western medical science), *Shi huo*, 1936, vol. 3, no. 2, pp. 43–53.

14 *The Lancet*, 12 March 1921, p. 552; and 22 May 1920, p. 1,142. For background to the British movement, see R. Porter and L. Hall, *The Facts of Life: The Creation of Sexual Knowledge in Britain, 1650–1950*, New Haven, Yale University Press, 1995, pp. 224–46; L. Hall, '"The English have hot-water bottles": the morganatic marriage between medicine and sexology in Britian since William Acton', in R. Porter and M. Teich (eds) *Sexual Knowledge, Sexual Science*, Cambridge, Cambridge University Press, 1995, pp. 350–66; *British Medical Journal*, 26 July 1913, pp. 194–5; 2 Aug. 1913, p. 269.

15 NCCVD, Minutes Fifth Annual General Meeting, 7 June 1920, Wellcome Library, Archives and Manuscripts, CMAC: SA/BSH/A.1/1.

16 *The Lancet*, 11 June 1921, p. 1,257.

17 Ibid.

18 *British Medical Journal*, 8 July 1921, p. 44.

19 *The Lancet*, 21 Jan. 1922, p. 140.

20 NCCVD, Minutes of Fifth Annual General Meeting, CMAC: SA/BSH/A.1/1.

21 NCCVD, Minutes of Executive Committee, 12 April 1920; 10 May 1920, CMAC: SA/BSH/A.2/4. The Treasury was prepared to commit £7,500.

22 Sybil (Mrs C.) Neville-Rolfe, formerly Mrs A. C. Gotto, went on to become the general secretary of the British Social Hygiene Council, as the NCCVD was renamed in 1925. She continued visiting colonial outposts, for example Jamaica, and publishing in the BSHC's journal, *Health and Empire*, into the 1930s. See 'Women and a cleaner world', *Millard's Review*, 25 Dec. 1920, vol. 15, no. 4, pp. 193–4; *Health and Empire*, Sept. 1932, vol. 7, no. 3, pp. 221–34. See also her obituary in *The Times*, 5 August 1955.

23 NCCVD, Minutes of Executive Committee, 4 Oct. 1920, SA/BSH/A.2/4.

24 According to the Commissioners, Colombo 'was the cleanest port visited and compared very favourably with any English port'. *British Medical Journal*, 14 May 1921, p. 717. As Colombo did not have a significant Chinese population, I have not included a discussion of their findings here.

25 NCCVD, Minutes of Executive Committee, 17 Nov. 1919, SA/BSH/A.2/4.

26 NCCVD, Minutes of Executive Committee, 1 Nov. 1920, SA/BSH/A.2/4. According to reports, the Commission received a 'warm welcome' across Canada and encouraged closer cooperation with the Canadian Council for Combatting VD who reorganized along the lines of the British National Council. *British Medical Journal*, 1 Jan. 1921, pp. 27–8.

27 'Vice conditions in Shanghai. Report of the Special Vice Committee', *Municipal Gazette*, 20 March 1920, vol. 13, no. 681, pp. 83–6.
28 Ibid., p. 86.
29 Shanghai Municipal Council, *Annual Report for the Year Ending 31 Dec. 1920*, Shanghai, Kelly & Walsh, 1921, pp. 256–60.
30 *North-China Herald*, 18 Dec. 1920; 24 Dec. 1920; 25 Dec. 1920.
31 *Millard's Review*, 25 Dec. 1920, vol. 15, no. 4, p. 196.
32 Shanghai Municipal Council, *Annual Report for the Year Ending 31 Dec. 1920*, pp. 262–7.
33 Shanghai Municipal Council, *Annual Report for the Year Ending 31 Dec. 1921*, Shanghai, Kelly & Walsh, 1921, p. 232.
34 NCCVD, Minutes of Executive Committee, 4 April 1921, SA/BSH/A.2/4.
35 F. Dikötter, *Sex, Culture and Modernity in China*, Hong Kong, University of Hong Kong Press, 1995.
36 *Hong Kong Confidential Report, National Council for Combatting Venereal Diseases Commissioners. Transmitted to the Colonial Office by the National Council. April 1921*, CO 129/472, pp. 356–57. Stubbs, the son of Bishop William Stubbs, Regius Professor of History, Oxford University, began his career as a civil servant in the Colonial Office in 1900 after graduating from Corpus Christi College. After special assignments in various colonies, he was Governor of Hong Kong from 1919 to 1925, arguably very difficult times. Unlike his predecessor and successor, who were both Hong Kong cadets and well-versed in Cantonese, Stubbs was viewed as a bit out of his depth (G. Endacott, 'Sir Reginald Stubbs – Governor in exciting times', *The China Mail*, 17 July 1965).
37 *Hong Kong Confidential Report*, p. 357.
38 *Conference Convened by His Excellency the Governor in the Council Chambers, Hong Kong, Friday 31 Dec. 1920*, CO 129/472, pp. 350–1.
39 *Hong Kong Confidential Report*, p. 357. Both Lau and Ho (Sir Robert Ho Tung's half brother) served as the only Chinese unofficial legislative councillors at that time. Lau generously contributed to the founding of the Helena May Institute for Women (which still exists on Garden Road) in 1914, for the welfare and accommodation of non-Chinese working women of the colony, a concern of the previous Governor's wife. Lau was also active in the *mui tsai* controversy (Lau Chu-pak, 'Girl slavery in Hong Kong', CO 129/467, pp. 250–2).
40 *Hong Kong Confidential Report*, p. 357.
41 For example, the Press commented: 'An official request that these lectures not be reported is our reason for the omission of any lengthy account of them', *South China Morning Post*, 8 Jan. 1921. *The Hong Kong Telegraph*, 7 Jan. 1921, reported: '[a]s desired, we abstain from recording the proceedings *in extenso*, but there can scarcely be any reason against giving an outline of the lecture, especially as Dr Hallam acknowledged the service rendered by the Press generally in opening its columns to a consideration of the evil'.
42 *Hong Kong Confidential Report*, pp. 357–8.
43 Ibid., pp. 358–9.
44 *British Medical Journal*, 9 July 1921, p. 45; CO 129/484, pp. 125–8; CO 129/484, pp. 258–9.
45 Miners, *Hong Kong under Imperial Rule*, p. 170.
46 *Singapore Confidential Report, National Council for Combatting Venereal Diseases Commission 1920*, CO 129/472, p. 438. This report was for the Colonial Office only and the paragraphs marked in red (the exposé of Governor Stubbs's communication with Guillemard) were considered confidential and omitted from the general report.
47 *Singapore Confidential Report*, p. 440.
48 Ibid., p. 445.
49 Ibid., pp. 443–5.

50 For an excellent discussion of the 'flesh trade' see Warren, *Ah Ku and Karayuki-San*, pp. 66–99. According to Warren, 80 per cent of the Chinese girls brought to Singapore in the 1880s were destined for the brothels.

51 Warren points out that the Po Leung Kuk in Singapore (like the Door of Hope in Shanghai or Peking) regularly arranged for the marriages of their charges, though the Singapore committee seemed to insist that the girls become 'first wives' (Warren, *Ah Ku and Karayuki-San*, pp. 336–8; *Singapore Confidential Report*, p. 444). What may have incensed the commissioners about this practice in Hong Kong was that members of the board of directors used it as a source for secondary wives, or concubines, who did not possess the familial rights or legal status conferred on primary wives. By custom, their children addressed the first wife as 'mother', and these concubines could be easily sent away or even sold. The commissioners also commented that the Hong Kong institution was 'popularly looked upon as a prison and managed on prison lines' (*Hong Kong Confidential Report*, p. 360).

52 *Singapore Confidential Report*, p. 440.

53 *Singapore, General Report of the National Council for Combatting Venereal Diseases Commissioners. Transmitted to the Colonial Office by the National Council, April 1921*, CO 129/472, pp. 451–62. *British Medical Journal*, 14 May 1921, p. 717.

54 Report of the Venereal Diseases Committee, *Straits Settlements Legislative Council Sessional Papers 1923*, pp. C286–327.

55 NCCVD, Minutes of Executive Committee, 2 May 1921; 6 June 1921; 29 June 1921, SA/BSH/A.2/5. Not deterred by the Under Secretary of State for the Colonial Office's response to their request, the NCCVD asked whether they might publish the reports, and if that was denied whether a question could be asked in the House 'as to the use which was to be made of the reports' (NCCVD, Minutes of Executive Committee, 25 July 1921, SA/BSH/A.2/5).

11

VENEREAL DISEASE, SEXUALITY AND SOCIETY IN UGANDA

Michael W. Tuck

Introduction

In response to a request from the governor of Uganda, in 1907 the British
Foreign Office sent a syphilis expert from the Royal Army Medical Corps
(RAMC) to report on the extent of venereal disease (VD) in the colony. The
expert, Colonel F. J. Lambkin, prepared a report by interviewing medical officials, missionaries and Ugandan chiefs, and he concluded that VD was rampant
and rapidly worsening. Although Lambkin's informants suggested a number of
reasons why VD was spreading swiftly, they tended to agree on two points:
syphilis was the most important VD in Uganda, and women were mainly
responsible for its outbreak and spread.[1]

European officials, missionaries and African politicians widely believed in an
uncontrolled epidemic of venereal syphilis, and they formulated responses based
on their perceptions of the disease. European and African beliefs reinforced one
another and resulted in the development of an understanding of VD in Uganda
which was based on ideas of gender, morality, race and uncontrolled sexuality.
British groups, from the RAMC to the National Council for Combatting Venereal
Diseases, influenced ideas about and policies towards the infected. European
views of African bodies and African sexuality affected definitions of VD, and
specific measures to combat syphilis were explicitly drawn from British experience.[2]

However, ideas and actions about VD in Uganda were not driven solely by
Europeans. Africans, especially élite African men, had their own ideas about
sexuality in their society which influenced their response to VD. Furthermore,
because of the nature of colonial rule in Uganda, African men had the power to
enforce policies. The British established a protectorate over the kingdom of
Buganda in 1893, and over the next decade expanded their rule over a wider
territory which would become the colony of Uganda.[3] The now province of
Buganda became the core of the colony and as a former kingdom maintained

some degree of autonomy. The British left in place a monarch (*kabaka*) and several senior politicians. Chiefs had the authority to enforce laws and collect taxes in their areas, and the upper level of chiefs formed a parliament which had the power to pass legislation for all of Buganda. African politicians eagerly exercised their powers as they tried to control VD and the diseased.

Although the concern in this chapter is mainly with social effects, it is impossible to separate social and medical aspects. The social response to VD was intended, in part, to ensure attendance of reluctant patients at the medical clinics. Socially, fears of VD influenced nearly every aspect of colonial society, from school curricula to a range of legislation, while medical responses to VD focused on issues of control – control of contagion through control of people. People with infectious diseases were barred from employment, and VD was used as an argument to enforce draconian laws concerning adultery and 'fornication'. In addition, the clinical experience was intended to reinforce the social messages about VD. How the efforts at medical and social control affected the population in Uganda needs to be explored in order to uncover more fully the impact that specific attitudes and beliefs had on people's lives. Seen in the context of colonialism (and colonial policy which depended on working through local chiefs), the response to VD resulted in social and legal restrictions on women and young men in particular.

Social discourse about VD

It is clear that the ideas which developed about VD had an impact on Ugandan perceptions of health and illness, and were widely accepted by 1955:

> Syphilis is popularly supposed to be a common disease in Uganda and large numbers of people come to hospitals and dispensaries demanding specific treatment with little or no justification.

> [...]An unfortunate idea has arisen that infertility, abortion, still-birth or death of offspring must be due to syphilis and a great demand is made by pregnant women for various anti-syphilitic injections. We consider it is important that proper health education should be instituted so that it is realised that much of the mortality and morbidity in mothers and babies is due to ignorance of nutrition, faulty personal or domestic hygiene, physical overwork or serious neglect of the child.[4]

It is not surprising that the above ideas were widespread in 1955, given that these were the messages being broadcast for most of the previous half century in Uganda. It is also understandable that Ugandans perceived close connections between women's reproductive health and syphilis, since that was a major focal point of public discourse.

When VD was raised as a serious threat in 1907, the first reactions by Ugandans were to define somehow the diseases and then explain their outbreak. After all, since venereal syphilis was not recognized as an illness by Ugandans prior to this, they could not define, explain or account for it. Europeans introduced to Uganda the concept of a group of diseases united by their transmission during immoral sexual activity, for 'venereal disease' connoted not just sexual transmission, but also the shameful nature of the sexual contact.[5] The eventual term for VD in Luganda became *endwadde ez'obukaba*, meaning illnesses of immorality, sinfulness or depravity, which more closely captured the sense of the word 'venereal' in VD.[6] The first European doctors to work on the anti-VD programme in Uganda addressed the senior African chiefs, explained the problem of syphilis to them, and the chiefs understood and agreed to help in the programme.[7] The chiefs readily understood and accepted the basics of the European explanation because these accorded with their view of the world and with prevailing ideas of illness. Because the VD scheme, like all of the colonial initiatives in Uganda, worked through the chiefs, their cooperation was essential for success. Furthermore, they were influential in the direction and scope the VD programme was to take and in the public discourse about VD.

The Ugandan chiefs – the male élite – had no trouble believing that their society was under threat by forces of rampant immorality and other undisciplined behaviour. This explanation fitted neatly with their views of a rapidly changing and chaotic society in which women and young men were resisting the control of older men. Prior to syphilis bursting onto the public stage, the African chiefs had been fighting a battle for years against what they saw as unrestrained sexuality and other social ills. While often expressed in the terms of Christian discourse, sexual control of young men and women had long been a purview of older African men. As such, they welcomed the idea that an epidemic resulted from this chaos since it offered a tangible link between their ideas of individual action and social disruption. And although most of the chiefs professed to be Christians, the concept of an epidemic resulting from people abandoning traditions and proper behaviour fitted with long-held African notions of retribution as a punishment for immoral conduct.

Fear of VD entered the existing discourse on the moral problems of the colony. In the African press, women were accused of acting in immoral ways and committing adultery with impunity, leading to VD and infertility.[8] Public discourse about sexuality, gender relations and social developments in general were all greatly influenced by perceptions of VD in society. From the time British colonial officials focused attention on VD in 1907, the discourse took on apocalyptic tones. Colonial officials were concerned with the impact that VD had on African population growth, and thus on the potential development of the colony. African concerns were broader, spanning issues of reproduction, gender relations and the general state of society, and paralleled those of British missionaries in Uganda who sought deeper explanations than colonial officials about the perceived outbreak of VD. Ugandans also sought explanations about the origins of diseases, how they spread through Uganda, and why they broke out when they did. Linkages between VD and race in colonial Uganda were complex and contradictory. In general, Europeans viewed Africans as both highly sexualized and diseased, but they were reluctant to blame African chiefs directly for the problem of VD. African men, on the other hand, tended to see syphilis in partic- ular as an imported disease, and attributed it to European or Asian visitors to Uganda who had access to African women. Asian views are missing from the historical record, but European officials and African men agreed that African women were the important link in disease transmission. The main explanation for disease outbreak which fitted with all views was the changing gender roles and sexual behaviours of women in Ugandan society.[9]

A connection between syphilis and women was strengthened by the European explanations offered. The idea of such a connection between syphilis and women was widespread in England, and as projected by Europeans in Buganda it supported the ideas about VD which were developing in the colony. Some European observers explicitly linked women and disease, such as the colonial doctor who attributed the spread of syphilis to 'the naturally immoral proclivities of the [Ugandan] women'.[10] European officials and African chiefs correlated the notion of syphilis as a condition or disease caused by immoral behaviour with the idea that immoral activity by women was widespread, thus ensuring that women would be the target of anti-syphilis efforts. As a direct result, the anti- syphilis information campaign focused on problems of women and immorality.

The colonial government and missionaries worked through schools, public lectures, films and other media to broadcast their views about VD and its dangers. An important aspect of the propaganda campaign was two widely distributed leaflets on VD written by the missionary doctors (and brothers) Albert and Jack Cook. Few if any Ugandan women were literate at this time and the Cooks, knowing this, wrote for African men. Both pamphlets depicted women as the sources of venereal infection, and thus representing a real danger to the predominantly male audience being addressed. Jack Cook (in a 1908 pamphlet on the causes of infant mortality) described VD as being those illnesses that 'infect people who couple with adulterous women *(nabakazi abobwenzi)*'.[11] The phrase *'abakazi abobwenzi'* was often used to refer to promiscuous or 'morally loose' women, not just women who committed adultery *per se*. In Albert Cook's description of venereal transmission (found in his 1921 pamphlet on VD), he traced infection to sex between a man and infected woman, and sometimes on to the man's wife and family. Albert Cook considered promiscuous women a source of contagion for many men. While he acknowledged that a man originally infected the woman, there was no concern for her well-being, only for the men she might go on to infect. 'If he [an infected man] couples with a promiscuous woman, he infects her, and she in turn will infect ten or more others and the problem spreads like wildfire.'[12]

These 'promiscuous' or 'loose' women were objectified as diseased creatures, and spoken of as one would an infected well. It was a problem to be taken care of, but not one which deserved the attention given to those people 'innocently' infected. An explanation for this was the dichotomous construction of African women by the British, who acted as if there were two kinds of women: virtuous wives who needed to be protected from disease, and prostitutes and loose women who were to be controlled and treated through legal means. Thus, there was no need to address women directly in these pamphlets. The virtuous, obedient wife was protected by her husband, as long as he knew the dangers of VD. Meanwhile, the immoral woman was corralled by the authorities under one of the laws regulating VD or prostitution which restricted the movements of women and allowed for the medical examination of women suspected of being infected. Men, even when infected from adulterous encounters, were not totally at fault because the blame was directed at the women who infected them.

Part of the anti-VD campaign was to create an unambiguous message about VD which could be spread through Uganda. The next steps were to ensure that the message was promoted in the clinical setting as well, and that all possible means were used to control sources of infection in the colony.

Medical response and its social effects

Until confronted by VD in 1907, medical personnel within the colony confined their attention to the health of army troops, and any conditions which could affect Europeans or long-term development plans for the colony. It was for this reason that venereal syphilis attracted the attention of officials in Kampala, Nairobi and London, who feared that it would leave Uganda with no population base from which to develop.[13] The resulting colonial response to the perceived epidemic of VD had a tremendous impact on the medical history of Uganda. The main government hospital, the network of rural dispensaries, the midwifery programmes started by the missions, and the education of medical assistants all had their origin in colonial anti-VD schemes. After the 1907 visit of Colonel Lambkin, the British government sent out three RAMC officers in 1908 to undertake a special venereal treatment programme in the colony.[14] That the first VD medical officers in Uganda came from the RAMC was significant because they modelled the anti-VD programme on that operating in the British army, with emphasis on compulsory attendance, examination and treatment, and regulatory measures to ensure compliance. Equally important were the Christian missions, who for decades operated the vast majority of the medical facilities for treating Ugandans, and who emphasized the immorality of those infected with VD. The government VD programme only became fully operational in 1913 with the completion of the facility at Mulago, outside of Kampala, and with the passage of various VD laws. Armed with both the legislative authority to prompt patients' attendance and the medical facility to treat them, the government doctors were ready to stem the tide of VD in Uganda. After a hiatus during the First World War, the VD programme achieved its full effects in the 1920s.

Those effects were as much – if not more – social rather than medical.

Patients avoided the largely ineffective and poisonous mercury therapies and often could not afford the more effective but expensive arsenicals.[15] Given the lack of appropriate drugs and the continuing reluctance of patients to seek and sustain treatment, doctors struggled to reach and treat the African population. How the Africans viewed these efforts can be seen in this description from a Ugandan scholar:

> The government clinic at Mulago was at first thought of as a haven. It was advertised throughout the country by the Protectorate government through the Baganda Council. ... Thousands of young and old people came out of their huts and villages hoping to be cured as soon as they arrived at the clinic. The treatment at the clinic was what the people expected. Whatever the treatment, it was known as *a ekalo*, or a giant needle. The needle or tube that was used terrified the people. Tale after tale spread all over the towns and villages that the white man was using a giant needle which he pushed inside the male organs after which a man was sexually incapacitated. The advertised remedy then was interpreted by the people as emasculation. From the medical point of view, there were cases that were beyond hope, and the men were sterilized. It was upon these scattered cases that the people mourned and lamented, and from these deduced that they were going to lose their organs. An exodus of socially diseased folks began. They ran out of town and went into hiding in the villages. There was one drug store in the country. Business picked up and the sale of venereal disease remedies skyrocketed.[16]

Not surprisingly, Ugandans sought and created alternatives to the unpleasant and costly treatment offered at government and missionary hospitals. Traditional medicine was available, although Western medicine was seen to be more effective and was thus preferred. Pharmacies offered Western medicine without the trouble of a medical examination or hospitalization. However, government officials regulated both of these choices and specifically prohibited pharmacies from dispensing medicine for VD. Not that regulations controlled everyone, as evidenced by two healers who were brought to trial in 1925 for causing the death of persons they had treated for VD with traditional medicine.[17] A similar case around 1930 resulted in the traditional healer being sentenced to four months of hard labour.[18]

The ordinance criminalizing VD treatment by non-registered practitioners was created in 1921 (and directly modelled on the British law) in response to pharmacies in Kampala 'extorting enormous sums from natives for so called cures for Venereal Diseases'.[19] Pharmacies advertised in local language newspapers to attract the business of Ugandans. Sometimes they published notices of particular medicines which they had in stock, and other times they simply advertised their status as dealers in European medicines, knowing that was enough to attract customers.[20] One pharmacy, Howse & McGeorge, carried arsenicals for syphilis and although they were supposed to supply only registered doctors, African patients managed to acquire them.[21]

When doctors did interact with patients, a major goal of the VD programme was to create a stigma about VD. European doctors felt that their biggest obstacles to controlling VD were the patients' ignorance about their condition and their apathy when informed of infection, and that if they could both inform patients and create some reaction to the diagnosis, their jobs would be easier. Missionary doctors in particular felt that African patients failed to show enough concern about their condition. However, this began to change after the First World War when the anti-VD programme became fully operational. In the words of the medical officer in charge in 1921:

> It is a tribute to the efficiency of anti-venereal disease measures that at length an awakening of a sense of social shame has begun to appear. One of the reasons given lately for non-attendance here by natives is that they do not want it known that they are attending a venereal disease hospital and that this fact is beginning to carry a stigma; this is really a great achievement in the educational direction and gives one to hope that the day when venereal disease will be regarded as a serious bar to marriage or intimate relations is not far distant.[22]

Doctors tried to create a stigma about VD directly and indirectly. Stigma was most immediately conveyed by doctors' attitudes towards their patients and by their explanation of their patients' medical condition. This was most explicit in the missionary hospitals. At Mengo Hospital, run by the Church Missionary Society, patients were expected to confess the sins which led to their infection, as in the case of a man diagnosed with syphilis. 'At first he denied having done any wrong', the doctor wrote in the chart, ' but had to admit that he had.' A similar effort at moralizing can be seen in the case of a young, unmarried woman who came into the hospital to give birth who was rebuked by the doctor for being 'apparently unconcerned that she had broken God's commandments'.[23]

Also clearly message-laden was the fee structure for injections and operations which penalized VD patients and reflected the notion that treatment for venereal illness should contain some type of penance or financial sacrifice. It was perhaps not surprising that the missionary Mengo Hospital decided in-patients should pay no fees except for circumcisions necessitated by venereal complaints.[24] The philosophy of punishment for venereal infection was widespread and widely accepted among doctors in East Africa. In 1914, the Uganda Division of the Uganda and East Africa Branch of the British Medical Association established the first guidelines for patient fees for doctors in the colony. Revealingly, they allowed deviations from the recommendations for 'venereal disease and injuries due to patients' own fault'.[25] Clearly, some doctors saw venereal infections as self-inflicted, except for certain categories of 'innocent' victims such as infants. Another proposed schedule of fees for medical personnel in Uganda, written in

1920, allowed doctors to charge double the normal fee for circumcision if the procedure was required as a result of a venereal infection.[26]

Policies such as the punitive fee structure and moral lectures contributed to the increasing reproach directed at people with VD. The stigma which patients at the colonial VD hospital (Mulago) faced was so widely recognized that it was one reason the senior African official gave in arguing for the conversion of Mulago into a general hospital. Apolo Kagwa, the prominent Muganda Katikiro (Prime Minister), reported to the government that people avoided Mulago because of the stigma they received as VD patients, and that with its conversion to a general hospital more VD patients would attend since it would not be known why they were there.[27] Patients were right to worry about stigmatization and labelling. Not only did they have to be concerned about being seen at the VD clinic or hospital, they must also have been aware that once diagnosed with a venereal infection, the medical officer would write a letter to their landlord or boss informing him. The purpose of the letter was to secure their cooperation in compelling the patient's regular attendance at the clinic, but the end result was to advertise to everyone who had VD.

VD and social legislation

Clearly the Ugandan élite and Europeans accepted the premise that VD was a problem, and discourse on VD became an important sub-text to discussions of sexuality and morality in Ugandan society. For example, Captain Sparkes of the RAMC, who was in charge of the VD scheme in 1909/10, complained that legislation was needed to solve one of the social problems which contributed to the spread of VD:

> In large centres like Kampala special legislative measures should be taken to deal with the number of loose women who are found wandering about prostituting. Many of these women are to be found living with the servants of Europeans, therefore no woman except the recognised wife of a servant should be allowed in the compounds, as I am certain that these women are a special source of danger to the community.[28]

A similar perspective was expressed by the Ugandan Prime Minister, Apolo Kagwa. In 1917, Kagwa ordered that 'all women who do not live with their husbands' be considered prostitutes, arrested, and expelled from the African capital. Only eighteen women were expelled, an indication that the perception of the danger was greater than the reality, or that enforcement efforts were not a government priority.[29] Sparkes did not give more details, but it would be interesting to know how he would have proposed establishing whether a woman was a 'recognised' wife. And although he refers to women 'wandering about prostituting' themselves, we see that the women concerned were in fact simply living with African men. However, it was enough to label them as prostitutes because they were probably not formally married to the men. For Sparkes and Kagwa the definition of what constituted prostitution was rather inexact. Any woman who appeared to be living outside of the social arrangements approved by either European or élite Ugandan men was in danger of being labelled a prostitute and targeted for medical intervention and legal sanctions. Underlying their arguments was the idea that the danger of VD represented sufficient cause to justify legislation.

A major impetus for VD laws came from the RAMC personnel who served in Uganda. As Levine pointed out, VD laws in England and in colonial India were designed for the protection of British soldiers, and the army doctors were familiar with and sympathetic to VD laws.[30] The first mention of legislation in Uganda was by Colonel Lambkin who proposed a law to punish people who concealed VD, but the medical staff of the colony vetoed the idea as being too difficult to implement. The later RAMC officers, including Captain Sparkes, sought legal means to force patients to attend clinics, and after much discussion, the government acquiesced. The colonial government enacted 'Venereal Disease Rules' under the Dangerous Diseases Ordinance of 1909, which allowed the government to declare syphilis a dangerous disease and establish sanitoria or hospitals to treat patients. 'The Townships (Venereal Diseases) Rules, 1913' were rules applicable to locations in the colony outside of Buganda, which had its own law.

In Buganda the chiefs and officials were also in favour of legislation, and the parliament of Buganda, the Lukiko, passed VD legislation in 1913 which was implemented in the province. It was this Buganda law which was most often used in the anti-VD campaign. The Colonial Office reviewed the VD laws before they went into effect and recognized that they might be controversial. One official noted that it sounded 'as if they were going to have the C.D. Acts in Uganda', but was informed that 'this differ[ed] from the old English C.D. acts in that it applie[d] to both sexes and [was] not limited to prostitutes'.[31] Technically, this was true, but since women were seen as the major problem, socially and medically, they were the main target of the laws. The Lukiko law of 1913 revealed the feelings of the Lukiko members towards VD and especially towards women in Buganda. In general, the law mandated that persons infected with VD must present themselves for treatment, continue treatment until cleared by a medical officer, and avoid all activities which might spread their disease. Syphilis and gonorrhoea were both covered although several of the clauses specifically exempted persons suffering the effects of non-infectious gonorrhoea.[32]

Special attention needs to be paid to two major laws, the Lukiko VD law of 1913 and the Adultery and Fornication Law of 1918, because they specifically addressed two issues related to sexuality which the Lukiko thought were important in Buganda. Apart from its focus on women, the VD law compelled people who were infected with VD to attend hospitals or dispensaries for treatment, and established mechanisms to ensure compliance. By working through registers of syphilitic patients, people could be tracked down by Ugandan assistants and forced, under threat of fines, to complete treatment. In order to ensure that those infected with VD sought early treatment, the law prohibited infected persons from undertaking employment or participating in market activities until they had a health certificate. Although the legislation established the right of doctors forcibly to examine or treat anyone they wished, the system relied on the cooperation of Ugandan officials. Chiefs and landowners were responsible for reporting infected persons and checking their certificates upon their return from treatment and, as an inducement, chiefs received a reward for every sick person they sent in.[33]

Many sections of the Lukiko VD law were written in general terms to apply to both men and women, including the requirement that persons obtain a certificate of medical clearance in order to work, and the rules about landlords and chiefs being required to report the names of all infected persons on their property.[34] However, groups of women in particular were rounded up for genital inspections, and the requirements for medical clearance were intended to target market women and young women who worked for Europeans.[35] In addition, the fact that the law concentrated on syphilis, which was seen as a disease of women, meant the law concentrated on women. Whereas the justification for the law was VD, this clearly controlled women's economic opportunities. Furthermore, there were sections of the law which were gender specific, and applied to prostitutes and other women, both pure and immoral. It is important to point out that the original law as passed by the Lukiko, and thus the official version, was in Luganda.[36] A language spoken by the Baganda, Luganda does not have gendered pronouns and it is therefore interesting to see how the words and phrases in Luganda were translated into the authorized English version in order to capture the intent of the Lukiko. Clause 17 of the law said:

> When any person is known to be a prostitute, and the Gombolola Chief has reason to believe that she may be an infected person, he shall send her forthwith to the nearest Medical Officer to be examined, and if it is found that she is quite free from venereal disease she shall go free, but if she is found to be an infected person she shall be liable to be kept in the Venereal Treatment Centre ... for the cure of her disease.[37]

The choice of the word 'prostitute' was probably due to European influence – Luganda did not have a distinct word for a prostitute until later when the word *malaya*, from Swahili, came to be used for women who were paid for sex. The Lukiko used the word *omwenzi*, which can be translated as 'fornicator' with no specific gender connotation. The word was also often used, as by Dr Jack Cook earlier in this chapter, to signify any woman considered to be promiscuous. The vague definition of prostitute allowed almost any woman to be subjected to the law, and thus would have been an aid in rounding up large numbers of women. One clause of the 1913 law referred to prostitution as 'adultery for gain', which foreshadowed a later law which defined a prostitute as 'any woman who habitually gives her body indiscriminately for profit or gain or who persistently indulges in promiscuous intercourse with men even though she derives no gain or profit thereby'.[38]

While the VD law was intended to round up immoral women for treatment, it also attempted to prevent the infection of 'innocent' girls. Clause 18 established fines for any knowingly infected person who had intercourse resulting in the transmission of VD, but the Lukiko decided that was insufficient and included a separate clause of further fines for 'any infected person who shall have sexual intercourse with an unmarried girl *who is not a prostitute*' (emphasis added).[39] Clearly 'prostitutes' were not deserving of this protection. It is apparent that, to the Lukiko, there were only two types of women who would be exposed to VD; they were either immoral adulterers or innocent, unmarried girls who were victims of men. The dual purpose here was to control those women who were a sexual threat to society, while at the same time bolstering men's ability to ensure that they could protect sexual access to other women.

Similar attitudes underpinned the 'Adultery and Fornication Law' of 1918.[40] The king of Buganda, Daudi Chwa, explained to the colonial administration the need for the law by arguing that 'it is proper to pass a Law to prevent fornication and protect the people in Buganda, so that the fornication may not be too excessive, because it greatly diminishes the increase of the nation: the women do not bear properly and they are very much infected by diseases through excessive fornication'.[41] Surprisingly, the 1918 law did not directly define adultery or fornication.[42] The eight clauses of the law mainly dealt with protecting women who were married, betrothed or minors. In addition, the law outlined punishments for rape and established the age of consent for women at age 15. There was no corresponding age for men. Ugandan legislators had tried for years to pass a law regulating sexual relations, including adultery and fornication, but the colonial government always vetoed their actions. It was not until the spectre of VD was raised that the law was finally approved.

Sexuality, society and AIDS

In Uganda, in recent years, there have been discussions and conflicts about sexuality, gender roles and marital relations just as there were earlier in the century. Urban women are still viewed as sexually dangerous and there is a great deal of concern about the proper deportment of urban women. The idea of an *omukyala omutufu* has developed around Kampala, meaning a 'proper woman', one who is disciplined and respectable, who dresses modestly, is in a long-term permanent relationship with a man, and is a reserved and respected wife and mother.[43] It is no coincidence that concerns about the roles and behaviours of women developed as Uganda confronted the problem of AIDS in the 1980s.[44]

We see definite parallels between the apocalyptic dialogue revolving around AIDS and the 'problem' of women in modern Uganda and the corresponding historical dialogue about syphilis. In both cases, the explanations of the diseases occurred in environments where sexuality, morality and the status of women were topics of anxiety. Furthermore, the social view of women was such that they were seen as different creatures from men. During the emergence of syphilis, European and Ugandan men talked about women as being inherently immoral and of a lower type than men. Similar views have been articulated with AIDS, such as the recent argument of a male correspondent to one local newspaper that women were a definite threat to men, and nearly a separate species.[45]

Evidence that people think of women as responsible for the spread of AIDS comes from a research study which was conducted in the Rakai district of Uganda, the area which is generally believed to be hardest hit by AIDS. Fifty-five Secondary school children were given the assignment of writing essays about AIDS, and an analysis of the writings found that forty-one of the essays 'suggested that the disease [AIDS] was spread by "immoral" women. In contrast, only three essays felt that the disease was spread by "immoral" older men visiting prostitutes and then turning to young girls'.[46] Although this material came from school children, it seemed to reflect the general views of society.

It is bad enough for women to be stigmatized or blamed for the spread of AIDS in the community, but there exists a danger that the blame could be codified into legal discrimination against women as a group. This is not an idle fear. A study of attitudes about AIDS among school teachers in Uganda found a strong belief that legislation would be an effective means of curbing the disease if it could be used to control certain groups of people, specifically prostitutes and newcomers to a community.[47] Clearly, these are the people viewed as responsible for the outbreak and spread of disease, and these are the groups whose liberties could be most at risk if Ugandans choose to react to threats of disease as they have in the past.[48]

NOTES

1 F. J. Lambkin, 'An outbreak of syphilis in a virgin soil: Notes on syphilis in the Uganda Protectorate', in D. Power and J. K. Murphy (eds) *A System of Syphilis*, vol. 2, London, Oxford University Press, 1908, pp. 339–55.

2 M. Vaughan, *Curing Their Ills: Colonial Power and African Illness*, Cambridge, Polity Press, 1991, pp. 129–42.

3 D. A. Low, 'The making and implementation of the Uganda Agreement of 1900', in D. A. Low and R. C. Pratt (eds) *Buganda and British Overrule*, Nairobi, Oxford University Press, 1970, pp. 3–159. The kingdom of Buganda is in southern Uganda along the shores of Lake Victoria. The people of Buganda are the Baganda, and their language is Luganda.

4 Committee to Examine Medical and Health Services in Uganda, *Report on Medical and Health Services in Uganda*, Entebbe, Government Printer, 1956, pp. 24, 57.

5 C. Quétel, *History of Syphilis*, Baltimore, Johns Hopkins University Press, 1992, pp. 3, 54.

6 J. D. Murphy, *Luganda–English Dictionary*, Washington, DC, The Catholic University of America Press, 1972, p. 36. Thanks to Andrew Byekwaso for discussing these translations with me.

7 F. J. Lambkin, 'Syphilis in the Uganda Protectorate', *Journal of the Royal Army Medical Corps*, 1908, vol. 11, pp. 159–60; and G. J. Keane, 'Notes on the treatment of syphilis in Uganda', *Journal of the Royal Army Medical Corps*, 1912, vol. 18, p. 45.

8 F. N. S. Kizito, 'Omusajja si malaya, omukazi ye malaya', *Gambuze*, 21 July 1933, p. 14.

9 *Lancet*, 3 Oct. 1908, pp. 1,022–3; B. M. Zimbe, 'Buganda ne Kabaka: Ebyafayo Eby'obwakabaka bwe Buganda' (Buganda and King: A Royal History of Buganda), translated by S. Musoke, unpublished typescript, Cooperative Africana Microfilm Project, n.d., pp. 130–1.

10 F. J. Lambkin, *Prevalence of Venereal Disease in the Uganda Protectorate*, African No. 917, London, Great Britain Colonial Office, 1908, p. 6.

11 J. H. Cook, *Okufa Okwabana Mu Buganda Bwekuli*, Entebbe, Government Printer, 1908, p. 3.

12 A. R. Cook, *Enwade Zo Bukaba Mu Buganda*, Entebbe, Government Printer, 1921, p. 4.

13 A. Beck, *A History of the British Medical Administration of East Africa, 1900–1950*, Cambridge, MA, Harvard University Press, 1970, pp. 7–16.

14 H. T. Treves and G. J. Keane, 'The treatment of syphilis in Uganda', *Journal of the Royal Army Medical Corps*, 1909, vol. 13, pp. 241–4.

15 For patient responses, see M. W. Tuck, 'Syphilis, sexuality, and social control: A history of venereal disease in colonial Uganda', Ph.D. diss., Northwestern University, 1997, especially ch. 5.

16 E. Balintuma Kalibala, 'The social structure of the Baganda tribe of East Africa', Ph.D. diss., Harvard University, 1946, pp. 510–12.

17 Letter from Attorney General, Entebbe, to Chief Secretary, 18 May 1925, No. 44/25; Legal: Venereal Disease Ordinance: Action under, Uganda National Archives, A46 uncatalogued.

18 P. S. LeGeyt, 'Witchcraft and native medicines', 1955, unpublished manuscript in Oxford Development Records Project, MSS. Afr. s.736, Rhodes House Library, Oxford University.

19 Report by Acting Attorney General of Uganda, 5 September 1921; Great Britain Colonial Office papers, CO 536/113/55945.

20 See adverts for Howse & McGeorge, Ltd., *Munno*, Jan. 1927, p. 14, and *Munno*, Feb. 1927, p. 14. Adverts for a shop in Wandegeya, near Mulago, ran in *Gambuze*, 6 Jan. 1933, p. 12; 10 Feb. 1933, p. 3.

21 Letter to A. R. Cook from Howse & McGeorge, Pharmacists, Kampala, 6 May 1925; Incoming General Correspondence 1924–30; 1925–30; 1925–35; Mengo Hospital Papers, Albert R. Cook Medical Library, Kampala, Uganda.

22 Major G. J. Keane, RAMC, 'A report on venereal disease measures in Uganda', appendix III in Uganda Protectorate, *Annual Medical and Sanitary Report for the year 1921*, Entebbe, Government Printer, 1922, p. 70.

23 Mengo Hospital Papers, in-patient case notes, 1910, patients 852 and 1434.

24 Report of the Mengo Hospital Medical Sub-conference, no date, Mengo Hospital Papers, copy letters from Dr A. R. Cook, 1909–12, 1916, 1917, 1921; letters received by Dr A. R. Cook, 1915–16, 1920–21.

25 Minutes of meeting of the Uganda Division of the Uganda & East Africa Branch of the British Medical Association, 23 Dec. 1914; Mengo Hospital Papers, Incoming Correspondence, 1914–16, box 1.

26 Fee schedule, 7 Feb. 1920, Mengo Hospital Papers, Incoming General Correspondence, 1919–21, 1925–30, including MTS and Kagwa.

27 Memo to the Chief Secretary of the Protectorate, Entebbe, from J. C. R. Sturrock, Provincial Commissioner, Buganda, 9 Feb. 1922; Medical: Mulago Hospital, Uganda National Archives, A46/2277.

28 Capt. W. M. B. Sparkes, RAMC, 'Report on the treatment of venereal diseases from January 27th 1909 to March 31st 1910', included in Uganda Protectorate, *Annual Medical and Sanitary Report for the year 1909*, Entebbe, Government Printer, 1910, p. 12.

29 P. C. W. Gutkind, *The Royal Capital of Buganda*, The Hague, Mouton & Co., 1963, p. 154.

30 P. Levine, 'Venereal disease, prostitution, and the politics of empire: The case of British India', *Journal of the History of Sexuality*, 1994, vol. 4, p. 602; see also P. Levine, this volume, ch. 9.

31 Great Britain Colonial Office Papers, August 1912, CO 536/51, Uganda 29206.

32 Reflecting the fact that gonorrhoea was thought to be less of a threat than syphilis, people diagnosed as being in the later stages of gonorrhoea were not subject to the penalties for marrying while infected: 'The Law for Preventing Venereal Disease, 1913', clause 19.

33 The legislation passed by the Lukiko was 'The Law for Preventing Venereal Disease, 1913'. It was published in Uganda Protectorate, Venereal Diseases Department, *Instructions for the Guidance of Officers in Charge of Venereal Treatment Centres*, Entebbe, Government Printer, 1913, pp. 15–20. Fees paid to chiefs are discussed on page 2 of the *Instructions*.

34 'The Law for Preventing Venereal Disease, 1913', clauses 4–9, and 14–16.

35 Abstract of letter from Dr Margaret Lamont to the Association for Moral and Social Hygiene, undated [1922], included in Great Britain Colonial Office, CO 536/123/8868.

36 E. S. Haydon, *Law and Justice in Buganda*, London, Butterworths, 1960, p. 27.

37 'The Law for Preventing Venereal Disease, 1913', clause 17.

38 This definition was used in 'The Law to Prevent Prostitution', enacted 1 April 1941, in D. Kingdon, *The Laws of the Uganda Protectorate*, London, Waterlow & Sons, 1951, vol. 7, pp. 1,255–6.

39 'The Law for Preventing Venereal Disease, 1913', clause 22.

40 'The Adultery and Fornication Law', 15 June 1918, in D. Kingdon, *The Laws of the Uganda Protectorate*, vol. 7, pp. 1,235–6.

41 'Buganda: Miscellaneous Laws enacted by the Lukiko', 4 Nov. 1915, Uganda National Archives, A45/194.

42 This question of definition was pointed out by a student of mine, Ms Joelle Gentner.

43 J. A. Ogden, ' "Producing" respect: the "proper woman" in postcolonial Kampala', in R. Werbner and T. Ranger (eds) *Postcolonial Identities in Africa*, London, Zed Books, 1996, pp. 174–9.

44 For responses to AIDS in the 1980s, see G. C. Bond and J. Vincent, 'AIDS in Uganda: The first decade', in G. C. Bond *et al.* (eds) *AIDS in Africa and the Caribbean*, Boulder, CO, Westview Press, 1997, pp. 85–97.

45 A. Wamara, letter to *New Vision*, 20 Jan. 1995, p. 7.

46 T. Barnett and P. Blaikie, *AIDS in Africa: Its Present and Future Impact*, London, Belhaven Press, 1992, p. 50.

47 J. Seely and J. Nabaitu, 'Knowledge about and attitudes to AIDS held by teachers in five schools in Kyamulibwa', unpublished working paper, 1990, cited in B. P. A. Olowo-Freers and T. G. Barton, *In Pursuit of Fulfilment: Studies of Cultural Diversity and Sexual Behaviour in Uganda*, Kisubi, Uganda, Marianum Press, 1992, p. 197.

48 For a general essay about women, gender, and AIDS in Uganda, see M. Nakateregga Kisekka, 'AIDS in Uganda as a gender issue', in E. D. Rothblum and E. Cole (eds) *Women's Mental Health in Africa*, New York, Haworth Press, 1990, pp. 35–53.

12

WOMEN, VENEREAL DISEASE AND THE CONTROL OF FEMALE SEXUALITY IN POST-WAR HAMBURG

Michaela Freund

Introduction

Shortly after her arrival in the port-city of Hamburg after the end of the Second World War, 15-year-old Eva was arrested by police officers on the charge of prostitution and spreading venereal disease (VD). Eva had grown up in the Eastern Provinces of Germany, from where she, her mother and her sisters escaped in the winter of 1944/45 and fled to Danzig, where Eva and her family separated. In Danzig, the young woman got to know German sailors who took her to Hamburg. There, she entered into sexual relationships with British soldiers and, according to a social worker, 'lived without identification papers and any food solely on sexual intercourse with members of the British force'. Her contact with British soldiers made her suspicious to Hamburg authorities and the British military government. The young woman was arrested, diagnosed with VD, and sent to a hospital.

After her cure, she was placed in a reformatory, from where she escaped to the Soviet zone of occupied Germany, where she was again arrested and sent off to hospital. In the following years, until the founding of the Federal Republic of Germany, Eva continued to wander 'from town to town and [lead] the life of a prostitute'. Several times she was locked up in reformatories and workhouses. When Eva was again arrested in Hamburg and diagnosed with VD, the young woman was sent to the notorious reformatory, Farmsen, in Hamburg. Because of her alleged 'lesbian leaning', she was confined to a special ward. In Farmsen, Eva received the same state care as that prescribed for registered prostitutes. Under this regime, 'immoral women' were not 'rehabilitated' as had been the case under the Weimar Republic, but, as under the Third Reich, treated by social workers as slave labour. In February 1951, when Eva turned 21 and West German democracy was in its second year, she was released from Farmsen.[1]

Eva was one of the women who in post-war Hamburg were assigned the

205

social identity of 'prostitute' and associated by Hamburg state authorities and the British military government with spreading VD. Hamburg's police officers, medical experts and welfare workers based their decision to persecute Eva as a prostitute on what they believed to be sound evidence. Because of her social background, her sexual relations to British soldiers, her history of VD, her mobility and her status as a refugee, welfare workers perceived Eva not as a 'normal' German woman, but defined her as an 'especially deranged prostitute'.[2]

Taking the case of Hamburg, this chapter explores how in the state fight against prostitution, the links between prostitution, promiscuity, and VD were (re-)established, maintained and adjusted to changing circumstances in post-war West Germany. By outlining the motives of German and British officials as well as their measures to find and to treat 'endangered' and 'dangerous' girls and women, it will delineate how Hamburg authorities and the British occupation forces came to perceive, name and make German girls and women into prostitutes, how they constructed prostitutes as the source and transmitters of 'the secret plague', and how they used discursive practices to control the sexuality of the general female population in post-war Hamburg.

Setting the stage: numbers and motives

In May 1945, Hamburg authorities noticed an increase in what they believed to be prostitution. They were, however, not so much concerned about an increase in what they defined as professional prostitution; instead they were worried about certain relationships between men and women which in the historiography of post-war Germany is usually called 'hunger prostitution'. Hamburg social workers perceived women's mobility as a prime indicator of this kind of prostitution. Thus, they voiced their concerns over women such as Eva, 'wandering from one zone to the next', and the influx of female refugees from Eastern Europe, the former Eastern territories of Germany and the Soviet zone of occupation into the port-city. Indeed, they viewed the arriving women, the great majority of whom were young and single, as a threat to the social order and moral fabric. The female social workers observed:

> These girls roamed the country, homeless, infected with scabies, diseases, and vermin, poorly dressed (without shoes and socks), no identification papers. They pushed into the city to disappear and to find their 'field of activity'. By prostitution (for food and cigarettes) and occasional thefts these women eke out an existence.[3]

The social workers branded the girls and women as the 'least valuable part of the female population', who 'knew how to obtain more convenient life conditions by entering into relationships with British soldiers'.[4] The welfare workers soon realized, however, that the relationships between German women and British soldiers were not limited to this 'least valuable part of the female population'. They now also noticed 'women, who had so far lived a well-ordered life, slipping into prostitution' and suspected girls and women from all classes and districts of Hamburg of seeking relationships with British soldiers.[5]

As studies on the history of women in post-war Germany have shown, many German girls and women in the immediate post-war years entered into relationships with Allied soldiers in order to obtain food, shelter and protection.[6] According to social workers in Hamburg, in some cases it was the husband who had talked his wife into a relationship with a British soldier because he wanted to have cigarettes.[7] While Hamburg's social workers seemed to be sympathetic to such behaviour by men, they condemned mothers for prostituting themselves in order to feed their children. In the eyes of the welfare workers, these women had failed not only as wives, because of their flawed morals, but, even worse, as mothers, because they had raised promiscuous daughters who brought home British soldiers.[8]

Regardless of why women engaged in sexual relationships with British men, state authorities were greatly alarmed. This was so because they linked prostitution not only with morals but also with the spread of VD. With the collapse of National Socialism and the occupation of Germany by the Allied Forces, the spread of VD became one of the greatest concerns not only of Hamburg authorities, but also of the British military government. Both German and British officials agreed that female promiscuity and prostitution were the main culprits for the spread of VD in post-war Hamburg.

It was not the professional prostitute, however, who was viewed as the primary cause of the spread of VD, as she was under rigid observation by state authorities. Professor G. Hopf, a medical doctor put in charge of the treatment of VD patients with penicillin by the British military government, pointed out: 'The prostitution does not in the least play such an important part in the spread of VD as is thought of by most people.' For years, as the physician noted, the number of infected prostitutes in Hamburg had been, as in 'most other big cities', 'very low'. 'The percentage of prostitutes found infected at the examinations which take place once or twice weekly, does not vary much and stays at approximately 0.8 per cent.'[9]

Instead, experts believed that all German girls and women with extramarital relationships with men, especially British soldiers, spread the 'secret plague', whether or not they frequently changed their partners, and irrespective of whether they took money or other material goods for sex. As a consequence, girls and women became the sole targets of state intervention by British and German officials.

It was not only the authorities' quest to control the spread of VD; they connected the presence of those whom they perceived to be promiscuous women with wider structural and social changes in Hamburg and Germany. Above all, women who dated British soldiers were accused of having betrayed their men and, even worse, the German *Volk* (people) in Germany's crisis years. After their husbands, sons and fathers had risked and even lost their lives at the front, and while they were now suffering as prisoners of war, German women were sleeping with the former enemy. Moreover, Hamburg authorities noticed that German women's behaviour in the post-war years often contradicted traditional gender roles, which had been undermined by defeat, occupation, fraternization and a post-war crisis of masculinity. Instead of complete families with the man as the breadwinner and authority and the woman as the submissive housewife and mother, they witnessed increasing rates of divorce[10] as a consequence of the long absences of their menfolk which resulted in women's infidelity.[11] They also noticed increases in promiscuity and other forms of 'immoral' behaviour. For example, in attempting to keep their pensions as war-widows, soldiers' widows decided to forego marriage with their new-found male partners and lived instead in so-called 'uncle-marriages', which, although viewed sympathetically in the general population, were eyed with suspicion by the authorities.[12]

Soon, politicians, social workers and religious experts called for a return to the 'proper' family. But after a long war and post-war years of shouldering responsibility solely by themselves, women had become sexually more autonomous and were no longer willing to live up to the rigid expectations of womanly behaviour; moreover, as noted above, many women could not afford to do so. In October 1946, there were seven million more women than men in occupied Germany.[13] Thus, a large number of German families were headed by women. Because so many young men had died or were still in prisoner-of-war camps, many young women could not hope to marry. Married women, not knowing whether their husbands were alive or not, could not remarry. State authorities, however, decided to ignore reality and chose to view women unwilling to subordinate themselves to the dominant moral norms and ideas as a great threat to the German patriarchal family. Defining them as the cause and expression of the moral, social and health crisis of post-war Germany, they chose them as their prime target of intervention.

The British authorities were also concerned about the relationships between their soldiers and German girls and women. Already, before the end of the war, the British military had considered ways of preventing fraternization between British soldiers and German women: 'It is thought that it would be possible to recruit from the liberated Allied countries volunteers for employment as hostesses/dance partners in amusement and dance centres in the larger military garrisons in Germany.'[14] They discarded plans, however, to bring Dutch and Belgian women into Germany. In spring 1946, British officials noticed that their fears had not been ungrounded as their soldiers became increasingly friendly with the Germans, especially with their girls and women. To higher military officials, the British military victory was endangered:

> The younger women's energies are concentrated on conquering the conqueror. Other Ranks in various occupation centres say 'they like the German women, they aren't half so bad, and anyhow we can't go on

hating each other for years and years if we're plonked down in their country to live among them'. Only one said 'I can't stand the German women – they are bossy and they are all "Gimme's" – it's give me this and give me that the whole time. They are out for all they can get and the only thing they give us is VD.'[15]

As the report states, this was the voice of one single soldier. The majority of them liked German women. Since many British soldiers who were stationed in Germany were young and inexperienced, they felt hardly any bitterness against Germans. This is also illustrated by a statement in the same report: 'After the lapse of a year German women having learned English rather than the British soldiers German, language problems are eased and the women are more than ever able to convince the British soldier that they as individual women are entirely blameless for all that is past.' Furthermore, the report stated that the women's attempts to convince British soldiers of their innocence were very successful.[16] The British soldiers, especially the younger ones, did not view German women as their enemies but as possible girlfriends and even mates. Thus, contact with German girls and women became a routine part of their lives.

While the British soldiers did not view German women as a threat, British officials viewed those relationships with a great deal of suspicion. The fear of the infection of British soldiers with VD and the association of German women and British soldiers led the British occupation force as well as the Hamburg authorities to use drastic measures in order to prevent such scenarios.

'The hunt for women': raids, ticket checks and other police measures

In post-war Hamburg, British and German officials joined ranks to control and correct women's sexual behaviour and morals. To achieve their goal of wiping out prostitution and to prevent sexual relationships between German women and British soldiers they developed an extensive web of surveillance that attempted to cover all girls and women considered at risk of becoming a prostitute and a vector of VD. On analysis, it is clear that these measures enabled welfare workers and police officers to discipline all German girls and women.

While state authorities believed the sexuality of professional prostitutes in brothels could be controlled by police officers and medical experts, they focused on those women who so far were under no state supervision. The women who had decided to work as professional prostitutes were in the eyes of the social workers lost souls, only a few of them being willing to return to a 'normal' life. But the women who were prostituting themselves without having registered at the *Zentrale Überwachungsstelle für Prostituierte* (Bureau for the Supervision of Prostitutes), an agency of the health office, and, more generally, women with sexual relationships with British soldiers or other foreign men such as Polish displaced persons – became the main targets of welfare workers and police officers.

According to a report of October 1945 by Hamburg welfare officers, Hamburg authorities and the British military government started their fight against the 'secret plague' as early as June 1945, just weeks after the British military had occupied the city state of Hamburg. As the most immediate measure to fight the spread of VD and prostitution, they targeted particular areas such as 'suspicious' bars, the ports, bunkers, and train, tram and bus stations. The raids were conducted by both British and German police vice squads and were directed exclusively at girls and women. In October 1945, one social worker described these raids as the 'systematic overhaul of restaurants by British and German police officers. All of the women who were in the company of men who were not their husbands, were loaded onto carts and examined for VD.'[17] The British police were particularly eager to cleanse Hamburg of VD because the military government feared that German women would infect British soldiers with gonorrhoea and syphilis. One case involved two young female teachers who came home from a church meeting late in the evening. As they passed Hamburg's main station on their way home, British police officers arrested them and brought them to the hospital in charge of VD examinations. There, the two young women were forcibly examined for VD.[18]

Such cases were not exceptional. German physicians, welfare workers, and the Hamburg public complained about the British zeal and the ineffective and indiscriminate manner of picking up girls and women of all ages.[19] Thus, in 1945, the British military police detained 4,667 women of whom 391 (8.4 per cent) were infected. The German morals police were more successful in their efforts to identify women who were actually infected: they had detained 1,896 women of whom 455 (23.8 per cent) were infected.[20] The low success rate of the British military police led to heated debates about British methods. German physicians complained that most of the arrested girls and women were not only not infected with syphilis or gonorrhoea, but that the military police even arrested virgins, some of whom were not even 14 years old.[21] Other officials complained that even women accompanied by their husbands were arrested and forced to undergo VD examinations.[22] Professor G. Hopf demanded that the military police should not only trace women, but men as well: 'If one goes so far as to suspect visitors of certain districts or cafés as being suffering from VD, the men are not less suspicious than the women.'[23]

Not only the medical experts complained about the British zeal to cleanse Hamburg of VD. The massive vice squad raids against German girls and women and their forcible examinations for VD enforced by the British military police did not go unnoticed by the welfare workers, the general population and local newspapers. In an article in the daily *Hamburger Volkszeitung* entitled 'Pursuit of Women', the reporter described an incident where German women were arrested by the British military police at the *Stephansplatz*, one of Hamburg's major public places. In an arbitrary fashion, mothers and young girls who were in the company of British soldiers were loaded onto trucks and taken for forcible VD examinations. The reporter observed a British soldier who had just lost his two female companions to the British military police. Yet, at the next corner, as the reporter noted sourly, the soldier merely solicited the company of another German woman. The report went on to say that the population was indignant as it was only women and not men who were taken for the medical examinations.[24]

Because of the massive arrests of German girls and women, the rooms of the Bureau for the Supervision of Prostitutes, where suspected women had to get their check-ups once or twice a week, were soon overcrowded. As a consequence, the British military police suggested separating the prostitutes from the girls and women arrested at the mass raids. For the medical examinations, they set up a bunker where females were taken for forcible examinations. Up to three times a day, British and German police brought women arrested on the charge of prostitution and the spreading of VD. The number of interviews conducted daily by the social office workers increased from ten to fifteen to over forty.[25]

From such figures it becomes obvious that in the course of British and Hamburg police raids, any German girl or woman in public who was unescorted, in the company of a man who was not her husband, or even in the company of her husband, became 'conspicuous' and ran the risk of being labelled a vector of VD and a possible prostitute. Based solely on their gender, girls and women were arrested by British and German police officers and taken for forcible VD examinations. How German girls and women were treated during the raids and the medical inspections was vividly described by the 20-year-old Ruth B. She was arrested when leaving a café at a quarter past nine in the evening. Ruth B. told Hamburg authorities about her experience:

> British police took my passport and together with a lot of other young girls I had to enter a closed cart divided into a lot of small cells. When we asked what this was all about we were not given an answer. Police took us to the Bunker at Dammtor where we had to undergo VD examinations. When we left the cart we had to walk through a line of British police officers who shone a flashlight in the face of every girl. When the examination was finished at one o'clock at night, nobody took care of us any longer. Since there was no public transportation at this time of the night, we were forced to walk home, to be precise to Blankenese or Rissen [a walk from the Bunker of at least three hours, M.F].[26]

Ruth B. stated that there were no female police officers present. The sexual harassment, social stigmatization and human degradation Ruth B. had to endure became the fate of thousands of German women in post-war Hamburg.

Although the British officials were convinced that the raids were quite effective and justified, they took the 'considerable resentment' of the Hamburg public into consideration.[27] And although 13.6 per cent of the women apprehended from April to June 1946 were found to be infected, in the second half of 1946, the British military government agreed to cease the so-called ticket checks. Furthermore, they decided to stop vice round-ups at larger cafés and to confine themselves to arresting only women known as prostitutes and 'obviously loitering for purposes of prostitution or in the company of British soldiers in circumstances giving rise to the probability of immoral purpose'.[28] In the event, a rise in the VD rate in the third quarter of 1946 led British officials to reinstate the Vice Squad. Although British military police did not strictly comply with such orders, a couple of months later German citizens still complained about the arrest of women and girls by British police officers.

As late as November 1946, Dr Albrecht of the Youth Bureau complained about the raids which 'disquieted the population and seriously disturbed the nervous systems of many a young girl. ... It is unbearable that e.g. at tram stops or in well-reputed restaurants indiscriminately all women are rounded up.' Albrecht suggested: 'If the papers are in order and the women come from districts above suspicion and give a respectable impression, or are accompanied by their husbands, a medical inspection should not be necessary and these women ought to be released as soon as possible.'[29]

Worried by all these complaints, the military government called for a conference with Hamburg authorities. At this conference on 12 December 1946, the British officials agreed to try out a new system for the ensuing two months, 'whereby the arrest of women would be entirely in the hands of the German police, with the exception of women reported by British soldiers as having passed the disease to them'.[30] Only a month later, in January 1947, the British military government decided that such raids were illegal and banned them completely.[31]

The German police, however, were neither willing to give up their power in the control of VD nor merely to assist welfare workers in cases where persons refused to go for treatment. They argued that there were areas of 'ill repute' where it was not proper for welfare workers to operate. Thus, possibly with the tacit consent of the British military authorities, Hamburg police continued to carry out raids until June 1947.[32] The actions of the Hamburg police department were backed by the Hamburg parliament (*Bürgerschaft*) and government (Senate), who in September 1947 demanded that German police should take part in the search for infected persons.[33]

The Allies were now in a 'catch-22' situation. On the one hand, the number of VD infections was increasing: while in Hamburg in 1946, there had been 1,062 people reported as infected with syphilis and 3,533 with gonorrhoea, this increased in 1947 to 3,873 cases of syphilis and 6,788 cases of gonorrhoea.[34] On the other hand, the Allies increasingly viewed raids as 'undemocratic'. They also agreed that the 1927 Weimar Act for the Combating of VD was no longer suited to present conditions.[35] As a consequence, they urged the legislative powers of the German *Länder* (states) to introduce a new law for fighting VD based on the Control Council Directive No. 52, a quadripartite directive (i.e. of all four Allies), which stated that the control of VD should be entirely in the hands of the public health and social welfare departments, not in those of the police.[36] The regional commissioners of the military governments were responsible for seeing that the German authorities implemented the directive's provisions. Hamburg instituted such a law in 1949. This was replaced by the West German Federal Act for Combating VD of 1953, which made the health offices fully responsible for fighting VD. The 1953 law continues to be in effect. Although the law is aimed at both men and women, female prostitutes and women with 'frequently' changing sexual partners have remained the main targets of state control.

The Allies' efforts dissatisfied the German police. To their chagrin, from 1948 onwards it was not they but welfare officers who checked bars, displaced persons' camps and ships with foreign sailors. In the same year, the British military government established a new British military police vice squad, which, with the help of one German welfare worker, investigated German girls and women who were named as sources of infection by British soldiers. Following Germany's Basic Law of 1949, the public health department reduced the vice squad from fifteen to four social workers.[37]

With the increasing use of penicillin, the number of VD infections began slowly to decrease from 1948 onward.[38] In Hamburg, the number of syphilis cases decreased from 3,873 in 1947 to 3,127 in 1948, and gonorrhoea cases were down from 6,788 to 6,299.[39] Despite such a drop in VD infections, the British military government became increasingly concerned not only about the health of the British soldiers and thus for the British people as a whole – with infertile fathers, infected British women and blind babies – but also with their morals. Thus, while the spread of VD might have been under control, in the opinion of British military officers the morals of the young British men and German women were not. Now, the British military government was

> much more concerned with convincing [British soldiers] that a happy
> and satisfactory family life as husbands and fathers in the years to come
> could have its best and most sure foundation on a life of self-control and
> fair living in the days of their youth.[40]

Senior officers most likely envisioned their charges' 'family life as husbands and fathers in the years to come' with British wives at their side and in the United Kingdom. However, while the British women were waiting, their men were seen as amusing themselves with the former enemy on the other side of the English Channel. As Elizabeth Heineman noted, army investigators had estimated that 50 to 90 percent of American troops, among them married servicemen, associated with German women in 1946.[41] This number might be too high for British troops, but the evidence suggests that a significant proportion of British soldiers formed liaisons and sought emotional contacts with German women.

In the opinion of British authorities, it was the German women who sought relationships with British soldiers. They dismissed reproaches by Germans that it was British soldiers who were initiating such relationships: 'Any suggestion of the right of a victor to express his victory in terms of possession of the bodies of German women is completely abhorent [*sic*] to our British way of thought.' Of course, they had sympathy with the moral lapses of German women:

> We are acutely aware of the many material and psychological difficulties confronting the German girls and young women of today. Poverty, over-crowding and the lack of German men of their own age. We know these difficulties; we are sympathetic towards them and we are explaining them to our soldiers.

Thus, the British officials asked their German colleagues to 'help us by securing among the German girls a standard of chastity and self-respect to match the ideals which we are trying to instil among our British soldiers'.[42]

'Treatment' by the *Pflegeamt*

To secure such a standard of chastity and self-respect among the German girls was the task of Hamburg's welfare workers of the *Pflegeamt*, the office that was in charge of the rehabilitation of prostitutes or suspected prostitutes. It was headed by Käthe Petersen. Together with her subordinates, she classified women's actions into the categories of 'prostitution', 'frequently changing sexual intercourse with monetary exchange', and 'frequently changing sexual intercourse without monetary exchange'. While these classifications covered a variety of different behaviours, the welfare workers used them interchangeably. They also interwove them with other meanings, such as carrying and spreading VD. Moreover, they altered these classifications in such a way as to include or exclude certain patterns of behaviour. Because it was difficult for state agencies such as the *Pflegeamt* to detect women's private sexual conduct, they looked for what they perceived to be indicators, such as 'neglected appearance', mobility and age.

A lot of the girls and women picked up by police and welfare workers were under-age refugees from the East and women wandering from one zone to the next. The group of girls and women the welfare workers were concerned about was diverse: 'From the hardworking girl who got into trouble to the sexually unrestrained tramp.'[43] In order to decide who was a respectable young woman gone astray as opposed to who was a hard-core, unrepentant, immoral person, the welfare workers interviewed them. Once they had found out more about the woman's social background, they decided about the kind of 'care' the woman was to receive. For the social workers, the key was to remove the women from corrupting conditions to institutions where they could be led back to the proper path of womanhood and be prepared for their future role as wife and mother.

One of those women receiving treatment from the *Pflegeamt* was Ingrid. In the summer of 1950 she was arrested by police officers in a bomb shelter. They brought the young woman to the police station, where she was questioned by a social worker of the Bureau for the Supervision of Prostitutes. In her report, the social worker described the former domestic servant as 'homeless and destitute and in a very dirty condition' and as 'unappetizing and without any discipline'. During the interview, the social worker noted, 'the woman scratched herself on her head and put her finger into her nose and mouth'. The social worker learned that Ingrid had wandered around, having 'varying acquaintances with men'. Moreover, Ingrid was pregnant but, as the social worker noted, 'was not able to give the name of the father'. Because Ingrid was not willing to have a medical examination and because of her neglected appearance and crude behaviour, the social worker was convinced that Ingrid was 'feeble-minded' or at least had some 'psychological disruption'.

Since Ingrid had 'varying acquaintances with men' and therefore varying sexual intercourse, her lifestyle in the mind of the welfare worker endangered other people through her transmission of VD. Ingrid was brought into a hospital. 'Since she was not willing to be examined, all of the smears had to be done while Ingrid was anaesthetized',[44] even though this action contravened human rights and West Germany's Basic Law of 1949. It is not clear whether this was standard practice in Hamburg's hospitals, although from the nonchalant, routine language of the social worker this appears to be so. It is clear, however, that the dignity and civil rights of girls and women in West Germany who were suspected of being prostitutes and vectors of VD were disregarded by Hamburg state authorities.

The practice of the *Pflegeamt* was criticized by both German and British officials. Professor Hopf was concerned that patients came to think 'that the treatment of VD is some sort of preparation for compulsory education. This, for instance, is the case when persons are being sent to approved schools or similar institutions immediately upon leaving the hospital and when doctors and their assistants have cooperated in such a way with the other authorities.' Thus, he believed that some people did not get voluntary treatment for VD because they were afraid of being sent to a reformatory afterwards. Furthermore, Hopf complained about the welfare workers' practice of making inquiries about the lifestyle of patients at their homes and from neighbours.[45] Mary Shaw, the VD expert of the Ministry of Health in the United Kingdom, was even harsher in her critique of the way in which Hamburg welfare workers approached the problems of VD. After her visit to the British zone in October 1948, she concluded:

> The whole approach to problems of Venereal Diseases is fundamentally different in Germany from that in this country and through it all runs a streak of cruelty which is all but dead here since it received its great blow in 1916 with the publication of the Final Report of the Royal Commission and the institution of the clinics as we know them today. The raiding of suspected areas and premises with compulsory treatment of women only is a one sided attack which ultimately does

nothing to prevent spread of infection; the conditions under which these women are kept are degrading and very little effort at rehabilitation seems to be being made.[46]

While Mary Shaw probably thought about integrating the women into society again, Hamburg's welfare workers had something different in mind. Strict supervision and punishment were their recipe for these 'immoral' girls and women. As soon as the women suspected of being infected with VD were taken into hospital, they were treated in a different way to 'normal' patients. The girls and women were not supervised by nurses, but by female prison warders, because, allegedly, nurses could not deal with such patients. Furthermore, the women had to be strictly supervised because they tried either to escape from hospital or to have contact with persons outside the hospital in an 'inadmissible way'. They were, for example, accompanied to the bathroom and to their medical check-ups by the prison warders. Therefore, the women were locked up and controlled twenty-four hours a day.

Just how tight the web of surveillance was spun around these young women is revealed by the process of legal incapacitation for women by which they were declared to be incapable of managing their own affairs. Welfare workers argued that an infection with VD was a sure sign that a woman was unable to lead a normal life and needed help. Because she did not have the ability to control her life, for her own benefit and that of society, it needed to be controlled by the state. In 1934, Käthe Petersen, the head of the *Pflegeamt*, had inaugurated the process of incapacitation in default of any law which could keep persons institutionalized for an indefinite period of time. From then on, Petersen, in cooperation with judges and physicians, had the power to deprive a woman of her freedom and to send her to the notorious reformatory, Farmsen. After the German unconditional surrender and the surrender of Hamburg to the British military, the practice of incapacitation was not discussed, but either with the tacit agreement or the ignorance of British officials, Hamburg authorities were to continue it well after the end of national socialism.

It was mainly the girls and women who were defined as prostitutes and vectors of VD who went through the process of incapacitation and who became the wards of Käthe Petersen. After the end of the Second World War, some 450 girls and women lived in open reformatories under the supervision of social workers. Another 300 were incapacitated and confined to Farmsen. In 1949, with the passing of West Germany's Basic Law, the practice of incapacitation became increasingly difficult, but not impossible. In cases where women 'posed a danger to the public and to themselves' and in cases of 'great demoralization' they could be stripped of their civil rights and kept in Farmsen.

Ingrid, the woman arrested in a bunker and subjected to a forced VD examination in the summer of 1950, was such a case. Her case worker believed that the young woman was 'unable to live on her own'. Like most women who were confined in Farmsen for two to four years, Ingrid had to stay for the maximum period until her release in the summer of 1954. As was the routine, she was found a job and remained under the surveillance of welfare workers. If the women repeatedly lost employment or 'returned to their earlier unrespectable way of living', they were returned to Farmsen and had to stay there for another year. This is what happened to Ingrid. Only a few months after her release, in September 1954, she was arrested again. This time police officers had picked her up in Hamburg's train station because she 'gave the impression of a tramp'. At the police station, Ingrid told the officer that she had left her job without permission from the welfare office. The police officer suspected that ever since, Ingrid had 'wandered around', financing her life 'through prostitution'. The social worker of the welfare office decided to take her into custody and to have her examined at the Bureau for Supervision of Prostitutes. Ingrid was then again sent to Farmsen where she had to stay for an indefinite period of time. This could have been a year, but it might have been much longer, as the case of one woman shows, who was confined to Farmsen for forty-two years – from 1942 until her death in 1984.[47]

Conclusion

Prostitution, promiscuity and VD were closely linked discursively in post-war Hamburg. The discourse on VD became a site on which medical experts, the police and social workers (re-)defined what constituted promiscuous behaviour and who constituted a prostitute. This chapter has examined how German girls and women like Eva, Ruth and Ingrid were defined and named 'loose women', prostitutes and spreaders of VD. The majority of those women had never in their lives worked as prostitutes but many of them had transgressed other social norms in ways that the officials felt were threatening to the social order.

Meanings of female sexuality and behaviour, notions of class, perceptions of women's bodies and their appearances, and theories about the genesis and spread of VD were interwoven in such ways that certain women were perceived as 'promiscuous' and named as 'prostitutes'; 'the amateur prostitute' especially was constructed as the diseased and polluted body and hence as the source and transmitter of VD. Consequently, girls and women so defined became the target of public supervision and state control.

As had already been the case in Weimar and Nazi Hamburg, the fight against prostitution and the spread of VD continued to be highly gendered. Girls and women continued to be regarded as the main vectors of VD. It was them and not, for example, British soldiers, who were forcibly examined for gonorrhoea and syphilis. All of the women had left the private sphere and had gone into the public domain as working women or to look for some form of amusement. Both the German and British authorities reacted by naming those women as 'prostitutes' and stigmatizing them as outcasts and deviants in need of punishment and rehabilitation. Through such regulation, they tried to lead the women back to the proper path of womanhood. However, the official message was directed not

only at the girls and women who had transgressed gender boundaries, but also –
as a warning – to all girls and women, telling them to stay on the path of proper
womanhood and not to disobey the boundaries of socially accepted femininity.

NOTES

1 Curriculum vitae of E. M. N., Staatsarchiv Hamburg (StA Hamburg), Sozialbehörde
   II, 136.00–4, Bd. 4.
2 Ibid.
3 Bericht über die Sammelvormundschaft, 1. April 1949, StA Hamburg, Sozialbehörde
   II, 012.10–10.
4 Monatlicher Kurzbericht der Fürsorgerin Aenne Prahl für Barmbeck-Uhlenhorst,
   5. August 1945, StA Hamburg, Sozialbehörde I, VG 30.69, Bd. III.
5 Lagebericht der Oberfürsorgerin Siemers für Flottbek-Othmarschen für die Monate
   November–Dezember 1945, StA Hamburg, Sozialbehörde II, 012.11–1, Bd. 1.
6 See R. Moeller, *Protecting Motherhood. Women and the Family in the Politics of Postwar West
   Germany*, London, University of London Press, 1993, pp. 23–5; H. Sander und B.
   Johr, *Befreier und Befreite, Krieg, Vergewaltigungen, Kinder*, München, Verlag Antje
   Kunstmann, 1992; K.-J. Ruhl, *Frauen in der Nachkriegszeit*, München, Deutscher
   Taschenbuch Verlag, 1988, p. 34; A. Tröger, 'Between rape and prostitution: survival
   strategies and possibilities of liberation of Berlin women in 1945–48', in J.
   Friedlander, A. Kessler-Harris and C. Smith-Rosenberg (eds) *Women in Culture and
   Politics: A Century of Change*, Bloomington, Ind., 1986, pp. 97–117; E. Heineman, 'The
   hour of the woman: Memories of Germany's "Crisis Years" and West German
   national identity', *American History Review*, April 1996, vol. 101, pp. 354–95.
7 Monatlicher Kurzbericht der Fürsorgerin Elfriede Mehliß für Blankenese vom August
   1945, StA Hamburg, Sozialbehörde I, VG 30.69, Bd. III.
8 Lagebericht für Harburg für den Monat August 1945, StA Hamburg, Sozialbehörde
   II, 012.11–1, Bd.1.
9 Prof. G. Hopf, 'Modern methods of tracing sources of infection of venereal diseases',
   translation of an article published in *The Doctor's Weekly* nos 59–60, 30 September
   1947, PRO (Public Record Office), FO 1014, 470.
10 The divorce rate climbed from only about nine divorces for 10,000 inhabitants in
   1939 up to almost nineteeen divorces for 10,000 inhabitants in 1948. U. Frevert,
   Frauen-Geschichte. Zwischen Bürgerlicher Verbesserung und Neuer Weiblichkeit, Frankfurt am
   Main, Suhrkamp, 1986, p. 252.
11 Lagebericht für Bergedorf, Vier- und Marschlande für die Monate November und
   Dezember 1945, StA Hamburg, Sozialbehörde II, 012.11–1, Bd. 1.
12 Frevert, *Frauen-Geschichte*, p. 252.
13 Heineman, 'The hour of the woman', p. 374.
14 Draft zur Non-Fraternization, o.D., PRO, FO 1038, Nr. 29.
15 'Appendix "Z" to Monthly Report for Period 1–30 April 1946', PRO, FO 1005, 1645.
16 Ibid.
17 Auszug aus der Niederschrift über die Besprechung der Sozialen Arbeitsgemeinschaft
   am 24 Oktober 1945, StA Hamburg, Sozialbehörde I, GF 33.10, Bd. 1.
18 Lagebericht des Fürsorgerinnendienstes der Sozialabteilung St. Georg, 25 Januar
   1946, StA Hamburg, Sozialbehörde II, 012.11–1, Bd. 1.
19 Jagd auf Frauen, in: *Hamburger Volkszeitung* no. 36, 3 August 1946, PRO, FO 1014,
   470.
20 Hopf, 'Modern methods of tracing sources of infection', PRO, FO 1014, 470.
21 Studie der Gesundheitsverwaltung über 'Die Verbreitung der Geschlechtskrankheiten
   in Hamburg', 15 Juli 1946, S. 4, StA Hamburg, Staatliche Pressestelle V, II M IV b.
22 Albrecht to military police, 27 November 1946, PRO, FO 1014, Nr. 470.

23 Hopf, 'Modern methods of tracing sources of infection', PRO, FO 1014, 470.
24 'Jagd auf Frauen' in: *Hamburger Volkszeitung* no. 36, 3 August 1946, PRO, FO 1014, 470.
25 Lagebericht des Pflegeamtes vom September/Oktober 1946, StA Hamburg, Sozialbehörde II, 012.11–1, Bd. 1.
26 Statement by Ruth B., n.d., translated by the author, PRO, FO 1014, 470.
27 Deputy Provost Marshal to Deputy Commander, 5 July 1946, PRO, FO 1014, 470.
28 Ibid.
29 Letter by Dr Albrecht, 27 November 1946, PRO, FO 1014, 470.
30 Letter on Public Health – VD by the Regional Commissioner, 12 December 1946, PRO, 1014, 470.
31 Public Health Technical Report for June 1947, PRO, FO 1050, 744.
32 Ibid.
33 Bürgermeister an die Militärregierung, 9 Sep. 1947, StA Hamburg, Verbindungstelle zur Militärregierung, III 1 Bd. 8.
34 Public Health Progress in Hansestadt Hamburg, n.d., PRO, FO 1050, Nr. 713.
35 While this law had abolished the state regulation of prostitution, it required that all women and men suspected of having promiscuous sexual intercourse should undergo a medical examination.
36 Regional Commissioner to *Bürgermaster*, 18 October 1947, PRO, FO 1014, 470.
37 Petersen zur Entwicklung des fürsorgerischen Streifendienstes vom 16.8. 1960, StA Hamburg, Gesundheitsbehörde, 564–06.16, Bd. II .
38 Monthly Report on Morale and Public Opinion for December 1947, Public Record Office, FO 1005, 1845.
39 Public Health Progress in Hansestadt Hamburg, n.d., PRO, FO 1050, Nr. 713.
40 VD Conference, 28 November 1947, PRO, FO 1014, 470.
41 Heineman, 'The hour of the woman', p. 381.
42 VD Conference, 28 November 1947, PRO, FO 1014, 470.
43 Bericht über die Pflegeamtsarbeit für das Jahr 1948, StA Hamburg, Sozialbehörde II, 012.10–10.
44 Einzelfallakte Nr. 1361, StA Hamburg, Gesundheitsbehörde, Bestand Sonderakten.
45 Hopf, 'Modern methods of tracing sources of infection', PRO, FO 1014, 470.
46 Report of visit to Germany (4 October–16 October 1948) by Dr Mary Shaw, PRO, FO 1050, 628.
47 Compare curriculum vitae of Käthe M. in B. Meister und R. Langholf, ' "Zweckmäßige Asozialenbehandlung". Entmündigung in der nationalsozialistischen Fürsorgepolitik', in A. Ebbinghaus (ed.) *Opfer und Täterinnen. Frauenbiographien des Nationalsozialismus*, Frankfurt am Main, Fischer, 1997, pp. 232–8.

13

'THE PRICE OF THE PERMISSIVE SOCIETY'

The epidemiology and control of VD and STDs in late-twentieth-century Scotland

Roger Davidson

Introduction

The development of VD and sexually transmitted disease (STD) policy and administration in twentieth-century Britain has attracted increasing attention from medical and social historians. Various strands of public health policy, along with their broader socio-medical implications, have been documented. Some studies have focused upon the emergence in interwar Britain of a state-funded, voluntary system of provisions for the diagnosis and treatment of VD.[1] Others have examined the lasting debate within government circles over the relative merits of moral education and medical prophylaxis as preventive strategies, highlighting the powerful moral agenda which has shaped institutional responses to VD.[2]

Further studies have focused upon the process by which VD has been deployed by legal and medical authorities to identify and proscribe dangerous (predominantly female) sexualities, perceived as a threat to racial health and national efficiency, and upon patterns of resistance from within feminist organizations.[3] Attention has also been paid to the significance of VD in defining the interface between military and civilian health and sexuality, and the impact of war on the surveillance and regulation of sexual behaviour.[4] Finally, several studies have analysed the impulses and constraints determining the course and outcome of campaigns for compulsory VD controls, including compulsory notification and treatment, or explored their implications for current issues of public health and civil liberties surrounding the threat of AIDS.[5]

For the most part, the focus of research has been on the first half of the twentieth century and on developments since 1980. In contrast, the intervening years have been largely neglected, despite the fact that both contemporaries and historians have portrayed this period as one of radical change in patterns of social intercourse and sexual behaviour.[6] This study sets out to examine the epidemiological debate and control strategies in Scotland regarding the classical venereal diseases and the new generation of STDs in the period 1948–80. It seeks to establish the degree to which these years witnessed a watershed in the discourse surrounding sexuality and disease or to what extent the so-called 'permissive society' retained conventional assumptions, taxonomies and moral agendas in its handling of sexually acquired diseases.

The epidemiological debate: 1948–80

Many strands of pre-war discourse surrounding VD survived well into later-twentieth-century Scottish society. In particular, the media and professional journals continued to identify VD with moral degeneration. As in the 1920s, it was widely believed in the 1950s that war had seriously eroded family and community controls and that its disinhibiting effects on patterns of sexual behaviour had profoundly 'demoralized' the nation.[7] Scottish venereologists shared the sentiments of Ambrose King, Adviser in VD to the Ministry of Health, that 'venereal disease was but one symptom of the general breakdown of moral order'.[8] Especial concern attached to the decline in the influence of religious values and commitment to the sanctity of marriage. Indeed, Robert Lees, Physician-in-Charge of Edinburgh's VD services in the period 1954–67, saw a clear connection between venereal infection and 'unions' that were only 'temporary and unblessed by Church!'.[9]

The long-established association between alcohol and promiscuity also resurfaced in post-war attempts by public health and church authorities to explain the incidence of VD. Thus, in the view of the Temperance and Morals Committee of the Church of Scotland, VD was one of many social problems arising from the influence of drink upon 'the censor of the conscience'.[10] Evidence from Glasgow in the late 1960s indicated that some 90 per cent of all VD cases had frequented a public house as a prelude to infective intercourse.[11] Seasonal fluctuations in the incidence of disease were also viewed in part as a function of drinking patterns, with the late-December/early-January peak commonly attributed to 'drunken parties at the festive season'.[12]

Meanwhile, as with the introduction of sulphonamides in the 1930s, fresh concerns were emerging about the impact of new penicillin-based chemotherapies on sexual behaviour. Venereologists were acutely aware of the moral dilemma posed by the widespread application of antibiotics. As R. C. L. Batchelor, Edinburgh's leading venereologist, observed in the mid-1950s, 'the myth of the miracle drug' with the prospect of a cure at state expense 'without discomfort or inconvenience', and with a much reduced opportunity for the clinician to regulate behaviour as part of therapy, had trivialized venereal infection in the minds of patients and undermined the impact of social hygiene propaganda.[13]

However, as in other countries, from the late 1950s, venereologists and public health officials in Scotland increasingly adopted a more sociological approach to the epidemiology of VD. Its incidence was explained less in terms of individual moral deficiencies and more in terms of the impact of a range of cultural, institutional and economic factors upon general patterns of sexual morality and behaviour. In the view of many social commentators, it was 'the price of the Permissive Society'.[14] Indeed, the central explanatory concepts informing medical and public debate over the rise of VD/STDs in late-twentieth-century Scotland were to become 'sexual promiscuity' and 'permissiveness'. The role of prostitution, with its epidemiological mind-set of a small cluster of feckless and vicious vectors, remained a *leitmotif* of public health reports, but it was steadily superseded by the spectre of widespread casual sex and an endless chain of infection.

In particular, certain 'high risk' groups were identified who were socially isolated due to marital or family disharmony, who were alienated from traditional values, and prey to a range of disinhibitants including alcohol, drugs such as cannabis and LSD, new forms of contraception, and a media 'obsessed with sexual permissiveness and gratification'.[15] Although attitude surveys on sexual issues continued to reveal a younger generation in Scotland that was 'conformist rather than permissive or hedonistic',[16] the burden of blame was commonly attached to teenage promiscuity. Scottish public health and church reports in the late 1950s and 1960s frequently identified the rise in teenage VD/STD cases with adolescent alienation from a morally bankrupt, acquisitive society. Concern was expressed at an emerging 'cult of sexual sensuality' among juveniles in the absence of 'parental and community restraint'. Venereologists lamented the health costs associated with the ensuing 'sensual licence' of Scottish youth, inflamed, it was claimed, by exposure to an increasingly permissive leisure and media culture.[17]

In addition, the casual attitude of teenagers towards venereal infection and medical therapy was identified as a major factor in the increase in the number of carriers and penicillin-resistant strains in the community. While it was reluctantly conceded that there was little evidence 'that the teddy boy cult ... or Rock 'an Roll' had any significant influence on the incidence of VD/STDs, its 'addicts' were typified as 'uncooperative in treatment' and lacking in 'the self-discipline necessary for cure'.[18] Such non-compliance with medical authority was often viewed as part of a broader breakdown in civil and moral order among Scottish youth.[19]

However, as previously, post-war moral panic surrounding the sexual hygiene of the young centred on the sexual promiscuity of teenage girls and young women. The potent image of asymptomatic, promiscuous girls as 'reservoirs of infection' haunting cafés, pubs, cinemas and dance-halls was widely projected in the media and public health literature.[20] The language of public health epidemiology still presented a largely passive role for male sexuality. According to senior venereologists in Edinburgh and Glasgow, it was female adolescent promiscuity that constituted 'the real danger' and a 'considerable nuisance and danger to seamen, servicemen, and mildly intoxicated youths'.[21] This asymmetry in perceptions of sexual behaviour and disease was powerfully reflected in contemporary analyses of the sources of infection, which enshrined the concept of women as the pro-active polluters well into the 1960s. Thus, Edinburgh's Public Health Department reports tabulated these sources as follows:[22]

Male infection	Female infection
prostitutes	prostitution
'amateur types'	promiscuous 'amateur' contact
marital partner	marital partner

Any reference to male 'clients' or 'consorts' was significantly absent. Equally noteworthy is the retention of a taxonomy that retains the highly stigmatic term 'amateur' (prostitution) for non-marital female sexual encounters.

Moreover, the emergence of a more social scientific interpretation of sexual behaviour and disease in the 1960s and 1970s served in many ways to reinforce this pathological view of female adolescent sexuality. Sexual promiscuity and VD/STDs among teenage girls became increasingly identified with a syndrome of distinctively female juvenile delinquency.[23] Girls were deemed to manifest their 'anti-social urges' primarily through promiscuity, with 'the ever-willing teenage girl' being 'the female equivalent of the skinhead in his bovver boots'.[24] Social psychologists also resurrected the linkages between VD, sexual permissiveness and mental instability that had so powerfully shaped inter-war responses to 'problem girls'.[25]

Inevitably, the debate surrounding female sexuality and the incidence of VD/STDs gave prominence to the increasing use by girls and young women of the 'pill'. The broad consensus among social commentators and medical practitioners by the early 1970s was that the pill had radically altered patterns of female sexual behaviour, thus promoting sexual promiscuity and disease. According to Robert Morton, President of the Medical Society for the Study of Venereal Diseases, whose views were shared by many Scottish venereologists, for the single person, the pill could 'be classified with the most dangerous of the polluting pesticides' and its use was 'more calamitous than anything precipitated by thalidomide'.[26]

In Scotland, the linkage between the pill and the rise in STDs was central to the broader campaign of the churches against the extension of family planning provisions for single women and girls. According to the Free Church's Committee on Public Questions, Religion and Morals in 1974, increasing sexual disease was due to 'Her Majesty's Government ... throwing open the flood-gates to fornication, adultery and promiscuity, making them risk-free on the NHS'.[27] In similar vein, it argued that in promoting 'a permissive life style', the ready availability of the contraceptive pill had 'violated the sanctity and beauty of sex' and, in the crisis of escalating VD rates, 'reaped the whirlwind for having sown to the wind'.[28] Such views echoed the concerns and assumptions not only of the other Scottish churches but also of a new 'Moral Right' within Scottish public health debates of the early 1970s.

Epidemiological debate drew on a similar mix of social concern and moral outrage in its treatment of the role of homosexual behaviour in the spread of VD/STDs. Early references to homosexual cases in Scottish reports on VD were largely cryptic and/or judgemental asides. Leading venereologists such as Batchelor and Lees did not subscribe to 'the modern view of homosexuality', and viewed it as a 'deviant' and dangerous 'perversion', driven by an 'aberrant instinct'.[29] In many respects, as the Scottish evidence before the Wolfenden Committee on Homosexual Offences and Prostitution had borne witness in the mid-1950s, such views were in accord with broad areas of Scottish public and professional opinion.[30]

The subsequent report in 1973 of the Gilloran Committee on Sexually Transmitted Diseases in Scotland did little to dispel prevailing prejudices when it identified 'passive homosexuals' as 'reservoirs of infection',[31] thus stigmatizing their sexuality as a source of pollution and disease in a fashion traditionally reserved for female prostitutes and 'good-time girls'. Although the proportion of syphilis and gonorrhoea cases at Scottish clinics recorded to have been 'transmitted homosexually' was far below that reported south of the border,[32] it was sufficient to fuel contemporary perceptions of homosexuals as an extremely promiscuous group whose casual sexual behaviour frustrated the best efforts of clinicians and contact tracers to contain the spread of disease.[33]

A marked contrast between the epidemiological debate on VD in post-war England and Scotland was the notable absence within Scottish health publications of allusions to immigration. This reflected the absence in Scotland of 'coloured, West Indian immigrants' who were viewed as major vectors of disease, especially gonorrhoea.[34] Yet, although it lacked the racial imagery of sexual politics in London and the industrial cities of the Midlands and north of England, the discussion of VD/STDs in Scotland was not entirely free of racial prejudice. Public health reports sustained the long tradition of stigmatizing 'foreign infections'. Thus, in the 1950s, Edinburgh's VD Department attributed the survival of syphilis in the city largely to the importation of infection from countries 'where Mars, Bacchus and Venus [were] still a formidable trio'.[35] Moreover, there were powerful xenophobic, if not racial, overtones in the condemnation by Scottish venereologists of the impact on the sexual mores of the younger generation of 'the worst type of American and negro films, booklets, music and dancing'.[36] They surfaced also in several diplomatic incidents when local clinicians and politicians publicly linked the spread of casual 'prostitution' and VD to the presence of American servicemen at the Polaris Base at Holy Loch and at airbases in Midlothian.[37]

The epidemiological debate surrounding VD/STDs in Scotland between the Second World War and the onset of HIV/AIDS continued to be shaped by a powerful set of moral fears, assumptions and stereotypes. Gradually there was, as in other countries, a shift in emphasis from diseased 'types' to patterns of individual sexual behaviour and their associated risk, but it was only a partial shift. Traditional patterns of scapegoating persisted within contemporary 'socio-logical' analyses of public health and the 'permissive society'. Moreover, in Scotland, church attitudes on sexual issues remained highly influential. As late as 1980, the General Assembly of the Free Church of Scotland endorsed the view that

> It will not do for cynical men to scoff at cleanliness as 'Victorian'. The categories of fornication, adultery, bestiality and sodomy are fully as meaningful as ever. To a holy God they are fully as offensive and punishable. *The increased incidence of certain sexually-transmitted diseases bears witness to the reality of God's just judgement.*[38]

The shaping of VD and STD controls: 1948–80

These powerful strands of both continuity and change displayed in the epidemi-ological debate surrounding VD and STDs in post-war Scotland were duly reflected in the shaping of disease control strategies.

Legal compulsion

The issue of legal controls for regulating sexual contacts and defaulters, which Scottish health authorities had campaigned for since 1918, continued to surface in the late 1940s and early 1950s.[39] In the 1960s, prompted by the rising inci-dence of gonorrhoea and non-specific STDs, the debate was reopened in the *Lancet* and in the House of Commons.[40] As late as 1968, Sir Myer Galpern, MP for Glasgow Shettleston, sought to introduce a bill to provide for the compulsory examination and treatment of persons suspected of suffering from venereal diseases.[41]

However, the Department of Health for Scotland (DHS) remained opposed to new legislation. In their view, the traditional arguments against legal controls still held good. They considered that the operation of the wartime Defence Regulation 33B during the period 1942–7 had not demonstrated the value of compulsion and that the reintroduction of similar powers would merely under-mine the confidence of patients and contacts in existing voluntary tracing procedures.[42] Concern was also expressed that it would revive an informer system with the danger of blackmail and with 'totalitarian' implications that were inimical to civil liberties, especially those of young women.[43] Moreover, by the 1960s, many of the younger generation of Scottish venereologists viewed compulsory measures as 'panic legislation' that would prove inoperable in a society where casual sex was increasingly prevalent and a 'target group of "culpable" vectors' no longer so clearly identifiable.

Yet, significant strands of socio-medical control did persist in post-war Scottish VD administration. There was a continuing anxiety to ensure that 'prostitutes' submitted to adequate treatment. R. C. L. Batchelor, Physician-in-Charge of Edinburgh's VD Services during the period 1934–54, had considerable sympathy with the prophylactoria of inter-war Russia in which prostitutes were institutionalized for treatment and moral rehabilitation.[44] Along with other more senior clinicians whose ideology had been shaped by pre-war eugenics and the social hygiene movement, he continued to identify promiscuity and prostitution with mental deficiency and to advocate the notification and confinement of 'moral defectives' for the purposes of reducing the reservoir of infection within the community.[45] His successor, Robert Lees, was also on record as advocating a more vigorous policy towards prostitution in the interests of social hygiene, recommending that police authorities, clinic social workers and prison medical officers should liaise in order to ensure the detention and intensive treatment of prostitutes.[46]

In fact, it was already common practice in Scotland for 'habitual prostitutes' appearing before the courts to be remanded in custody for medical examination under the Criminal Justice Act. Although Scottish Law Officers subsequently ruled that such powers had been intended as an aid to sentencing and not infectious disease prevention and could not be used purely as a public health measure, in some Scottish cities, all women convicted of prostitution continued to be referred to the VD clinics irrespective of whether they had any symptoms.[47] However, as the focus of epidemiological debate shifted in the 1960s and 1970s from prostitution to the effects of greater sexual permissiveness within society, calls for the closer regulation of prostitution on public health grounds became less strident.

Meanwhile, the regulation of the sexual behaviour of 'problem girls' that had so exercised health officials in inter-war Scotland remained an integral part of VD and STD administration. Prior to the 1970s, girls (but not boys) committed to remand homes and approved schools under the Children and Young Persons (Scotland) Act were routinely examined for venereal infections on their first admission and on any readmission after absconding or home visits.[48] Whereas young persons of either sex might be brought to the juvenile courts for suspected promiscuity, in practice it was girls 'deemed to be promiscuous' or 'exposed to moral danger' who were targeted and referred to the clinics. In the late 1960s, some 56 per cent of female patients under 18 years of age attending the Edinburgh clinic were referred by approved schools and remand homes.[49] While physical compulsion was never contemplated, formal permission was rarely sought from the girls for vaginal examinations as they were perceived to be 'rebellious and unco-operative'.[50]

However, by the late 1960s, there was growing unease among Scottish venereologists; first, that it was 'possible for a group of girls to be continuously segregated because of sexual behaviour which [was] not in itself punishable in other persons', and secondly, that the medical expertise of venereologists was being deployed as part of coercive procedures of social work departments designed to control juvenile promiscuity.[51] The recommendation of the Latey

Committee on the Age of Majority that the age of consent for medical treatment should be lowered to 16, coupled with the introduction of children's panels
under the Social Work (Scotland) Act of 1968, altered the situation. Girls might
still be subject to supervision orders and residential care for moral offences and
sexual promiscuity but the VD services were no longer an integral part of such
procedures.[52]

Health education

Meanwhile, despite dramatic changes in post-war society, Scottish health education initiatives had also remained heavily influenced by a traditional moral
epidemiology regarding sexual behaviour and disease. The VD posters and literature distributed in the late 1940s and 1950s continued to enshrine many of the
assumptions and stereotypes that had shaped interwar propaganda. There was a
continuing stress on VD as a racial pollutant, as a disease undermining the virtue
and efficiency of the nation and the mental and physical health of future generations.[53] Likewise, it continued to be identified in propaganda materials with
dysfunctional extramarital sex in which moral and physical degeneracy were inti-
mately related. As before, infidelity and infection, medical risk and moral
culpability, were conflated, with syphilis and gonorrhoea the 'homebreakers,
bringing suspicion and danger to family life'.[54]

Moreover, the discourse of VD propaganda still remained strongly gendered,
representing young women as the primary protectors/destroyers of the moral
health and efficiency of the nation. Thus, central to the plot of *The People at
No. 19*, a health education documentary produced by the Central Office of
Information and frequently screened in Scotland in the late 1940s, was the infidelity of the young wife during the war leading to syphilitic infection. Typically,
the overriding concern was less for her health *per se* and more for the health of
the unborn child and the peace of mind of her husband. Even 'the natural
sexual attraction of a chaste girl' had the 'power' to pollute for, according to the
Scottish Council for Health Education: 'She should remember that a man whose
desires have been excited without being satisfied may be driven to that type of
woman who merely gratifies the man's physical sex hunger which has been so
unfairly aroused' and who 'too often give him venereal disease'.[55] Similarly,
again echoing interwar representations, while male VD was depicted as a
'shadow on health', female VD was 'a shadow on happiness', a lasting degradation of social reputation and domestic fulfilment with wide-ranging moral
overtones.[56]

When, in response to the rising incidence of gonorrhoea, official sex education materials were upgraded in the early 1960s, their tone was less
discriminatory. However, they continued to imply a model of infection that
located blame within the female body. Thus, a leaflet issued in 1962 warned that
the 'sexual adventurer' was

sooner or later ... bound to come into contact with the infectious, and so runs a continuing risk. .... [A] girl may be perfectly clean in the ordinary sense of the word and yet have in her body millions of the invisible germs of gonorrhoea or syphilis, or perhaps both.[57]

Only limited progress in raising public awareness of VD and in affecting patterns of sexual behaviour appears to have been achieved by health education initiatives in Scotland. VD became increasingly overshadowed in health education programmes by other issues such as mass radiography for TB, polio immunization and air pollution. In addition, there was resistance from publicans and ballroom owners to displaying literature and posters relating to VD, on the grounds that it was offensive to their clientele and would attract obscene graffiti. As a result, both spatially and symbolically, VD continued to be 'thought of and dealt with' mainly 'on a lavatorial level'.[58] At the same time, the issue of sex education in schools remained highly contentious, especially in areas with sectarian differences.[59] Many parents and teachers feared that it would actively promote promiscuity, and there was little consensus on the appropriate content, timing and method of sex instruction.

However, in the late 1960s, rising public concern with sexual promiscuity and STDs led the newly established Scottish Health Education Unit to issue a new set of posters and information materials focusing on the dangers of casual sex and targeted at the venues of youth culture.[60] The main poster depicted youngsters in a dance-hall setting with the wording 'It's the first time they've met, but any casual sex encounter is a risk.' It reflected the shift in epidemiology from a preoccupation with a few critical vector groups, such as prostitutes, radiating disease, to the endless chain of infection created by the casual sex of a promiscuous generation. The central message of the new materials was that 'people who [were] too easy [were] too dangerous' because of their previous sexual contacts. There was more gender symmetry in their wording, but the posters still depicted the female contact in red – the traditional colour coding for pollution and moral danger employed in VD propaganda since the 1920s. Moreover, the hidden threat of vaginal infection was still deployed in order to pathologize female sexuality. Thus, one poster designed for male lavatories in public houses read: 'Sex – and her. Is she easy? – Then she's dangerous. Women often don't know when they have VD – but they can give it to you during intimacy. You don't know who she was with last.'[61]

Thereafter, moral issues and taxonomies continued to shape VD/STD information literature. The leaflets of the 1970s focused as much on social behaviour as on medical symptoms, with the key vectors identified as those who 'had intercourse without the *normal* courtship'.[62] Concepts of 'virtue' and 'vice' and 'deviance' still figured prominently in the warnings that venereologists sought to convey in public health reports. As Weeks has noted: 'Even the most liberal texts tended to endorse a "stages" view of sexual development, which was either to be happily resolved in heterosexual monogamy or unhappily resolved in sadness and isolation',[63] and official discourse continued, despite the more 'permissive' society of the 1960s, to view 'safe' female sexual activity as primarily a procreative duty rather than a recreational pleasure.[64]

Meanwhile, health education materials did little to dispel the ignorance and stigma that continued to surround the role of 'homosexual' behaviour in the spread of STDs. From the mid-1970s, Scottish venereologists made increasing efforts to publicize the risks of casual gay sex, but it is significant that, when writing or lecturing on the subject, they often felt compelled to use a pseudonym for fear of attracting adverse publicity or offending the medical establishment.[65]

Perhaps the most revealing testimony to the lasting moral agenda underpinning later-twentieth-century health education in Scotland was the absence of any reference to the use of condoms for protective purposes. Many leading postwar venereologists shared the view of the Scottish churches that while the freer public availability of condoms might reduce the incidence of VD, it would create 'unnecessary temptation' and merely reinforce the 'growing dissociation ... of sex relationships from the sanctities and responsibilities of married life'.[66] From the 1960s, some clinicians and contact tracers routinely advocated protected sex in their confidential advice to patients. However, mindful of the censorious attitude of the media, of church and civic leaders, and of the medical establishment, such advice remained strictly off-the-record.[67]

The Department of Health for Scotland did consider including contraceptive advice in its VD publicity in the early 1960s, but decided that it would provoke widespread opposition and render health education even more of a sectarian issue in the west of Scotland.[68] Such considerations became increasingly persuasive as the whole issue of contraceptive advice and facilities for single girls and women moved to the forefront of Scottish civic debate in the early 1970s.[69]

As a result, health education continued to rely on moral prophylaxis in its approach to VD. The concept of 'safe sex' as articulated in VD posters and literature remained firmly associated with concepts of courtship and marriage and sexual fidelity rather than with the use of 'precautions'. As many clinicians and health administrators increasingly recognized, given this ideology of prevention and the evident shift in the pattern of sexual behaviour within British society, there were severe limits to the degree to which health education might contain the rising incidence of VD/STDs. Any real success in VD/STD control would have also to depend on tracing the chain of infection and identifying infected contacts for treatment.

Contact tracing

The most significant development in VD/STD controls in late-twentieth-century Scotland was the growth of an increasingly sophisticated system of contact epidemiology. A limited system of contact tracing had been introduced during the interwar period and subsequently expanded during the Second World War with emergency powers under Defence Regulation 33B.[70] However, until the

1960s, little further progress was made. During the 1950s, tracing was primarily restricted to female contacts identified by the armed forces or by police or child welfare authorities. Tracing was conducted in a very *ad hoc* and uncoordinated fashion and during the period 1948–60, in the major cities, only about 10 per cent of the contacts of men diagnosed with acute VD were followed up.[71]

A range of constraints operated upon contact-tracing provisions. Concern over the legal status of contact tracing under Scots Law continued to inhibit the VD policy of the DHS. Law Officers advised that existing statute would not protect health authorities from action for damages under Scots Law for slander or for 'injury done to feelings', should information be divulged for the purposes of contact tracing. As a result, while the Department advised VD medical officers in confidence that 'contact tracing should be conducted as vigorously as ever', they felt unable to issue formal guidelines.[72]

In addition, the division of responsibilities for VD under the National Health Service (Scotland) Act, 1947, with diagnosis and treatment the responsibility of the Regional Hospital Boards and issues of epidemiology and prevention remaining within the remit of the Local Authority Health Departments, served to disrupt existing contact-tracing services. For their part, the Regional Hospital Boards accorded venereology low status as a specialty. They did not feel that additional resourcing of contact tracing was justified and increasingly took the view that the availability of fast-acting antibiotics had reduced the urgency for 'follow up' procedures.[73] Many health administrators continued to adopt a 'Calvinistic' judgementalism towards those infected with VD and considered the issue to be the responsibility of local health authorities. The latter were keen to upgrade contact tracing but were concerned at the ability of their tracers to obtain medical information from hospital authorities and at the lack of legal protection for their activities.[74]

Despite the reactive approach of the DHS (reconstituted as the Scottish Home and Health Department (SHHD) in 1962) towards contact tracing, local initiatives *were* undertaken within the major Scottish cities during the 1960s, primarily in response to the rising incidence of gonorrhoea in women and teenage girls. More systematic interrogation of infected patients was instituted and additional staff dedicated to contact tracing. The focus of 'social work' in the clinics shifted from the traditional preoccupation with 'defaulters' to tracking down the 'hidden pool of infection within the community'.[75] However, this continued to be represented as primarily a female phenomenon and particular attention continued to be paid to identifying the 'inmates' of the more notorious brothels and tracing prostitutes operating in the docks.[76] Tracers routinely visited bars, nightclubs and cafés and each VD department gradually built up

> a dossier of promiscuous people, usually women ... compiled from the descriptions of those who ... attended, together with their habits, haunts, and family background; from reports of other health visitors of

possible problem families in their districts; and from newspaper reports
of women drunk and disorderly, in court for soliciting or prostitution.[77]

As a result, by 1970, nearly 50 per cent of primary contacts named in male VD
clinics in Edinburgh and Glasgow were being traced and persuaded to attend for
treatment and over 40 per cent of all first-time female patients attended clinics in
response to contact tracing, as compared with 16 per cent in 1951.[78]

However, such advances continued to be frustrated until the early 1980s by an
enduring lack of funding and staff resources, reflecting the broader struggle of
venereology to maintain its professional identity and status as a specialty within
the Scottish health services.[79] The SHHD came under prolonged pressure to
adopt a more aggressive policy towards contact tracing. A Scottish Medical
Advisory Committee Report in the mid-1960s pressed for more intensive contact
tracing by social workers, especially among younger age groups. According to its
report, contact tracing was not being pursued systematically in Scotland outside
Edinburgh and Glasgow, due to a lack of resources, poor liaison between
medical social workers and the VD clinics, and the failure of Regional Hospital
Boards to make full use of local authority health visitors.[80] Added pressure came
from the issue in 1968 by the Ministry of Health for England and Wales of fresh
regulations and guidelines designed to facilitate contact tracing by extending
statutory protection for the disclosure of information and to upgrade tracing
procedures as a means of 'breaking the chain of infection'. Finally, the report of
the Gilloran Committee on Sexually Transmitted Diseases in Scotland,
published in 1973, stressed the importance of improved contact tracing in
controlling the spread of STDs, and in particular, in securing medical treatment
for the 'promiscuous females' and 'passive homosexuals' who, it argued, constituted the major 'reservoirs of infection'.[81]

Although it eventually issued a guidance booklet on VD in 1975 which
stressed the importance of contact tracing, and some form of practical training
for contact tracers was gradually introduced, the SHHD remained resistant to
issuing any major directive to the health authorities.[82] Its officials voiced continuing doubts as to the wisdom of openly promoting procedures vulnerable to
action for damages under Scots Law. Moreover, during the 1970s, the Department was preoccupied with the reorganization of the health services and was
reluctant to endorse recommendations involving additional resources in a period
of severe financial restraint. An additional constraint was the lack of consensus
within the medical and social work professions as to the desirable mix of medical
and counselling skills required for effective contact tracing. As in other areas of
STD work, contact-tracing policy was strongly shaped by the contest for recognition and status between professional groups within medicine and society. As a
result, although the SHHD conducted a more focused review of contact-tracing
facilities in the mid-1980s, as Scotland entered the era of HIV and AIDS, provisions for contact tracing remained extremely variable and chronically
under-resourced.

ROGER DAVIDSON

Conclusion

The social history of VD and STDs in late-twentieth-century Scotland is as much a story of moral regulation as it is of public health. The medical and legal discourses surrounding sexually acquired diseases in the period 1948–80 continued to be shaped by more general community concerns to regulate sexual behaviour and public morality. Despite the impact of new chemotherapies and sociological insights, public debate over VD and STDs was still informed, and indeed triggered, as much by moral anxieties over the erosion of community and family values, as by the medical dimensions of the problem, and taxonomies of guilt and moral culpability continued to circumscribe the social response to such diseases. In this context, the lasting role of the churches in defining the moral climate of Scottish civil society and of local magistrates and church elders in sustaining 'the remarkable influence of puritanical religion' and 'an illiberal presbyterian theocracy' was critical.[83]

To some extent, there *was* a 'democratization' of the discourses shaping medical practice and policy towards VD and STDs in post-war Scotland. The previous association of class, 'wantonness' and unhygienic sexual behaviour largely disappeared from the rhetoric of public health reports and health education literature, partly in response to the broadening social distribution of patients attending the special clinics. However, in Scotland, as in many other countries, the process of moral regulation, in which VD had played such a central role, continued to be heavily gendered. As previously, while legitimate medical arguments might be advanced for viewing women as 'reservoirs' of infection, it was also very much a social construction built upon long-standing cultural beliefs of 'woman as polluter'. Although, after the 1950s, the social epidemiology of VD shifted, at least in part, from the rhetoric of 'prostitution' to 'promiscuity' and 'high-risk behaviour' and the concept of a few core vectors was succeeded by that of a chain or network of infection, female sexuality and sexual behaviour remained the focus of public concern over the incidence of VD and STDs. New theories of sexual delinquency merely added a patina of scientific respectability to traditional fears identifying female sexual 'precocity' with pollution. Thus, despite 'the permissive movement', the processes by which medical, sociological and legal discourses surrounding VD in late-nineteenth-century and early-twentieth-century society had criminalized and pathologized sexually active single women clearly remained operative, albeit in more coded forms.

Another clear strand of continuity lay in the determination of post-war health educationalists and VD administrators to regulate the sexual urges of the young. Throughout the early twentieth century, public health debate surrounding VD had been informed by acute concern at the apparent breakdown of family and community controls upon the sexual behaviour of adolescents. Shifts in the lifestyle of juveniles, occasioned by changes in income and consumption patterns and by the onset of new forms of leisure and entertainment, were perceived as a threat to the rational, sober, responsible sexuality expressed within marriage, that was necessary for social stability and racial

232

health. Again in the 1960s and 1970s, contemporary debate over VD policy was used to articulate such anxieties and VD figures were widely presented as part of a wider 'social pathology' of youth culture. Although, as Weeks has argued, this was not just a 'simple resurrection of old themes' and a new moral authoritarianism had emerged by the late 1970s,[84] there remained a substantial legacy from the socio-medical discourses that had for so long surrounded VD.

Other continuities are visible. Many of the logistical and ideological constraints upon VD control strategies prior to the Second World War continued to operate. As for much of the interwar period, the VD services in post-war Scotland were marginalized both in health politics and within the medical profession itself, with clinicians stigmatized as 'outcasts' in the eyes of 'colleagues and laity'.[85] The enduring problem of resourcing control strategies such as health education and contact tracing reflected this ongoing struggle of venereology to maintain its professional identity and status as a specialty within the Scottish health services. However, the slow and often erratic development of control procedures in late-twentieth-century Scotland was also a function of broader ideological concern over medico-legal issues of personal liberty, confidentiality and the inquisitorial role of the state in protecting public health. Once again, even within the sexual politics of the 'permissive society', the terms of the debate had shifted very little. They remained anchored within a traditional dialogue between libertarianism and public health imperatives over the governance of dangerous sexualities.

NOTES

1 See, e.g., D. Evans, 'Tackling the "Hideous Scourge": The creation of the venereal disease treatment centres in early twentieth-century Britain', *Social History of Medicine*, 1992, vol. 5, pp. 413–33.

2 See, e.g., B. A. Towers, 'Health education policy 1916–26: venereal disease and the prophylaxis dilemma', *Medical History*, 1980, vol. 24, pp. 70–87.

3 See, e.g., L. Bland, ' "Guardians of the race", or "vampires upon 'the nation's health"?: Female sexuality and its regulation in early twentieth-century Britain', in E. Whitelegg *et al.* (eds) *The Changing Experience of Women*, Oxford, Martin Robertson, 1982, pp. 375–88.

4 See, e.g., L. Hall, ' "War always brings it on": War, STDs, the military, and the civil population in Britain 1850–1950', in R. Cooter, M. Harrison and S. Sturdy (eds) *Medicine and Modern Warfare*, Amsterdam/Atlanta, Rodopi Press, 1999, pp. 205–23; M. Harrison, 'The British army and the problem of venereal disease in France and Egypt during the First World War', *Medical History*, 1995, vol. 34, pp. 133–58.

5 See, e.g., R. Davidson, ' "A scourge to be firmly gripped": The campaign for VD controls in interwar Scotland', *Social History of Medicine*, 1993, vol. 6, pp. 213–35; D. Porter and R. Porter, 'The enforcement of health: The British debate', in E. Fee and D. M. Fox (eds) *AIDS: The Burdens of History*, Berkeley/London, University of California Press, 1988, pp. 97–115.

6 See, e.g., F. Bédarida, *A Social History of England 1851–1975*, London, Methuen, 1979, ch. 10; A. Marwick, *British Society Since 1945*, London, Allen Lane, third edition, 1996, ch. 15.

7 C. Haste, *Rules of Desire: Sex in Britain: World War I to the Present*, London, Chatto & Windus, 1992, p. 143.

8 Edinburgh Health and Social Services Department (EHSSD), *Annual Report*, 1967, p. 73.
9 Edinburgh Public Health Department (EPHD), *Annual Report*, 1958, p. 196.
10 *Report of Committee on Temperance and Morals to General Assembly of the Church of Scotland*, 1960, pp. 419–20.
11 B. P. W. Wells and C. B. S. Schofield, ' "Target" sites for anti-VD propaganda', *Health Bulletin*, 1970, vol. 28, no. 1, p. 76.
12 See, e.g., EPHD, *Annual Report*, 1957, p. 152.
13 R. C. L. Batchelor, 'Recent developments in venereology', *Edinburgh Medical Journal*, 1954, vol. 61, pp. 367–8.
14 See, e.g., *Glasgow Herald*, 3 Oct. 1972.
15 *Report of Joint Sub-Committee on Sexually Transmitted Diseases*, Edinburgh, HMSO, 1973, p. 14.
16 *The Scotsman*, 28 April 1976.
17 See especially, EPHD, *Annual Report*, 1959, pp. 142–3; C. B. S. Schofield, *Sexually Transmitted Diseases*, Edinburgh, Churchill Livingstone, third edition, 1979, pp. 35–7.
18 EPHD, *Annual Report*, 1956, p. 157; 1962, p. 156.
19 See, e.g., *Glasgow Herald*, 15 May 1971.
20 See, e.g., EHSSD, *Annual Report*, 1969, p. 71.
21 EPHD, *Annual Report*, 1956, p. 156; C. B. S Schofield cited in *Sunday Mirror*, 15 June 1970.
22 EPHD, *Annual Reports*, 1958–60.
23 EHSSD, *Annual Report*, 1968, pp. 66–7; 1969, p. 71.
24 Schofield, *Sexually Transmitted Diseases*, Edinburgh, Churchill Livingstone, second edition, 1975, pp. 43–4.
25 Ibid., pp. 44–6.
26 R. S. Morton, *Sexual Freedom and Venereal Disease*, London, Owen, 1971, pp. 90–1.
27 *Reports to the General Assembly of the Free Church of Scotland*, 1974, p. 146.
28 Ibid., 1975, p. 155.
29 R. C. L. Batchelor Papers, 'Changing concepts and changing patterns in venereology', Lecture Notes, 21 Oct. 1963, pp. 13–16; EPHD, *Annual Report*, 1961, p. 144.
30 See National Archives of Scotland (NAS), HH57/1287, Papers relating to Wolfenden Committee, 1955–7.
31 *Report of Joint Sub-Committee on Sexually Transmitted Diseases*, HMSO, 1973, p. 2.
32 British Co-operative Clinical Group, 'Homosexuality and venereal disease in the United Kingdom', *British Journal of Venereal Diseases (BJVD)*, 1973, vol. 49, pp. 329–34.
33 See, e.g., Batchelor, 'Changing concepts'; *Glasgow Herald*, 10 May 1968, p. 9.
34 See, e.g., British Medical Association, *Report on Venereal Disease and Young People*, London, BMA, 1964, p. 23.
35 EPHD, *Annual Report*, 1952, p. 99.
36 EPHD, *Annual Report*, 1959, pp. 142–3.
37 *Scottish Daily Express*, 20 Oct. 1960, 27 June 1963.
38 *Reports to the General Assembly of the Free Church of Scotland*, 1980, p. 146. My emphasis.
39 See, e.g., EPHD, *Annual Report*, 1949, p. 96.
40 *Lancet*, 1966, vol. 2, p. 1,289; 1967, vol. 1, p. 159; *Hansard*, 662, cols 291–4, 3 July 1962.
41 *Hansard*, 774, col. 511, 27 Nov. 1968; 780, cols 944–76, 21 March 1969.
42 On the operation of Defence Regulation 33B, see also Lesley Hall and David Evans, this volume, chs 7 and 14.
43 NAS, HH 58/66/93, Memorandum on control of venereal diseases: Compulsory examination and treatment, 20 June 1962.
44 R. C. L. Batchelor Papers, 'Changing concepts and changing patterns in venereology'; on Russian procedures, see also Frances Bernstein, this volume, ch. 6.

45 R. C. L. Batchelor and M. Murrell, *Venereal Diseases Described for Nurses*, Edinburgh, E. & S. Livingstone, 1951, pp. 196, 202–3.
46 Robert Lees, 'VD – some reflections of a venereologist', *BJVD*, 1950, vol. 26, p. 160.
47 NAS, HH 57/568, Treatment of venereal diseases in prison: General questions.
48 D. H. H. Robertson and G. George, 'Medical and legal problems in the treatment of delinquent girls in Scotland: II. Sexually transmitted disease in girls in custodial institutions', *BJVD*, 1970, vol. 46, pp. 46–51.
49 J. M. Hunter and M. Neilson, 'Sexually transmitted diseases in Edinburgh: Patients under 18 years of age', *Health Bulletin*, 1980, vol. 38, no. 1, p. 24.
50 Medical Society for the Study of Venereal Diseases, Scottish Branch, Correspondence.
51 D. H. H. Robertson, 'Medical and legal problems in the treatment of delinquent girls in Scotland: I. Girls in custodial institutions', *BJVD*, 1969, vol. 45, pp. 135–6.
52 Ibid., pp. 132–5; Hunter and Neilson, 'Sexually transmitted diseases', p. 24.
53 See, e.g., NAS, HH 48/65/6, DHS Circular 17/1945.
54 NAS, HH 58/66/74b, DHS Poster: 'Syphilis and gonorrhoea are homebreakers', 1952.
55 *Women in War and Peace*, Edinburgh, SCHE, 1948.
56 NAS, HH 58/66, Official VD posters.
57 NAS, HH 58/112/11, Draft of leaflet: 'A personal word', March 1962.
58 'Publicity Material on VD', *Health Bulletin*, 1970, vol. 23, no. 1, p. 6.
59 NAS, HH 61/1099, Health education in schools 1960–6.
60 Wells and Schofield, ' "Target" sites', pp. 75–7.
61 *Health Bulletin*, 1970, vol. 28, no. 1, p. 6.
62 See, e.g., Health Education Board for Scotland Library, SHEU Circular no. 1, 5 Jan. 1970.
63 J. Weeks, *Sex, Politics and Society: The Regulation of Sexuality since 1800*, London, Longman, second edition, 1989, p. 256.
64 R. Davenport-Hines, *Sex, Death and Punishment, Attitudes to Sex and Sexuality in Britain since the Renaissance*, London, Fontana, 1991, pp. 275–6.
65 Interview with retired consultant venereologist, 2 June 1998.
66 *Church of Scotland Report to the General Assembly: Annual Reports of Committee on Church and Nation*, 1947, p. 316; 1950, p. 349.
67 Interview with retired consultant venereologist, 9 April 1997.
68 NAS, HH 58/66, Minute I. N. Sutherland, 17 Oct. 1961.
69 NAS, HH 61/970/29, Family planning and health education discussion paper, Nov. 1970.
70 R. Davidson, 'Searching for "Mary, Glasgow": Contact tracing for sexually transmitted diseases in twentieth-century Scotland', *Social History of Medicine*, 1996, vol. 9, pp. 196–206.
71 EPHD, *Annual Reports*, 1948–60; *Annual Reports of MOH for Glasgow*, 1948–60.
72 NAS, HH 58/66, Minutes and correspondence on contact tracing, 1948–62.
73 See, e.g., British Medical Association Archives, Venereologists Group Committee, 26 Feb. 1953, Memorandum by R. Lees.
74 NAS, HH 58/66, Minutes and correspondence on contact tracing, 1948–62.
75 EPHD, *Annual Report*, 1962, p. 144; EHSSD, *Annual Report*, 1967, p. 77.
76 Ibid., 1966, p. 133.
77 Schofield, *Sexually Transmitted Diseases*, 1975 edition, p. 28.
78 EHSSD, *Annual Report*, 1970, p. 58.
79 For details, see Davidson, 'Searching for "Mary Glasgow" ', pp. 206–12.
80 NAS, HH 104/35/75, Report of working party, Oct. 1965.
81 *Report of Joint Sub-Committee on Sexually Transmitted Diseases*, 1973, pp. 2, 6, 14–15.

82 NAS, HH 104/36, Correspondence relating to sexually transmitted diseases: Gilloran Report, 1975–80.

83 C. G. Brown, *The People in the Pews: Religion and Society in Scotland since 1780*, Dundee, Economic and Social History Society of Scotland, 1993, pp. 44–5. For similarities with the Dutch experience, see A. Mooij, *Out of Otherness: Characters and Narrators in the Dutch Venereal Disease Debates 1850–1940*, Amsterdam, Rodopi Press, 1998.

84 Weeks, *Sex, Politics and Society*, pp. 236, 277.

85 A. S. Wigfield, 'The emergence of the consultant venereologist', *BJVD*, 1972, vol. 48, p. 550.

14

SEXUALLY TRANSMITTED DISEASE POLICY IN THE ENGLISH NATIONAL HEALTH SERVICE, 1948–2000

Continuity and social change

David Evans

The introduction of the United Kingdom's National Health Service in 1948 is generally accepted to be the most enduring legacy of the Labour government elected at the end of the Second World War.[1] The fiftieth anniversary of the NHS in 1998 stimulated much commentary on the successes and limitations of this major social experiment.[2] The NHS was established in an attempt to address long-recognized inequalities in access to health care. It brought together previously poorly coordinated voluntary and local authority hospital services, local authority community health services and private general practitioners, in a tax-financed but cash-limited system promising universal access to health care largely free at the point of service. However, one aspect of the introduction of the NHS has received little attention: the incorporation of sexually transmitted disease (called venereal disease until the 1970s) services into the NHS. Previous research has not explored in detail the relationship between wider health policy (in particular, the introduction and development of the NHS), social change and STD policy between 1948 and 2000.[3] There is, for example, no mention of the incorporation of STD services into the NHS in Webster's otherwise definitive two-volume history of the NHS.[4]

The historiography of twentieth-century STD policy in the UK has been dominated by discussions of the impact of the rising incidence of STDs during both world wars, and related policy debates on coercive measures, usually directed at prostitutes and women labelled as 'promiscuous'.[5] This emphasis is widely shared within social history and reflects in particular the view of feminist scholars who have seen legislation and other policy responses to STDs and prostitution as forms of social control, particularly directed towards young working-class women. As other contributions to this volume illustrate, this focus on the social control of young women's sexuality has recently been extended to encompass a broader analysis of stigmatization and social control related to class, generation and ethnicity.

This chapter, however, advances a somewhat different thesis. It is argued that English STD policy in the twentieth century, and particularly in the years of the NHS, 1948–2000, was not characterized by an ethos of social control. The limited coercive measures half-heartedly implemented during the two world wars were not typical of English policy during the century. The two wars together account for barely ten years, and long periods of domestic peace have been much more the norm in the UK during the century. The basic principles of UK STD services – open access, treatment free at the point of service, confidentiality and non-coercion – were formulated by the Royal Commission on Venereal Diseases during the early years of the First World War and established as national policy at the creation of the 'venereal disease treatment centres' in 1916.[6] These principles survived largely unchanged despite the short periods of intense pressure for policy change during both world wars. Where war issues impinged, they were largely confined to issues of enforced notification and clinic attendance, where a degree of coercion was introduced during both world wars. In the Second World War, Regulation 33B of the Defence (General) Regulations, 1942 allowed for any sexual contact named by two or more patients with STDs to be required to attend for diagnosis and treatment.[7] It was almost exclusively applied to women, but never applied to large numbers and was allowed to lapse in 1947 despite the record levels of civilian STD cases experienced during demobilization.[8] Regulation 33B certainly was repressive, and may be seen as part of a pattern of regulation directed towards young women, but it was not characteristic of STD policy in peace time during the century. Moreover, post-war English STD policy was decreasingly concerned with prostitution, with prostitutes largely disappearing from official and medical discourse as a significant source of STD infection.

Thus, the coercion represented by regulation 33B was very much the exception to the broad thrust of STD policy both before and after the establishment of the NHS. Despite the radical social change that has occurred between 1948 and 2000, this period has been characterized by a high degree of policy continuity with the principles of open access, free treatment, confidentiality and non-coercion established in 1916. Equally, policy throughout this period has been characterized by an attitude of benign neglect during which there was little policy development or resource commitment, punctuated by short periods where changing epidemiological patterns or media scares stimulated political interest.

What, then, was the state of English and Welsh (separate legislation covered Scotland)[9] STD services following the end of the Second World War prior to the establishment of the NHS? From 1916, county and borough councils had been required to ensure provision of free and confidential STD treatment with central government providing 75 per cent of the costs. The Local Government Act of 1929 gave local authorities a large amount of discretion in how they organized these treatment centres.[10] Treatment centres were mainly based in general hospitals, with a few clinics, especially in London, in local authority facilities. The medical officers in charge of the clinics were appointed by the hospitals or local authorities and were usually not required to have an extensive specialist knowledge of STDs. The national requirement was for medical officers to have attended an STD clinic for 130 hours of 'training' (which did not require taking or passing any examination). A 1939 survey found that only 36 of 259 medical officers in 156 provincial centres and 11 of 98 London medical officers were specialists in venereal disease.[11] Accommodation was often highly unsatisfactory – 'so cramped and ill-ventilated, situated in the basement of buildings'.[12] Laboratory facilities were often also poor. For medical staff, there was no recognized specialist training, while medical officers in provincial centres often worked in isolation, with poor career prospects. The great majority of medical officers were men, although the need to offer women the opportunity of consulting a female doctor had long been recognized within the Ministry of Health.[13] General practitioners enrolled under the Ministry of Health were also allowed to treat patients for STDs in their own surgeries, as were hospital consultants working in a private capacity.

The steady decline in the incidence of STDs over the 1930s had contributed to a lessening of policy interest in the treatment of STDs before the Second World War. Demobilization at the end of the war led inevitably to a rapid increase in civilian STD rates. The numbers of male civilians newly diagnosed with STDs peaked in 1946 with over 50,000 cases (compared with just under 37,000 in 1938).[14] However, the introduction during the war of penicillin for the treatment of syphilis and gonorrhoea revolutionized treatment and enabled the centres effectively to treat both STDs for the first time. The relatively short course of penicillin treatment compared with pre-war therapies reduced the total number of attendances required. It took time before all medical officers were convinced of the effectiveness of penicillin for both syphilis and gonorrhoea, but within a few years it was the treatment of choice at the vast majority of centres. The end of the war saw the release to civilian life of a substantial number of venereologists who had been employed in the armed forces. These ex-service doctors had substantial experience of the use of penicillin in the treatment of both syphilis and gonorrhoea, at a time when the drug was hard to come by in civilian practice. This influx of experienced ex-forces doctors probably contributed to the rapid acceptance of penicillin treatment for STDs in civilian practice, and the concomitant consolidation of a medical rather than socio-moral model of STD control.

Thus, the upsurge in STDs and the availability of skilled doctors with a new and effective treatment was the context for the incorporation of STD services into the new NHS. The creation of the NHS was a central objective of the 1945 Labour government and a bill to establish the new service was first introduced in 1946. The proposals put forward by Aneurin Bevan, the new Minister of Health, included the nationalization of the voluntary hospitals, the extension of

salaried medical practice and the creation of Regional Hospital Boards governing
the hospitals and accountable to the Ministry of Health. The heated confronta-
tions between the Labour government and elements within the medical
profession (who resented greater state control) over the structure of the new
service, and the terms and conditions of doctors, are well known.[15] However,
this conflict did not include debate over the incorporation of the STD clinics
into the NHS. As a largely centrally funded service with national guidelines and
monitoring, employing salaried specialists, the STD service already operated in
practice as an embryonic National Health Service. There was no apparent opposition to incorporation in the NHS within the STD service. The limited
commentary which appeared in medical journals welcomed the advent of the
NHS and the 'wonderful opportunity offered for improving the present venereal
disease service'.[16] The creation of Regional Hospital Boards was seen as offering
the opportunity of creating regional consultant posts who would support treatment centres, supervise general practitioners offering STD services, promote
liaison with social services regarding contact tracing and organize educational
conferences.[17]

To the extent to which STD policy was a subject of controversy in the period
leading up to the establishment of the NHS, debate focused on long-running
disagreements over the effectiveness and ethics of coercion and notification.
From the beginning of the service in 1916, the Ministry of Health had taken the
view that coercion and notification would be counter-productive as they would
discourage those at risk of STDs from attending for diagnosis and treatment. A
small but vocal band of MPs, peers, doctors and other social hygienists had
unsuccessfully challenged this policy during the 1920s and 1930s. Concerns
about rising rates of STDs during the Second World War, particularly among
Allied governments, persuaded the government to override Ministry of Health
objectives and introduce Regulation 33B. However, in the early post-war years,
the Ministry of Health quickly reverted to its longer-term policy of non-coercion
and the calls for the continuation of Regulation 33B were brushed aside. Once
again, there was an explicit central policy rejection of moralizing and punitive
practices. Although moralizing and stigmatizing attitudes can of course be found
in the writings of individual venereologists and policy-makers, there is little
evidence of active policy measures which might be construed as explicit attempts
at social control related to STDs. From the late 1940s, the key STD control
mechanism promoted by the Ministry was the tracing of sexual contacts through
the voluntary cooperation of patients, supplemented by professional contact
tracers. As the Chief Medical Officer reiterated in his report for 1955:

> It cannot be repeated too often that the control of venereal disease
> depends largely on successful contact tracing. Though the original
> patient is usually the most effective agent for this purpose, cases often
> arise where this is not so. Here the services of an experienced worker
> can be invaluable ... and it is important that whoever undertakes this

work should be in close and constant contact with patients as well as clinicians.[18]

Such contact tracing may have been experienced by patients as a form of social control, but there is little or no direct evidence on patients' perceptions and views of the degree of informal compulsion they may have undergone. At the most, this was a relatively weak form of social control compared to more explicitly regulatory and coercive regimes.

The NHS Act of 1946 transferred control of voluntary and local authority hospitals to the Ministry of Health. New Regional Hospital Boards, Hospital Management Committees and Boards of Governors (for teaching hospitals) were created to manage on behalf of the Minister of Health what was now the third largest non-military organization in Britain with around 500,000 employees or contractors. The establishment of these new bodies and the transfer of all hospitals and their endowments to the state were huge and complex administrative tasks. The 'appointed day' of 5 July 1948 arrived before the new management bodies had taken effective control of their groups and before contracts for consultants and other hospital staff were finalized.[19]

Within these massive organizational changes, little attention was given to STD services. STD clinics were incorporated into the NHS with the hospitals in which they were largely based, but no specific provision was made for them in the NHS Act. The only specific statutory action taken by the Ministry of Health with regard to STDs and the new NHS was to issue a one-page statutory instrument reapplying the principle of confidentiality of information about persons attending treatment centres.[20] The duty of confidentiality, placed on local authorities by the Public Health (Venereal Disease) Regulations 1916, was revoked by the NHS Act as the STD clinics were transferred out of local authority control into the NHS. Although the Ministry of Health initially considered confidentiality in NHS STD clinics to be adequately covered by more general principles of medical confidentiality, the statutory instrument was issued in response to continued expressions of concern by some parliamentarians.

The incorporation of the STD clinics into the NHS raised little comment in STD circles. There is no mention of the change in the annual reports of the Chief Medical Officer despite the continued appearance of a section on 'venereal diseases' throughout the 1940s and 1950s. MPs and peers gave little attention to the organization of STD services in this period, and no criticisms were made of the integration of the STD clinics into the NHS. Similarly, after one positive assessment of incorporation in the *British Journal of Venereal Diseases* in 1947 just prior to the establishment of the NHS,[21] there was no further substantive discussion of the issue in the medical press during the late 1940s or early 1950s.

Despite this lack of discussion, inclusion in the NHS did consolidate the position of STD services and the medical officers who ran them. Prior to 1948, relatively few venereal disease medical officers were accorded a status similar to that of other medical specialists within hospitals. With the advent of the NHS, many more venereologists were given consultant status. As one venereologist later recounted:

> With this transfer I think it is agreed that the status of the clinics and the doctors who served them improved beyond measure. From that date the venereologist was given the opportunity of taking his place in the hospital team on an equal footing with his colleagues in other specialities.[22]

This is perhaps an excessively optimistic account, for questions raised in parliament at the time[23] and the obituaries of several venereologists in the 1950s and 1960s record the resistance they encountered in 1948 among some hospital medical staff to their appointment to consultant posts. One major teaching hospital, the Middlesex Hospital, rejected the advice of the consultant dermatologist who ran its syphilis clinic, and refused to appoint a venereologist to improve the fragmented care experienced by patients until 1963.[24] Integration in the NHS did not in itself reduce the stigma still associated with the STD clinic or its treatment as a 'Cinderella service'.

One benefit of incorporation for STD services was the transfer of funding arrangements from local authorities to the Regional Hospital Boards and Boards of Governors of Teaching Hospitals. Venereologists had long complained both about local authorities' miserly attitudes towards the funding of STD services, and about the Ministry of Health's central funding mechanism. The five-year block funding arrangement for STD services meant that local authorities were not reimbursed for increased usage or improvements in services from central funds until the next grant period. This was a major disincentive for local authorities to invest in improved services. With integration into the NHS, Regional Hospital Boards and Boards of Governors of Teaching Hospitals had wide discretion in allocating and spending their central grants. The result was a considerable rise in the salaries of STD specialists and some improvement in the equipment and premises of clinics.[25]

Prior to the establishment of the NHS, many venereologists had been calling for a national VD service to improve liaison between clinics and the quality of provision by smaller part-time clinics.[26] The Ministry of Health advised the newly constituted Boards to appoint regional advisers or advisory committees in venereology to assist them in deciding on STD service policy. Some Regional Hospital Boards appointed regional advisers, usually senior consultants from major teaching hospitals.

A further implication of inclusion in the NHS was the separation of STD services from the preventative public health function of local authority medical officers of health. Prior to the NHS, medical officers of health had been responsible for STD treatment services as well as prevention under the 1929 Local Government Act. With STD treatment passing to the NHS in 1948, and with medical officers of health losing their responsibilities for hospital health services, their interest and expertise in STDs quickly diminished.[27] Thus, the main policy tool for the control of STDs, contact tracing, was divorced from those medical officers who traditionally would have had a concern with communicable diseases and population health. Although there were notable local examples of STD clinicians and medical officers of health working together on STD control after 1948, these do appear to be exceptional.

At the inception of the NHS, the Ministry of Health emphasized the need for specialist STD hospital services. A circular from the Ministry stated emphatically that 'the diagnosis and treatment of venereal diseases constitute a separate clinical specialty, and should not be left to become a minor interest of specialists in other fields'.[28] However, a number of factors over the subsequent decade appeared to threaten the existence of venereology as a hospital specialty.[29] First and foremost, the numbers of new STD infections decreased rapidly after the peak year of 1946. In 1955, new cases of syphilis were less than 5 per cent of those in 1946. The decline in the number of cases of gonorrhoea was less marked but still significant, with figures falling well below even pre-war levels. Secondly, the introduction of penicillin had significantly reduced the level of technical skill required to treat both syphilis and gonorrhoea. General practitioners and other non-STD specialists might equally use penicillin to treat STDs. Thirdly, the impact of the falling incidence of STDs and the perceived lack of clinical challenge engendered by penicillin led to a lack of interest in the specialty among medical graduates. Venereologists were so concerned by this that there were suggestions that the UK STD service should combine with colonial services to ensure adequate training.[30] All three of these factors contributed to hospital authorities downgrading the specialty, the closure of clinics and failure to reappoint venereologists on the retirement of older consultants.

By 1955, a review of specialist medical services by the Ministry of Health found that the VD service was maintained by only ninety-three consultants and seventy-nine senior hospital medical officers. The proportion of consultants was considerably lower than that of the specialist services as a whole, and the number of venereologists had declined while the overall number of specialists had increased. Venereologists were generally older than other specialists with many approaching retirement. Despite this favourable job market, there were only nine senior registrars in training as venereologists in 1955.[31]

Thus, by the mid-1950s, venereologists were increasingly concerned that their specialty was at risk from official indifference and neglect, at least at the regional and hospital levels. In terms of central policy, however, there were no significant changes to the strategy adopted by the Ministry of Health from the inception of the NHS in 1948. The heated national debates about patient charges in the NHS, and the change of government in 1951, did not affect the STD services. Patients attending STD services were exempted from the prescription charges introduced in 1952.[32]

Epidemiological and social change began to place new demands on the STD service during the mid-1950s. In 1955, the first evidence in England and Wales since the Second World War emerged of consistently increasing rates of STDs. A slight increase in the incidence of new cases of syphilis and gonorrhoea during the second half of the 1950s was followed by a more substantial increase in gonorrhoea.[33] Rates of gonorrhoea would continue to increase through to the mid-1960s, while rates of non-gonococcal urethritis (which was gradually recognized as causing serious disease) increased throughout the 1950s and 1960s. Other STDs, including chlamydia, genital warts and genital herpes, were increasingly identified and found to be steadily increasing during the 1960s.

From the 1950s, venereologists began to take an interest in the changing social demography of STDs. Two major social changes began to impact upon STD clinics during the 1950s. The first was the increase in black immigration from the New Commonwealth. The first published mention of STDs among black immigrant populations occurred in the *British Journal of Venereal Diseases* in 1950. In the journal's account of the July 1950 meeting of the Medical Society for the Study of Venereal Disease, Robert Lees, VD Medical Officer for Leeds, is recorded as commenting that

> The coloured men who spread venereal disease presented a very acute problem, especially in London and the large seaports. These persons came from communities with a very high rate of venereal infection, and many arrived in Great Britain already infected. They certainly had not the moral or social training which would enable them to live as decent members of a civilized society, and they were very badly assimilated into the community.[34]

As this quotation illustrates, there were a number of racist and stereotypical attitudes and beliefs expressed by policy-makers and venereologists about black men, and considerations of race increasingly played an important part in shaping the way the STD problem was defined and formulated. However, these attitudes do not appear to have led to race-specific policy choices, except to generate an interest in statistical studies of the relative incidence of STDs among different ethnic groups. In 1951, the Chief Medical Officer noted that 'a considerable increase in the number of African, West Indian and Asiatic patients has been noted in many of the larger urban centres'.[35] An early study of the incidence of gonorrhoea by the British Cooperative Clinical Group (a newly established venereology research group) undertook an analysis of gonorrhoea by place of birth. By the mid-1950s, such studies were showing that approximately 25 per cent of cases of gonorrhoea in men were among West Indian immigrants.[36] Many of these studies commented on the youth of their UK-born (i.e. presumed white) female sexual contacts.

This focus of concern on sexual relations between black immigrant men and white women was not of course the first time that issues of race and sex troubled the British government. During the Second World War, the government had been acutely concerned over sexual relations between black American GIs and white British women.[37] A number of measures were taken to discourage white women from socializing with black GIs, and consideration was given to more extreme actions including the segregation of black units. One of several areas of official anxiety during the war was the alleged loss of sexual self-control by young white women involved with black GIs. Discussions of STDs among black immigrant populations in the 1950s demonstrate similar anxieties about the 'problem' of sexually uncontrolled young white women who engaged in sexual activity with black men. However, the policy context in the 1950s was very different. With a growing awareness of the complexity of race relations issues, NHS policy-makers were not keen to address this 'problem' explicitly. Within the STD service, public discussion by clinicians of the issue focused on the inevitability of high rates of STDs in black men. This was seen to be due both to the importation of STDs from colonial areas with high rates and the immigrants' sexual promiscuity related to separation from wives and families. Promiscuity is of course an ill-defined and value-laden concept rather than a precise epidemiological one. There was no evidence provided in the BCCG studies or other reports that black men had more sexual contacts than whites, although this was the clear perception of clinicians. Whether due to importation or promiscuity, the underlying factor was seen to be a 'social problem' outside the remit of the STD service. The policy response was not race specific; rather, the control of STDs among West Indian immigrants depended on the same voluntarist approach to contact tracing and treatment as was applied to the rest of the population. While it is likely that many black patients experienced racist attitudes among clinic staff, it is difficult to interpret the formation or implementation of STD policy in the context of race as in any significant way an aspect of social control.

The second major social change during the 1950s to impact the STD service was the increasing social recognition of the existence of homosexuality. The first UK articles on 'the problem of the homosexual with venereal disease' appeared in 1948-9[38] and by the mid-1950s, venereologists were publicly acknowledging the increasing proportion of STD infections found among homosexual men, particularly in parts of London where homosexuals were found to account for around 60 per cent of new syphilitic infections.[39] The publication of the Wolfenden Report on Homosexual Offences and Prostitution in 1957 illustrated the slow sea change in attitudes towards the criminalization of male homosexual activity. After prolonged parliamentary and public debate, the Wolfenden Report led to legislation partially decriminalizing homosexual activity in 1967. During the late 1950s and 1960s, homosexual men were increasingly using STD clinics, and increasingly willing to discuss openly their sexual contacts and to attend for treatment.[40] The advent of the gay liberation movement in the late 1960s and 1970s led to the creation of a more self-confident 'out' gay community with a number of activist and campaigning groups. Sexual liberation became an important component of gay life; many sexually active gay men came to regard

245

attendance at STD clinics as a regular, if inconvenient, aspect of sexual life.[41] As with black immigrants, the control of STDs among gay men was based on the same voluntarist principles of open access and non-coercion applied to the rest of the population. Again, there were a number of examples of what would now be regarded as homophobic and stigmatizing attitudes expressed by policy-makers and venereologists, but little evidence of STD policy as a mechanism for the social control of gay men.

There is little documentary evidence on how patients experienced STD services. There is some evidence that people found infection by STDs to be stig-matizing, and on occasion the attitudes of clinic staff contributed to this sense of stigmatization.[42] The writings of venereologists demonstrate that many shared essentially negative views of young women's sexuality and concerns about STDs as a symptom of moral decay. This may have contributed to informal and implicit processes of social control, but once again it did not change the funda-mental characteristics of STD policy.

By the mid-1960s, the number of attendances at STD clinics was increasing dramatically. The 'sexual revolution' of the 'permissive society', the advent of the oral contraceptive pill and the declining popularity of the condom all contributed to an increase of STDs, particularly viral infections. The increased incidence of STDs was seen in official circles as 'primarily a reflection of sexual promiscuity in the population'; rather than prostitutes, however, the main social groups now seen to be responsible were teenagers, immigrants, asymptomatic promiscuous women and homosexuals.[43] Policy on STDs, however, continued to be characterized by benign neglect. Clinics were 'bursting at the seams' with the same old problems of poor conditions, overcrowding and difficulty in attracting a younger generation of doctors to an increasingly 'Cinderella' service. Various attempts were made within the profession to increase its status, notably through an increase in research activity from the early 1970s, and the appointment of the first chair in genitourinary medicine at the Middlesex Hospital in 1979. Clinics were increasingly renamed departments of 'genitourinary medicine'. As pres-sures increased on STD clinics during the 1970s, the Department of Health and Social Security (DHSS) carried out various limited enquiries into the premises and workload of clinics, and encouraged local health authorities to improve conditions in those found to be inadequate. Additional senior registrar and regis-trar posts were approved and more central funding made available for STD-related research.[44] Despite these initiatives, STD services remained 'Cinderella' services within the NHS. Difficulties continued in recruiting consul-tants to STD posts and increasingly posts were filled by 'overseas' (i.e. non-white) doctors.[45]

There was very little legislative activity regarding STDs. In 1968, a new statu-tory instrument was issued by the DHSS clarifying the rules governing the confidentiality of contact tracing.[46] These regulations were further clarified in 1974 in another statutory instrument necessitated by the 1973 NHS Re-organi-zation Act.[47] The 1974 and 1982 reorganizations of the NHS and the introduction of general management in the mid-1980s did not otherwise impact directly on STD services. Central guidance to the STD service was largely concerned with improvements to the system for contact tracing. A 1968 DHSS memorandum gave detailed advice to clinic authorities on the procedures for contact tracing.[48] In 1980, a comprehensive handbook on contact tracing was published by the Health Education Council.[49]

It was not until the mid-1980s that STD services returned to anywhere near the centre of the health policy agenda. In 1981, the first UK death was reported in the *Lancet* from a condition which would become known as AIDS. Over the next few years there was a steady increase in the number of deaths from AIDS in the UK, particularly among gay men. Epidemiological data from the USA, where AIDS was first recognized and spread rapidly, strongly indicated that AIDS was often caused by a sexually transmitted organism. In 1984, the organism, HIV, was identified by French scientists and in 1985 a blood test for the virus was developed. The recognition that HIV was a sexually transmitted organism and the impact on the gay community which had long used STD clinics meant that STD clinics were at the forefront of the response to the new epidemic, particularly in London.

The policy response to AIDS in the early 1980s has been described as 'policy making from below'.[50] The initial response came largely from within the gay community with the establishment of campaigning and support groups. A small number of clinicians, the 'samurai of AIDS', some but by no means all STD specialists, working at London teaching hospitals with AIDS patients, pushed AIDS up the NHS priority agenda.[51] Outside the STD world there were strong media pressures for a punitive and coercive approach to AIDS, with suggestions for compulsory notification and, more extremely, detention.

The response of the Conservative government of Margaret Thatcher to AIDS was slow to be articulated. AIDS first appeared to the government as a public policy problem with regard to the Blood Transfusion Service, where decisions needed to be taken about excluding 'at risk' donors and universal testing during 1983–5. When media and public pressure forced the government to consider wider policy issues during 1984–5, there was a period of uncertainty during which policy options, including new coercive notification measures, were debated. By 1985, however, the traditional liberal approach to STD policy had been reaffirmed. As with the 'traditional' STDs, the view was taken that notification and other coercive measures would dissuade people at risk from seeking testing and treatment for HIV/AIDS. Senior STD clinicians involved in AIDS were central to the scientific and policy debates within and around government that dictated the liberal policy response.[52]

The impact of HIV/AIDS had far-reaching implications for STD services. From 1985, large sums of money began to flow into HIV/AIDS service development, much of it into STD clinics. Ring-fenced AIDS funding increased from £6.3 million in 1985 to £25.1 million in 1987/88 to £126 million in 1990/91.[53] The decision in 1987 to offer the public confidential HIV testing at STD clinics

DAVID EVANS

meant that even clinics with few or no HIV/AIDS patients suddenly found themselves with generous funding for new or improved premises, additional staff and other benefits. A review of STD clinic workloads published in 1988 made a number of recommendations for improvements, which became the basis for Department of Health guidance to health authorities.[54] The scientific and clinical challenges of HIV/AIDS meant that for the first time since before the advent of penicillin, STD services were able to attract able young junior doctors and develop prestigious research projects. The presence of a relatively young and articulate group of patients, and a gay community-based voluntary sector, meant that STD services began to develop new partnerships and ways of working. By the early 1990s, many STD clinics had been transformed almost out of recognition compared with the 'Cinderella' services that had existed for much of the previous seventy years. The emphasis placed on STDs as one of five priority areas in the 1992 *Health of the Nation* White Paper demonstrated their centrality to health policy in the early 1990s.[55]

At the same time, the most far-reaching reform to the NHS since its inception was being introduced by the Conservative government. Previous NHS reorganizations in 1974 and in the early and mid-1980s had essentially restructured the layers of NHS bureaucracy. The 1991 NHS reforms sought to replace bureaucratic NHS decision-making with market mechanisms in an *internal* or *quasi-market*.[56] Health authorities which had previously managed hospitals and community health services were given the responsibility of purchasing services on behalf of their resident populations. Responsibility for service management was transferred to newly created NHS Trusts. In principle, the quasi-market gave purchasers the opportunity to improve service quality through choice between competing providers, who might expand or lose business from different purchasers.

However, in practice, the impact of the 1991 reforms on STD services was not significant. For health authorities, STD services were a relatively small specialty. They had only limited routine intelligence on population health needs and on the quality and outcomes of STD services, and usually only one local provider. Given their limited resources and the extensive government demands made on them in more politically sensitive areas (e.g. reducing hospital waiting lists), health authorities had little incentive to prioritize STD services. In practice, health authorities did not seek to use their theoretical 'purchasing power' to effect changes in STD services. Budgets for STD services were usually historically determined rather than needs-based, and were much more influenced by decisions about the central allocation of AIDS monies than by the operation of the NHS quasi-market. As with a number of other specialist services in the quasi-market, contracting was based much more on relationships and trust than on market mechanisms.[57]

By 1993/94, STD services began once again to move down the list of central government health priorities. During the mid-1990s, the centrally determined ring-fenced HIV/AIDS allocation was discontinued for treatment and care, and

gradually reduced for prevention. A number of regional HIV/AIDS coordina-
tion and management posts disappeared with the abolition of Regional Health
Authorities in 1996. HIV/AIDS and STDs did not figure in the 1999 English
White Paper, *Saving Lives: Our Healthier Nation*,[58] as they had previously done in
the 1992 *Health of the Nation* White Paper.[59] The failure of the predicted UK
HIV/AIDS epidemic to materialize enabled policy-makers to revert to the policy
of benign neglect towards STD services which they had pursued since the end of
the Second World War.

English STD policy throughout the period 1948-2000 was characterized by a
high degree of continuity despite the radical social and organizational change
that occurred during this period. The fundamental principles of policy – open
access, treatment free at the point of service, confidentiality and non-coercion –
were incorporated into the NHS at its creation and have remained essentially
unchanged. Unlike the experiences recounted in this volume relating to other
European and colonial societies, and in other time periods, there is little evidence
in England in this period to justify a view of STD policy as a form of social
control. Despite anxieties and stigmatizing attitudes about promiscuity, young
women's sexuality, homosexuality and black sexuality, such attitudes did not
change the central aspects of STD policy. The policy response to STDs
continued to reflect a medical rather than a socio-moral model throughout the
period. There was a continued and explicit policy rejection of any form of coercion. The notes of a meeting called by the Chief Medical Officer in 1961 to
discuss concerns about the rise in STDs among young people summarize the
consensus nicely: 'There must be no appearance of "persecuting teenagers" as a
group.'[60] One brief challenge to this policy continuity occurred with media and
popular demands for coercion in the early days of the AIDS crisis. However, a
powerful alliance of civil servants and clinicians ensured the continuation of the
long-established official consensus. The fear in official circles of a major AIDS
epidemic acted as an important catalyst for a substantial increase in resources for
traditional STD services. These AIDS allocations had the short-term effect of
rescuing STD services from the poor funding and policy neglect which had characterized the NHS period. However, AIDS itself was the product of a complex
interplay between a range of long-term social changes including economic glob-
alization, post-colonial population movements, cheaper international travel and
gay liberation. Thus, via the vector of HIV/AIDS, wider social change has had
a significant, albeit limited impact on STD policy in the UK. By contrast, the
major structural changes to UK health services, including the establishment of
the NHS in 1948 and the introduction of the quasi-market in 1991, caused
hardly a ripple to the continuity of STD policy.

NOTES

1 C. Webster, *The Health Services since the War*, Volume I, *Problems of Health Care; The
  National Health Service Before 1957*, London, HMSO, 1988.

2 I. Loudon, J. Horder and C. Webster (eds) *General Practice Under the National Health Service, 1948–1997*, Oxford, Clarendon Press, 1998; C. Webster, *The National Health Service*, Oxford, Oxford University Press, 1998; M. Powell, *Evaluating the National Health Service*, Buckingham, Open University Press, 1997.

3 But see L. Hall, '"The Cinderella of Medicine": sexually transmitted diseases in Britain in the nineteenth and twentieth centuries', *Genitourinary Medicine*, 1993, vol. 69, pp. 314–19.

4 Webster, *The Health Services since the War*, Volume I; C. Webster, *The Health Services since the War*, Volume II, *Government and Health Care; The British National Health Service, 1958–1979*, London, HMSO, 1996.

5 E. Beardsley, 'Allied against sin: American and British responses to VD in World War One', *Medical History*, 1976, vol. 20, pp. 189–202; S. Buckley, 'The failure to resolve the problem of venereal disease among the troops in Britain during World War One', in B. Bond and I. Roy (eds) *War and Society*, vol. 2, London, Croom Helm, 1977; R. Davidson, 'The impact of World War II on civilian VD policy in Scotland', *Scottish Historical Review*, 1996, vol. 75, pp. 72–97; R. Davidson, 'Searching for "Mary Glasgow": Contact tracing for sexually transmitted diseases in twentieth-century Scotland', *Social History of Medicine*, 1996, vol. 9, pp. 195–214; M. Harrison, 'The British Army and the problem of venereal disease in France and Egypt during the First World War', *Medical History*, 1995, vol. 39, pp. 133–58; S. Rose, 'Girls and GIs: Sex and diplomacy in Second World War Britain', *International History Review*, 1997, vol. 46, 146–60.

6 D. Evans, 'Tackling the "Hideous Scourge": the creation of the venereal disease treatment centres in early twentieth-century Britain', *Social History of Medicine*, 1992, vol. 5, pp. 413–33.

7 Davidson, 'The impact of World War II'; see also L. Hall, this volume, ch. 7.

8 *Report of the Chief Medical Officer on the State of the Public Health for the year ending 31st December 1947* (PP, 1948–9, xvi), p. 642.

9 For developments in Scotland, see R. Davidson, this volume, ch. 13.

10 L. Harrison, 'The control of venereal diseases under the National Health Service', *British Journal of Venereal Diseases*, 1947, vol. 23, pp. 145–54.

11 Harrison, 'The control of venereal diseases', p. 146.

12 I. Price, 'Is a new deal in the control of venereal disease necessary?', *British Journal of Venereal Diseases*, 1944, vol. 20, pp. 19–30.

13 Evans, 'Tackling the "Hideous Scourge"', p. 427.

14 *Report of the CMO for 1947*, p. 754.

15 Webster, *The Health Services since the War*, Volume I.

16 Harrison, 'The control of venereal diseases', p. 145.

17 Ibid., p. 147.

18 *Report of the Chief Medical Officer on the State of the Public Health for the year ending 31st December 1955* (PP, 1956–7, xii), p. 736.

19 Webster, *The Health Services since the War*, Volume I, p. 123.

20 The National Health Service (Venereal Diseases) Regulations, 1948, Statutory Instrument 1948/2517, p. 2,303; on the treatment of venereology within the early National Health Service, see also L. Hall and R. Davidson, this volume, chs 7 and 13.

21 Harrison, 'The control of venereal diseases'.

22 G. McElligott, 'Venereal disease and the public health', *British Journal of Venereal Diseases*, 1960, vol. 36, p. 211.

23 Anonymous, 'Parliamentary Reports', *British Medical Journal*, 1949, vol. II, p. 338.

24 M. Adler, 'History of the development of a service for the venereal diseases', *Journal of the Royal Society of Medicine*, 1982, vol. 75, p. 126.

25 McElligott, 'Venereal disease and the public health', p. 211.

26 Price, 'Is a new deal in the control of venereal disease necessary?'; Harrison, 'The control of venereal diseases'.

27 J. Lewis, *What Price Community Medicine? The Philosophy, Practice and Politics of Public Health Since 1919*, Brighton, Wheatsheaf Books, 1986.

28 R. Lees, 'The teaching of venereology', *British Journal of Venereal Diseases*, 1949, vol. 25, p. 16.

29 A. King, ' "These dying diseases": venereology in decline?', *The Lancet*, 1958, vol. 1, pp. 651–7.

30 Lees, 'The teaching of venereology', p. 25.

31 King, ' "These dying diseases" ', p. 656.

32 Webster, *The Health Services since the War*, Volume I, p. 195.

33 *Report of the Chief Medical Officer on the State of the Public Health for the year ending 31st December 1956* (PP, 1957–8, xiv), p. 543.

34 R. Lees, 'VD – Some random reflections of a venereologist', *British Journal of Venereal Diseases*, 1950, vol. 26, p. 163.

35 *Report of the Chief Medical Officer on the State of the Public Health for the year ending 31st December 1950* (PP, 1951–2, xv), p. 308.

36 R. Willcox, 'Immigration and venereal disease in England and Wales', *British Journal of Venereal Diseases*, 1970, vol. 46, pp. 412–21.

37 Rose, 'Girls and GIs', pp. 146–60.

38 F. McDonald, 'The problem of the homosexual with venereal disease', *British Journal of Venereal Diseases*, 1949, vol. 25, pp. 13–15.

39 *Report of the Chief Medical Officer on the State of the Public Health for the year ending 31st December 1957* (PP, 1958–9, xv), p. 252.

40 M. Waugh, 'Studies on the recent epidemiology of early syphilis in West London', *British Journal of Venereal Diseases*, 1972, vol. 48, p. 538.

41 Chief Medical Officer, *On the State of the Public Health, 1980*, London, HMSO, 1981, p. 62.

42 A. Dalzell-Ward, C. Nicol and C. Haworth, 'Group discussion with male VD patients', *British Journal of Venereal Diseases*, 1960, vol. 36, pp. 106–12; D. Evans and C. Farquhar, 'An interview based approach to seeking user views in genitourinary medicine', *Genitourinary Medicine*, 1992, vol. 72, pp. 223–6.

43 Public Record Office (PRO): MH 55/2324, Ministry of Health minutes, 8 December 1960.

44 Chief Medical Officer, *On the State of the Public Health, 1973*, London, HMSO, 1974, pp. 51–2.

45 R. Catterall, 'Education of physicians in the sexually transmitted diseases in the United Kingdom', *British Journal of Venereal Diseases*, 1976, vol. 52, p. 98.

46 The National Health Service (Venereal Diseases) Regulations, 1968, Statutory Instrument 1968/1624, p. 4,449.

47 The National Health Service (Venereal Diseases) Regulations, 1974, Statutory Instrument 1974/29, p. 111.

48 Department of Health and Social Security, *Memorandum HM(68)84*, 1968.

49 Health Education Council, *Handbook on Contact Tracing in Sexually Transmitted Diseases*, London, Health Education Council, 1980.

50 V. Berridge, *AIDS in the UK: The Making of Policy, 1981–1994*, Oxford, Oxford University Press, 1996.

51 Ibid., p. 27.

52 Ibid., pp. 69–70.

53 Ibid.

54 Department of Health, *Report of the Working Group to Examine Workloads in Genito-Urinary Medicine Clinics (The Monks Report)*, London, Department of Health, 1988.

55 Secretaries of State for Health, *The Health of the Nation*, London, HMSO, 1992.

56 R. Flynn and G. Williams (eds) *Contracting for Health*, Oxford, Oxford University Press, 1997.
57 D. Evans, 'The impact of a quasi-market on sexually transmitted disease services in the UK', *Social Science and Medicine*, 1999, vol. 49, pp. 1,287–98.
58 Secretary of State for Health, *Saving Lives: Our Healthier Nation*, London, Stationery Office, 1999.
59 Secretaries of State for Health, *The Health of the Nation*.
60 PRO, MH 55/2325, Notes of an informal meeting on venereal disease held by the Chief Medical Officer, 13 April 1961.

INDEX

King, Ambrose 221
Kirchner, Martin 78
Kitchener, Lord 125
Krafft-Ebing, Richard von 52

Ladies' National Association for the
    Repeal of the Contagious Diseases Acts
    121
Lambkin, F.J. 191, 195, 199
Lancet, The 131, 168, 173, 177, 225, 247
Lanza, Giovanni 142
Larson, Pier M. 173–4
latent germs, theory of 23
Latey Committee on the Age of Majority
    227
law 3, 7–8; Britain 122, 127, 132, 176,
    237, 246 (*see also* Contagious Diseases
    Acts); Germany 7, 78, 83–8, 212–13;
    Italy 8, 137–52 *passim*; Scotland 225–7,
    229–30, 232; Spain 63, 66, 68–9;
    Sweden 4, 7–8, 31, 39–40, 41; Uganda
    7, 192, 198–201, 202; *see also* crime;
    regulationism
Lees, Robert 221, 224, 226, 244
Lennmalm, Frithiof 35
Levi, Ettore 145
Levi-Luxardo, Italo 147
Levine, P. 2, 199
Lewis, M. 3
Ligue des droits de l'homme 24, 26
Liszt, Franz von 84
literature, VD in 5, 80, 122
lock hospitals 45, 138, 166, 175
Lombroso, Cesare 11, 140
London Women's Suffrage Society 123
Long, Charles W. 122
Luciani, Luigi 142
Lupton, Deborah 161

McClintock, Anne 163
McHugh, P. 1
Madagascar 173–4
Malaya 173; *see also* Federated Malay
    States; Singapore
male elite, Uganda 12, 191–202
male sexuality 10–11; British views 121,
    123, 124, 132; Dutch views 48, 51–2,
    56; Italian views 11, 139, 143, 145,
    147, 148; Russia 112–13; Spain 70
Malmroth, Carl 33
Manderson, Lenore 173
Marcus, Karl 38

Mario, Jessie White 141
Marks, Lara 161
marriage 40, 65; Britain 122, 123–4, 221;
    Germany 86–7; Italy 146, 150, 151–2;
    Uganda 201
Martindale, Louisa 123
masturbation 52, 99, 139, 169n5
Mauritius 162
Mazzini, Giuseppe 141
Medical Society for the Study of Venereal
    Diseases 129, 244
medicine 3, 6, 9, 12; Britain 120–32 *passim*,
    176, 237–49; and control of female
    sexuality in Hamburg 207, 210,
    215–16, 217; Chinese *versus* Western
    175, 181, 182; colonial context 11,
    160–9, 173–4, 178–86; and
    epidemiological debate in Scotland
    221–33; Germany 77–88 *passim*; images
    in Russian health-education posters
    96–116 *passim*; Italy 137–54 *passim*;
    Spanish social medicine 61–75; Sweden
    29–41 *passim*; Uganda 192, 193, 194,
    195–8; *versus* political organization in
    Netherlands 12, 45–56; *see also* public
    health; treatment and care; venereology
mercury treatment 7, 45, 54, 88, 196
Merlin, Lina 147, 148–9
Middlesex Hospital 242, 246
military concern 4, 7, 11; Britain 1, 2, 121,
    122, 125, 130–2, 166–7, 199, 205–14,
    220; colonies 162, 167, 168–9, 199;
    Germany 83, 84–5; Italy 11, 137, 144,
    152; Netherlands 44, 58n16; Russia 93;
    Spain 11, 62, 70
missionaries 174, 193, 194, 195, 197
Möller, Magnus 32, 33, 35
Monlau, Pedro Felipe 63
Montanelli, Indro 148
Mooij, A. 3, 4
moral approach 3, 6, 9, 12; Britain 10,
    121, 123, 161, 162, 176–7, 213–14,
    220, 246, 247; colonies 11, 164; France
    17–27; Germany 77, 78–83, 87; Italy
    137, 139, 142–3, 144, 146, 147, 149,
    150, 152, 154; Netherlands 48, 50, 51,
    56; Scotland 221, 223–4, 227, 228,
    229, 232, 233; Spain 61, 62–3, 65, 71;
    Sweden 30, 38; Uganda 191, 193, 194,
    195, 197, 202
Morning Post 124–5
Morris, Sir Malcolm 124

SUNY BROCKPORT

3 2815 00869 7552

RA 644 .V4 S3675 2001

Sex, sin, and suffering

DATE DUE

NOV 2 1 2005		
MAY 1 6 2008		
JAN 1 6 2009		
MAR 0 5 2012		
OCT 0 3 2013		
GAYLORD		PRINTED IN U.S.A.